RECLAIMING
OUR ROOTS

RECLAIMING OUR ROOTS

AN INCLUSIVE INTRODUCTION TO CHURCH HISTORY

VOLUME I
THE LATE FIRST CENTURY TO THE EVE OF THE REFORMATION

MARK ELLINGSEN

TRINITY PRESS INTERNATIONAL
HARRISBURG, PENNSYLVANIA

Trinity Press International, P.O. Box 1321, Harrisburg, PA 17105
Trinity Press International is a division of the Morehouse Group.

Cover design: Rick Snizik

Library of Congress Cataloging-in-Publication Data
Ellingsen, Mark, 1949-
    Reclaiming our roots : an inclusive introduction to church history
/ Mark Ellingsen.
        p.   cm.
    Includes bibliographical references and index.
    Contents: v. 1, The late first century to the eve of the
Reformation.
    ISBN 1-56338-275-X (pbk. : alk. paper)
    1. Church history.   I. Title.
BR145.2.E435 1999
270 – dc21   99-29536

Printed in the United States of America

07 08 09   10 9 8 7 6 5 4 3

For
Interdenominational Theological Center
and all its wonderful community members

CONTENTS

ACKNOWLEDGMENTS

In some respects I have found that writing this segment of a volume is the most pleasurable task of the process. This book and the second volume of this series are no exception. Although in some sense an author works alone, I have never experienced loneliness when I write. The room in which I write is filled with friends, both figuratively and literally. How wonderful it is, then, publicly to thank these people about whom I care and to whom I have been indebted.

Anyone who writes about the history of the Church and loves the Church is in the company of friends when he writes about the giants of the faith. To a great extent this volume and its companion are books about my roots. However this reflection on roots was occasioned by my responsibilities within a very special part of the Christian community — the Interdenominational Theological Center and the historic African American church it serves. This two-volume series has its origins in the lectures I have delivered over the years in the Center's introductory courses on church history. As such, both books continue to bear the marks of my oral presentations and of the wonderful students whom I have been privileged to teach in this very special institution.

Anyone who has taught such courses knows how much the students teach the teacher. On so many occasions I have changed my perspective on material, clarified my thinking, due to insightful interventions of the quality students who matriculate at the Center. Many of them who read the book will be able to recognize that it is they who wrote a portion of the work. What a pleasure it is, then, to thank them not just in these acknowledgments but also by dedicating this book to them.

In addition to these coauthors I also recognize my colleagues from the Center, whose support, provocative insights regarding the African American church, and encouragement to explore the implications of the history of the Church for globalizing a theological curriculum have been essential elements in the writing process. Thank you wonderful colleagues!

My family spent the most time with me in the room in which I wrote and edited. An occasional good conversation with my children, my mother, and my wife, Betsey, in the middle of a paragraph that needed more work and further reflection had a way of making the writing process a lot more fun. In the case of Betsey, her contribution as editor and conversation partner has been especially profound (though we both got a lot of help in editing this time from Ruthann Dwyer). Besides being my best friend and wife of twenty-six years, Betsey truly has been my primary coauthor over the years, and that includes this time too. I have plans in the next volume more duly to thank her for her contributions. But we have both agreed that this book, which to some extent concerns itself with the reclaiming of Christianity's African roots, is more aptly dedicated to the very special sons and daughters of Africa whom I have the pleasure of serving at the black church's largest and premier theological center.

WHY CHURCH HISTORY

There is virtually no school of Christian theological education anywhere in the world that does not require the study of church history. Church leaders are not considered adequately prepared unless they know something of the heritage of the Church. Why is the study of the history of the Church deemed so essential? Seminary students regularly ask this question. Courses in biblical studies seem immediately relevant for ministry, as do courses in practical theology. Justifying the study of theology and ethics as necessary preparation for ministry is not difficult either. However, to convince seminary students and biblically concerned laity of the relevance of church history is a much more difficult matter. Church history appears to be little more than an exercise in intellectual trivia, with scant relevance for the parish.

In response to these criticisms, I must be candid about my perspective. I have always found church history to be a relevant resource for ministry. Of course, we encounter colleagues in ministry who claim that church history is of little use to them (and, besides, they have forgotten most of what they had learned in seminary anyway). Nevertheless, pastors like myself who love church history have found ourselves living off the discipline as a constant source of inspiration and as a conversation partner in sermon preparation, in the leadership of Christian education events, and in the day-to-day decisions pastors are always making about priorities and pastoral care.

Why (and how) has church history played such an important role in my ministry? Why has the Church agreed on the importance of this discipline for the preparation of its leaders? In a sense, this entire book and its companion volume — written as an introduction to church history for students of theology, undergraduates, and interested laity — are my response to these questions. It is my firm conviction that when readers truly enter into dialogue with the giants of the faith and the decisive historical events examined in this two-volume work, many of their questions regarding relevance will vanish.

The key stipulation here is "dialogue." If the history of the Church is approached with an attitude that it is merely a collection of facts to learn, sure enough, the material will not come alive and will not be relevant. Students of church history need to enter into conversation with the great theologians of the past — argue with them and/or assess the degree to which the students' own theological commitments are indebted to these great mentors. Students also need to imagine what life and ministry were like in centuries past in order to appreciate why the Church took certain decisions or reacted as it did. In short, church history only comes alive and is relevant when we "live" with the data, when we make it our own.

In fact, Christians are people who live with the "stuff" of church history. They are people formed by communities (and in many cases by families) that are living incarnations of the core data of the discipline. The use of a creed in worship (or its disuse), the style of interactions laypersons have with their clergy, the character of Sunday school, and the laity's perceptions of what it takes to live Christianly on the job are all functions of the living relevance of the material dealt with by the discipline of church history. Living the Christian life is an ongoing dialogue with church history.

Providing opportunities for dialogue with the wealth of Christian history and reclaiming dimensions of the heritage that have been neglected make this textbook and its companion volume unique. This reference to wealth, to the richness of Christian roots, points to a fundamental principle of my scholarship that provides the organizing principle of these volumes. The Church has a richly diverse heritage, which, in the interest of making more simple what is complex and as a reflection of the cultural-intellectual presuppositions of many Western historians, has too often been repressed in introductory presentations.

Wealth and diversity are blessings, but they can also be a curse. Many options can be bewildering and confusing. It is that way with the history of Christianity. Readers who want a neat picture of the Church's history need to obtain some of the standard Western, male-oriented narratives that largely neglect Eastern Christianity, the Church in Asia and Africa, women, or other usually marginalized groups. This is not that sort of Western male-oriented book. It and its companion volume are marked by their exploration of the theology and church life of regions that other textbooks usually ignore. In that sense, these books can help the Church reclaim its roots. Efforts in many church history textbooks used in Western settings to simplify the complex for those new to the discipline have achieved their aims at a price. They have cost the Church wealth, diversity, and inclusiveness.

This book and its companion are not about to abandon readers in the chaos that is history. First and foremost, this is a textbook, not a book for experts in the field. Thus to help the student, at some points I have prepared lists or employed formal typologies of the views of persons and developments that were contemporary, explaining each, one at a time, rather than merely narrating the events of the years during which each existed. What such an approach forfeits in storytelling, it gains in clarity and depth of analysis.

This volume and its companion are distinct from other church history texts in offering material and study helps for readers to master the material and to learn to think theologically for themselves. Rather than organizing the material neatly, I have preferred to present it in all its rich diversity, providing readers with some formal categories and tools (in the form of open-ended questions) to guide them in dialoguing with the Church's history and in thinking about it for themselves. I shall explain these tools in more detail subsequently.

The study of church history helps make its students more sophisticated Christian theologians. Students of church history have dealt with the wealth of Christian history and made it their own by clarifying and systematicizing the diversity themselves. They have learned to think systematically and do it for themselves.

These initial reflections on the relevance of church history deserve more systematic elaboration. I have identified at least four distinct roles for the discipline of church history in ministry: as community building, as safety patrol, as an instrument of liberation, and as a source of theological creativity.

CHURCH HISTORY AS COMMUNITY BUILDING

The preceding reflections on the ongoing impact that ecclesiastical decisions and theologians of the past continue to have on the Church suggest a different paradigm for describing church history. Practitioners of this discipline are not "intellectuals" (in the narrow sense of engaging in activities removed from "real life"). Rather, church historians are more like storytellers or family elders, who spin the tales and lore of the old days. Practitioners of the discipline are the family member or neighbor who can spot a feature on your face (or in your thought) and link it to some (spiritual) relative, recounting the tales of that father or mother of yesteryear in such a way that he or she comes alive. Those of us privileged to have grown up in such a family or community where the stories of kin are still living realities know how wonderfully illuminating it is, how many fresh insights about oneself can be received, when who we are is seen as a reflection of our forebears' hopes and dreams.

One is not alone, not without support, when one's talents, dreams, and even misfortunes are interpreted in relation to loved ones and forebears who have gone before. For example, I am consistently strengthened in my commitments to the political and spiritual values of my own worldview when I reflect on the nurture I received growing up in a home shaped by the egalitarian politics of modern Norway and the feeling-oriented Pietism typical of my grandparents' and my mother's southern Norwegian homeland. In my own particular way, I am just walking in their shoes, an heir to the family jewels.

Given the pluralism of Western society at the turn of the millennium and the Church's present status as an increasingly minority community in our post-Christian context, its members need this kind of awareness of their roots and identity. Relatively recent congregational studies of thriving churches have revealed that those parishes that best nurture a sense of identity and heritage through adult educational programs tend to be the most thriving and are most inclined to nurture spiritual maturity among their members. Broader socioecclesiastical analyses further confirm this insight.

In American society (and elsewhere in the West), people feel increasingly bereft of a sense of community and seem more and more to function as isolated questers for a sense of self. Is it any wonder that theologically conservative church movements and/or ethnically distinct denominations are growing faster and exerting more social impact in this context than those mainline denominations most inclined to identify with the prevailing sociocultural trends? The theologically conservative (Evangelical) movements tend to offer a sense of community not found in the ecclesiastical institutions more fully "mainstreamed." How have they built such communal sense? They have done so by highlighting their uniqueness from society as a whole and by nurturing in members (or capitalizing on) a sense that their "family tree" is distinct from the whole of society. This same formula also seems to explain the phenomenal present growth of the Church in the Southern Hemisphere, as in these regions to be a Christian is to belong to a community that sets one apart from society as a whole.

Given these dynamics of church growth and effective Christian nurture, it is evident how the material of church history can contribute to a sense of communal heritage and identity so essential to the development of vibrant congregational and denominational life. Even many of the Western mainline and historically ethnic denominations are recognizing this. Calls for a renewed sense of denominational identity and heritage are very much on the front burner of many denominational offices. This agenda is also one of the newest trends in the study of church history.

Why, then, church history? To some extent church history is about denominational/confessional identity, that is, helping Christians understand and appreciate the uniqueness of their particular branch of

Christianity so that they can come to know who they truly are. Our account of the history of the Church since biblical times endeavors to provide this element, summarizing at appropriate points in the narrative the distinct beliefs and heritage of each of the major denominational and (when appropriate) ethnic Christian heritages.

Such preoccupation with denominational/confessional identity represents no relapse into a narrow parochialism. This is evident from the fact that, save for the Eastern Orthodox–Roman Catholic Schism and the Monophysite churches' schism with the Catholic Church dealt with in this volume, the question of denominational distinctions does not preoccupy our attention until the second volume of this series. This way of treating the data entails that the concern with denominational and ethnic uniqueness emerges only in the broader context of catholic (universal) consensus that Christians have shared virtually unbroken for centuries and still share today. To celebrate my unique Lutheran identity is not to divorce myself from the fellowship I share with the Roman Catholic, African Monophysite, or Pentecostal traditions.

Church history offers its students insights into their identity, a knowledge of what they share in common with their kin (learnings necessary for thriving communities), and with it a kind of self-confidence without which ventures of fellowship with other Christians and society as a whole are not possible. Only if you know who you are (know your roots) can you risk encounter with your neighbor.

CHURCH HISTORY AS SAFETY PATROL

The Church may or may not be infallible (the succeeding narrative will provide enough data for readers to make their own judgment about this), but all would agree that certain segments of its membership have made mistakes. In anticipating the next mistakes likely to be found in the Church and the role church history might play in safeguarding the Church from such errors, a particularly distinguished African theologian of the late fourth to early fifth centuries, Augustine, has offered some profound insights. (Readers will note how important the contributions of prominent African Christians have been to the final formulation of many universally accepted doctrines and practices.)

Augustine was the foremost early formulator of a view of human nature that has gained catholic endorsement by the Church. As a primary formulator of the doctrine of original sin, he taught that human beings (even Christians) since the Fall are mired in sin. Just as we did through Adam in the Garden of Eden, human beings are always bound to go astray (*Against Two Letters of the Pelagians* IV.IV.7; I.VIII; cf.

Gen. 3; Rom. 5:12; 7:14–23). Since the Fall, human beings, it seems, are inclined to make the same mistakes over and over again. Given these dynamics, studying how the Church has dealt with its past mistakes is invaluable in helping us catch their modern versions before they get out of hand. The study of ancient heresies and the Church's interaction with them also provides guidance today in the struggle to minister to those exposed to these modern versions of those old mistakes.

What makes church history relevant? Such study gives access to the great minds of the past, access to your roots, in the ongoing struggle against the perversity and waywardness of false Christian teachings and social injustices. The more sense of heritage you have imbibed, the more sense of solidarity you feel with your Christian brothers and sisters of the past, then the more chance the Christian movement has to succeed.

CHURCH HISTORY AS AN INSTRUMENT OF LIBERATION

Several modern Latin American theologians who represent a perspective called "liberation theology" have suggested another aspect of the relevance of church history for the Christian ministry. Their point, especially as it is implied in remarks by Juan Luis Segundo,[1] is that the Church needs to study church history because a historical perspective is necessary in order to understand the present and all its injustices to the poor. The study of history involves stepping out of your own shoes, to live in a world foreign to your own. It involves looking at the world the way someone else did. The commitment to study church history entails that most of the time we are to live in a world very different from the one you and I know. It is not the world of capitalism, multimedia, automobiles, and air conditioning. In this book, we will travel in slower, more chaotic, more ordered worlds. Our job is to live in those worlds.

What is gained from all this for ministry? Our own world will look a little different from this other perspective in which we must endeavor to reside. Moreover, we are likely to see things in our world that we have never seen before. (At least that can happen to you if you really try to think like Athanasius and Augustine or like a Reformation woman, Martin Luther, John Calvin, Susanna Wesley, Charles Mason, or Martin Luther King). From this new perspective, we may stop taking some things for granted that we were taking before, see new problems, and perhaps find new answers.

---

1. Juan Luis Segundo, *The Liberation of Theology*, trans. John Drury (Maryknoll, N.Y.: Orbis, 1976), 19, 9.

The discipline in which one must be engaged when doing history, learning how to think like and to walk in the shoes of somebody else, is what Christian ministry is all about. In the parish or the specialized ministry in which we serve or are preparing to serve, we need to know how to walk in the other person's shoes, to empathize with them, to hurt or to celebrate with them. Another reason for the study of church history, then, is to provide opportunities for learning to empathize with people who do not come from your world — skills that good ministers must have.

CHURCH HISTORY AS A SOURCE OF THEOLOGICAL CREATIVITY

One final reason for the study of church history has to do with drawing on the wisdom of my Christian neighbor and on the wisdom of the geniuses of the Church. I know from personal experience that this argument for the relevance of church history will resonate with anyone who has served in parish ministry in the same location for several years.

After three years in the same pulpit, pastors will probably find themselves less creative than they thought they were. They are likely to be running out of fresh, original things to say in the pulpit, in Sunday school, in Bible studies, and in the newsletter. (One of the greatest American theologians of our century, Reinhold Niebuhr, said almost the same thing about himself and his ministry in *Leaves from the Notebook of a Tamed Cynic.*) After just eight or nine months in a parish, you have probably told all the stories and used all the examples you know and shared all your insights. Then what do you do?

What helped me was reading church history in the parish. Reading the work of the giants — Augustine, Athanasius, Tertullian, Martin Luther, John Calvin, John Wesley, Karl Barth, Reinhold Niebuhr, Georgia Harkness, John Mbiti, and Martin Luther King Jr. — is how the new insights came. These parents in the faith can offer insights that we are likely never to have gained on our own. From them, pastors can acquire new ideas for sermons about the meaning of Bible texts. It is through such study that church leaders and their congregations can get their batteries charged. The study of church history is a most relevant discipline for church leaders who know that they need help in keeping fresh.

•

None of the benefits of the study of church history that I have outlined are likely to accrue — that is, readers are probably doomed to come away from reading these texts with little more than a sense of their offering mere book learning — if readers fail to engage the material and do not try to make it their own. One needs to engage the figures and events of the Church's history, dialogue with their proposals, and second-guess the Church's solutions. Role-play is a helpful way that I have found to make the material come alive. Sometimes dialogue on a contemporary problem may be a way to proceed. For example, what would King, Wesley, Luther, and Clement of Rome propose for dealing with America's welfare crisis? How would Origen, Tertullian, and Calvin deal with the new religious pluralism in America?

These reflections allow me to introduce explicitly the tools I am providing to help readers learn how to order and dialogue with the wealth of church history. To facilitate the process of appropriation, each chapter, especially in the final section, includes several questions about the events, persons, and movements discussed in the chapter. The questions, not merely concerned with the mastery of facts, guide readers in developing their own theological perspective in relation to the material covered. They help readers reclaim the rich diversity of Christian roots and order the wealth. These questions are deliberately open-ended and do not lend themselves to quick and simple answers. They do not require expertise, but they will require long periods of reflection and a willingness to live with the material. Instructors might use these questions (or formulate their own) as a means of assisting the process of educating students to think theologically about both the tradition and present realities. Sensitivity to these pedagogical matters is one of the distinguishing characteristics of this introduction to church history.

The sort of contemporary dialogue with the past that I suggest presupposes that one has first taken the historical figures and events being considered on their own terms and in their own context. This commitment implies that we have actually read the works of the giants of the Church's past. Study of the primary sources is absolutely essential. To that end, I have prepared texts that facilitate such study. At every point in each chapter when theological commitments are attributed to the persons considered, primary-source documentation is provided. These references give readers a starting point for investigating the actual writings of the theologian on the subject in question. As such, this book and its companion volume are invitations and tools for facilitating an actual encounter between readers and the great theologians of the past.

Even when this feature of the textbook in your hands is taken into account, I nevertheless urge a careful and limited use of it. Like every other survey of the rich history of the Church, it shortchanges readers. It can only function adequately as an introduction to church history when its readers are keeping the author and his interpretations "honest" by supplementing the text with ample readings in the primary sources themselves.

CHAPTER 1

THE BEGINNINGS OF CHRISTIANITY
INCLUDING THE GENTILES

No history of Christianity can begin without some attention to the historical-cultural context in which Christianity began. Much of its subsequent history, particularly those events covered in the next chapters, is a direct consequence of Christianity's origins as a first-century Jewish sect in a "backwater" province of the Roman Empire.

The setting of most of the biblical accounts in Palestine (the Jewish Holy Land) is a stark reminder that Christianity and the fate of its adherents are intimately connected with the Jewish people and their heritage. One must never forget — though segments of the Church in different historical contexts sought to forget it — that Jesus and all his first followers were Jews. Paul, in Romans 11:17–24, says that Gentile Christians (the vast majority of members of the Church throughout history) have been grafted into the root that is Judaism, grafted into the Jewish heritage. Subsequently in the chapter he says, "And so all Israel will be saved" (v. 26).

OLD TESTAMENT PRECEDENTS

The Bible makes it evident that Palestine has long been a land of strife and suffering. In ancient times this turmoil was a function of its geographical position at the crossroads of the most important trade routes that joined Egypt and Mesopotamia, the two dominant civilizations of ancient times in the region, as well as the trade routes between Arabia and Asia Minor. As empires came and went in the region, they repeatedly cast a covetous eye on this strip of land.

The early history of the Hebrew people in Israel as reported in the Old Testament may be divided into six periods: (1) the settlement in the land after the Exodus late in the thirteenth century B.C.; (2) the amphictyony, as reported in the Book of Judges, when each of the tribes or regions in Israel that the Hebrews had settled had its own local ruler, or judge (some historians maintain that this may have been a period in which twelve unrelated peoples, each with their own tribal gods, gradually began to recognize their mutual affinities and to adopt common religious practices); (3) the United Kingdom, the period when all of the Hebrew tribes were united not only under a single God but also under a single ruler — Saul, David, and Solomon; (4) the "civil war," or secession of the northern tribes (assuming the name "Israel") from the tribe of Judah, which remained loyal to Solomon's heir; (5) the conquests of Samaria (the capital of the Northern Kingdom) and Jerusalem by the Assyrians and Babylonians, respectively; and (6) the return and rebuilding of the Temple during a period of Persian domination. Generally speaking the Old Testament narrative concludes prior to Alexander the Great's fourth-century B.C. conquest of Persia. This military accomplishment in turn made this Macedonian the ruler of Palestine. His victory had important cultural implications, which if not properly understood can distort our understanding of the earliest stages of Christianity.

ALEXANDER THE GREAT, THE PROGRAM OF HELLENIZATION, AND HEBREW REACTION

Alexander's conquests had an ideological basis. He did not wish simply to conquer the world; he also wanted to unite it by spreading the insights of Greek civilization throughout the region (a strategy that has come to be called "Hellenization"). As a result, the territories of his empire developed a mix of the elements of classical Greek culture with those of civilizations he had conquered. The indigenization of this cultural outlook became important subsequently for the propagation of Christianity in the next centuries. Alexander's strategy provided a unity for the eastern Mediterranean basin, which made it easier for a common gospel to be preached than would have been possible had each of its regional cultures maintained its own distinct culture.

Many Jews during the period of Macedonia's domination did not regard Hellenism as a blessing. Hellenistic ideology consisted in equating and mixing the gods of different nations. The most devout Hebrews generally regarded this as a threat to their faith. The history of Palestine from the time of Alexander until the destruction of Jerusalem by the Roman Empire in A.D. 70 is properly understood as a struggle between Hellenizing pressures against continuing faithfulness to Hebraic traditions.

The Maccabees' family led a revolt in the second century B.C., which marks the high point in the Hebrew struggle against Hellenism. The account of this revolt appears in several books of the Apocrypha. It is a great story. For roughly a century the Maccabees were able to restore Israel's independence. Eventually, though, their successors also succumbed to the Hellenizing pressures of the Seleucid dynasty (the royal house that presided over the northern and eastern part of Alexander's empire following his death). After some turbulence in Israel over these dynamics, Rome intervened in 63 B.C., which explains how Roman power was in place by the time of Jesus.

ROMAN RULE AND JEWISH REACTION

In general, the Roman Empire governed by means of tolerant policies. The local religion and most of the customs of the people whom they had conquered were permitted to remain in place. In Israel, the Roman government permitted descendants of the Maccabees some authority, using several of them to govern the land. Even Herod, appointed the puppet ruler of the region by Rome in 40 B.C., had a distant relation to the Maccabees through marriage. His Hellenizing policies met much Jewish resistance.

The Jewish reaction in this period to Roman Hellenizing assumed several forms. Hebrews of like-minded concern organized themselves into several distinct groups: Zealots, Pharisees, Sadducees, and Essenes.

Zealots. This radical party tenaciously opposed Roman rule, usually advocating or employing revolutionary, if not military, means of liberation (see Acts 5:36–37). The Zealots played a leadership role in the Jewish insurrection of A.D. 66, which failed and resulted in the destruction of the Jerusalem Temple four years later.

Pharisees. In this era, the Pharisees were the best known of the Jewish parties both because of numerous Gospel reports about their interactions with Jesus (e.g., Matt. 12, 16, 21–23; Mark 2, 7; Luke 7, 11, 14; John 7–11) and because they shaped modern Judaism. This party of common Jews did not enjoy much material prosperity from Roman rule. They advocated faithfulness to the Law and the careful study of it for its everyday implications. As such, the Pharisaic party was very important in helping Judaism adjust to the new cultural context. Quite critical of the Pharisees, conservatives (like the Sadducees) regarded them as innovative, citing as evidence the Pharisees' adoption of a belief in angels and in the final resurrection. It is likely that Jesus had roots in and affinities to the Pharisaic party. In moving among common people as he did, Jesus was more likely to rub shoulders with Pharisees than with other Jewish groups.

Sadducees. A more conservative, upper-class group of Jews, the Sadducees were more oriented to the old-style worship of the Temple in Jerusalem. Their political conservatism helped them gain favor with their Roman rulers (Acts 4:1–3; 23:6–8).

Essenes. An ascetic sect, the Essenes were also apocalyptic (believing in the imminent, cataclysmic final destruction of evil). Many interpreters attribute the Dead Sea Scrolls to them. We might think of the Essenes as forerunners of modern sects. They were certain that the end was coming but were also dedicated to practicing a very strict version of Judaism. Some historians believe that a number of the *heresies* (false teachings or distortions of the Word of God) that the early Church encountered derived from this community.

All of these parties were characterized by an eschatological orientation. (*Eschatology* refers to the end times.) Early Christianity's eschatological orientation may have its roots in them. For evidence of this eschatological orientation, consider Matthew 4:17, where it is stated that from the time of John the Baptist's death Jesus' preaching centered on the imminent dawn of the kingdom of God.

CONSEQUENCES OF THE JEWISH DIASPORA

For centuries before the birth of Jesus, since the Babylonian captivity of the early sixth century B.C. (2 Kings 24:10–17), the number of Jews living away from Israel (Diaspora Judaism) increased. This phenomenon was of crucial importance for the spread of Christianity because the Diaspora Jewish community was one of the main avenues through which the new faith expanded.

One characteristic of Diaspora Jewish communities was that most of their members had forgotten the language of their ancestors. A translation of the Hebrew Scriptures into a language accessible to their membership was a necessity. Alexander the Great's program had made Greek the common language of much of the Mediterranean. Consequently a Greek translation of the Hebrew Scriptures was necessary. Out of this context came the first translation of the Hebrew Bible into Greek, the *Septuagint*, which means "version of seventy." According to Jewish legend, this translation is so called because it was the product of seventy Jewish scholars who worked on it independently and whose translations miraculously agreed. The aim of the legend was to verify the later claim that the translation itself was divinely inspired.

The Septuagint proved enormously important for the development of Christianity, providing a ready-made medium for translating the message to Gentiles. Indeed, this translation of the Hebrew Scriptures is the version most often quoted by New Testament writers and therefore profoundly influenced early Christian vocabulary. For example, consider the title "Christ." Not found in the Masoretic text, it is the Greek term that appears in the Septuagint as a translation of the Hebrew term "Anointed One" or "Messiah."

A second characteristic of Diaspora Judaism was its need to enter into dialogue with Hellenistic philosophy, to engage in *apologetics* (rational arguments) on behalf of Judaism. The city of Alexandria was a hotbed of this kind of activity. Indeed, much of the cutting-edge work in apologetics in early Christianity came out of this Egyptian city, and the prime Jewish apologist was an Alexandrian named Philo (ca. 20 B.C.–ca. A.D. 50).

A contemporary of Jesus, Philo argued that the best in Greek philosophy agreed with Hebrew Scriptures; the difference, he claimed, was that Scripture speaks figuratively (*On the Account of the World's Creation Given by Moses*). Early Christians came to employ precisely this kind of allegorical interpretation for such apologetic purposes. Philo was primarily in dialogue with Neoplatonism, which was a later, revised version of Plato's philosophy. However, the philosophical school of Stoicism also influenced him, as evidenced in his endorsement of the concept of the Logos (cf. VI; John 1).

EARLY CHRISTIANITY'S CULTURAL AND INTELLECTUAL DEBTS TO THE ROMAN EMPIRE

Early Christianity's cultural context in the Graeco-Roman world was definitely a factor in accounting for the faith's success. The Roman Empire's political unity allowed Christians to travel in a way that would have been impossible due to harassment by bandits and pirates only a few decades before. The empire's political unity was also good for trade, which in turn mandated travel by ordinary people. Many Christians, not just missionaries, were regularly on the road during this period. They too spread the gospel (Acts 8:1ff.). The development of the Septuagint was another factor contributing to Christianity's success.

Two philosophical traditions prominent in the empire, both of which influenced Philo and the Diaspora Judaism of the era, also proved useful for advancing the gospel. Not unlike Philo, some Christians began employing the categories of Neoplatonism and Stoicism in order to gain intellectual credibility for the claims of the new faith.

NEOPLATONISM

After a period of losing influence in the Roman Empire as a whole, Platonism — the philosophy of the ancient Greek Plato (428–348 B.C.) — made a comeback early in the second century A.D. This revivification was really a modification of Plato's thought and has been termed "Neoplatonism." Plato believed that the physical world was comprised of fleeting things and so was not eternal. True reality was to be found in the universal forms that individual entities share in common. For example, he might argue, readers of this book share the common universal form of humanness. We can discern correct data and observations contained in this book because these particular truths participate in the universal form of "Truth." As essentially spiritual in nature, such forms are eternal (*Republic* VI,VII; *Parmenides*). Plato even spoke of humans as being composed of an eternal soul (*Phaedo* VI,XIV).

The new cultural climate, due to the influence of the rise of various mystery religions in this period, fostered an emphasis on the immediacy of internal human experience. This manifested in a quasi-religious philosophical preoccupation with the anxieties of sensual, bodily existence and, in response to these anxieties, in the articulation of strategies for restoring the soul to its original state of contemplation. Portrayed as a kind of salvation, such restoration was a different emphasis from that found in the philosophy of Plato and the other ancient Greeks, whose primary preoccupation was with understanding or explaining the world. However, Platonic categories, particularly in distinguishing the world of the senses from the world of ideas, were congenial to these new cultural trends. Consequently the revivification of Plato's thought by these philosophers of the Roman Empire in service of a new agenda is hardly surprising.

Given these commitments, Neoplatonists criticized the polytheistic gods of the Greek pantheon in favor of a supreme, immutable being in which is encompassed all other forms.[1] There is an obvious compatibility between the Christian faith and this Neoplatonic belief in a supreme, immutable being. Compatibilities between this philosophy and the teachings of the Church are evident in some of its other affirmations. In view of these compatibilities and the increasing popularization of the Neoplatonic agenda among the Roman Empire's elite, it is hardly surprising that early Christians adopted a number of Neoplatonic themes. (Of course, appropriation of the Neoplatonic concept of the immutability of God may have been to Christianity's detriment given the interactivist view of God portrayed by the Old Testament; see Gen. 6:6–7; Exod. 32:14; 1 Sam. 15:11,35.)

STOICISM

This philosophical school, whose precise origins are a matter of debate, eventually became a dominant philosophy in the Roman Empire and was even propounded by one of the most prominent emperors of the

---

1. Plotinus *Enneads* VI Trac. IX.

second century. Stoicism advocated high moral standards and a willingness to endure without passion what is given by the ever-enduring laws of nature.[2] These emphases made Stoicism most attractive to early Christians with their concern about responsible lifestyle and obedience.

As a consequence of their materialistic, pantheistic orientation and insistence on the universality of the law of reason, Stoics at least implicitly critiqued the religions of the empire and offered a critique of parochialism. Stoics believed that they were citizens of the world.[3] As such, Stoicism provided a congenial conceptuality to early Christians when they sought to draw members from all races after agreeing to admit Gentiles. The issue of receiving Gentiles was, as is well known, a crucial, difficult decision to which we shall soon turn. We have already noted the Stoic endorsement of the concept of Logos — that is, the idea that all rational creatures participate in universal Reason — and its obvious resonance with Christian teaching.[4]

GNOSTICISM

Another cultural current that affected the early Church is Gnosticism (1 Tim. 4:3–5; 6:20; 1 John). It is sufficient at this point simply to note that this loosely organized movement derives its name from the Greek word *gnōsis*, which means "knowledge." Gnostics believed that they possessed a special mystical knowledge, reserved only for the elite, that would release them from imprisonment in the material world (the body).[5] As early as the late first century, Christians were rejecting these and their associated body-denying claims in the New Testament epistles cited above.

EARLY CHRISTIANITY AND ITS RELATIONSHIP WITH JUDAISM

The first Christians did not consider themselves part of a new religion. They were still Jews in their own mind, convinced that Jesus had fulfilled their ancient faith. This is why they continued to keep the Hebrew Sabbath and to worship in the Temple (Acts 2:46; 13:14; 21:26; 25:8).

---

2. Diogenes Laertius, in *Stoicorum veterum fragmenta* I:179a; III:4; *Manual of Epictetus* 12.
3. Marcus Aurelius *Meditations*, bk. 7.9; Philo and Seneca, in *Stoicorum veterum fragmenta* II:532; III:351.
4. Cf. Cleanthes *Hymn to Zeus*; John 1.
5. *Poimandres*; Nag Hammadi texts, *On the Origin of the World*.

To this they added observance of Sunday to celebrate Jesus' Resurrection; they conducted Communion services (breaking of bread) at that time but did so with a spirit of celebration and joy (Acts 2:46). Only later did worship become more centered on the Cross.

The earliest Jerusalem Christians may not have been as unified as we like to think. References in Acts 6:1 and elsewhere (see Acts 11:20–21) are made to "Hellenists" and "Hebrews" in the body of Christ. Obviously conflict flared between these groups. Since Gentiles had not yet been admitted to Christianity at this stage in Luke's narrative, the distinction can only be based on different attitudes of the groups towards Hellenization. The appointment of the Seven (deacons) was perhaps an effort to give the Hellenized party a more visible leadership role, for all of the Seven (in Acts 6:5) have Greek names.

Hellenistic Jewish Christians probably received harsher treatment from Jewish elders than the "Hebraic" Christians. How else can one explain Stephen's martyrdom (Acts 7:54–60)? They also seem to have functioned as the earliest bridge builders for Christians to the Gentiles (Acts 11:19–21). Of course, eventually such Gentile converts overshadowed the earlier Jewish Christian community.

Hellenistic Christians, the first Christians to be persecuted, were also the first to flee and set up churches outside Jerusalem (Acts 8). This opened the door for a mission to the Gentiles. Paul's work should be understood in this context. Indeed, the work of Hellenistic Christians in setting up churches extended not just to Athens (Acts 17:34), Corinth (Acts 18:1–17), and Rome (Acts 28:15; Rom. 1:7). They also carried on successful evangelism work in such distant and prominent cities as Antioch (Acts 11:19–21), where the Syrian Church to this day claims to be rooted in Peter's ministry, as well as in Damascus (Acts 9:10) and Alexandria (Acts 18:24–25), a product allegedly of the missionary work of Mark. An interesting pattern may be observed in the traditions concerning the founding of these churches. Churches in these and other important cities of the empire claimed apostolic origins, which entailed that credit for this evangelistic work was given to the "Hebraic," not just to the "Hellenistic," parties, even though in fact the latter had been more actively engaged in missionary work.

One can document the presence of Christianity in Africa in the first centuries of the Christian Era in Ethiopia, at least as early as the fourth century when two young Phoenician Christians, Frumentius and Aedesius, introduced King Ezana to Christianity. Eventually he became a convert. Syrian Orthodox missionaries (the Nine Saints) converted the land as a whole in the late fifth century. However, Ethiopians themselves root the origins of Christianity in their land from the conversion of the Ethiopian eunuch by Philip (Acts 8:27–39). In fact, links to the biblical witness are said to be as ancient as the visit of the queen of Sheba to Solomon, who is believed to have answered all her desires by providing her with a male heir (1 Kings 10:1–13). The presence of a tribe of black Jews, the Falashas, who have played an important part in the history of Ethiopia and the Ethiopian Orthodox Church, is indisputable.

When considering other regions not typically regarded as early Christianity's cradle, but in which nonetheless the Church was planted in the first centuries, one should not overlook India. There is a tradition that Bartholomew and Thomas did missionary work there establishing the community of Malabar Christians, which has existed at least since the sixth century A.D. (perhaps founded by a mission of the Syrian church).

It is evident that Paul was not the mission developer of every prominent church in the first century. In fact, in many cases he was not the first to bring the gospel even to the regions he visited (Acts 18:23; 28:13–15). His importance for the early Church seems much more related to his role as a writer for the cause of the mission to the Gentiles than as an evangelist/missionary. The controversy he occasioned concerning the admission of the Gentiles was not readily solved to everyone's satisfaction and may never have really been solved in New Testament times. A study of Acts 11–15 and Galatians renders the validity of that observation readily apparent.

The eventual predominance of the Pauline side in the dispute over the admission of Gentiles to the Church is evident in the character of Christian literature. Every prominent postbiblical writer of the early Church was a Gentile. This trend differs radically from the New Testament, whose authors, with but the one exception of Luke, were apparently Jews. Such a development is symptomatic of the radical change in postbiblical Christianity. For the first Christians, continuity with Judaism was crucial. They and most of their contemporaries regarded the Church and Judaism as parts of the same family, in a relationship like one has with one's own mother. With predominant Gentile membership, though, the theological agenda shifted to establishing discontinuity with Judaism, almost like relating to one's mother-in-law. As we move into the second century and beyond, Christians came to regard the Jewish heritage of their faith as a burden or as offensive.

These new developments entailed that Christian faith was no longer merely a syncretistic version of Judaism. For the sake of unity in the empire, Roman authorities were inclined to countenance syncretistic faiths, which combined insights from different religions. Adherents of these faiths did not undermine the empire's unity since they would be open to finding truths in all the faiths of the empire. When Christianity no longer qualified for such a "safe category," it began to receive more attention from Roman authorities, coming to be viewed with more suspicion, which eventually culminated in persecutions (to be considered in the next chapter).

These developments, as well as Herod Agrippa's persecution of certain Jerusalem Christians (notably James the son of Zebedee and Peter; Acts 12:1–19) and the need for the Jerusalem Christians to distance themselves from a growing Hebrew nationalism that eventually led to Jerusalem's destruction by Roman forces in A.D. 70, resulted in the scattering and isolation of the Jewish Christian community. Victimized by heretical tendencies and the suspicions of the dominant Gentile segment of the Church, it faded away, probably by the fifth century. However, as our concluding considerations will suggest, this form of Christianity may not be dead entirely.

CONCLUSION: IS CHRISTIANITY REALLY A WESTERN RELIGION? IF NOT, WHY ARE OUR CHURCHES NOT MORE LIKE THE MOST ANCIENT ONES IN ASIA AND AFRICA?

In each chapter, as previously indicated, the concluding section frames a question for readers with the express intent of prodding them to come to some conclusion about the issue addressed. Each of these issues is framed with an eye towards helping readers develop their own theological perspective. In this chapter, we need to examine our own theological and cultural presuppositions about the Christian faith. Most readers are likely to approach Christianity with the assumption that it is a Western religion, which, though it may have originated in the ancient Near East, has its real strength and most profound cultural impact in Europe and in North America. Christianity in Asia and Africa, we have been led to believe, is a product of the modern missionary movement or of the Roman Empire's "Christianization" of North Africa in the third century. With these assumptions some argue that Christianity is a religion of the white man imposed on Africans and Indian people. Islam and Hinduism are said to be more authentic to the cultural heritage of these regions.

We have noted some historical data that call these assumptions into question. Christianity has ancient roots in Africa, Syria, and India. Churches in these regions are nearly a millennium older than the churches to which Protestant readers belong. They are older than Islam and so are more indigenous to these regions. These facts issue several challenges to readers who belong to Western church denominations (Roman Catholicism and Protestant denominations).

Why have the Western churches been so ignorant of the presence of ancient churches in these regions of the Southern Hemisphere? Why have we thought of these regions as unchurched and requiring evangelization? Given the venerability of these branches of Christendom, it seems about time that we began to take their unique teachings and practices more seriously in the formation of our own theologies. The preceding proposal becomes all the more provocative when we consider the character of one of these churches, the Ethiopian Orthodox Church, which seems to embody characteristics unique to the most ancient version of Christianity, Jewish Christianity. We can only appreciate the unique character of this church, though, if we consider it in relation to its sister church, the Coptic Orthodox Church, and to the Eastern Orthodox tradition as a whole.

THE NATURE OF AFRICAN ORTHODOXY AND THE EASTERN ORTHODOX FAMILY

Eastern Orthodoxy refers to those churches originating in regions that in the first centuries were more under the sphere of influence of Constantinople than of Rome. We have already noted the alleged apostolic origins of all of these churches. Even newer Orthodox ecclesiastical bodies, such as the Greek Orthodox Church and Russian Orthodox Church, claim apostolic foundation insofar as all of them maintain that their ministries are in the apostolic line. In making this claim, they affirm *apostolic succession* (the belief that every bishop ever consecrated has been consecrated by a bishop who was himself consecrated by a bishop, and this line of succession can be traced back to one of the apostles). For theological-historical reasons, nearly all of them tend towards some form of hierarchical dependence, not on the bishop of Rome (the Roman Catholic papacy), but on the ecumenical patriarch (bishop) of Constantinople (at least regarding this episcopal office as "first among equals"). As in the Roman Catholic tradition, such bishops are celibate; however, the Orthodox tradition does differentiate itself from Rome in allowing for married clergy as parish priests.

At least six other theological commonalties are shared by almost all of the Orthodox churches:

Authority of tradition. Where there is consensus in the Church over time about a particular teaching or practice, then we are to treat it as infallibly authoritative. This commitment in turn entails that the style of these churches' theology is oriented, not so much toward the latest theological trends, but rather toward consideration of the writings of the first Christian theologians (the so-called Church Fathers, whom we begin considering in the next chapter).

Liturgical forms of worship. Given the preceding commitment, it is not surprising that worship in these churches would be structured around very ancient orders of worship called "liturgies" (prescribed forms of worship in which the basic structure of the service does not change from week to week). Notably in the case of the African churches, these liturgies typically reflect the cultural forms of their region of origin. These liturgies are distinct from, though at many points similar to, the liturgies of Western churches. They are also much longer than the Western liturgies: A typical Orthodox Sunday service runs several hours (with a sermon much briefer than the typical Protestant sermon). Worshipers are free to come and go during the service.

Related to worship styles is the use of a distinctly Christian calendar for the church year. Worship and devotional life are structured around certain festivals (Easter, Pentecost, Epiphany, Christmas, assorted saints' days, etc.), much like in liturgically oriented churches of the West. One important difference is the date for the celebration of Christmas. For reasons we shall subsequently examine, the Orthodox Church celebrates the birth of Christ, not on December 25, but on January 6 (the Festival of the Epiphany).

Rejection of the Filioque. Like the Roman Catholic Church and many Protestant churches, the Orthodox churches acknowledge the authority of the Nicene Creed. However, unlike these Western churches, the Eastern churches do not include the phrase, in the final article of the creed pertaining to the Holy Spirit, that the Spirit proceeds from the Father "and the Son" (*filioque* in the original Latin amendment of the creed). On firm historical grounds, the Orthodox churches maintain that the phrase is an addition to the original Nicene Creed and so should be rejected as tampering.

Belief in seven sacraments and the real presence. Orthodoxy practices the same number of sacraments as the Roman Catholic Church recognizes: baptism, Lord's Supper (Eucharist), confession, confirmation, ordination, marriage, and last rites (extreme unction). Also like the Roman Catholic tradition, these churches do not regard the sacraments as mere symbols but believe that Christ is actually present in the visible elements of the rites. However, the Orthodox churches are less inclined than the West to try to speculate or to explain the nature of Christ's presence, tending simply to speak of it as a mystery (*mysterion*).

The understanding of salvation as theōsis *(deification).* The Orthodox churches, unlike those of the West, tend to describe salvation as the process of becoming godlike. In this regard, they are indebted to the insights of Irenaeus, a great second-century bishop of Lyons and theologian of the Church who developed the idea that in salvation "God became man, so man could become like God" (*Against Here-*

sies V.xxi.I; Clement of Alexandria *Exhortation to the Greeks* I.8.4; 2 Pet. 1:4).

Belief in the unity of church and state. In view of the preceding commitment — the belief that God is working to divinize the whole of reality — it is not surprising that the Orthodox reject any two-sphere thinking that would posit a separation of church and state. Rather, the state is regarded as sharing in the divine energies that have been introduced into the material world through the Incarnation. As such, the state is seen not just as divinely instituted but as doing the Will of God. Rulers are divine agents, even functioning as defenders of the faith. Historically these commitments have manifested in situations in which the Orthodox Church has been the guardian of national identity and the ruler's principal ally, as has been the case in Ethiopia (under the regime of Haile Selassie), Greece, and Serbia. The drawback of such a model is that it can lead to the church's submission to the state, as seems to have been typically the case in Russia under Communist rule.

•

Generally speaking, with only a few exceptions (notably in Africa), each of the Orthodox churches understands itself to be in communion with each other, under the authority of the ecumenical patriarch of Constantinople. They tend to be divided, though, by national boundaries. Thus Greece has its own church, as do Syria, Russia, and Egypt, etc. In each case they claim to be apostolically founded. We have already observed this in the case of the Coptic Church and the Ethiopian Orthodox Church. However neither of them, for reasons that we shall soon observe, is in formal fellowship with the Eastern Orthodox family of churches and their acknowledgment of the authority of the ecumenical patriarchate of Constantinople. (In fact, the Coptic Church even has its own pope, the patriarch of Alexandria.) Likewise several other Orthodox bodies, notably the Armenian Apostolic Church and the Syrian Orthodox Church, are not in fellowship with the ecumenical patriarch and the rest of the Orthodox churches. The issue in the cases of all of these dissident churches is that none of them endorses the ecumenically agreed-upon idea, maintained by all the other Orthodox churches, that Jesus has two natures — a divine nature and a human nature.

With regard to the Ethiopian and Coptic churches, there is a longtime sisterly relationship between the two, with the Coptic Church functioning in a kind of motherly role. These close ties extend at least as far back as the fourth century, when Frumentius was consecrated as Ethiopia's first bishop by Athanasius, the bishop of Alexandria. This created a situation in which the Ethiopian Church functioned essentially as a diocese of the Coptic Church, with all its bishops (usually Egyptian) appointed by the patriarch of Alexandria until 1958. Since that time, largely as a result of the growing sense of nationalism under Haile Selassie (1891–1975), it became *autocephalous* (independent, but still belonging to the Alexandrian dioceses).

This kind of relationship between two churches in the first centuries is in keeping with the early Coptic Church's missionary orientation. Its missionary endeavors in Africa and in other regions outside the continent were no doubt related to Egypt's role as a trade center in the ancient world. In connection with this missionary role, it is necessary to address the implicit supposition of much Western scholarship that Egyptian culture is more Arian than African. The Negroid influence in the Nile Valley in premodern Egypt cannot be denied. Egyptian people are a mixture of many peoples. Those in the south have notably darker skin than in the north. Consequently the earliest Christians in that region must have been black. Even if this point is contested, it is impossible to deny indigenous African participation in the church in the case of the Ethiopian Orthodox Church.

The Coptic Church and the Ethiopian Orthodox Church have been linked together historically by unique theological commitments, one of which has separated them from the rest of the Christian world. While other churches, including the Eastern Orthodox churches, endorsed the teachings of the Council of Chalcedon held in 451 concerning Christology (the council pronounced Christ recognized in "two natures, without confusion..., without separation"), the Coptic Church and its sister churches (including the Ethiopian Orthodox, Syrian Orthodox, and Armenian Apostolic churches) have assumed a Monophysite Christology. That is, they have rejected the council's formulation in favor of insisting that Christ is truly one, of one nature. Another Orthodox ecclesiastical body, the Assyrian Church, claiming to be in the apostolic line with the early Assyrian Christians of Nineveh, has likewise been estranged from the catholic community over its view of Christ (Christology). Sometimes identifying itself as the Church of the East and of the Assyrians, it has endorsed the Nestorian heresy, which held that if Christ is divine and human, he must be two persons in one. Unlike in the Orthodox tradition, the Assyrian Church is averse to the use of icons and images, does not practice the sacrament of confession, and does not venerate Mary.

In subsequent chapters we shall examine the origins of the divergent Christologies of these churches and the reasons why the Church as a whole rejected them. For the present, suffice it to note that Monophysitism and Nestorianism seem more commonsensical and reasonable than the two natures formulation. Readers are invited to reflect on what is at stake for themselves and their churches in rejecting these two heresies. One contemporary theological argument on behalf of the

Monophysite position, advanced by theologians of the Ethiopian Orthodox Church, seems particularly provocative. The Incarnation, it is argued, is rather like what happens when wine (signifying Christ's divine nature) is mixed with water (signifying his human nature). Christ is divine and human like the liquid in a cup is water and wine. But just as when water is mixed with wine, one still has wine, so Christ is one. The Christology of the African Orthodox and other Monophysite (Oriental Orthodox) churches may deserve a second look by catholic Christianity, or at least readers need to gain clarity on why it is so important to attribute two natures to Christ.

•

The overwhelming majority of Egypt's Christians (over 90 percent) belong to the Coptic Orthodox Church. However, even though it is very much a minority in Egypt, it is still a most influential minority in an Islamic nation. Some historians have suggested that part of the reason for the success of the Moslem invasion in the seventh century in Egypt and Syria was related to the Monophysite commitment of the Coptic Church. Too much effort to defend these lands by the Byzantine emperor led to papal warnings about the emperor's aiding and abetting heretics, so he backed off. The Near East, Egypt, and most of the rest of North Africa henceforth became Moslem lands. This cultural and historical isolation occasioned by the Islamic conquest is a major factor accounting for why Western civilization has been so ignorant of the historic African churches.

For all its commonalties with the Eastern Orthodox tradition, the Coptic Church is not just unique with regard to its Christology. It employs the Liturgy of Saint Mark, while most of the Orthodox churches employ their own national version of the Liturgy of Saint Chrysostom. The Coptic liturgy is still in the indigenous Coptic language (no longer widely spoken among Egyptian Christians, where Arabic is the language of the street) with unique adaptations. Another unique feature of Coptic Orthodoxy is the significant impact of monasticism (living a life of self-denial in the desert) on the church. Though perhaps declining in numbers today, it has suffered no decline of influence on the church's theology or polity. Bishops and patriarchs are always and only selected from monastic communities.

The Ethiopian Orthodox Church, by contrast, is the majority religious body in its homeland, intimately related to the social and cultural patterns of Ethiopia. This is not the case with regard to the other Oriental Orthodox churches we have been considering. They are minority churches. The Syrian Orthodox Church, once the national church of Syria, was severely decimated by fourteenth-century Mongol invasions and by massacres at the hands of the Turks in the twentieth century. Less than a quarter of a million in membership in the region of its homeland, the church has spread worldwide. The Malabar Christians of India (claiming to be part of the community begun by Thomas in the first century) are part of the Syrian Church. The Armenian Apostolic Church is largely an exodus church of several million in exile from a homeland that has been occupied by foreign powers and severely persecuted by these powers. The Assyrian Church survived after the Moslem invasion by hiding in the mountains of North Kurdistan. It members were driven from this exile site in the twentieth century; what is left of the small community lives mainly in Syria, Iraq, and Lebanon.

IS ETHIOPIAN ORTHODOXY A JEWISH CHRISTIANITY?

True enough, the Ethiopian Church is thoroughly indigenized, a truly African church. That is not to say, however, that it is a church of Gentiles with no regard for Jewish roots. Quite the contrary, it is in this religious body that we may come closest to encountering Jewish Christianity in a modern form.

We have already noted the presence of the tribe of black Jews in Ethiopia, the so-called Falasha, whose presence has been highly influential on Ethiopian society and yet who have endured much persecution, at least since the fifteenth century. In any case, Jewish influence in Ethiopia seems evident in the church. For example, circumcision is prescribed. The Sabbath is observed on Saturdays, while regular worship occurs on Sundays. Numerous items of food are shunned by the Ethiopian Orthodox faithful as unclean, in a manner not unlike Jewish kosher obligations. Old Testament feasts are prominent in the liturgical calendar. Walls around traditional churches and the clear architectural separation of the altar from the nave are reminiscent of demarcations that separated the outer court, inner court, and Holy of Holies in Solomon's Temple (cf. 1 Kings 6–7; Deut. 14:3–21; Lev. 11:2–23).

The preservation of these elements compatible with original Jewish Christianity is indeed striking. Even if these practices are the result of gradual adoption, rather than ancient survivals, they do raise the intriguing possibility that the Ethiopian Orthodox Church might be more in touch with the New Testament version of Christianity (with the disciples' Jewish Christian faith) than any other segment of Christendom. Even the church's Monophysite commitments do not seem to render its belief structure any less venerable. After all, the first disciples never unambiguously talked about two natures of Christ.

Several other characteristics of the church are also intriguing. Monasticism is as influential in Ethiopian Orthodoxy as in the case of the

Coptic Church. Church life is characterized by a large number of clerical professions; a significant number are priests, but many are without much formal training (by Western standards). Typical of African culture, a high view of ministry with much deference given to the priest also characterizes church life. As with all Orthodox churches, women are not ordained. They are permitted to worship in most churches, but not in all because a former empress desecrated one of these buildings. Devotion to Mary is also an important part of Ethiopian Orthodox spiritual life. Some historians suspect that such devotional practices may be rooted in the pre-Christian indigenous worship of the Egyptian goddess Isis.

Fasting for long periods, sometimes 250 days without meat and all forms of animal products, is a common form of devotional practice for priests. Even laity are obligated to fast 180 days according to such rubrics. Pilgrimages to Jerusalem are also a feature of Ethiopian Orthodox spirituality. Some scholars speculate that this practice emerged as a kind of counterpart to the pilgrimages of Ethiopian Moslems to Mecca. The Ethiopian Church recognizes confirmation and the anointing of the sick as sacraments, though, according to reports, they are scarcely practiced. Penance, including a generic confession of sin, is normally given only to the dying.

Perhaps because of the difficulties of establishing a churchwide communications network or as a vestige of the lack of a native hierarchy during the centuries of direction by the Coptic Church, Ethiopian Orthodoxy has a weak hierarchical organization. This has entailed a great deal of local church independence with little liturgical uniformity. Indeed, the church's Jewish Christian orientation is stunningly combined with apparently characteristic African styles of worship.

The Ethiopian Orthodox Church's use of the liturgy of Alexandria (the Liturgy of Saint Mark) is characteristic of some other Orthodox churches. Typical of Orthodox liturgies, the service takes several hours to complete, with worshipers coming and going in the midst of worship being accepted practice. An archaic, older language (Geez) is employed in the worship. The music is also indigenous, with roots in sixth-century Ethiopian worship. Elaborate indigenous vestments are worn by priests. The liturgy includes the use of drums, dancing, and hand clapping. The parallels to traditional African American worship forms are striking. Of course, in some Ethiopian Orthodox congregations these parallels are not so apparent, as hand clapping or dancing are not practiced. This is likely a function of the previously observed absence of liturgical uniformity in the church.

In any case, liturgical dancing is central to Ethiopian Orthodox worship. Indeed, there is a distinct order in the church, the *Dabtera*, whose function is to be engaged in ceremonial dance as well as other assisting functions. Ethiopian Orthodox practice clearly embodies many characteristics often associated with African culture by Afro-centric scholarship. However, the church's other unique characteristics, notably its use of a historic liturgy (rather than a free-worship style) and its Jewish Christian orientation, raise new insights about what it might mean to be a Christian profoundly influenced by African culture.

The theology of the Ethiopian Orthodox Church is perhaps nowhere more clearly articulated than in a text derived from its monastic tradition, the *Wisdom of the Elders of Ethiopia*. It is fitting to close with a sample:

> About discretion and patience. They told how some men, having heard of Abba Agaton's reputation, came to him with the intention of testing his discretion and patience, to see if he could be made angry.
>
> They said to him, "Are you Agaton? We have heard what a great fornicator you are!"
>
> He gave thanks and said to them, "That is quite correct, that's just what I am!"
>
> Again they said, "Are you the Agaton who is such a slanderer and calumniator of men?"
>
> "Yes," he said, "that's who I am."
>
> Then they said to him, "Are you not Agaton the heretic?"
>
> At this he answered and said, "No, I am not! A heretic I have never been!" And was he angry!
>
> So they inquired further and said to him, "Tell us why you willingly bore what we said at first, but our last remark you will not tolerate at all?"
>
> He replied, "I took what you said first, because it was good for me to do so; but were I to declare myself a heretic, I would be separating myself from the Lord!"
>
> Hearing this statement, they marveled at him and went away edified.

We have here the gospel of justification by grace through faith in a nutshell. An interesting question is raised if one considers that a church body like the Ethiopian Orthodox tradition can produce this kind of grace-filled proclamation, coupled with a strong concern for discipline in the Christian life, a worship style that embodies the very best aesthetic elements of its indigenous culture, and a view of Christ that seems more commonsensical than the idea of Christ's having two natures, and has kept alive the Jewish Christian heritage to a degree that no other Christian communion has. It seems well worth asking anew why our churches have not appropriated these themes, why they have neglected them in favor of the "Western" versions of Christianity with which most readers of this volume are best acquainted.

This textbook and its companion volume aim to provide an account of how our churches reached their present theological positions and practices, why the (African and Jewish) agendas of Ethiopian Orthodoxy and those of Eastern Orthodoxy as a whole have not impacted the church bodies of most readers. The challenge to readers is to evaluate whether this process has been good for their churches or whether something precious has been lost. Church history challenges us to evaluate the heritage of our traditions, to examine critically the theological baggage we carry.

CHAPTER 2

A LIBERATING, OPEN "JEWISH" MOVEMENT?

The distancing of the Church from its Jewish roots, largely occasioned by its marked increase in Gentile membership, had significant consequences for increasing tensions between the Church and the Roman Empire. The end result was the initiation of the empire's persecutions of Christians. Rome really approved of most of the religions in the empire with syncretistic elements that combined with other religions, for such commitments effectively supported unity in the empire. At first Christianity seemed to fit that bill, as a sect of Judaism. However, with its increasing Gentile membership and the desire of many Christians to distance the Church from the emerging militant Jewish nationalism in the first century, the uniqueness of Christianity became more problematic to the empire. Persecutions were waiting to happen.

It is important to clarify the persecutions of the early centuries. They played an important role in helping the Church clarify its identity. They also help highlight the important role women played in the early Church.

THE PERSECUTIONS OF THE FIRST TWO CENTURIES

To be sure there were some instances of persecution in biblical times. Jewish leaders in Jerusalem instituted persecution of the disciples and had Stephen stoned (Acts 4:1–31; 5:12–42; 6:8–8:1). Herod Agrippa, the grandson of the original King Herod, a Roman puppet in Judea, instituted a persecution sometime in the fifth decade of the Christian Era. He had James, the brother of Christ, killed, and he harassed Peter (Acts 12). First Peter (1:6; 2:19; 5:9–10) does refer to the suffering of Christians, but it is more likely that the suffering was not so much the result of an official persecution as it was social discrimination. Only the Book of Revelation reports an official empirewide persecution very late in the first century. Consequently it is well to backtrack and recount the various empirewide persecutions. Each had its own agenda, its own distinct impact on the early Church, and each was initiated by a particular emperor.

UNDER NERO

A despised, perhaps mentally deranged, ruler, Nero (A.D. 37–68) was the instigator of the first harsh empirewide persecution. His rationale for persecuting Christians in the seventh and eighth decades of the Christian Era had little to do with justice. He had been suspected of setting fire to Rome and perhaps turned to Christians as scapegoats to exonerate himself. During this period there are reports of a woman of high social standing, Pomponia Graecina, who was brought to trial for her Christian commitment.

In A.D. 68 Nero was deposed by a rebellion and subsequently committed suicide. The persecution ceased, but his edicts against Christians were never rescinded.

UNDER DOMITIAN

Domitian (A.D. 51–96) renewed the persecutions late in the first century. He loved and respected Roman traditions and sought to restore their declining influence. Christians and Jews stood in the way of his dream, as they rejected the Roman gods. He charged them with being pagans or atheists because they worshiped an invisible God. The persecution he initiated in Asia Minor in this period apparently led to the writing of the Book of Revelation. There is, however, some controversy among historians whether he actually led a persecution. His reign ended much as Nero's did, and so for several years following his death Christians enjoyed relative peace.

UNDER TRAJAN

Persecution intensified under Trajan (A.D. 53–117) in the early decades of the second century. He established a policy of persecuting Christians, which occasioned the torture of two female Christian ministers. This occurred in a region of the Roman Empire (the northern shore of present-day Turkey) so populated by Christians that pagan temples were almost deserted. The women were at the least deacons, but they were probably ministers. The fact that there were female ministers at this early date in the history of the Church should be highlighted.

Essentially, Trajan's policy was that the state should not actively seek out Christians; however, if they were accused and refused to recant, they should be punished. This did not preclude the possibility of pardon if they were willing to worship the Roman gods. Trajan's policy remained in place throughout the second century and for part of the third century.

Given the long period in which Trajan's policy governed the empire, its effects on the Church and the general knowledge that Roman leaders had of Christianity demand consideration. First, though, we close with the final major periods of persecution initiated during the centuries covered in this chapter.

UNDER MARCUS AURELIUS

Marcus Aurelius (A.D. 121–80), the great scholarly emperor-philosopher, intensified persecutions in the latter half of the second century. Given his high ideals and scholarly nature, it may seem surprising that he presided over this program of persecution. We must remember at this point, though, that this great Stoic intellect was a Roman citizen, not a modern man. Like his peers, Aurelius was superstitious and consulted seers. Early in his reign, the empire endured a number of disasters. Seers convinced the emperor that Christians were to blame, for they had brought the wrath of the gods on the empire. In addition, Aurelius was committed to bringing about revival of the old Roman religion. He was also apparently irritated by the stubbornness with which Christians held their beliefs. After Aurelius died in A.D. 180, the severity of the persecution was tempered under his successor, Commodus. The civil war that followed his reign gave Christians more respite until A.D. 193.

UNDER SEPTIMIUS SEVERUS

Septimius Severus (A.D. 146–211) came to power as the new century was dawning. He was very committed to instituting religious harmony and cultural unity in order to avoid further civil war and preclude barbarian invasions, which had begun to trouble the empire. He aimed to achieve this with a policy promoting syncretism that would bring together all the various religions and philosophies in the empire by subsuming all gods under the Unconquered Sun reigning over all. The policy met resistance from Jews and Christians, and the emperor responded by outlawing all conversions to Christianity. After his death in A.D. 211, the policy remained in place, but its enforcement was not rigorous until 249.

THE IMAGE OF CHRISTIANITY
IN THE FIRST CENTURIES

As late as the second century, what was known about the religion of the Christians was still quite scant, and so decisions made by most of the rulers to persecute them were not based on accurate facts. Christians were charged with paganism. In addition, it was also widely known that

Christians gathered before dawn to sing to Christ "as to a god," joined together in oaths concerning upright moral behavior, and gathered for a common meal. Later this meal was regarded as a love feast. Because Christians referred to each other as "brother" and "sister," even married couples, the popular mind-set in the Roman Empire came to consider Christian love feasts as orgies.

Other rumors aimed at discrediting Christianity were rooted either in sociocultural dynamics or in intellectual reservations toward it. Sociocultural dynamics influenced many citizens of the Roman Empire to criticize the prominent role that the early Church gave women and children. Good citizens of the empire were also critical of Christians for their lack of education and their cultural crudeness (Phil. 4:1–3; 1 Cor. 1:26; Rom. 16:1; Acts 16:11–15; Mark 9:36–37). Of course, there must have been some upper-class Christians in the first centuries, as evidenced by the trial of the upper-class woman Pomponia Graecina for professing Christ. To a great extent, though, the persecutions in the empire of Christians were rooted in class prejudice.

Intellectual reservations to Christianity in this period stemmed from the perceived inviable character of the Judeo-Christian view of God. In contrast to the classical view of the Good as eternally unchanging, this Christian God was always meddling in human affairs, affected by what transpired. In the following chapter, we consider early Christian efforts to deal with such a critique.

MARTYRDOM IN THE EARLY CHURCH

Although there had been earlier martyrs for the faith, it was during the period when the Roman Empire implemented the persecution policies of Trajan that we encounter narratives or autobiographical comments of early Christian martyrs, specifically of Ignatius and Polycarp, which help to illuminate the early Church's view of martyrdom and what that says about its developing theology. Courage is certainly evident in these martyrs' witness. Ignatius (ca. 35–ca. 107), bishop of Antioch, was probably martyred sometime late in the first decade of the second century. He was an old man and saw his death as an opportunity to make a witness. Indeed, he welcomed martyrdom, asking the Christians in Rome not to try to free him:

> If you remain silent about me,
> I shall become a word of God.
> But if you allow yourselves to
> be swayed by the love in which

> you hold my flesh, I shall
> again be no more than a
> human voice.
> (*Letter to the Romans* 2.1)

The time of reckoning for Polycarp (ca. 69–ca. 155), bishop of Smyrna, a younger friend of Ignatius's, came nearly fifty years later. The empire proconsul pleaded with him to recant. His response is again heroic:

> But the Proconsul urged him
> and said, "Swear, and I will
> release thee; curse the Christ."
> And Polycarp said, "Eighty and
> six years have I served Him, and
> He hath done me no wrong; how
> can I blaspheme my king who
> saved me?"
> (*Martyrdom of Polycarp* IX)

A crucial question is how the early Church regarded martyrdom — whether as a personal human act of courage or as God's act. The question is most relevant for helping us deal with the crucial theological question of what sort of understanding of salvation and of the gospel predominated among early Christians. Did they subscribe to a grace-filled gospel (a version of the gospel in which salvation need not be earned by the believer's deeds and strength but is totally a gift of God)?

Germane to this question, we note that Ignatius believed in a God who wills everything that is (*Letter to the Romans*, Address). Polycarp apparently was inspired to his martyrdom by a voice from heaven urging strength (*Martyrdom of Polycarp* IX). A later martyr, Perpetua (ca. 181–203) said that the Holy Spirit instructed her, presumably in preparation for her martyrdom. The Spirit wanted her to request nothing from the baptismal waters except endurance of physical suffering (*Martyrdom of Perpetua* 3). Her repeated visions indicate that she was in constant conversation with God regarding her preparation for martyrdom (4ff.). It is evident that for these early Christians, martyrdom was not something chosen by the martyr's courageous will. God chooses and strengthens those who are to endure martyrdom. It is ultimately God's act, not the martyr's own.

During the persecutions instituted by Aurelius, the greatest Christian scholar of the time, Justin Martyr (ca. 100–ca. 165), died. Another victim was the widow Felicitas and her seven sons. Her status as a "widow" was likely an office of the Church. Such widows were probably Christian women set aside by the Church in order to devote themselves full-time to its work, with the understanding that the Church would offer support. (This is in accord with 1 Tim. 5:3–16 and Acts 6:1.) Felicitas is reported to have witnessed boldly to the Roman prefect working her case by claiming, "While I live, I shall defeat you; and if you kill me in my death I shall defeat you all the more."That the Church has preserved the memory of Felicitas's courage and that the Roman Empire took the time to pursue her case offer more suggestions that women had a prominent role in the early Church.

Another prominent woman martyr of the early Church was the aforementioned African Christian named Perpetua, as was her servant Felicitas. Perpetua was martyred during Septimius Severus's persecution of Christians seeking converts. The fact that Tertullian (ca. 160–ca. 225), one of the most famous theologians of the era, wrote the account of their martyrdom is another indication of Perpetua's influence in the early Church (and perhaps of the influence of women in general).

We have noted a number of instances in which women played a more or less prominent role in the Church. This important issue and the role that the early Church's developing theology may have played in enhancing or frustrating women's leadership roles require more detailed attention. First, though, it is necessary to consider these dynamics in the context of the prevailing thinking in the Church of the first centuries. This entails examining the theological commitments of the so-called Apostolic Fathers (a general designation for the very first postbiblical theological writings of the Church). We characterize their collective views as "Jewish Christian theology."

JEWISH CHRISTIAN THEOLOGY

In view of the decision of the New Testament's Jerusalem Council (Acts 15:1–35) and its implementation of admitting Gentiles into Christianity, it seems odd to think that a Jewish Christian theology dominated thought forms of the early Church. By *Jewish Christian theology*, we do not refer to institutional associations between Christianity and Judaism or to persons of Jewish ethnicity. Rather, the reference is to an early form of Christian theology beginning in the second century that employs Jewish categories. The work of the Apostolic Fathers represents this style of theology. Specifically, we refer to the work of Clement of Rome (probably the third bishop of Rome) and Ignatius of Antioch, a manual of instruction on worship called the *Didache*, the late-first-century *Letter of Barnabas* (probably written by a Christian from Alexandria), and the second-century apocalyptic work the *Shepherd of Hermas*.

Precisely why these Gentile authors came to rely so heavily on Jewish modes of thought, at the expense of Pauline emphases, is to some extent shrouded in mystery. Perhaps it was in response to the declining loyalty towards Judaism that developed in the late first and second centuries (eventually culminating in Gnostic heresies like those of Marcion, with which we shall deal in chap. 4). It may also have been related to the need to develop structures of ethics, liturgy, and polity (i.e., the manner of organizing the church). A Christianization of many features of Judaism was a way that the early Church met these needs. At any rate, we can say unequivocally that within the mainstream of orthodox Christianity, the Jewish heritage remained ever visible, and for its continuance the development of Jewish Christian theology played no small part.

Collectively we may summarize the theological commitments of the Apostolic Fathers and Jewish Christian theology in terms of six characteristics. Practitioners of this theological approach:

1. Employed theological categories in a thoroughly Jewish, unsystematic way. (In a sense, this unsystematic character grows out of Judaism, whose mind-set is not systematic. This commitment also entailed that Jewish Christian theology did not much engage the prevailing Hellenistic philosophy of the day.)

2. Were more concerned with practice and discipline than with doctrine. (This commitment also reflects the Jewish mind-set.)

3. Employed the Old Testament as authoritative. (As in the first century, much of the content of the New Testament was transmitted orally; an officially accepted New Testament canon was still in the Church's future.)

4. Appreciated that humans can be good or evil. (This commitment entailed that good and evil were deemed spiritual powers.)

5. Were strongly preoccupied with ecclesiology, that is, the Church. (The theme of the Church universal, not just particular churches, comes to the fore. The doctrine is considered, then, in a cosmological framework.)

6. Exalted Christ in unsystematic categories, but ones often set in a cosmological framework.

Given the Jewish orientation of this theological mind-set, one other possible feature warrants attention. As Judaism is preoccupied with obedience to the law, do we find inordinate legal tendencies in Jewish Christian theology?

The situational character of the literature entails that the writings of the Apostolic Fathers do not provide a full insight into the Christian thinking of the era. It is, however, the best we have.

CLEMENT OF ROME

As one of the first bishops of Rome, Clement is thought to have had some connections with Peter. His major authentic piece, *Letter to the Church in Corinth* (also called *1 Clement*), was written to settle some disputes (1,3,44) among the Corinthians, probably in A.D. 80 (though many date it nearly twenty years later). Almost immediately the document gives attention to persecutions that the Church had endured in Rome (Address), including the martyrdom of Peter and Paul (5.3ff.), and persecution of two women, Danaids and Dirces (6.2). In this text, then, we encounter another example of attention being paid to women in the early Church.

Clement does claim that we are justified, not by ourselves and our piety, but by faith (32.4). God's love covers a multitude of sins. He takes hold of us, elects us (49). Affirmations like this of God's unconditional grace are softened somewhat elsewhere by Clement. He claims that Christ will bring about the resurrection of those who served him in holiness (26). We *must turn* to God to receive repentance (7.5). In addition to these comments and the claim that Abraham was blessed by his works (31.2), which suggest divine-human cooperation or even human responsibility for salvation, Clement commends some very strict ritual observances (40–41). Perhaps the most problematic compromise of the priority of divine grace, though, is the text's claim that whoever humbly and without regret carries out the commandments of God will be enrolled among those saved (58.2).

Clement seems confused about the nature of grace and about whether salvation is ultimately a matter of perks. He placed emphasis on what the believer must do to fulfill the demands of God's law, and like the other Apostolic Fathers, he relegated Christ to the role of a mere teacher or example for the faithful (36).

Jewish sensibilities reflect in Clement's positing a very high view of Scripture, to the point of endorsing something like its infallibility (45). Liturgically, he advocated the confession of sins (51.1). Such Jewish sensibilities are also apparent in the polity he endorsed. Clement refers to a threefold ministry — bishops, deacons, and presbyters/priests (41–44). This model for ordering ministries, still embodied today in both Roman Catholic and Eastern Orthodox churches, was already incarnate in the Church of the first century.

Apparently Clement was responding to efforts in Corinth to remove bishops illicitly (44). (Controversy in the Church, discontent with its leaders, is an old story.) In response, Clement asserted a high view of clerical authority. In this context he posited something like apostolic succession. The concept is a very ancient one, first clearly articulated in the mid-second century by Hegesippus, a Christian writer who opposed an early heresy in the Church called "Gnosticism" (Matt. 16:18–19; 1 Tim. 5:22). When there has been turmoil in the Church, it is in these contexts that a high view of ministry has been articulated as a resource to bring about order. Readers should reflect on whether overall that has been good for the Church.

A "re-Judaization" of Christianity is evident throughout Clement's work. It surfaces in his endorsement of a priesthood and sacrificial cult (32.2; 40). These are not features of the New Testament church. However, the concept of priest and sacrifices are essential elements of the religion of the Hebrews. We also find Clement refer to "laity" in these texts, perhaps the first time the designation was made. Such terminology is clearly indicative of an elevation of the priest's authority. Clement's reference to Christ's role as High Priest (36.1) also suggests such a re-Judaizing process insofar as the Hebrew preoccupation with ritual sacrifice is further incorporated into Christianity by this christological image.

IGNATIUS

We have already noted that Ignatius was a late-first-century bishop of Antioch. He is said to have been an auditor of John's and was a good friend of Polycarp's. He died a martyr.

Ignatius was one of the first to talk of Jesus in language suggesting that he had two natures (a doctrinal affirmation not authoritatively formulated for centuries). He spoke of Christ as both flesh and spirit, born and not born, God in man, etc. (*Letter to the Ephesians* 7.2; 20.2). One of the first references to the virgin birth appears in his corpus (18.2; *Letter to the Smyrneans* 1.1). Ignatius was also one of the first to endorse a view of Christ's atoning work as a destruction of evil (the so-called classic view of the atonement; *Letter to the Ephesians* 19.3).

The writings of the Antiochene bishop also suggest an affirmation of the threefold ministry (*Letter to the Magnesians* 2; *Letter to the Trallians* 3.1). Granted, the distinctions may not be clear, as at one point the tasks Ignatius assigns to deacons (dispensers of the mysteries of Christ, not of food and drink) sound more like tasks of presbyters. Such an affirmation of the threefold ministry raises a crucial point: If the threefold ministry is evident in the New Testament (1 Tim. 3; 4:14; 5) and in the early Church, should not all contemporary ecclesiastical communions likewise endorse such a polity?

Ignatius posits a very high view of the episcopacy and of ministry in general. He claims that without deacons, presbyters, bishops, there is no Church (*Letter to the Trallians* 3.1). Christians are to follow the bishop as Christ followed the Father, follow the presbytery as they would the apostles, and respect the deacons as they would the commandment of God. There is no valid worship or sacraments, he claimed, without the bishop (*Letter to the Smyrneans* 8.1). Moreover, the bishop should not be opposed (*Letter to the Ephesians* 5.3). The idea that the presbyters hold the authority of the apostles suggests apostolic succession. It is interesting to note here and in Clement's writings how apostolic succession functions to assert the unity of the Church in the midst of chaos and division (*Letter to the Philadelphians* 1–3; 8). Some suggest that in his *Letter to the Romans* (Address), Ignatius endorsed the primacy of the Roman church. This overall concern with unity may indicate the impact of Stoicism on his thought.

Although eschatological urgency diminished in the post–New Testament era, Ignatius did not forget it. In his *Letter to the Ephesians* (11) he claimed that the last days are here. A similar preoccupation reflects in other writings of the Apostolic Fathers (*Didache* 16.3). Though Ignatius refers to our election (*Letter to the Ephesians*, Address), his letters place more emphasis on keeping the Commandments and earning salvation. Love, he said, makes one worthy of God (*Letter to the Romans*, Address).

Despite the endorsement by the Antiochene bishop of themes consistent with Judaism in his strong affirmation of a set-apart clerical leadership (priesthood) and a concern with obedience to the law for attaining salvation, by no means did he unequivocally endorse Judaism. In fact, he engaged in a polemic with Judaism, and in that context he effectively disinherited the Jews in the sense of asserting that Judaism is based on Christianity (*Letter to the Magnesians* 10.3).

THE DIDACHE

This document was an early Church manual of instruction on worship (appearing in at least one ancient version in Coptic, which could suggest Egyptian origins). It commences, though, with a Manual of Conduct. The document clearly embodies very legalistic strictures on how to live, asserting that one either lives according to the way of life or the way of death. (Some scholars have suggested that this reference to the two ways may refer to a Jewish Essene document.) Preoccupation with lifestyle standards is evident as the *Didache* urges the practice of Christian virtues like abstinence, shunning idolatry, patience, humility, and goodness. Readers are likewise urged to hate hypocrisy and boastfulness (1–5). The document's claim that we should evaluate teachers by the kind of behavior their teaching engenders and evaluate prophets by their lifestyle suggests legalistic propensities (11). With regard to the view of the ministry endorsed, the document speaks of bishops and deacons (15).

Concerning the *Didache*'s instructions on worship, one can discern the origins of the baptismal practices of many churches. Immersion is not taught as mandatory. The rite was to be administered, it is stated, in the name of the Father, Son, and Holy Spirit (7). For the Apostolic Fathers in general, purification happens in baptism, but not crucifixion of sin, as in subsequent Western Christianity.

With regard to Communion/Eucharist, weekly celebration is reported as standard practice (14). One wonders why this ancient practice has been so neglected by most Protestants. It is important to note that the rite is identified as a sacrifice (14). The *Didache* sets the stage for the Middle Ages' view of the Mass as a sacrifice. There are suggestions in the document that the Eucharist is regarded as only a symbol. For example, the document's prescribed Thanksgiving Prayer refers only to "spiritual food and drink," and there is no reference to Christ's bodily presence (10). Such images are distinct from suggestions of Christ's real presence in the rite offered by Ignatius, who claimed that the Eucharist is "the flesh of our Savior Jesus Christ" (*Letter to the Smyrneans* 7). If modern Christians cannot agree on the status of the Communion elements, is that because the early Church also could not? Perhaps it is simply the case that this debate on the status of the elements was not a problem in the early Church. In any case, the *Didache*'s preoccupation with worship forms is characteristically Jewish, not typical of the Pentecostal enthusiasm in Acts. In that sense, we see again a re-Judaizing of Christianity in the document.

THE LETTER OF BARNABAS

There is general consensus that the *Letter of Barnabas*, likely written by an Alexandrian Christian, is un-Pauline, even if it was traditionally linked with Paul's companion Barnabas (Acts 9:27; 12:25). The document does speak of renewal through forgiveness of sins (6.11). On the other hand, it is also very critical of the faith's Jewish roots. Much of its doctrinal section (1–17) is devoted to an allegorical interpretation of the Hebrew Bible. Strictures on eating pork are interpreted as directives to believers not to join men who are like pigs, men who sometimes remember their master and at other times forget him (10.3). In fact, one can discern hints of the sort of anti-Judaism later developed by Marcion as the document claims that Israel never really had an authentic covenant with God (14.3–4). Yet elsewhere the works righteousness appears (possibly with insights explicitly drawn from the Jewish community), as the document, much like the *Didache*, refers to two ways of life, exhorting believers to an appropriate lifestyle (18–21).

Some have identified the *Letter of Barnabas*, with its use of allegorical interpretation and reliance on Neoplatonic philosophical assumptions, as a forerunner of the Alexandrian school of theology, which came to fruition in the next century and continued to be a force with which to be reckoned throughout the period of the early Church. These emphases in the epistle are undeniably suggestive of the great Alexandrian Jewish philosopher Philo. As such, the epistle demonstrates again how deeply indebted the writings of the Apostolic Fathers are to Jewish suppositions.

THE SHEPHERD OF HERMAS

This apocalyptic work by Hermas, the second-century former Christian slave, later wealthy merchant, and brother of a pope, is concerned primarily with the problem posed by sins committed after baptism. Manuscripts of the work have been found in Ethiopia, so it clearly had an influence on early Christianity there. Its final form may have been the result of a number of interpolations or additions by subsequent editors.

Perhaps reflecting Stoic influences, or at least that philosophy's preoccupation with human unity, the treatise embodies a concern about unity/harmony in the Church (I.III.V.1; III.IX.XVII.4). The document grants the possibility of repentance for sins after baptism, or at least a second chance (II.IV.III.1). However, the possibility of seeing God is still said to be dependent on preserving purity and holiness (II.IV.IV.1). Also, as in later Catholicism, the document claims that it is possible to do more than the commandment of God requires, and so to gain merits (III.V.III.3). Again it sounds like Judaism: one must do something to be redeemed.

An interesting christological nuance appears in the work. The Holy Spirit is identified with the Son of God (III.IX.I.1). This entails breaking with the static Greek view of God, for on Hermas's grounds, the Spirit (and so God) is immersed in, affected by, historical time by virtue of becoming one with the man Jesus. Such views regarding the effect that historical interactions with creation has on God is more typical of Jewish rather than Greek thought (Gen. 6:6–7; Exod. 32:14; 1 Sam. 15:11).

RETURN TO JEWISH ROOTS?

The Jewish Christian theology of the Apostolic Fathers again raises issues discussed in the previous chapter regarding the authority that venerable traditions in the Church, such as the Jewish Christian orientation of Ethiopian Orthodoxy, ought to have for today. Granted, this literature is un-Pauline, not generally emphasizing the work of Christ in saving the faithful. However, it could be argued that the Apostolic Fathers' concern with the human contribution to redemption is not problematic as long as we keep in mind that no distinction between the sovereignty of God (divine initiative) and human responsibility is made in Judaism. In that case, the Church need not be so preoccupied with concerns about works righteousness as it has throughout its history since the time of Augustine (354–430).

Indeed, perhaps we need to challenge Augustine's condemnation of salvation by works (*On Rebuke and Grace* I.2; see chap. 9) for effectively shattering for Western Christianity the Jewish synthesis that Christianity received in the first centuries from the re-Judaization process. If so, we will need to conclude that many of the struggles in which subsequent Christianity engaged (including the emergence of Protestantism) were mistakes that the Church should have avoided. In addition, readers will need to agree that the re-Judaizing process of the early Church must be allowed to continue. On the other hand, those put off by the version of the gospel put forth by the Apostolic Fathers with concerns that these ancient ones with their many moralisms have inadvertently robbed God of the glory due for saving us may be more inclined to evaluate the early Church's return to Jewish roots as a bit too extreme.

At the very least, it must be conceded that re-Judaizing had a profound (perhaps a positive) impact in helping the Church organize its leadership and its ritual practices. Is Christianity not better off when it goes back to Jewish roots? The New Testament witness will not allow Christianity to reject these roots totally. Paul's Epistle to the Romans (11:1–2, 26–29) ever reminds us that the Jews have not been rejected, that they are still of the covenant into which Gentile Christians have been grafted. If the Jewish Christian theology of the early Church did not do an adequate job in affirming this, how can we contemporary Christians do it better?

CONCLUSION:
DID THE EARLY CHURCH PROCLAIM
A GRACE-FILLED, LIBERATING GOSPEL?

The question of the gospel put forth by the Apostolic Fathers is not without significance for our other major concern in the chapter — the role of women in the early Church. Both issues (grace and liberation) pertain to the question of the extent to which the message of the gospel (Exod. 3:9–10; John 8:36; Gal. 5:1) was adequately proclaimed and whether a failure in one is related to a compromise of the gospel's liberating power in another way. If women did not have a prominent role in the early Church, could that relate to the legalistic propensities of the re-Judaization process?

Thus far we have noted a number of prominent women in the post-biblical era, especially martyrs, and have marveled at their courage. By preserving tales of their martyrdom, the Church has acknowledged the prominence of Perpetua and her friend Felicitas, another Felicitas (martyred under the persecution of Marcus Aurelius), Pomponia Graecina, and the two female ministers persecuted under Trajan's reign. The fact that the famed Tertullian is likely the author of the account of Perpetua's and Felicitas's martyrdom gives credence to their renown, and so is presumably indicative of the prominent role that women played in the early Church.

Contrary to much popular opinion, prominent roles for women in the Church seem to have New Testament precedents. Clearly Jesus had a ministry directed towards women, contrary to the patriarchal public social expectations in the Roman Empire of his day. For example, it is reported that he "loved" Mary and Martha (John 11:5). The more historically reliable Synoptic Gospels indicate that there were many women, in addition to Mary Magdalene and Mary the mother of James, who followed Jesus (Mark 15:40–41). Many New Testament scholars have argued that Jesus' own feminist/womanist sympathies are evident not only in such attention given to women (and also in the attention of Jesus' followers, who continued to recount his interactions with these women) but also in the strictures Jesus issued against divorce. His main point in condemning divorce and remarriage, it is argued, was to ensure that the patriarchal practices of his day, which only gave men the right to initiate divorce, could no longer victimize women (Matt. 19:3–9; cf. Deut. 24:1). Not to be overlooked in highlighting the role of women among Jesus' followers is the fact that women are reported to have been the first witnesses of his Resurrection (Matt. 28; Mark 16; Luke 24; John 20). When we note that Paul believed that seeing the Risen Lord rendered one an apostle (1 Cor. 9:1), does it not follow that these women might be deemed apostles?

The prominent role of women seems to have continued in the post-Easter community. The tradition of Jesus' directing ministry to women was continued (Acts 5:14; 8:3; 13:50; 16:13–19, 40; 17:4). Paul was led to claim that in Christ there is neither male nor female (Gal. 3:26–29). In addition, there are numerous reports of prominent women leaders in the Church. The list of these first-century women in ministry follows:

unmarried (virgin) daughters of Philip who prophesy (Acts 21:9)

Tabitha (or Dorcas), who was healed, and the "widows" present when the healing occurred (Acts 9:36–43)

Priscilla the wife of Aquila (Acts 18:18, 26; Rom. 16:3–4)

Phoebe (Rom. 16:1–2)

Lydia (Acts 16:14–15, 40)

Julia and Nereus's sister (Rom. 16:15)

Nympha (Col. 4:15), Apphia (Philem. 2), and Mary the mother of John Mark (Acts 12:12), all of whom had the church meet in their houses

the women and Mary the mother of Jesus (Acts 1:14)

Euodia and Syntyche (Phil. 4:2–3)

We also find New Testament texts that identify specific ecclesiastical offices held by women: (1) deacon (possibly translated "minister?" Rom. 16:1); (2) widow (1 Tim. 5:3–16); and (3) virgin (1 Cor. 7:25). The latter two were likely offices for women practicing celibacy and devoting themselves full-time to ministries of service to the church, such as prayer (in the case of widows) and prophecy (in the case of some virgins). (One cannot but speculate whether the order of nuns could have had biblical origins in these offices.) By the third century, the order of widows had disappeared, replaced by "deaconesses." Also intriguing are references to those women noted above (Nympha, Apphia, Mary the mother of John Mark, Lydia, and Priscilla) in whose homes the church congregated.

Recent scholarship suggests that the mores of the Roman Empire and pre-Roman Egypt were such that women were granted significant authority in the household. This entailed that women in these regions did not hold narrowly circumscribed roles. Managing the household was an executive position that involved the direction of male and female servants and laborers as well as the production and distribution of what was produced in the fields and by servants skilled in the production of crafts. In holding responsibility for distribution of these products, these women householders often traveled, bought, sold, and negotiated contracts.

Given these cultural suppositions, it is argued, when the church met in households, it naturally began to develop its polity along such household lines. Consequently, women householders could be expected to have played a similarly prominent, administrative leadership role in the New Testament church. It does not seem then like a fallacious jump to suspect that when the church met in the household of a woman, she exercised leadership in that particular church. New Testament references to the prominent tasks performed and ecclesiastical offices held by women seem to provide verification. This would also have been a logical development insofar as a study of ancient inscriptions indicates that women played prominent leadership roles in some of the Jewish synagogues during this era.

This sort of ecclesiastical leadership was apparently exercised by women in the first two centuries after biblical times. This may account for the early Church's recollection of the prominent women and the roles they played. In addition, we note that given the economic influence that women of wealthy households played in the empire, a number of such wealthy Christian women functioned as dispensers of patronage to the Church. In at least one case, in third-century Syria, Queen Zenobia not only supported one of the region's theologians (Paul of Samosata) but also appointed the region's bishop. In addition, we have evidence of women holding ecclesiastical offices in this post–New Testament period. Pliny, the Roman governor of Bythinia, mentions two slave women who were ministers of a Christian community in the region. Cyprian (in the third century) mentions a woman presbyter in Cappadocia. A fourth-century Egyptian papyrus refers to a Christian woman, Kyria, as a teacher. One finds references as late as the turn of the fifth century to the ordination of deaconesses (*Apostolic Canons*, Ep. 10) and an identification of their tasks as ministers to other women (*Apostolic Constitutions* 3.16.1; 2.26.6).

Given these indications of women's leadership in the early Church, some hard "patriarchal" facts remain to be considered. None of the twelve disciples were women. There is no record of a woman functioning as a bishop. None of the Apostolic Fathers or theologians of the early Church were women. In addition, we have the strongly patriarchal texts of the New Testament with which to contend. Man is said to be the head of a woman (1 Cor. 11:3), and women are expressly subordinated to men (1 Cor. 11:8–9, 12). Explicit directives concerning women's dress are also prescribed (1 Cor. 11:5–6); likewise, women are directed to remain silent in church (1 Cor. 14:34–36). Given these strictures, it is hardly surprising to find in the deutero-Pauline Pastoral Epistles explicit prohibitions of a teaching role for women (1 Tim. 2:11–15).

What are we to make of this Pauline and deutero-Pauline anti-feminism? This question is even more troubling in view of the promising feminist/womanist themes and practices that we have already observed. Upon considering several possibilities, readers finally must make their own historical-theological judgments.

One possibility is that Christianity is essentially patriarchal in character, a vestige of its Hebrew roots, and so can never function as a liberating religion for women and other minorities. More gospel-friendly interpretations with regard to the Pauline literature and the New Testament witness might be to note the obvious contradictions between their and Jesus' own overall liberating message and the patriarchalism of the particular texts that we have identified. It may be, as some scholars have noted, that by its liberating message and practice Christianity was being confused with mystery religions in the Roman Empire that practiced women's equality. Consequently, it was in Christianity's best interest to distinguish itself from these religious sects by demonstrating to Roman citizens that it shared many of their basic values and mores, including patriarchal attitudes toward gender. (In the public square, rather than in matters pertaining to the household, Roman culture was patriarchal.) If that be the case, a contemporary interpreter of these more patriarchal texts could have some warrant for reading them critically, without diminishing the authority of the biblical witness as a whole. One could maintain that they are time bound to a particular missionary context for the Church (the need to present Christianity in an intellectually and socially acceptable way to a fundamentally patriarchal society) that no longer demands our attention. If anything, the agenda today in most Western societies is just the opposite: the need to present the gospel in a credible way to societies in which patriarchalism is unacceptable. As such, the problematic texts are not relevant to our context.

Even if the validity of such arguments is granted, the historian of Christianity still encounters problems with the charge of patriarchalism. We have observed that the patriarchal propensities of Paul and even of the deutero-Pauline literature of the first century apparently did not put an end to the leadership of women in the Church, at least not when the Church was largely a household phenomenon of the private sphere. However, by the time that Christianity became the established religion of the Roman Empire in the fourth century (see chap. 6), women's leadership became progressively less visible, although we have identified some references to women deaconesses exercising clerical functions. Even the offices of widow and virgin seem to have died out. Why this development transpired requires attention.

Some decisions of councils (gatherings of bishops meeting to make ecclesiastical decisions on behalf of the whole Church), especially those inspired by African church leaders, may be significant. The Council of Elvira (ca. 300 A.D.) posited numerous strictures on women, such as the excommunication of women who have left a Christian husband, even if he had been philandering or was ever engaged in prostitution (*Canons* 9,12). Although clergy with wives are acknowledged, it is required that they remain celibate (33). The Council of Neocaesarea (ca.

314–25) came very close to an outright insistence on clerical celibacy. It advocated removal of presbyters who were married (*Canons* 1).

The councils displayed an increasingly negative view towards women, and African Christian precedents for such attitudes are readily identifiable in the work of two of the region's greatest early theologians. It is difficult to conclude that they were not factors in the less prominent role for women in church leadership that characterized the Church from that time until the modern period. Tertullian and Origen (ca. 185–ca. 254), whose theologies we shall examine in more detail in the next several chapters, forbade a woman to speak in church, as in the Pauline literature (Tertullian *On Baptism* XVII; Origen *Fragments on I Corinthians*). There is much to suggest that the reason for the strictures these two placed on women was much akin to the rationale for the Pauline positions. Both were working in a region where Gnosticism and Montanism (early Christian heresies) were having a great impact. The Gnostics and Montanists, as we shall observe, were quite egalitarian with regard to women's leadership. Consequently, a good way to distinguish Orthodox Christianity from these sects was to ensure that the women of the Church were not unduly engaged in it but were playing a role analogous to the public role that most women of the region customarily played.

Another possible reason for the declining visibility of women's leadership in the early Church beginning with the fourth century is the sociological factors associated with the establishment of Christianity as the favored religion of the Roman Empire. When the Church was no longer confined to the household (the "private" sphere) but was a truly public institution, then its leadership needed to be exercised only by males, for in the context of the Roman Empire's culture, the rightful sphere for women was the private, not the public, sphere.

Yet an additional possible factor in the declining role for women might be the Jewish Christian theology that dominated the Church beginning late in the first century. The insistence that its proponents characteristically placed on obeying the commandments of God as the means to salvation (an apparent compromise of the grace-filled version of the gospel proclaimed in the Pauline corpus) tends to create a dynamic whereby what a person was (not just what he/she did) mattered before God. From that standpoint, a next logical step would be to make distinctions between genders, some (males) being more qualified to stand before God in worship. Might it be the case that only when the gospel of justification by grace apart from works of the law (Gal. 2:16) is proclaimed can it be that in Christ there is neither male nor female (Gal. 3:28)? For only when merit does not count before God are the distinctions between humanity of no account, and only then is the gospel truly a liberating proclamation.

As we have noted, the emergence of Jewish Christian theology was just one, not the sole, manifestation of a process of re-Judaization in the Church in the post–New Testament era. We have also observed the development in this period of an ecclesiastical hierarchy along the lines of the Jewish priesthood. Insofar as Judaism sanctioned no women priests (Exod. 28:1), could it be that a priestly hierarchical polity (such as the threefold ministry of bishop, presbyter, and deacon, which came to characterize the early Church and still prevails in many denominations today) is inherently patriarchal?

Even if the rise of Jewish Christian theology, the re-Judaization of Christianity at the expense of Pauline themes, was not the sole factor in the declining role of women in the early Church after New Testament times, challenges must be issued to these developments. Could it be that the dominance of this theological ethos and the development of an ecclesiastical hierarchy along Jewish priestly lines precluded any possibility of forestalling the retreat from women's leadership that was being occasioned by other dynamics? These are hard questions for readers attracted to theological emphases like the Apostolic Fathers' concern about Christian responsibility (the role of works in salvation) and belonging to churches with episcopal polities. There is something about this theological-ecclesiastical perspective that requires amendment in order for the Church to avoid being co-opted by reactionary social currents. Sorting out these questions is crucial for the development of a socially conscious theological perspective.

CHAPTER 3

DEFENDING THE FAITH

THE FIRST CHRISTIAN APOLOGISTS

By the middle of the second century, the Church was entering a new phase. Though Christianity was by no means the established religion of the Roman Empire, church life was markedly different from what it was in the previous century. Christianity had become sufficiently established that its leaders could attend to the critiques and questions of the empire's citizenry. The new circumstances opened the way for the development of new theological styles, which have effectively enriched the Church with more theological diversity. Addressing these challenges was a group of theologians who have come to be known as the Apologists. They are so called because they wrote "apologies" for the Christian faith — that is, efforts to make sense of the faith, to show its credibility to the cultured despisers.

EARLY CRITICISMS OF CHRISTIANITY

There is little doubt that a number of the earliest criticisms of Christianity were related to class prejudices. Recall that good Roman citizens were likely to look down upon poor, largely lower-class Christians.[1] Even the more substantive criticisms were somewhat class-related. The cultured and sophisticated of the empire could not conceive of the possibility, as Christians claimed, that one could derive truth, not from Greek or Roman thought, but from primitive Jews.

In that connection, the picture of God that Christians adopted from Judaism was mind-boggling to good, decent law-abiding Roman citizens. It was bad enough that these Jews and the Christian sect believed in a spiritual reality that was anathema to the Roman mind — an "invisible god." And they were downright atheistic in orientation, rejecting worship of the Roman pantheon of gods visibly depicted in various

---

1. Celsus *True Word*.

statues. Failure to engage in good, wholesome civic activities like the worship of these true gods of the empire was just one more indication of the extremist character of this new Jewish sect. The Christian hang-up with venerating the Roman gods, claiming that such rituals were idolatrous, was perceived by many Roman citizens as antisocial. Such unpatriotic behavior was further manifest in the pacifism of a number, though perhaps not all, of these Christians. (It was not until late in the second century that the Christian ideal of pacifism was articulated; the North African Church Father Tertullian did so in *On Idolatry* [19.1–3]. Consequently, contrary to the assessments of many scholars, we must assume that pacifism was by no means regularly or unanimously affirmed by early Christians.)

Even if proper, open-minded citizens of the Roman Empire were to grant that the God of the Christians was invisible, along the lines that Hellenized Romans construed the universal forms like the Good, Truth, and Beauty (as invisible and eternal), the Judeo-Christian vision was still intellectually untenable. Christians had endorsed the unacceptable (by Roman standards) Jewish portrayal of a God, who like some kind of a busybody, is always messing around in human affairs, even to the point of being affected by them. Recall, the universal forms of ancient Greek philosophy, the philosophy that dominated the Roman Empire in this period, were construed as unchanging. Little wonder, then, that Christianity was discredited in such an intellectual context. It posited a God who was clearly inferior to the universal forms.

How could the Church respond to these and related critiques? With the pressures of persecutions increasingly lessened, it was now sufficiently secure to respond to such sociocultural, intellectual challenges. Addressing these matters was the work of the Apologists. The core question for them in arguing for the credibility of Christian faith was to address the classical pagan culture and the Hellenistic philosophical commitments that surrounded them. The Church needed to address the question of whether the work of Plato, Aristotle, and the Stoics revealed any truth and, if so, how this could be reconciled with the gospel.

Questions like these are by no means irrelevant in the contemporary context. Although theologians in our era may not need to dialogue as directly with classical Greek philosophy as did the Apologists, the contemporary context for theology has many analogies to the middle of the second century. Christians in that context, like today, were encountering a pagan culture. Likewise the concern of the second-century church to address questions about the intellectual credibility of faith, to address the general cultural climate that regarded Christians as outcasts, is not much different from the agenda the Church (at least in the Western world) faces today.

THE GREAT CLASSICAL OPTIONS
IN THEOLOGICAL METHODOLOGY

Two distinct apologetic approaches emerged for dealing with the critiques and challenges of the pagan culture and Hellenistic philosophy. To this day these approaches continue to constitute a typology for theological method (how to relate the Word of God to the sociocultural context), which can be useful to contemporary students trying to sort out their own theological commitments. We may differentiate the two distinct methodological approaches by designating one as the *correlationist approach* (those apologists systematically committed to linking or building bridges between the gospel and Hellenistic culture) and the other as the *orthodox model* (those critical of building such bridges, for fear that faith might be distorted by such efforts).

THE CORRELATIONIST APPROACH

Justin Martyr and like-minded Apologists such as Clement of Alexandria, Athenagoras, and Tatian were committed to the correlation of the Word of God and the insights of the Hellenistic culture of their day. In some respects their methodological commitments were indebted to the African Jewish heritage, as they were deeply indebted to apologetic efforts on behalf of Judaism that the great Alexandrian Jewish philosopher Philo had launched a century earlier. The dependence of these Apologists on his thought is readily apparent.

Justin Martyr. The trailblazer of the correlationist approach was unquestionably Justin Martyr (ca. 100–ca. 165). Born of Greek pagan parents and trained as a teacher of Platonic philosophy, Justin came to Christianity through a study of the philosophical traditions of his day. He later opened the first Christian school in Rome. It is reported that he was martyred for refusing to offer token sacrifices to the Roman gods during the persecution instituted by Marcus Aurelius.

Essentially, Justin argued that Christian teaching is merely an expression of the truths of reason, insofar as Christians are really expounding the same truths that the classical philosophers held (*First Apology* 23). Borrowing the concept of the Logos as world-soul from Plato (*Timaeus* 36–38) and Stoicism, Justin identified Christ with the Logos/reason in whom all human beings participate, which entails that humanity is in touch with Christ intuitively. Whatever human beings understand correctly belongs to Christianity, since it is a "seeing darkly" through the Word that has been implanted in humanity through reason. Those who live in accord with rational principles (as the Greek philosophers did) are really anonymous Christians (*First Apology* 5,46)! From these arguments, Justin proceeded to claim that the Greek philosophers got their ideas on the immortality of the soul and other truths from the biblical prophets. The seeds of truth are in all human beings. However, Justin insisted, through Christian faith even the uneducated can know these truths (44,60).

Various theologians throughout history have repeated again and again the essence of Justin Martyr's correlationist approach as they endeavored to offer a theology that understands its principal task as apologetics, presenting Christian faith in the most intellectually attractive way possible. This theological approach has been especially dominant among the Western church's major theologians since the eighteenth century. Like Justin, such theologians typically begin with one of the most intellectually credible philosophical systems of the day. The categories of this system of thought are understood as an accurate description of the way things really are in the world. Given this supposition, they then present Christian doctrines in the conceptuality of the intellectually credible philosophical system with which they began.

We see these methodological moves operative in Justin's theology. He appropriated the Platonic philosophical system, which was so widely endorsed among the intellectual elite of his day. He then proceeded to translate/correlate the core doctrines of the faith into Platonic categories. Thus, Christ, as Son of God, is translated into the Platonic (not the distinctively Johannine) notion of Logos.

Justin sought to offer an apologetic defense of the Christian faith in other, related ways. Typical of other Roman-oriented (Western) apologists, in contrast to Eastern theologians, Justin also argued for Christianity's credibility on grounds of its social function. Christians, he contended, because of their belief that no wicked deed can be hidden from God, can make significant contributions to the Roman Empire by instilling public virtue (*First Apology* 12). This sort of argument for Christianity's credibility is clearly in accord with the correlationist approach. An intellectually respectable system of thought, the importance of moral virtue for the success of the empire, is introduced. Then one presents Christian faith in relation to these moral categories; faith is construed in terms of its moral contribution to the empire.

Another kind of argument for Christianity's credibility that Justin mounted is an argument from prophecy. Christian claims about Christ, he maintained, were fulfillments of what had been predicted in Old Testament times (*First Apology* 30–53; *Dialogue with Trypho*). The argument here proceeds not so much on the basis of some prior commitment to the authority of the Jewish tradition, as if conformity to its precepts would merit intellectual credibility for Christianity. Rather, the argument seems to presuppose a prior rationalist worldview — the idea that something fulfilling a prediction in advance demonstrates the kind of consistency that warrants the credibility of believing in both the prophecy and the fulfillment. Christian claims regarding Christ and Old Testament prophecies, when considered together, conform to this prior rational/logical worldview. Consequently, the veracity of both seems a credible conclusion.

The correlation of a prior worldview and the claims of the gospel in order to verify the truth/credibility of the Christian faith is at the heart of Justin's theology and the correlationist approach he embodies. Other dimensions of Justin's theology should, and subsequently will, be noted. First, though, we need to consider the arguments of other second-century Apologists who employed something like the correlationist approach.

Clement of Alexandria. Like Justin, Clement of Alexandria (ca. 150–ca. 215) was the child of pagan parents. After his conversion to Christianity, he embarked on a life of questing for deeper instruction in the faith. This brought him to one of the most renowned catechetical schools of the early Church, the one based in Alexandria. His talents as a student in the school eventually led to his appointment as its second teacher. He succeeded Pantaenus (d. ca. 190), a renowned scholar who left the school to undertake a mission to the intellectuals in India. After years as a successful teacher, Clement was forced to flee Egypt in 202 during the persecutions of Septimius Severus. Authorities never permitted him to return to Africa from this exile.

Clement's reliance on something like the correlationist approach is evident in his claim that philosophy is a preparation for religion (*Stromata* I.V.28). Society seems to pose the questions that, in Clement's view, the gospel answers. In this sense he correlates the Word of God with his social context, though he was perhaps more cautious in his correlation than was Justin.

Clement echoed many of Justin's constructive theological proposals. One could argue that Clement was not more cautious than Justin insofar as the idea of philosophy as preparation for the gospel could be regarded as elevating philosophy to the status of divine revelation, just as the Old Testament revelation given to the Hebrews was preparation for the gospel (*Stromata* I.XX; VI.V; VI.VIII). Indeed, Clement did claim that the truth of philosophy is the result of a revelation by God (VI.V) or at least that the philosophers received their best ideas from the Hebrews (I.XX).

Clement identified Christ with the Logos, much as Justin did. He never proceeded, though, to claim that all rational human beings intuitively know Christian truths (*Stromata* VII.Iff.). Clement did concede elsewhere, however, that all human beings, particularly men engaged in intellectual pursuits, are bestowed with a certain divine emanation, which gives some insight into divine truth (*Exhortation to the Heathen* VI).

To the degree that it is reflected in Clement's thought, whatever cautiousness he had about correlation was probably a function of the distrust of Greek philosophy that many of his contemporaries in the Church felt. The Gnostic heresy, which emerged from an illicit use of such philosophy, had a strong impact on the Church. (See the next chapter for details.) In fact, Clement even devoted attention to refuting the teachings of this heresy (*Stromata* VI.IV; VI.IX–X).

Athenagoras. Also a second-century Apologist, Athenagoras was a contemporary of Justin Martyr's. Though we know very little about the life of Athenagoras, we do know that he shared Justin's concern to defend Christianity from criticism by the general culture. It is unreasonable, he argued, to label Christians "atheists" simply because they have distinguished God from matter (*A Plea for the Christians* 4,10). The similarities between Athenagoras and Justin Martyr also extend to their Christologies, as both identified Christ with the Logos (10). The correlation of Greek philosophy and the Word of God is again clearly evident in this contemporary of Justin's.

Tatian. A native of Syria and likely a contemporary of Athenagoras's, Tatian (b. ca. 120) did not become a Christian until he was quite mature. He went to Rome, where he became a pupil of Justin Martyr's. (Late in his life he returned to the East and founded the Aquarii, a sect that was so extreme in its asceticism as to be suspected of Gnosticism. However, we will only consider his thought during his orthodox period.)

Tatian's apologetic bent is obvious from his insistence that faith is rational. He seems to argue for the existence of God on the basis of what one can observe from the visible things of the world (*Address to the Greeks* XXI,4). (The use of similar arguments by later theologians is identified as the cosmological argument for the existence of God.) However, Tatian's correlationist propensities are not just in evidence in the correlation he posited between human rationality and the gospel. Like his teacher, he relied on Greek philosophical concepts (such as Logos) and correlated them with his exposition of the faith. He also correlated Greek thought with the faith by applying his Hellenized culture's critique of Christianity as "barbaric" to classical Greek thought itself. After all, the Greeks, he contended, have rather barbarian ideas associated with their pantheon of gods (V,XL).

THE ORTHODOX MODEL

The endeavor to correlate the Word of God with the latest intellectually credible sociocultural trends was clearly the predominant approach employed by the Apologists, but there were serious objections to this approach, and an alternative developed. Tertullian is without question the premier proponent in this period of the orthodox model of theology. One may also properly categorize an anonymous Christian epistle of this period, the *Letter to Diognetus*, the earliest work of Christian apologetics, as a representative of this model. Methodologically this theological approach represents an almost (perhaps self-consciously) total repudiation of the correlationist approach.

Tertullian. Quintus Septimius Florens Tertullianus (ca. 160–ca. 225) is a most imposing figure in the early Church. Born in Carthage of pagan parents, this North African studied law and became a lawyer of no little repute. His legal training continued to be reflected in his thought and life even after his conversion and evolution as a Christian writer.

We can observe Tertullian's love of Roman law and its fine points in his theology. Indeed, his training in Roman law manifests itself in the very way the Apologist did theology and wrote it. He was, for example, perhaps the first Christian theologian to write in Latin. His theological style also reflects the adversarial character of the practice of law. Though engaged in apologetics, he did not aim to build bridges between the Word and the surrounding cultural currents, as Justin Martyr and the other correlationists did. Tertullian was more inclined to attack the adversary, to attack the sociocultural pagan currents in which he lived (*Apology* 11ff.).

Tertullian's view of the Christian life evidences a pronounced legalistic tone. Though he does not seem to have been an ordained priest, he practiced his own spiritual life with rigor. It was likely this legalistic exactitude with which he himself sought to live out his faith that led him late in life to join the Montanist sect (a rigorous heretical movement, which will be described and analyzed in chap. 4).

Tertullian best summarizes his methodological commitments regarding theology — his skepticism of philosophy and the correlationist approach — in his famed utterance in the *Prescriptions against Heretics* (7). He wrote:

> It is this philosophy which is the subject-matter of this world's wisdom, that rash interpreter of the divine nature and order. In fact, heresies are themselves prompted by philosophy.... What is there in common between Athens and Jerusalem? What between the Academy and the Church? What between heretics and Christians?

Philosophy inspires heresy, Tertullian claimed. We must keep the gospel pure from both.

Given these commitments, Tertullian needed some standard or criterion by which to judge what the gospel teaches. He insisted that truth
was given to the apostles. They have collectively delivered to the Church
a creed or rule of faith as a norm for the Church in critiquing its own
teachings (*Prescriptions against Heretics* 9–14). It is interesting to observe that many of the themes that would later make their way into the
formulation of the Nicene Creed appear in Tertullian's version of the
rule of faith.

Tertullian's skepticism of philosophy and the correlationist approach
led him to posit a paradoxical relationship between faith and reason.
Faith's claims are most credible, he argued, when they offend reason
(*On the Flesh of Christ* 5). This is not to suggest, however, that Tertullian was an incorrigible anti-intellectual, but rather that he practiced
apologetics in an unsystematic, ad hoc way. For example, at one point
in his writings he conceded, much like Tatian, that nature suggests to
reason that God is the Creator (*Shows* 2.4). He also held that nature
reveals the standards of right and wrong to both Christians and non-
Christians (*On the Crown* 6). Tertullian did not deny that there indeed
may be an overlap between faith and philosophy. When that happens,
though, it is almost by divine accident (*Incarnation of the Logos*, Apol.
XXI). One cannot proceed, as the correlationists did, to relate the gospel to the latest academic trends in a systematic fashion, for the risk is
a distortion of the Word.

The Letter to Diognetus. Regarding the identity of its author as well
as its historical context, the *Letter to Diognetus* is shrouded in historical
mystery. It is clearly an apologetic work in the sense that it endeavors to make Christianity intellectually credible in its original historical
context, primarily by arguing for the unique role Christians play in society. However, its invocation of Pauline themes, uncharacteristic of the
Apostolic Fathers and the first Apologists, distances its methodological
commitments from those of the correlationists.

The paradoxical character of Christian faith, which Tertullian emphasized, is evident in this epistle. Christians are said to live in the
fatherland — but as foreigners. They are flesh — but do not live after
the flesh. They love all men — but are persecuted (5). The paradoxical
character of faith is in part demanded by the nature of the world, which
is said to be filled with deceit and error (10.7). In a sense, this sort
of paradoxical relation with the world makes possible a more powerful Christian witness. Recognition of such paradox is not typical of the
correlation method of Justin Martyr and his colleagues.

Maintaining a theme suggestive of Augustine and Protestant Reformers like Martin Luther, the epistle states that God, as a God of love,
is recognized in our iniquity (9.2). The epistle also shares Tertullian's

suspicions of philosophy (8). As such, with Tertullian, it represents eloquently an important alternative to the correlationist approach of the other Apologists.

OTHER THEOLOGICAL COMMITMENTS
OF THE APOLOGISTS

In addition to the positions the Apologists took on the questions of theological method (how to *do* apologetics), which we have been considering, some of their observations on other theological issues represent important steps in the subsequent development of Christian thought. For example, Tertullian's approach to biblical interpretation in relation to typical correlationist methods is worthy of attention. He seems to operate with a sophisticated literalistic approach to Scripture; that is, he interprets literally those portions of Scripture that demand such interpretation. By contrast, a number of the correlationists interpret the Bible allegorically.[2]

We have previously noted Tertullian's legalistic propensities. Christ is said to proclaim the law. In fact the law is so central for this African Father that he claims that no one can be a Christian without persevering to the end (*Prescriptions against Heretics* 9,7). Tied with these emphases is an affirmation of the freedom of the will (*Against Marcion* II.V).

These non-Pauline themes characterized the theology of most of the Apostolic Fathers. It is consequently hardly surprising that Tertullian, with his "orthodox" commitments, endorsed them. What to make of these themes in our post-Augustinian context is another problem. Some scholars have argued that the emphasis on freedom and responsibility that characterized the Apologists and their predecessors was their reaction to the generally accepted belief among the masses in the Roman Empire that the predetermination of the stars undercut human freedom. In any case, redeeming "Augustinian" features of Tertullian's thought are his claims that Adam is the originator of our sin (*Exhortation to Chastity* II) and that we are actually regenerated in the baptismal event (*On Baptism* I).

Tertullian took a number of other interesting and important positions. He affirmed both apostolic succession and the priesthood of all believers, which is a reminder to us that these distinct emphases are not necessarily in conflict (*Prescriptions against Heretics* 21; *Exhortation to Chastity* VII). Long before the Church clarified its formal position on the nature of Christ, Tertullian was perhaps the first Christian we know

2. Tertullian *Against Marcion* IV.XIX.6; cf. Clement *Stromata* VI.XV.

of to speak of Christ as one person with two substances, or natures
(*Against Praxeas* XXVII).

The African Father also offered significant trinitarian reflections in
the era before the Church adopted the doctrine of the Trinity. Dealing with the relationship between the Father and the Son, he claims
that Father and Son are distinguished, not by virtue of "substance,"
but in virtue of "personality." They are one in sharing the same work
(*Against Praxeas* XII,XXII). Father, Son, and Holy Spirit are said to be
"Three Persons," yet one (II). Elsewhere in another intriguing observation, Tertullian claims that the Son is generated from the Father as a ray
is generated by the sun, and that as the sun is in the ray, so Father and
Son share the same substance (*Apology* 21). These concrete descriptions
of the relations of the first two persons of the Godhead may yet be helpful nearly nineteen centuries later as the Church continues to struggle to
find language for communicating the trinitarian vision.

We have already noted the Pauline themes reflected in the *Letter to
Diognetus*. Consequently, it is perhaps somewhat surprising (though not
really given the overall theological profile of the Church at that time) to
find the epistle still affirming some role for the human will in the process of salvation. God is said to have sent his Son to "persuade," not
to "compel" us (7). The epistle also reflects other Pauline themes not
previously noted. While emphasizing the loving character of God, the
letter maintains that our sins are covered by an external righteousness.
Much as Augustine and the Protestant Reformers would subsequently
affirm, a "blessed exchange" of the believer's wickedness for Christ's
righteousness is said to transpire in faith. Christ takes our wickedness
to the Cross so that we might receive his righteousness and redemption
(9). The *Letter to Diognetus* is clearly a rich, too-much-overlooked resource for those working in the Augustinian theological heritage and its
Protestant manifestations.

Justin Martyr offered some important insights about the ethos of the
early Church in the course of his efforts to provide apologetic arguments
on behalf of the Christian faith. Among these insights include affirmations
of baptismal regeneration and the real presence of Christ in the Eucharist,
as well as an insistence on a legitimate role for deacons in distribut-
ing the sacrament to those who are absent from worship (*First Apology*
61,65–67). In addition, Justin provided an outline of an early liturgy (67).

Several of Justin's other commitments are more controversial. He
endorsed the kind of legalistic propensities (the belief that we can con-
tribute to our own salvation by our deeds) that typifies most of the
Apologists. For example, he affirms free will, as well as insisting that
God only accepts those who imitate good things (*First Apology* 10,43).
Even more problematic is Justin's advocacy of the censure of Jews (63).

Warts and all, though, Justin Martyr is still clearly one of the most profound Christian theologians of this and every other era.

Clement of Alexandria provides another important insight concerning the correlationists' approach to theology. We have noted his reliance on an allegorical method of interpretation. Although not all of the other correlationists of the era explicitly embraced this method of biblical interpretation, there is a sense in which the correlationist commitment to construing the real meaning of the Word of God in terms of the language and thought forms of some other currently intellectually credible conceptuality demands a reliance on allegorical interpretation. Such theological moves entail that we will necessarily bypass the literal sense of Scripture, claiming that the conceptual system of thought chosen to explicate the Christian faith best expresses the spiritual/deeper meaning of the Bible's literal sense. This sort of hermeneutical approach is precisely what allegory seeks to do.

Tertullian warns that such a methodological approach to theology inevitably leads to the distortion of the Word of God. At least in the case of Clement there are suggestions that this is borne out on at least one doctrine, Christology. Despite the importance the doctrine plays for him, on at least one occasion he has problems affirming the full humanity of Christ (*Stromata* VI.IX). Nevertheless, despite this shortcoming, Clement of Alexandria is a most substantial theologian. He was probably the first Christian thinker to teach the doctrine of creation out of nothing (*creatio ex nihilo*), refuting the Greek idea that matter is eternal (*Exhortation to the Greeks* IV). Tertullian subsequently developed this affirmation more fully in *Against Hermogenes*.

Athenagoras typifies the theology of most of the early Apologists, not just in his endorsement of the correlationist approach but also in his treatment of fundamental Christian themes. For example, his thought exhibits the legalistic propensities of most of his fellow theologians. He claims that the law, the threat of punishment, motivates good works (*Supplication for the Christians* 31). He also offers profound reflections on the relationship of Father, Son, and Holy Spirit. Prefiguring similar conceptions of the Trinity articulated by Augustine and later in the eighteenth century by Jonathan Edwards, he claims that the Holy Spirit binds Father and Son together in a unity (10). Such a portrait may still make an important contribution to the Church today, as it provides a helpful conceptual model for describing the oneness of the Triune God.

The apologetic efforts of Tatian were significant for the early Church's evolving reflections on *soteriology* (the doctrine of salvation). He refers to the indwelling of the Spirit in the believer. The Spirit is said to create a union between the Lord and the believer (*Address to the Greeks* 13,15). Such conceptions suggest Pauline themes that undercut the legalism we have observed in so many of the early Church's theological reflections. It is evident that the Apologists of the first centuries offer rich insights for doing Christian theology in our own present context.

CONCLUSION:
SHOULD WE HEED TERTULLIAN'S WARNINGS?

The debate between Justin Martyr and Tertullian regarding the most appropriate theological method is one that students of theology have repeated throughout Christian history. Readers of this book should enter into this debate. It is essentially a debate about whether the heart of the theological task is to present the Christian faith in the most intellectually credible way possible.

If presenting Christian faith in the most intellectually credible way possible is in fact the central task of theology, then readers are well advised to endorse Justin Martyr's method. As he did, we would be wise to select an intellectually credible philosophical system or worldview (like capitalism, psychology, the latest business-management techniques) and systematically correlate the gospel with it. One accomplishes this by translating all Christian doctrines into the conceptualities of the intellectually credible worldview selected.

The alternative approach to theology concurs with Tertullian that such theological moves will inevitably distort the Word of God. Readers are inclined to follow his orthodox approach if they regard theology first and foremost on the basis of the literal sense of Scripture, unconcerned about correlating the Word with the latest intellectual fashion. Another way of posing the debate between these two theological approaches pertains to whether one believes that contemporary experience is best understood in light of the gospel or contends that the gospel should be interpreted first in light of our contemporary experience.

Readers are heartily encouraged to reflect on these questions and try to determine which theological approach considered in this chapter seems most congenial. Those who come to terms with these issues will launch themselves well along the road toward sorting out their own individual theological positions.

We have noted how the increasingly stabilized position of the Church in the second century provided an opportunity for Christians to engage in the sort of sophisticated theologizing considered in this chapter. Such prosperity also gave the Church the opportunity to reflect on its teachings in new ways. Creative theologizing has its vices and virtues. It can, as Tertullian noted, lead to heretical distortions of the gospel. This is the story we consider in the next chapter.

CHAPTER 4

STRUGGLES AGAINST HERESY

The early Church encountered problems other than the external challenges of dialogue with secular Hellenistic culture. In developing a formal apologetic theology, it began to confront internal challenges, false teachings threatening to undermine the gospel. In the Church's responses to these heresies, new theological insights developed.

The topic of heresy is the business of all Christians, at least those who subscribe to the catholic heritage, for the ancient heresies are still in the air and, as such, remain threats to the gospel. Most of these heresies had their origins in philosophical and cultural ideas that were floating around in the Hellenistic society of the Roman Empire of the day. In a sense this was very typical, for virtually all of the heresies that the Church has confronted originated in sociocultural trends that were dominant at the time that the heresy emerged.

Given this background, one can better understand Tertullian's warnings about reliance on philosophy and his conclusion that mixing such human wisdom with the gospel inevitably leads to heresy (*Prescriptions against Heretics* 7). Is he correct that the use of reason and the latest social insights distort the gospel? Or is it rather the case that the so-called heresies of the early Church convey many sound biblical insights, that the reason for their condemnation was mostly related to ecclesiastical politics, that in fact contemporary Christians can have much to learn from these heresies? Let us approach these heresies first with an open ⟵ mind and try to assess whether the Church might have made a mistake in condemning them.

GNOSTICISM

Gnosticism is a general title used to designate various dualistic, syncretistic mystery religions that invaded Hellenistic culture from the Orient. It had a special impact in North Africa, and so some scholars have speculated about its being rooted in African spirituality.

Some, but not all, Gnostics held Christian commitments. Virtually all contended that humanity's heavenly element, the soul, was imprisoned in the body. Thus, one could only achieve true spirituality, they thought, through *gnōsis*, which involves renouncing the evils of fleshly existence. (Similarities to Neoplatonism are striking at this point.) Gnostics believed that only they could obtain this true spirituality, as in their view the larger class of humans was purely corporal with no soul.[1]

Gnostics emphasized this spirit-matter distinction even more sharply when they posited the distinction between the Supreme God of spiritual things and the Creator God (a spiritual being who had fallen into error and as a result had created material things imprisoning sparks of the spirit made by the Supreme God in material things).[2] Consequently, the world is not what the Supreme God intended. In fact, it is an aberration of the spirit, from which spiritual beings yearn to be released.

According to the Gnostics, a messenger was required to bring the knowledge (gnosis) that would save by facilitating release. For Christian Gnostics, this messenger is Christ.[3] Thus, the Gnostic heresy had christological implications; essentially it entailed Docetism (a belief that the Savior only had the appearance of a man).[4] Such an affirmation was a logical outcome of the Gnostic devaluation of the material creation. It is generally believed that the piety of the Gnostic movement took two forms. Some Gnostics completely denied the flesh and lived as ascetics. Others are said to have lived as libertines (living only for the day).

Some scholars have argued that a factor in enhancing the attractiveness of Gnosticism among Christians in this period was the kind of Judaism that was influencing the Church. With its emphasis on mysteries, Essene Judaism — the Jewish sectarian community that generated the Dead Sea Scrolls (DSS) — is thought to be a contributing factor in paving the way for the acceptance of such heresies as Gnosticism. For example, the *Birth of Noah* (8–9) refers to "mysteries," such as the mysterious knowledge of the Gnostics, and the *Manual of Discipline* (iii.13–iv.26) speaks of two spirits in man, each generated from a different source, in ways most suggestive of the Gnostic body-soul dualism rooted in different spiritual emanations.

Some analysts of American society and American religion claim that gnosticism still prevails in our context. Not unlike the Gnostics, Americans hold the belief that knowledge (education) is the key to a good life. (It is common to refer to the new "knowledge society" and its indus-

---

1. *Gospel of Thomas* II.32; Irenaeus *Against Heresies* I.V.6; I.XXI.4; I.XXIV.1,5.
2. *Tripartite Tractate* I.51ff.; *On the Origin of the World* II.97ff.; Irenaeus *Against Heresies* I.XXVI.1; I.XXIV.3–4.
3. Irenaeus *Against Heresies* I.XXIV.4.
4. Ibid., I.XXIV.1–2; 2 John 7.

tries.) Some American gnostics throw in a little libertinism. American religion likewise exhibits gnostic characteristics in its spirituality. American Christians are often so caught up in the pursuit of holiness (or psychological well-being) that they forget the goodness of God's creation. The ecological crisis and the Church's relative silence about it illustrate this point. Of course, in a society unduly preoccupied with materialism, could the gnostic disdain for the corporal be a healthy corrective?

THE CHURCH'S RESPONSE

The Church has struggled with Gnosticism since biblical times. The Epistle of 1 John (and perhaps Col. 2) was probably written against Gnostics. It is likely that Philip's encounter with Simon (reported in Acts 8:9–24) is an account of an early confrontation between the Church and Gnosticism.

In early post–New Testament times there are ample examples of the Church's efforts to refute Gnostic teaching. Irenaeus, whose life and work we shall explore later in this chapter, Clement of Alexandria, and Justin Martyr claimed that true gnosis is available to all through Christ.[5] Irenaeus also maintained the goodness of creation and its completion in deification (being made godlike) (*Against Heresies* IV.18.4–5). The *Letter to Diognetus* (7) affirmed the redeeming Son's role in creation. Thus, creation must be good. Tertullian made the same claim in the rule of faith (*Prescriptions against Heretics* 13). There is even some possibility that in the city of Rome a baptismal creed was developed as early as the mid-second century to refute Gnosticism; the formulation eventually evolved into our contemporary versions of the Nicene Creed and the Apostles' Creed.

The confession of the goodness of creation and of God's role in it and the rejection of secret, privileged saving knowledge have been perduring marks of Christian faith since the Church's confrontation with Gnosticism. Readers should reflect on whether (and if so, why) these have been sufficient reasons to reject gnostic elitism and spirituality in its present forms. Insofar as the reliance on creedal formulations in church life also seems to have its origin in the Church's confrontation with Gnosticism and other heresies, we must consider the adequacy of this sort of response to the contemporary heresies that faith must encounter.

---

5. Irenaeus *Against Heresies* III.IV.1; Clement of Alexandria *Stromata* II.IV; V.I; Justin Martyr *First Apology* 60.

MARCION

Marcion was a mid-second-century heretic from the northeastern regions of Asia Minor who became heavily involved in the early Church's efforts to distance itself from Judaism for apologetic purposes. Recall the discussion in earlier chapters regarding what was at stake for the Church in creating such distance between itself and Judaism. Marcion also may have been reacting to the neglect of Paul and the legalistic orientation that characterized the "re-Judaization" of Christianity.

In his efforts to assert the newness of the gospel, Marcion went too far. For him (as for the Gnostics, with whom he shared much in common), the gospel negated the world. He could not reconcile the existence of evil in the world with the goodness of the gospel and its God. Therefore, he concluded, this good and excellent God of the gospel could not be the Creator, which led him to posit a second god, Jehovah, a judgmental and harsh god who created the world. It was this god, he maintained, about whom the Jews spoke.[6] The movement that Marcion's teachings initiated actually formed a formidable rival church.

THE CHURCH'S RESPONSE

Marcion effectively disenfranchised the Jewish canon and its heritage. This result, as well as Marcion's efforts at amending several New Testament books, led the Church to respond to his challenge by establishing the biblical canon. Without intending it, Marcion effectively provided the impulse for the Church's identification of the books to be included in the canon.

To be sure, there was no canon, no Bible, as we know it until the end of the second century or later, and the process was an ad hoc, informal one. Though one can identify some earlier lists of books of Scripture, the first list to contain all the books of our Bible was written by Athanasius in A.D. 367. There was wide agreement about the authority of Paul's letters (which had been used widely in worship in various churches), Acts, and the Synoptic Gospels (which were regarded, if not as firsthand accounts, as works of those who were intimate with the apostles). However, controversies arose concerning the other books eventually included in the canon, and at times the writings of some of the Apostolic Fathers and even Gnostic literature were given serious consideration and treated as authoritative. Finally two African councils (Hippo in 393 and Carthage in 397) approved Athanasius's version (supplemented by ad-

---

6. Irenaeus *Against Heresies* I.XXVII.2.

ditional books that have come to be known as the Apocrypha), the full
canon as the Roman Catholic Church has it today.

It is true that the inclusion of the Apocrypha was not uniform in the
early Church after the mid-third century. Theologians after Athanasius
who influenced the Eastern churches more than the Western ones rejected it. Nevertheless, the Church's reception of the decisions of these
African councils regarding the books of the Bible has been virtually, but
not completely, executed. In the Western church, at least in Germany,
the *Letter to the Laodicians* was included in the biblical canon until
late in the Middle Ages. The Armenian Apostolic Church has recognized
and continues to accept a third letter of Paul to the Corinthians. All of
the Eastern Orthodox churches have come to endorse several additional
apocryphal books not included in the Catholic canon — Psalm 131 as
well as 3 Maccabees and 4 Maccabees.

The comments in various ancient texts, written prior to the formal
establishment of the New Testament canon, regarding the texts considered authoritative are most instructive. When one reads the Muratorian
Canon and observations by Papias and Irenaeus, it is evident that many
of modern biblical scholarship's ideas about the aims and origins of the
New Testament books and about the authenticity of Mark's Gospel in
comparison to the other Gospels have very ancient roots.[7]

Marcion was also refuted in other ways, with arguments most
compatible with the Church's rationale for rejecting a sister heresy,
Gnosticism. Irenaeus offers another noteworthy critique of the Marcionite heresy (*Against Heresies* I.XXVII.2–3). He claims that it posits
only salvation of the soul, not of the body.

Marcion provided a notable threat to the Church catholic because the
churches he founded lasted several centuries. Ultimately what he did was
to pose in its most radical form the question with which we observed
the Church struggle since its inception: What is the proper relationship
between the gospel and its Jewish roots? One alternative is to establish close ties between them, as has Jewish Christian theology and the
Ethiopian Orthodox Church. Other Christians have concluded that the
freedom of the gospel and the proclamation of God's unconditional love
are best served by severing the ties to Judaism as much as possible.

DOCETISM

Both Gnosticism and the Marcionite heresy were Docetic (a term derived from the Greek word meaning "to seem"). Essentially Docetism

---

7. See Eusebius *Church History* 3.39; Irenaeus *Against Heresies* III.I.1.

amounts to a denial of Christ's true humanity because a good and holy God could not become incarnate in evil flesh. It is reported that proponents of this heresy tended to withdraw themselves from the Eucharist because in their view the earthly elements of the sacrament could not be the flesh of Jesus.[8] (Such suppositions are most compatible with the suppositions of Platonism.) Are there not some today who talk about Jesus in such ethereal terms that it is as if Christ were not human? Docetism still seems to be thriving.

At stake in Docetism is Christ's redemption of our sins. That is, if Christ were not really human, his death has not really removed our sin, and God cannot truly empathize with us in our sufferings, for he has not truly walked in our shoes. The early version of the creed previously noted, which primarily addressed the Gnostic and Marcionite heresies, also addressed this heresy. The creed's reference to Christ's being born of the Virgin Mary was intended to affirm that Jesus was actually born and did not simply "appear" on earth.

With Docetism, the Church was pressed for the first time in a formal way to articulate the mystery of the Incarnation — how Jesus can be divine and human and still be one. Throughout its subsequent history we will observe the Church's struggle with this issue. Where it ceases to struggle, Docetism typically reemerges.

MODALISM/SABELLIANISM

Sabellius was the great third-century Roman advocate of modalism/Sabellianism, which teaches that Christ was merely a mode of God; that is, Father, Son, and Spirit were construed as merely temporary modes or manifestations of God, not really distinct. They fulfill their mission and return to the divine monad.[9]

It is important to come to terms with precisely what was at stake in the Church's negative reaction to modalism. Tertullian offered the criticism that the heresy taught that the Father must have suffered, a teaching that is called "Patripassianism" (*Against Praxeas* I). It is not exactly clear what is lost in the teaching except a repudiation of classical Greek philosophical assumptions that an eternal God cannot change. Of course, had the Church not condemned modalism, it would have forfeited God's communal nature. Also, upholding the heresy might render some biblical texts that seem to subordinate the Son to the Father (Mark 14:36; John 14:28) difficult to interpret. However, given the dif-

---

8. Ignatius *Letter to the Smyrneans* 7.
9. Epiphanius of Salamis *Against Eighty Heresies* 62.1.

ficulties that affirming God's threeness in one has posed for the Church, *Well...*
would not the modalist view have been a preferable, more reasonable
model? Readers need to consider what is at stake for them in affirming
the trinitarian vision of God rather than the modalist view.

EBIONITISM

Despite the influx of Gentiles in the post-Pauline era, Jewish Christianity
persisted. A number of its adherents maintained orthodox Christian beliefs and simply continued to observe the regulations of the Mosaic law.
A more radical segment of this Jewish Christian sect, though, challenged
the prevailing view of Christ and even challenged the authority of Paul.[10]
This group came to be termed "Ebionite," a word whose etymological
origin relates to the Hebrew word for "poor" (*ebyon*). Ebionitism was
probably never a very widespread movement; it seems to have disappeared as the Church continued to become more Gentile and the Jewish
Christian community virtually disappeared.

Some scholars believe that the Essenes influenced the Ebionite movement, for both posited a Gnostic-like principle of good and evil as forces
in the cosmos.[11] The Ebionites also maintained that the Good is revealed through its prophet, who has been incarnate several times, most
recently in Jesus by adoption.[12] Essentially the Ebionites held an adoptionist Christology; that is, Jesus became the Son of God by adoption
when he received the Holy Spirit. Many held that the Spirit left Jesus at
the time of death, which is how the Father could raise Jesus.[13]

Why is the Ebionite view problematic? It effectively maintained that
God did not really suffer. But if God did not suffer, then it seems that
God was not really the agent of salvation. Or is it too barbaric, not
sufficiently respectful of divine majesty, to think of God as suffering?
Another challenge raised by the movement concerns the uniqueness of
Jesus Christ: Was Christ really unique in history, or was he merely what
the Jewish community has always claimed the Messiah would be like (so
that he can be understood *only* in that context, as one in a line of Israel's
prophets)? Precisely how unique is Jesus' ministry? How one answers
that question is intimately related to one's assessment of the validity of
the Ebionite movement.

The early church was also critical of the movement's maintenance
of certain Jewish practices. However it is not readily apparent that the

---

10. Irenaeus *Against Heresies* I.XXVI.2.
11. See the Ebionite *Preaching of Peter* 2.15–17; *Manual of Discipline* iii.13–iv.26.
12. *Preaching of Peter* 2.15–17.
13. Irenaeus *Against Heresies* I.XXVI.1.

Church would be damaged or the gospel ill-served by this. Has the continuing preservation of Jewish practices hurt Ethiopian Orthodoxy over the centuries?

MONTANISM

Montanism was a second-century apocalyptic movement, named for its founder, Montanus, whose adherents believed that the Church must continue to anticipate Christ's imminent return and refrain from structuring itself in more permanent forms. Even its critics such as Hippolytus (ca. 170–ca. 236), a Roman presbyter, conceded that the movement was essentially orthodox in character, at least in its early stages (*Refutation of All the Heresies* viii.19).

Apparently Montanus and his followers came to believe that the Spirit had been withdrawn from the Church because of its moral laxity. This view coupled with rising persecutions fostered an apocalyptic sensibility among them that was ripe for belief in extraordinary manifestations of the Spirit. Outbreaks of prophetic ecstasy, including speaking in tongues, characterized the movement.[14] In a sense, it was a postbiblical Pentecostal movement.

Around A.D. 207, Tertullian, that staunch opponent of heresy, joined the Montanist movement. Above all, its moral rigor seems to have attracted him. Also his orthodoxy, rooted in New Testament faith, may have attracted him to the Pentecostal manifestations typical of the New Testament church (Acts 2; 1 Cor. 14). We have also previously considered that Perpetua, the third-century female martyr, was also likely a Montanist. The prophetic visions she experienced and the fact that Tertullian is probably the author of the account of her martyrdom seem to render this conclusion likely (*Martyrdom of Perpetua* 4,8,11–12).

From the outset of the movement, women, notably Priscilla and Maximilla, were placed in positions of significant leadership.[15] Throughout the history of the Church, when women have been permitted to exercise leadership, this has typically occurred in movements of the Church, like Montanism, that were not established. For example, in the early stages of the modern Pentecostal movement, when it was largely a movement of the poor and disenfranchised in America, leadership opportunities were conferred on women. (One thinks of the International Church of the Foursquare Gospel, a Pentecostal body, founded by a woman — Aimee Semple McPherson.)

---

14. Eusebius *Church History* 4.16.7.
15. Hippolytus *Refutation of All the Heresies* viii.19.

Montanism was a radical Pentecostalism in that adherents tended to speak of the Holy Spirit in the first person. It is even reported that they spoke in trinitarian formulations.[16] Indeed, Montanism made an important contribution to the Church in rekindling awareness of the Holy Spirit and the Spirit's contribution to the life of the believer, as well as an awareness of its personal character and relation to the Father and Son. There is some indication that prophetic utterances had not entirely disappeared among orthodox Christians in the second century, but they were becoming rarer and rarer.[17]

THE CHURCH'S RESPONSE

Montanism was not formally condemned; it just died a slow death. It would be intriguing to find out precisely why, and some scholars have speculated that it may have lapsed into a kind of idolatry, divinizing its founders. The Montanist movement was probably curtailed in Rome. No doubt, the failure to see the eschaton achieved was a factor in its demise. As we have noted, though, it did rekindle the Church's awareness of the Spirit. One might say that its mission was accomplished.

Why was Montanism a problem for the Church? It effectively challenged the emerging structure of the Church, as church structures are not necessary if the end is near. Montanism also undermined the significance of Jesus and the New Testament events, insofar as its adherents claimed to have received new revelations. Such claims entail that the New Testament events are not ultimately authoritative but are just one stage in the history of salvation. How can Pentecostalism avoid such difficulties? Perhaps it is not inappropriate to relativize the authority of the *of* New Testament and to believe that present revelations of the Spirit are *the...* likewise authoritative. In that case Montanism may not really be such an aberration of the gospel.

APOSTOLIC SUCCESSION: THE BEST ANTIDOTE TO THE HERESIES OF CONTEMPORARY SECULARISM?

Church structure was emerging in the first centuries of the Christian Era. Apostolic succession, as we have noted, has very ancient roots in

---

16. Epiphanius of Salamis *Against Eighty Heresies* 48.II.1,9; Didymus the Blind *On the Trinity* 3.41.

17. Justin Martyr *Dialogue with Trypho* LXXXII, LXXXVIII; Irenaeus *Against Heresies* II.XXII.4.

the post–New Testament Church. Clement of Rome, Tertullian, and Irenaeus affirmed it.[18] The same period bears witness to the development of a fixed order of worship (a liturgy).[19] These structures, especially apostolic succession and the authority it conferred on the Church's leaders, were probably the single most important dynamic in refuting heresy. What Jesus wanted conferred would be found among successors of the disciples. Consequently, the argument proceeded, because these successors denied the new teaching, the Church was right to conclude that it is unlikely that such teaching is in accord with Christ.

The development of apostolic succession was simply the logical outcome of the general tendency of churches in most of the prominent cities of the Roman Empire to claim to have been founded by one or more of the apostles. Of course, it is not readily proven that the churches in each of these major cities, including Rome, Alexandria, and Antioch, can substantiate their claim to apostolic founding or that they were in fact presided over by bishops (at least not by individuals holding an office distinct from elders) during the first decades of their existence. Why else would the late-first-century New Testament Epistles have so few references to bishops and not address them specifically in introductory greetings? Nevertheless, at a very early date in the life of the Church, the high prestige that the bishops of these churches enjoyed made the claims to apostolic succession easy for the faithful to believe.

Such prestige was further strengthened by even stronger claims on behalf of the episcopal authority of church leaders, like Irenaeus, who asserted that only presbyters in apostolic line should be obeyed (*Against Heresies* IV.XXVI.2). Ignatius, recall, insisted that the faithful "follow the Bishop as Jesus Christ followed the Father" (*Letter to the Smyrneans* 8). Cyprian, the third-century bishop of Carthage, claimed that if one is not with the bishop, he is not in the Church. Furthermore, he asserted, the Church is in the bishop (*Epistles* LXVIII/LXVI.8). We have here rather resounding affirmations of episcopal authority.

Another by-product of the evolution of apostolic succession in response to the heresies is that it facilitated a sense of unity among the various local churches. Each was now appealing to a common source — the apostolic tradition — in refuting false teachings. It could be claimed against the heresies that the Church everywhere and throughout the decades (since the time of the apostles) had taught contrary to the views of the heretics. It is in this sense, then, that we observe the roots of a catholic (universal) self-understanding in the Church. It is hardly sur-

---

18. Clement of Rome *Letter to the Church in Corinth* 42–44; Tertullian *Prescriptions against Heretics* 20–21; Irenaeus *Against Heresies* III.III.1; IV.XXVI.2.
    19. Justin Martyr *First Apology* 65–67; *Didache.*

prising that it was in this period (at least by the late second century) that the Church began to refer to itself as "catholic."

The term "catholic" does not just mean "universal"; it also means "according to the whole." The Church's appeal to an apostolic tradition to refute heresy was catholic in this second sense of the term's meaning. The Church was willing to consider as true teaching only what all of the apostles and their successors agreed upon, not the allegedly secret teaching just given to one of the apostles, as the heretics claimed was the source for their new ideas. We also have in these commitments the seeds for a kind of Christian egalitarianism, which would be later developed in the Reformation. Insofar as Christian teaching belongs to the whole, it is public and so accessible to all the faithful; it is not just the business of the elite.

Given the success that the affirmation of apostolic succession and a high view of the episcopacy had in helping the early Church clamp down on heresy and in facilitating a stronger sense of unity or catholicity among the churches, would not the same polity work effectively today against the ravages of secularism? Is part of the Church's contemporary problem of being co-opted by the latest winds of change a function of the breakdown of clerical authority, which is itself related to the rejection of this sort of polity by Protestant churches?

DEIFICATION (SALVATION AS BECOMING LIKE GOD): ARE THE WESTERN CHURCHES MISSING SOMETHING?

One cannot address this concluding topic until we examine more systematically the theology of Irenaeus of Lyons (ca. 130–202), one of the great early Christian theologians, who, in response to some of the heresies we have considered, first formulated something like the concept of deification, which is also called *theōsis* (*Against Heresies* V.Pref.; V.XXXVI.3). Later theologians like Origen and Athanasius more fully developed the concept of salvation as becoming like God because in Christ God first became man, dispersing the divine energies in human flesh.[20] A contemporary of Irenaeus, Clement of Alexandria also offered reflections suggesting the concept of deification, as he asserted that "the Logos of God had become man so that you might learn how a man may become God."[21]

Born in Asia Minor (present-day Turkey), Irenaeus was a disciple of Polycarp's (*Against Heresies* III.III.4) and was perhaps one of the

---

20. Origen *Against Celsus* III.XXVIII; Athanasius *On the Incarnation* 54.
21. Clement of Alexandria *Exhortation to the Heathen* XII, IX.

students of Justin Martyr. Irenaeus was brought to serve as a sort of missionary in Lyons, France. During a persecution, its bishop was martyred, and Irenaeus was called to serve.

Unlike a number of his contemporaries, Irenaeus was not an Apologist or speculative theologian; he was rather a pastor who sought to keep the flock away from heresy. He was especially preoccupied with refuting Gnosticism (and somewhat with Marcion). His writings are important sources of information about these heresies and also offer important critiques of them. However, Irenaeus was no rough-and-ready polemicist. His project was merely to point to, with great cosmic profundity, the love of God.

Before proceeding to Irenaeus's refutation of Gnosticism, by means of the doctrine of *theōsis* and its related concept of recapitulation, let us examine a few of his most important other theological commitments. For Irenaeus, Scripture is perfect (*Against Heresies* II.XXVIII.1). Fundamentalists did not invent this teaching, it seems. Such an insight poses questions for those of us committed to the use of historical-critical insights for biblical interpretation (which, as we shall see in the second volume, are themselves historically conditioned). Have we "fallen" from the faith of the ancient Church by our implicit critique of Scripture's inerrancy? On the other hand, Irenaeus is nothing like a Protestant who advocates *sola scriptura*. He appeals to apostolic succession as a way of ruling out heresies, arguing contrary to the Gnostics that if the apostles had had any secret knowledge, they would have passed it on to their successors (III.III.1; IV.XXXIII.8). Consider with suspicion, he advised, those teachers who are not in the apostolic line (IV.XXVI.2). In essence, then, he appeals to both Scripture and tradition as authorities for Church teaching (III.II.1–2). Faith makes even barbarians wise (III.IV.1).

Not unlike the Stoics, who may have influenced him, Irenaeus stressed the unity of God's people in the midst of their cultural diversity (*Against Heresies* I.X.1). In proclaiming such unity, he asserts the primacy of the Roman church, claiming that all churches must agree with it (III.III.1). Irenaeus's preoccupation with the unity of the Church in refuting heresies surfaces in other ways. Not unlike Tertullian, he posits a "rule of faith," a nascent creed (I.X.1). It may be that what he cited was the ancient Roman baptismal creed noted earlier. Certainly the similarities between it and the later Nicene and Apostles' Creeds are a striking testimony to the continuity of Christian faith over the centuries.

Given Irenaeus's continuities with the tradition before him, it is not surprising to find in him certain legalistic propensities, such as his claim that God will confer life on those who keep his Commandments (*Against Heresies* I.X.1). A similar continuity with the past is revealed in

Irenaeus's treatment of the atonement (the doctrine that addresses why Jesus had to die or engage in ministry in order to redeem humanity, to set things right). He endorses a view we observed earlier in Ignatius, the idea of Christ as a ransom for the devil, overcoming the devil (V.I.1), but there is no reference here to the need to buy off an angry God, to make recompense.[22] It is another testimony to Irenaeus's testimony to the loving character of God.

Turning finally to Irenaeus's endorsement of something like deification, we must understand it in relation to his view of recapitulation, which emerges from his inextricable commitment to connect salvation/ redemption to creation. Such commitments, of course, emerge from his concern to refute Gnosticism, which had effectively negated creation in its quest for salvation. Irenaeus's theological commitments that follow take the form of a narrative, as recapitulation makes for a kind of "narrative theology."

According to Irenaeus, God created humans as the crown of creation, part of a process leading to a final goal with humans to be increasingly conformed to the divine will and nature. But humans were not created in this final perfection (deification), for one angel, Satan, is said to have become jealous and sought to thwart the Incarnation as a model for making humans in the divine image. With the introduction of sin, a new purpose emerged in God's plan to become incarnate in a man; the Word would also have to redeem humanity (*Against Heresies* V.I).

Jesus then became incarnate as a second Adam, recapitulating the first, now totally renewing human nature with divine energy so it might become incorruptible, that is, like God (*Against Heresies* V.I.2; III.XVII.6; III.XVIII.1). As Irenaeus put it, "Christ... became what we are, so that He might bring us to be what He Himself is" (V.Pref.). To be sure, becoming what Christ and God is in himself does not entail being lost in the divine or being the same as God. Deification refers to a process that is ever growing; we are always on the way towards becoming like God. In this process, humans are said to have a free will. Irenaeus's affirmation of this point is his refutation of the determinism implied by Gnosticism's teachings of the entrapment of the soul in the body and the inherent inability of some to achieve spiritual knowledge (IV.XXXVII).

Irenaeus and others who endorse deification unambiguously affirm the goodness of creation, for on these grounds the redeeming Word has been involved in creation from the beginning (*Against Heresies* III.XVIII.). This entails that there must be a continuity between creation and redemption, an affirmation that foreshadows the Council of Nicea and its catholic consensus. Gnostic, classical Greek, and other world-

---

22. Cf. Ignatius *Letter to the Ephesians* 19.

views that effectively negate the goodness of the physical world cannot stand in face of such theological commitments. Furthermore, it seems fair to say that Irenaeus's theology, if not the view of salvation as deification in general, offers stronger testimony to the Resurrection than the Cross. There are indications that such an emphasis was characteristic of the Christian worship of the first centuries, which does not seem to have been very Cross oriented (Acts 2:46).

To construe salvation as deification is to depict a process. To the extent that a process like deification involves movement and action, as is characteristic of narratives, proponents of salvation as deification can be said to engage in a narrative theology. We noted in chapter 1 that this is the primary way of describing redemption that prevails in the Eastern Orthodox churches, including the Oriental Orthodox churches, such as the Coptic Church and the Ethiopian Orthodox Church. It is the model of describing salvation that prevailed among most of the theologians of the early Church. In fact, the impact of this view on the theologians of the early Church, particularly on the Cappadocians (to be considered in chap. 10), entails that salvation as deification may underlie the theology of John Wesley and the Methodist tradition, insofar as Wesley was deeply indebted to these theologians. To claim that "God became man, so we might become like God" may not be so foreign to the pieties of readers of this volume after all. In another sense, though, the concept is quite foreign to readers associated with most other denominations with Western origins. Since Augustine, the Western church, concerned to distinguish the acts of God from human works, has avoided the concept of deification.

In addition to the reliance of the ancient African churches on the concept of deification, affinities between this sort of understanding of salvation, and African spirituality are even more pronounced when one considers that the idea of demon possession is characteristic of African religion. It is not difficult to move from belief in possession by demons to belief in being possessed by the divine energies engendered in the deification process. A family resemblance also exists between the ancient Egyptian belief in the divinity of the king and Christian contention that all the faithful are becoming like God.

Deification also offers insight in interpreting theological remarks of early Christian theologians, including those by Irenaeus, that suggest we must do something to merit salvation. When the salvation process is understood as deification, then the whole human being, including all human works, is infused with the divine energies. The Incarnation has so closely united divinity and humanity that the divine is inextricably linked to human nature as a whole. Human nature, and so human actions, can no longer transpire without the divine nature. There is no such thing as a human work that is not infused with divine energies. The distinction between God's work and human work is ultimately artificial.

Has the concept of deification successfully overcome concerns about placing too much emphasis on human works in the salvation process? To the degree it has, the distinction between God's work and our own work, which played such a major role in the Church's great debate about works righteousness (see the Pelagian controversy in chap. 9), may be ultimately artificial, not worth the Church's concern. Is it only because Western churches have not maintained the theme of deification that concerns with legalism and works righteousness emerged?

Questions need to be raised about whether such a vision of Christian life and salvation is idolatrous in its claim that believers might become *like God*. Or is deification a biblical concept? Consider 2 Peter 1:4. Western churches need to consider whether their general neglect of this concept has deprived them of a resource for intimately linking God's work of salvation in Christ to the hope for transformation of the whole created order. Is the "individualistic" piety manifest in many Western churches, and frequently lamented, the result of this neglect?

CHAPTER 5

LIFE IN
THE EARLY CHURCH

The church structure that emerged in the first centuries of the Christian Era was directly related to the need to refute heresy. The affirmation of apostolic succession was an important ingredient in establishing sufficient authority for the bishops' teachings to ensure that the Church as a whole rejected the early heresies. The next steps in the evolution of church structure (polity) in the early Church came with the nascent stages of the development of papal primacy.

Claims to papal primacy have a very ancient history. In the mid-third century, Cyprian of Carthage argued for the primacy of Peter for the sake of the unity of the Church (*Unity of the Catholic Church* 4–5; *Epistles* LXXII/LXXIII.7). We have already observed the even stronger affirmation by Irenaeus in his claim that because of the Roman church's position of leadership and authority, every church must agree with it (*Against Heresies* III.III.1). Quite early in the Church's history, then, its appeal to episcopal authority and apostolic succession to clamp down on heresy was linked to claims for Roman, if not papal, primacy.

The Church recognized the dangers in merely appealing to the individual's faith or the individual's own interpretation of Scripture as the source and norm for its teaching, but that meant the Church as a whole (that is, someone speaking for the whole Church on its behalf) must be able to offer the authoritative interpretations. Theology by committee does not usually produce profound results. Can those who are attracted to the need for the Church to posit authoritative interpretations of the gospel and a stronger view of clerical authority as antidotes to the anything-goes ethos of contemporary Western society really have that apart from acknowledgment of a center of authority? Are there not good historical reasons for locating that center in Rome? (We will consider these questions in more detail below in chap. 8.)

WAS ORIGEN A HERETIC
OR A CREATIVE ORTHODOX THEOLOGIAN?

In the previous chapter, we closed with a consideration of the thought of one of the early Church's great theological thinkers, Irenaeus. It is well to consider next another great theologian of the following generation and the first systematic theologian of the Church — Origen (ca. 185–ca. 254). Though Origen was a man of the elite echelons of the early Church, his life and thought reflected and subsequently influenced the daily life of the Church in the second and third centuries.

Origen was apparently a native of Alexandria, that center of culture and capital of Christian apologetics (esp. of the correlationist approach). In fact, he was a student of Clement's. Origen's parents were Christians; his father suffered martyrdom during the persecution of Septimius Severus.

Origen himself was not merely a Christian scholar; he was a man who lived his faith. He yearned for his own martyrdom, which in his context, recall, was the ultimate witness that one could make for the faith. He avoided this fate while still a youth during the persecution in which his father lost his life only because his mother hid his clothes, forcing him to remain at home. He eventually died a martyr, anyway, in the persecution initiated in the mid-third century by Emperor Decius (the next persecution of Christians following that of Severus).

THEOLOGICAL METHOD

It is hardly surprising to learn that Origen characteristically employed the theological approach of his teacher, Clement. This approach became so characteristic of theology done in Alexandria that it is customary to speak of an Alexandrian school of theology. An alternative theological approach with origins in Antioch (to be considered in subsequent chapters) came to be its principal rival.

It was characteristic of Alexandria to employ the correlationist approach to theology. Recall, this method involves the commitment systematically to correlate the gospel with the philosophy of the day, in the case of the Alexandrians to correlate the gospel with Neoplatonism. This commitment in turn entails the use of an allegorical method of biblical interpretation, which views the meaning of Scripture as more than its literal sense (the plain meaning of a text).[1] Allegorists presuppose that hidden underneath the words' literal sense is a deeper, more pro-

---

1. Origen *On First Principles* I.Pref.3ff.; I.VII.4; IV.III.4–5.

found spiritual meaning that the words are yearning to express. In fact, the literal meaning of a text — its actual words — is even frequently deemed a barrier to the deeper spiritual meaning. Such commitments are a logical outcome of the correlationist aim to translate the Bible into the categories of another philosophy. If you bypass a text's literal sense, it is easier to say that it meant to speak the philosophical truth you claim it intends — that the more philosophical meaning is hidden under the text's literal sense and is waiting to be liberated by proper spiritual interpretation.

Origen's method may be just what we need for our time. It provides a way of making sense of Scripture, of arguing for its spiritual value, even when it is not historically accurate in what it reports. Origen himself concedes that not all biblical accounts happened as reported (*On First Principles* IV.II.5; IV.III.5). Whenever modern interpreters seek to claim a spiritual meaning for Scripture while negating its literal sense by denying its historical accuracy, they are employing a kind of allegorical approach. Readers should evaluate their own reactions to the method of allegorical interpretation, trying to determine why they believe as they do, whether they ever use its allegorical models of interpretation, and why or why not.

Despite his apologetic propensities, Origen was very concerned about the quality of Christian life. The purpose of Christian knowledge, he claims, is to "call men to lead a good and blessed life" (*On First Principles* I.Pref.1). One must base this knowledge on the unmistakable basics of the faith, the "first principles." Consequently, not unlike a number of other theologians noted earlier, Origen's starting point is a "rule of faith," an early version of the Nicene Creed (I.Pref.4).

FIRST PRINCIPLES: CORE THEOLOGICAL AFFIRMATIONS

Long before the Church officially authorized such a doctrine, Origen affirmed something like the concept of Christ's having two natures (*On First Principles* I.II.1). He closely related the two natures in a way characteristic of the Alexandrian school, that is, by positing a communication of idioms (*communicatio idiomatum*), the idea that anything attributed to one of Christ's natures may be attributed to the other (II.VI.3). Every Christian must come to terms with this claim — whether to believe it or not. As we shall begin to see in subsequent chapters, the Church has been engaged in a debate on this matter at least since the fourth or fifth century.

Also with regard to Christology, Origen followed his correlationist predecessors in one very basic affirmation. Like them, he spoke of Christ as Logos, as (universal) Reason in which all rational beings partake (I.III.6).[2]

CONTROVERSIAL COMMITMENTS

Although Origen's treatment of the relationship between the Father and the Son raised many controversies after his death, it is not necessarily the most suspect of his controversial positions. He refers to something like an eternal generation of the Son, as well as of the Spirit, by the Father (*On First Principles* I.II.3,13). Generally speaking it can be said that he placed more emphasis on the distinction of the Father and the Son than on their unity, to the point of even once referring to the Logos as a creature (IV.I.1; I.III.5). This emphasis will help us better understand why later heretics (esp. the Arians), who were not inclined to affirm the full deity of the Son, claimed Origen's writings as an ally.

With regard to the doctrine of God, Origen's reliance on allegorical interpretation and Platonic thought also led him to claim that God has no body and is impassable, since on Platonic grounds that which is truly spiritual is distinct from the things of the body (II.IV.3–4). Of course, these affirmations were not problematic in Origen's Alexandrian context, though they would later become controversial.

More controversial was Origen's positing of two creations. Both of them transpired, he claimed, because of sin. In a qualified sense he also seems to have at least implied that the creation process as a whole is eternal (*On First Principles* I.IV.4). First, according to Origen, there was the spiritual creation, which then fell, followed by the creation of the material world. (Might one cite a certain reading of Isa. 66:22 in support of these reflections?) The physical creation involved the placing of the preexisting soul into a body (I.VII.4). The first, spiritual creation was itself the result of sin. Souls were created when minds, which in eternity had been in unity with the Logos, desired their own individuality because of their discontent with being part of the whole (II.VIII.3). The physical creation had become necessary because those souls with excessive spiritual defects, desiring the most individuality and seeking to distance themselves from the divine love, required grosser, more solid bodies (I.VIII.4; III.V.4). (Could Rom. 8:5–12 be used to support his argument at this point?) In making these points, Origen seems very much in dialogue with Gnosticism. Souls with the most inclination to evil became incarnate in humans. When a soul is truly evil, it is clothed as an animal body. The affinities to Eastern religions, except for a per-

---

2. It is interesting to note that Origen referred to the Logos (by implication the Son of God) in the feminine gender (*On First Principles* I.II.2).

haps slightly more positive construction of the material creation, are obvious here.

An affirmation that was less controversial in the context of the early Church, but has been nonetheless controversial for Christians ever since the time of Augustine, was Origen's insistence that human beings have a free will, though he did concede that spiritual powers may influence it (*On First Principles* I.Pref.5). To be sure, he affirmed that salvation is a gift of God; however, he also insisted that we must cooperate with grace (III.I.18–19). Ultimately he construed life as a kind of trial in which by making use of freedom, we might return to the harmony of intellectual beings (I.VI.3). Christ overcomes our weakness by overcoming the power of the devil and granting illumination (*Commentary on the Gospel of in Matthew* XIV.8). Nevertheless, Origen still claimed that God judges and grants rewards based on merit concerning progress made in imitating and participating in God (*On First Principles* I.VI.2).

Despite Origen's concern about the practice of the Christian life and the individual Christian's responsibility for one's own salvation, the overall cosmological-philosophical scheme in which he places the content of the Christian faith led him to affirm the salvation of all rational creatures (*apokatastasis*), even of the devil (*On First Principles* III.VI.5; see 1 Pet. 3:19; 4:6; 1 Tim. 2:4). Nothing guarantees, though, that the cycle of fall and restoration might not repeat again (II.I.3; II.III.3ff.; II.VIII.3). The ideal is that all would become one. When diversity first transpired through spiritual defects of minds, matter was created because it lent itself to fashioning such diversity. God created such diversity so that none would be lost, in order that the final aim of the complete restoration of all in unity might be achieved (III.VI.4–5). Salvation is nonexistent unless it includes every rational being. Whether we agree or disagree with the Christian character of such an affirmation, all can agree that Origen has sketched a truly majestic vision.

ASSESSMENT

With theological proposals such as the ones noted, it is hardly surprising that Origen was a most controversial figure. His influence was widespread among adherents of the Alexandrian school. Later we will have occasion to note his impact on Eusebius of Caesarea (ca. 260–ca. 340) and the "official theology" he articulated. Particularly after Origen's death, his views, especially his vehement denial of God's having a body, set off sharp controversies among early practitioners of monasticism. The controversy spread to the point of involving a number of eminent late-fourth-century bishops. A council held in Alexandria in A.D. 400 and another in 553 in Constantinople condemned a list of views attributed to him. (Part of the problem was that a number of Christians who were eventually condemned as heretics, the Arians, came to co-opt Origen's views on the relation between the Father and the Son.)

Controversy even followed Origen in his lifetime. In addition to his defiance of the Roman Empire, which resulted in his martyrdom, in the final two decades of his life he became engaged in a controversy with his bishop in Alexandria, due to Origen's receiving ordination at the hands of a bishop in Caesarea. Exiled from Alexandria, Origen established a catechetical school in Caesarea, which came to rival the famed catechetical school in Alexandria, where he had originally taught.

In itself, controversy is not a bad thing. Sometimes the theologians who contributed most to the advancement of the cause of the gospel were those whose views came under the most fire. The concluding issue for our purposes must be for readers to evaluate Origen's theology for themselves — to determine whether Origen presents us with a creative orthodoxy or a heresy.

THIRD-CENTURY PERSECUTIONS

Since we have considered debates among the early Church's intellectual elite, it is now appropriate to examine what life was like for ordinary Christians in the third century. We pick up the story of the persecutions endured by the Church where we left off with the narrative of earlier persecutions, in the mid-third century or a little earlier. Recall that the earlier persecutions were instituted by Nero, Domitian, Trajan, Marcus Aurelius, and finally by Septimius Severus early in the third century. From that time until the reign of Constantine in A.D. 306, the history of the Church in the Roman Empire was one of ups and downs.

THE PERSECUTIONS OF DECIUS AND VALERIAN:
THE PROBLEM OF WHAT TO DO WITH THE LAPSED

Reigning in a period of crisis and uncertainty in the Roman Empire, Decius came to power in A.D. 249. His preoccupation was to restore Rome to its ancient glory. In his view, that entailed restoring the ancestral religion to the empire. With the Edict of Decius in 250, which demanded the practice of sacrifice to the gods, Decius aimed not so much to persecute Christians as to force them to practice idolatry. Gallus succeeded Decius in 251, setting his predecessor's policies aside. Christians were safe, but not for long. Valerian, a compatriot of Decius, ascended the throne from 253 to 260, ordering sacrifices to the gods, and later forbade Christians to assemble. After the capture of Gallus by the Persians, the Church enjoyed forty years of relative peace.

The Church was then faced with the problem of what to do with those who had lapsed in the period of these persecutions. In order to avoid persecution, some Christians had purchased certificates that testified they had offered pagan sacrifices. Of course, they had not actually performed such sacrifices. Other Christians (who came to be known as Confessors) had confessed the faith in face of the persecution, thus gaining great stature in the Church as a result of their courage. In North Africa especially these confessors claimed authority to determine which of the lapsed should be restored; however, such authority usually rested with the bishops.

The controversy was especially poignant when one of the lapsed was a bishop. One of them, Cyprian of Carthage (d. 258), had lost some stature by fleeing his diocese during the persecution of Decius. Allegedly he did so in order to be able to continue guiding the flock through correspondence. (One should perhaps not be too quick to accuse him of cowardice since he offered his life in martyrdom under the Valerian persecution.) When Cyprian returned to Carthage at the end of the persecution, his authority was severely undermined.

One challenge to Cyprian came from a number of the Confessors who advocated the readmission to Christian fellowship of all who had lapsed and offered a sacrifice to the false gods. With his authority challenged, Cyprian convened a synod (a meeting of all the bishops in a local region) to set policy on readmission of the lapsed. Three decisions were made. (1) Those who had purchased certificates but actually performed no sacrifice to the Roman gods were immediately to be readmitted to the Church. (2) Those who had sacrificed could only be readmitted at death if they repented or withstood another persecution. (3) Those who had sacrificed and were unrepentant could never be readmitted. Cyprian insisted on setting policies regulating readmission of the lapsed because of his understanding of the Church and his belief that it must be united. Intimately connected with these policies was Cyprian's belief that "outside the Church, no salvation" (*Epistles* LXXII/LXIII.21), for the Church is the mother of the faithful, the nurturer of faith (*Unity of the Catholic Church* 5–6). Cyprian's stance has been a most controversial one for Christians. Is there really no hope for the salvation of those outside the Church?

In the preceding chapters we noted that Cyprian was a primary spokesman for clerical authority and, particularly, episcopal authority. His concern with regulating restoration of the lapsed opened the way to the development of the penitential system and the sacrament of confession.

THE NOVATIAN HERESY

The Novatian heresy was a reaction against such policies of restoration. Novatian (d. ca. 257) was a Roman presbyter who argued that the restoration policy in Rome was too permissive. Mere repentance was not sufficient in his view. Novatian also had difficulties with modalism and in order to refute it, so stressed the distinction between Father and Son as to unwittingly set the stage for the Arian heresy (*On the Trinity* 17,27).

Novatian's position on the Roman Church's policy of restoring the lapsed is most reminiscent of an earlier controversy that was initiated very early in the third century by the Roman presbyter and noted theologian Hippolytus (ca. 170–ca. 236). He argued, contrary to the Roman bishop Callistus (d. ca. 222), that fornicators ought not be forgiven (*On Heresies* 9.12.20). Ultimately the more permissive views of Callistus prevailed.

The heresy of Hippolytus did not long endure, though the parallel position of Novatian endured much longer by joining the resistance to Cyprian's policies. This raises a challenge to the more permissive positions of the churches that have carried the catholic tradition since the fourth century: Why should the Church not be so strict with the lapsed?

FINAL PRE-CONSTANTINIAN PERSECUTIONS

As noted, the Church was at peace until the fourth century. Valerian's reign as emperor ended in 259 or 260, when he was succeeded by Gallienus, who basically reversed his predecessor's policies. Gallienus restored Christian basilicas and granted freedom of worship.[3] The Church enjoyed peace until Diocletian's reign began in 284. These were troubled times for the Roman Empire, and Diocletian played an important role in reorganizing it after a period of turbulence. He accomplished this task largely by sharing the emperorship with a team of three others. The strategy was that this would curtail civil wars previously wracking the empire over succession.

At first Diocletian was friendly towards Christians and may have been one himself. At least his wife and daughter are reported to have been confirmands. A controversy began to develop, though, over whether Christians should be expelled from the Roman army. (This indicates that, contrary to much popular opinion, the early Christians were not all pacifists.) Diocletian's junior (assistant) emperor, Galerius, clearly influenced him in the decision, which led to a number of abuses in the

---

3. Eusebius *Church History* VII.XIII.2.

dismissal process. Some Christians were persecuted; some lost their lives. Diocletian was also persuaded to strip Christians of any government position they held. The next step was the repeal of Gallienus's Edict, which had protected Christian freedom of worship. Thereafter, churches were razed, and Christian meetings were forbidden.[4] Edicts were issued decreeing that all denizens of the empire should offer sacrifice to the idols.[5]

After much subsequent turmoil occasioned by Galerius's attempt to gain control of the empire without sharing the leadership, Maximinus Daia, one of his proteges, even tried to restore pagan worship during the years of 308 to 311.[6] On his deathbed in A.D. 311, Galerius did recant this policy.[7]

Under Diocletian's scheme of shared power, Constantine held territory in the West. He and Galerius were locked in a power struggle. Constantine did not advocate the persecution of Christians as Galerius had prior to his death. Constantine's eventual emergence as leader was begun in earnest after he had defeated one of his rival emperors (Maxentius, who held Rome), following a vision in which Constantine was instructed to have his soldiers bear the first two letters of the Latin equivalent of the name "Christ" on their shields. Many believe that this was a kind of conversion experience for Constantine. In any case, following the victory, he met with two other coemperors, and they agreed to the 313 Edict of Milan, which put an end to all persecution of Christians. Essentially the edict gave Christians the freedom of religion and decreed that their places of worship be returned to them.[8] In the next chapter we consider in more detail the implications of all this for Christianity, whether its eventual establishment was a good or a bad thing for the Church.

LIFE IN THE CHURCH OF THE THIRD CENTURY

In some respects, daily life in the Church in the third century was not unlike what it had been in the previous one hundred years. However, in other respects some significant new developments were transpiring as the Church became more and more part of the establishment.

By the third century, members of the Roman Empire's elite increasingly joined the Church. However, Christians in this era were still largely

---

4. Ibid., 9.10.8; 7.2.4.
5. Eusebius *Martyrs or Palestine* 3.2.
6. Ibid., 9.2.
7. Eusebius *Church History* VIII.XVII.6–10.
8. Lactantius *Deaths of the Persecutors* 48.2–11.

drawn from lower socioeconomic classes. But despite this continuity with the past, changes were in the ecclesiastical air. Certain houses began to be used exclusively for worship. Thus by the mid-third century, the first churches had been developed.

The Christian calendar as we know it today was coming to full development in this period. The weekly calendar included Sunday (a celebration of Easter), Wednesday, and Friday (days of fasting and penance). Soon Easter, Lent (a period of preparation through catechetical instruction prior to baptisms, which were held on Easter), Pentecost, and Epiphany (the baptism and later the birth of Jesus) were commemorated. Christmas came to be celebrated on December 25 only later in the fourth century in the Latin West in an effort to "baptize" a pagan festival in the empire. The Eastern Orthodox Church has retained the older date (January 6) for the festival. Controversy emerged (and still continues) over the date of Easter, that is, whether it should always be set in accord with Passover.

Concurrent with, if not prior to, these developments, was the commemoration of the anniversary of the death of certain eminent martyrs, a practice that evolved into the identification of a cult of saints (deceased Christians thought to have lived notably holy lives) and the commemoration of saints' days. In the next century, after Christianity became the establishment religion under Constantine, churches began to be built over the sites of these martyrdoms. The next step would be the veneration of certain alleged relics of these martyrs. The whole process was further expedited by a pilgrimage to Jerusalem undertaken by Constantine's mother, Helena (ca. 255–ca. 330) in A.D. 326. While there she supervised the founding of churches built on sites in the Holy Land that were crucial to Jesus' life and ministry.

We have noted earlier indications of the development of liturgies in the Church. There are evidences dating as early as A.D. 22 of a eucharistic liturgy from an Egyptian Church order that closely resembles many modern liturgies. The regular use of such liturgies, or at least their rudiments, in worship was becoming more and more typical by the third century.

The Cross was still not very important for piety in this period and was not the symbol of Christianity, which was a celebrative, resurrection faith. Rather, the fish functioned as the chief Christian symbol because the Greek term for "fish" (*ichthys*) is composed of the first letter of each word in the Greek phrase of "Jesus Christ, Son of God, Savior."

The threefold order of ministry, which we observed unfolding as early as in the thought of the Apostolic Fathers became catholic practice early in the second century. Women were playing less and less of a role in leadership, so that by the third century the leadership of the Church was entirely male. Again the question must be raised about whether the decline in women's ecclesiastical leadership could be related to the centralization of authority (the emphasis on apostolic succession). This also raises anew the question of whether an episcopal polity is inherently sexist. Perhaps the increased ecclesiastical patriarchalism is a matter of the Church becoming more a part of the establishment. When that happens (not just in the period of the early Church but, as we shall see, throughout history), women's leadership role is compromised.

The early Church's missionary methods are intriguing in light of the modern preoccupation with church-growth programs. Revivals and community surveys were unknown to the first Christians. Theirs was not a bucolic religion (a religion that only thrives in rural or small-town areas). Rather, the Church's greatest growth was in the cities through informal contacts and through debates. Whenever it enjoyed periods of freedom from persecution, early Christianity was fundamentally a religion of the public square. Martyrdom and miracle working were always apparently its most successful evangelistic tools. Are there lessons we can learn about evangelism from the early Church?

CONCLUSION:
SEVEN SACRAMENTS? ARE THEY ALL LEGITIMATELY ROOTED IN THE PRACTICE OF THE EARLY CHURCH?

If, indeed, all seven rites of the Roman Catholic and Orthodox churches are rooted in the early Church, should not all our churches endorse them? This is a crucial question for (Protestant) readers to consider as we proceed with a review of the historical origins of each of the seven rites.

BAPTISM

There is no indisputable evidence for the baptism of infants in the first centuries of the Church's life prior to the third century. Proponents of infant baptism could appeal to the "household baptisms" reported in the New Testament (Acts 16:15; 1 Cor. 1:16), though it could be argued that in a patriarchal setting women and children were not included as full members of a household. (Of course, we have observed that women, and so perhaps also children, did not play such a negligible role in the households of the Roman Empire.) We know indisputably that infant baptism was administered in the Carthage of Tertullian to children of Christian parents, as there are records of his lamenting the practice (*On*

Baptism XVIII). Presumably the fear of many in the early Church was that sins committed after baptism would not be forgiven, and so it was better to postpone the rite (Heb. 6:4). In a short time after Tertullian's third-century observations, two of his younger contemporaries actually advocated infant baptism in order to remove the sin in which children are born.[9]

Two other standard baptismal practices of the early Church should be noted. We have previously observed an openness to dipping, not just to immersion, in the *Didache* (7). The ancient practice was apparently to baptize only once a year, on Easter.

Although the theologians of the early Church rarely explicitly addressed the doctrine of baptism, those who did seem to have taught that the rite actually conferred regeneration and forgiveness of sins.[10] Cyprian of Carthage associated baptism with the gift of the Holy Spirit (*Epistles* LXXIII/LXXIV.5; Titus 3:5). Does this evidence rule out the possibility that the early Church ever considered baptism as a mere symbol of a spiritual reality, as a symbol of the baptism of the Holy Spirit?

CONFESSION

We have already observed how the Church's penitential system and the rite of confession developed from the Hippolytan and Novatian controversies concerning what should be done about baptized Christians who sin. Tertullian explicitly referred to external, visible acts of confession (*On Repentance* IX.1–2), as did the *Didache* (4.14) even earlier. As early as 589 the Third Council of Toledo expressly referred to private confession as a sacrament. For a biblical basis for the rite, one might appeal to Luke 7:36–40, 44–48 and Matthew 18:18.

THE LORD'S SUPPER

The celebration of the Lord's Supper by the followers of Christ (probably in the context of a full meal) dates back to Jesus' own lifetime (Mark 14:12–25; Acts 2:46–47; 1 Cor. 11:17–34). However, new circumstances — responses to the general criticisms in the Roman Empire of the rite as an orgiastic love feast as well as the warnings of Paul in 1 Corinthians — had an impact on the rite. Collectively they combined to transform it and its setting into something more typical of the way in which most churches celebrate the sacrament today.

---

9. Cyprian of Carthage *Epistles* LVIII/LXIV.5; Origen *Homilies on the Gospel of Luke* 14.5.
10. Tertullian *On Baptism* I,X,XV; Irenaeus *Fragments* XXXIV; Rom. 6.

An early custom of Christians, perhaps dating back to the first century, was to celebrate Communion at the tombs of the faithful, especially of the martyrs. Could this be the origin of the Roman Catholic practice of saying the Mass on behalf of the dead? There are at least indications that it is a practice with very ancient roots.

A belief that Christ is really present in the consecrated bread and wine was endorsed by Ignatius (*Letter to the Smyrneans* 7). Irenaeus spoke of Christ's real presence in the sacrament in such a way that its earthly elements are not denied, which is a kind of proto-Lutheran or proto-Calvinistic view (*Against Heresies* 4.XVIII.4–5). Likewise Justin Martyr made a similar point (*First Apology* 66).

Liturgically oriented traditions with a high sacramentology have great allies in the practices of the early Church. Even the Roman Catholic idea of the Mass as a sacrifice has precedents in this period, at least in Irenaeus (*Against Heresies* 4.XVIII.4) and Cyprian of Carthage (*Epistles* LXII/LXIII.14).

We have already observed the evolution of early eucharistic liturgies, parts of which are still employed to this day. Note that the *Didache* (14) indicates that weekly Communion was the normal practice in the early Church. Given these historical precedents, one wonders why that practice has not been continued in most segments of Protestantism.

CONFIRMATION

Confirmation (the training of candidates for receiving baptism) was practiced at least as soon as the early fourth century. Late in the second century Theophilus of Antioch apparently referred to a rite of worship that brought the period of training to a close, as evidenced by his claim that we are Christians through anointment with oil, which presumably refers to the rite of confirmation (*To Autolycus* I.XII). In this period the Church believed that such anointing conferred the gift of the Holy Spirit, enhancing the baptismal rite in which the forgiveness of sins was provided. Likewise Tertullian referred to the rite, claiming that we are thoroughly anointed with oil after coming from the place of washing (*On Baptism* VII.1). We can discern explicit references as early as 441 in the Synod of Orange to the rite of confirmation as we know it today. The biblical basis usually cited for the practice of this rite is Acts 8:14–19.

ORDINATION

We have already observed numerous early affirmations of apostolic succession: espoused by Cyprian (*Epistles* XXVI/XXVIII.1), by Irenaeus

(*Against Heresies* 3.XXXIII.8), and by Tertullian (*Prescriptions against Heretics* 32). Such stances seem to presuppose the sacrament of ordination, as there must have been some ceremony of worship whereby God visibly passes on the succession through the laying on of hands. One can discern an acknowledgment of this rite by Tertullian in the *Prescriptions against Heretics* (32). Also to be noted is a third-century description of the rite by Hippolytus of Rome (*Apostolic Tradition* 2–4). For a biblical basis for the sacrament, Acts 13:2–3 and 1 Timothy 4:14 are normally cited.

EXTREME UNCTION/LAST RITES

Extreme unction — the anointing of the sick for purposes of invoking divine sanction for healing (the original purpose of the sacrament) — seems to have been practiced at least as early as the third century. There are certain hints of the rite in comments by Origen, though he may have been referring to confession, not extreme unction (*Homilies on Leviticus* II.4). As a biblical basis for the practice, one might appeal to James 5:14–15.

MARRIAGE

Marriage in the Roman Empire was a civil and private matter. Yet very early, Christians sought to insist that Christians needed to receive some form of divine (or ecclesiastical) blessing for the institution. Ignatius said men and women who wish to marry should secure the consent of the bishop (*Letter to Polycarp* V.1). Tertullian insisted on marriages being professed in the presence of the Church (*On Modesty* IV.4). The New Testament authorization that is usually cited for considering the rite a sacrament is John 2:1–11.

DOES A NEW SITUATION JUSTIFY DOCTRINAL DEVELOPMENT?

What are the methodological implications of what one makes of the seven sacraments, that is, whether one deems that all seven are sufficiently legitimately rooted in the ancient practice of the Church? If they are so rooted, why do not all Christians recognize these rites as sacraments? Or did the early Church make a mistake in practicing these rites? The answer one gives to these questions says much about one's own theology, about whether ancient practices and teachings of the Church carry any authoritative weight for contemporary theology and church practice. Or should we just read our Bibles, not caring about the practice of the early Church?

Granted, these rites, as we have them in their present form, are the result of an evolutionary process. They evolved as the Church confronted new situations that were not quite like those in biblical times. By the fourth century, the Church was dramatically entering a new era. It is to that new day we turn in the next chapter.

CHAPTER 6

THE ESTABLISHMENT
OF CHRISTIANITY AND THE
DEVELOPMENT OF MONASTICISM

At this point in the narrative of the history of the Church we come to a most crucial juncture: Christianity finally becomes part of the establishment. In one sense, with the establishment of Christianity as the favored religion of the Roman Empire, the struggles were over. In another sense, the problems were just beginning. In this period one of the most important doctrinal formulations in the history of the Church was developed, the Trinity doctrine. As had happened at other crucial moments of doctrinal formulation, this authoritative doctrine emerged as a response to a problem, specifically the challenge of Arianism.

Before we look at the complex issues that arose from Arianism's challenge (in chap. 7), it is first necessary to set the sociocultural background for the debate that led to the formulation of the Trinity doctrine. The political sphere had much to do with occasioning the desirability of getting Christians to agree about the nature of God. In fact, even the ultimate formulation of the Trinity doctrine was not without political influence.

The establishment of Christianity as *the* religion of the Roman Empire had other implications for the Church and its everyday life. In the first place, it can be said that the establishment of Christianity created exciting new opportunities for propagating the gospel and living it. But we need to ask whether that was a good thing or whether the older ways and Christian lifestyles were more in keeping with the biblical witness. As the established religion of the empire, the Church gained more members. But does greater quantity always translate into higher quality?

For some Christians of the period under consideration, the answer to both of the preceding questions was a resounding no! These Christians proceeded to found a new alternative ecclesiastical institution, monasticism, in response to the changes that the establishment of Christianity as the religion of the empire had effected. For this reason, the development of monasticism requires attention. We should assess whether monasticism is a distortion of the faith or an African enrichment of the gospel. First, though, we shall continue the narrative from the last chapter concerning Constantine's emergence as the sole emperor of the Roman Empire.

THE CONSTANTINIAN ERA

As noted in chapter 5, Constantine emerged as the sole leader of the Roman Empire through his conquest of Rome in A.D. 313, defeating his rival Maxentius, allegedly as a result of placing a Christian symbol on the shields of his soldiers. The success of this venture and the vision that inspired him to employ the Christian symbol were the turning points in his conversion to Christianity.

There is much dispute among historians about the sincerity of Constantine's conversion. Clearly it was tied to political motivations. We do know that Constantine, as part of his political responsibilities, continued to participate in pagan rites after his conversion. He did not have any other options given his commitments to establishing unity in the Roman Empire among all its people and traditions. Moreover, though Constantine never formally placed himself under the direction of Christian teachers or bishops and considered himself the bishop of bishops, he did have prominent Christians in his entourage. However, Constantine never really joined the Church: he was never formally catechized and was not baptized until he lay on his deathbed. But this deathbed request and the fact that his conversion to Christianity prior to his seizing of Rome would not have been politically advantageous (as most of his support within the city came from the old Roman aristocracy) seem to support the contention that Constantine truly believed that God would reward him for his faithfulness and his beneficence to Christians.

In any case, it cannot be denied that Constantine believed that Christianity, the unity among Christians, could contribute to cementing the unity of the Roman Empire. These sentiments were explicitly expressed by Constantine in 313 in a letter to Anulius in which Constantine granted Christian clergy exemption from public duties and asserted his conviction that Christianity is good for the state.[1] Is it really the case that Christianity is good for the state?

---

1. Eusebius *Church History* 10.7.

CONSTANTINE IN CONTROL

We return to the narrative of Constantine's reign as emperor in order to understand precisely the process by which he established Christianity as the official religion of the empire and precisely what that entailed. The context is necessary to help us evaluate whether this establishment was indeed good for the Church.

In the previous chapter we noted that Constantine along with his fellow emperor Licinius (in 313 he had not yet seized sole rule of the Roman Empire) issued a decree called the "Edict of Milan." This decree gave Christians freedom of religion. The actual establishment of Christianity as the favored or official religion of the Roman Empire was still in the future, and that development was intimately linked to Constantine's emergence as sole legitimate leader of the empire.

We do know that Constantine was an able statesman and tactician. After his conquest of Maxentius, which gave Constantine control of Rome, he was the uncontested ruler of the entire western half of the empire, while the eastern half was ruled by two other coemperors. Constantine attempted to build a coalition with one, Licinius, in order to vanquish the other. This eventually succeeded in eliminating the third, Maximinus Daia. Constantine's aims, though, were to bring the whole empire under his dominion.

Most Christians lived in the eastern region of the empire ruled by Licinius. (We are reminded anew that Christianity in its origins is no Western religion.) Having signed the Edict of Milan with Constantine, Licinius was not persecuting his Christian subjects. However, various controversies involving Christians in the region led him to use force to assure peace, which in turn led the church in the region to begin thinking of Constantine as the true "defender of the faith." This dynamic led Licinius to suspect the Christians of treason, which resulted in his taking measures against them, effectively drawing the church more into the arms of Constantine. With an excuse to move against Licinius, the perceived persecutor of the faith, Constantine could posture himself as its defender. Eventually the whole empire came into Constantine's hands.

As a result of his military campaigns in the eastern part of the Roman Empire, Constantine became impressed with the strategic location of Byzantium. For this and for at least one other significant reason, he decided (claiming it was at the direction of a revelation from God) to establish the empire's capital in Byzantium, renaming it Constantinople (the "city of Constantine"). It would be the "New Rome." Constantine's decision was partly tactical, locating the center of power in a strategically important area. However no less a consideration was to negate the influence of the Roman Senate, which largely opposed his Christian agenda, objecting to the eclipse of ancient gods and privileges that this agenda entailed. In a sense, the new capital was a way to bypass the Senate's opposition. Its members' objections would no longer be voices from the center of power.

The relocation of the capital had significant consequences for the Church. Moving the capital of the empire to Constantinople had the effect of making the bishop of Rome, in the absence of the emperor, the most prestigious officeholder in the city. This was an important step towards papal authority. It transformed the office of the bishop of Rome (eventually the papacy) into a political leader.

Constantine's taking up residence in Constantinople also had an impact on the office of the bishop of that city, effectively making it a much more influential position. This ecclesiastical-political development proved to be very important in the Eastern Orthodox schism of the eleventh century and the subsequent evolution of the polity of Eastern Orthodox churches.

THE ESTABLISHMENT OF CHRISTIANITY

As previously noted, a major motivation in Constantine's efforts to establish Christianity was his sense that the unity he believed he observed among Christians would bolster a sense of unity in the empire. (The Church does not seem to have ever been as united as he thought.) What he did specifically after coming to power would change Christianity, Western civilization, and eastern Europe forever.

After guaranteeing freedom of religion, Constantine established Christianity as the Roman Empire's official religion in steps. He decreed that empire funds should subsidize Christian clergy and granted them deferments from government service. Subsequently he even instituted legislation in favor of the Church at the expense of other religions and engineered legislation granting state recognition of Sunday. Most interestingly, he even intervened in Church discipline matters.

The status Constantine conferred on Christianity as a religion sanctioned by the state created a new era for the Church, which has continued into the twentieth century. It is common to speak of a Constantinian era for the Church in this period, an era that only now may be coming to an end. The *Constantinian era* refers to the period when the Church became part of the establishment, when cultural values and expectations were so altered that it became socially, if not also politically and economically, advantageous to be a Christian. In a Constantinian society, membership in the Church and citizenship in society were virtually synonymous/identical. The American Church throughout its life span, if not western society in general, has existed in the Constantinian era. Are we now — with secularism and its values all over the media and a general cultural attitude that Christianity is not "where it's at" — entering a post-Constantinian era?

WHEN CHRISTIANITY BECAME AN ESTABLISHED RELIGION, WAS IT GOOD FOR THE CHURCH?

Without doubt, there are positive aspects to the establishment of Christianity. When the Church is part of the establishment, wide exposure and media accessibility are almost guaranteed. One thinks of the sort of media access that western European state churches enjoy. It is also prudent to reflect on the positive impact Christian values might have on a society. Some social historians have even speculated that the reason why Western civilization has achieved its advanced levels of technology, high standards of living, and democratic governmental systems of humane power sharing is because of the impact of Christianity and its value systems on it.

American and European readers, even those who belong to minority cultures in these regions, should consider the intimate connections between Christianity and Western society since the time of Constantine. Christianity has been in the air such readers have breathed their whole lives, inevitably intertwined with the extended family histories in which they have been nurtured. Given the way in which their lives have been so saturated by things Christian in Western society, American and European readers should seriously consider whether they would be Christian had they not lived in the Constantinian era. (Is it not the case that even Christians belonging to minority cultures in these regions, like the African American Church, are in their own way as enmeshed in the Constantinian paradigm as are the British by the Church of England or white citizens of the American South are by the Southern Baptist Convention?) There is certainly rich evangelistic potential for an established church, one that embodies the Constantinian paradigm of identifying Christian values with good citizenship. There are sound arguments for maintaining that it was and still is good for the Church that Constantine established Christianity as the Roman Empire's favored faith.

On the negative side, one must consider whether the quality of membership has really improved as a result of the Constantinian paradigm. Is church life as vibrant in Europe and the Americas as it was in the pre-Constantinian era or in regions of the Southern Hemisphere, where today Christianity has not been the established religion? Insofar as the

Constantinian era has been typified by government interference in religion, has not the era, even in regions theoretically committed to the separation of church and state, been bad for the Church, effectively relegating Christianity to the status of a mere handmaiden of the host cultures' power brokers and opinion makers?

If the Constantinian establishment of Christianity has been harmful for the Church, we must consider the question of what would be an effective contemporary alternative to it. If we are indeed moving into a post-Constantinian era, where being an upright denizen of Western society does not necessarily include identification with the Church, how should the Church position itself vis-à-vis the culture?

MONASTIC REACTION
TO THE CONSTANTINIAN ESTABLISHMENT

With the establishment of Christianity by Constantine, the days of martyrdom were over. Consequently, the energy and commitment that had previously been devoted to martyrdom were focused in new directions. For some giants of the faith, talents were directed to theological reflection, and some of the Church's greatest theology was done in the fourth century — by people like Athanasius (ca. 296–373), the Cappadocian Fathers (see chap. 10 for an identification), Jerome (ca. 342–420), and Augustine (354–430). Other Christians directed their high levels of commitment instead to monasticism, a kind of substitute martyrdom. Consequently the era was marked by the flocking of hundreds of the Christian faithful to the Egyptian desert. There they intended to flee from human society, renouncing the pleasures of the body for the things of the spirit — just as the martyrs had done, or so it was perceived by the early church.

Although the practice of a monastic lifestyle was not unheard of prior to the Constantinian era, its mass appeal and marked growth were clearly related to the discontent of many Christians with the impact that the Constantinian establishment of Christianity was having on the Church. Predictably, the establishment of Christianity had sparked a tendency for the Church to accommodate itself to Roman culture. Such accommodationist propensities manifested in new attitudes towards wealth and a desire to build elaborate churches after the fashion of Roman architecture. In the latter enterprise, Constantine and his mother, Helena, through her supervision of the founding basilicas in the Holy Land, played a crucial role. Another outcome of these new dynamics was that the Church began to employ music in worship without its previous reservations about the possible undue pagan influence that inclusion of musical instruments might connote. After all, the Church now saw itself as more a part of Roman culture, free to give expression to the culture's highest aspirations.

The accommodationist dynamics had an impact on the quality of church membership. The Church grew markedly in numbers, but long-time members perceived many of the converts as not caring too deeply about the faith. More and more, the Church was coming to be an institution of the powerful and the privileged. Bishops joined the grab for power, sometimes competing with each other for the plum assignments. Given these dynamics of the Church's increased wealth, power, and well-being, it is readily apparent why the monastic lifestyle represented a reaction that appealed to many among the faithful who yearned for the days when being a Christian mandated commitment and sacrifice. Consequently many monks in this period were disgruntled exiles to the desert, disgusted by attitudes towards the wealth and the lax membership standards of the imperial church.

As noted, monasticism had pre-Constantinian roots. The impulse was enhanced by Paul's references to the freedom of single life (1 Cor. 7:32–35) and Jesus' claim that in the Kingdom "they neither marry nor are given in marriage" (Matt. 22:30). We have also noted that Christian women held the offices of widow and virgin in the early Church and that these offices may have been forerunners of monastic institutions. In addition, general cultural dynamics at the time seem to have been hospitable to the monastic impulse. Stoic doctrine held passions to be the enemy of wisdom. Greek philosophy regarded the self as imprisoned in the body. Several religions in the Mediterranean basin included sacred virgins and celibate priests. All of these factors had an impact on the early Church and doubtless contributed to the further development of Christian monasticism.

MONASTIC INSTITUTIONS, LIFESTYLES, AND BELIEFS

Although monasticism emerged in several regions of the Roman Empire, its greatest growth was in the Egyptian deserts. Paul of Thebes (d. ca. 340) and Anthony (ca. 251–356), said to be the first two monks of the African desert, were made renowned by the oral traditions of the desert and by the writings of Jerome and Athanasius, respectively. The word "monk" derives from the Greek word *monachos*, meaning "solitary." The early monks sought solitude, completely removing themselves from the distractions of society that made it difficult to practice the Christian life. Solitary monks were called "anchorites."

Although Anthony was not the first of the desert monks, his life of Anthony is sufficiently typical of early monastic existence to warrant attention. One can refer to him as the patriarch of monasticism, insofar as he (or at least the traditions about him) made monasticism a truly catholic movement. A native of central Egypt, Anthony was the uneducated son of well-to-do peasant Christians. As a young man he was moved by a reading in church of Matthew 19:21, concerning Jesus' call to sell all and give to the poor. It changed Anthony's life, inspiring him to dispose of all his property and give it to the poor. About fifteen years later, these commitments led him to a complete renunciation of all things, and so he retreated to the desert, where he was tutored in the monastic life by an older father.[2]

Conflict with demonic powers is a theme regularly emphasized in the traditions about Anthony as well as about other early monks.[3] It is also typical of pre-Christian African religions and so may further serve to suggest the African roots of monasticism. Likewise Anthony shares with other monks a reputation of being a healer or worker of miracles.

There was a strong sense of sin in Anthony, though not so strong in his case as to entail belief in original sin.[4] (Other early monks such as Longinus, Moses the Negro, and Matoes do affirm an even stronger view of sin, something like the doctrine of original sin and its insistence that sin permeates every corner of a person's life.)[5] In fact, Anthony shared a view of salvation that was typical of theologians of the pre-Constantinian era: he believed that humans have a free will and can choose to obey God's precepts, thereby ensuring salvation (in The Sayings of the Desert Fathers 1,3,33). He also seems to have affirmed something like salvation as deification.[6] To these soteriological themes he added a different emphasis, which is shared with other monks — the possibility that in the desert we might strive for perfection.[7] (This theme became important in the theology of some post-Constantinian theologians who in turn had significant impact on the Methodist movement in its origins.)

One should not discount the theological implications of the influence of Matthew 19:21 on Anthony and perhaps on other early monks. Is a desire to earn eternal life (legalism) underlying the monastic motive, or is it motivated more by trust in God (as per Matt. 6:34)? There are some passages in early monastic literature that suggest the former.[8] That

---

2. Athanasius Life of St. Anthony 3–4.
3. Ibid., 5–7,35–46,52; cf. Macarius the Great, in The Sayings of the Desert Fathers 11.
4. Anthony, in The Sayings of the Desert Fathers 1.
5. Longinus, in ibid., 5; Moses the Negro, in ibid., 2; Matoes, in ibid., 2–4.
6. Athanasius Life of St. Anthony 74.
7. Ibid., 20; Macarius the Great, in The Sayings of the Desert Fathers 33.
8. Anthony, in The Sayings of the Desert Fathers 33; Apophthegmata Patrum 33; Arsenius, in ibid., 1; Ammonas, in ibid., 4.

the monks would have seen a relationship between monastic life and the attainment of salvation is certainly consistent with their emphasis on free will's role in gaining salvation.

There are definitely some indications in the early monastic traditions of spiritual pride among the monks, which even manifested itself in express criticisms of the episcopacy. That is, some monks felt that because their life was holier, they (and not bishops) should determine Christian teaching (*Paternicon aethiopice* 92). On the other hand, one can identify numerous testimonies of the monks' spiritual humility and their faith in a sovereign, loving God of grace, who is the agent of salvation.[9] Indications of pride and testimonies of humility are combined with stirring commitments to avoid judging one's neighbor.[10] On the whole, then, early monastic theology seems to reflect the sort of mix that one can observe collectively in the writings of the theologians of the first centuries from the Apostolic Fathers to the time of Augustine: there is a clear emphasis on the believer's role/responsibility in attaining salvation, and yet this is combined with Pauline testimonies to what God has done to bring this about.

MONASTIC LIFE

It is useful to move from these theological considerations to the daily lives of the desert monks. What would a visitor (and there were many spiritual pilgrims who went to the desert to be inspired by the monks or just for the sake of sheer curiosity) have found? Such travelers would likely have not been too isolated, despite the barren conditions of the territory. In fact, it was a cosmopolitan world they were entering. No matter from where in the Roman Empire one came, it was likely that communication with one of the monks would be possible. At least one of the monks whom the visitor encountered would have had national origins in the visitor's home region. Monasticism in the African desert was truly an international movement.

This cosmopolitan character of monasticism is not meant to convey that life in the desert was anything but simple, sometimes harsh. Some monks could be observed cultivating their own gardens for subsistence farming. Most earned a living by weaving baskets and mats. Almost always, devotional exercises were practiced while working. The diet of the desert was hardly sumptuous — bread, with some fruit, vegetables, and

---

9. Athanasius *Life of St. Anthony* 84,56; Anthony, in *The Sayings of the Desert Fathers* 6,32; Macarius the Egyptian, in ibid., 2. Recall the quotation from the *Wisdom of the Elders of Ethiopia*, cited in chap. 1.

10. Moses the Negro, in *The Sayings of the Desert Fathers* 2; Paphnutius, in ibid., 1.

oil, was standard fare. As part of their spiritual discipline, some monks even refrained from more lavish fare when it was offered.

To the extent that there was a nomadic character to the anchoritic lifestyle, limited belongings were the order of the day. A monk was likely to own and carry nothing more than clothes and a mat on which to sleep. Because of the monks' distrust of possessions, suspicion of owning books was also typical, out of fear that it could lead to pride. Bereft of such intellectual resources, the monks taught each other the Bible by memorization and exchanged wise spiritual anecdotes. Though the monks were not theologians in a formal sense, but more typically possessed a simple faith, many were immersed in the controversies surrounding Origen's theology, particularly his rejection of all anthropomorphisms concerning God. Indeed, the majority of the monks probably repudiated Origen's views on the subject.

Many of the laypeople committed to monasticism rejected the priesthood; indeed, the movement tended to be anticlerical. In the desert one met very few clerics. Consequently some anchorites would go for years without receiving Communion. The silence of private meditation and renunciation were the primary ways to enhance spirituality in the desert.

Although the original model for monastic spiritual life in the desert was solitude, those exploring or newly undertaking the monastic life typically sought a spiritual father (*abba*) whose deep spirituality would communicate life-giving words and inspiration. This practice quite logically created a climate in which it was inevitable that forms of communal monasticism (cenobitic monasticism) would develop. Its origins too, then, seem intimately related to Africa, since its most influential early proponent, though probably not the creator of the very first monastic community, was a third- and fourth-century Egyptian, Pachomius (ca. 290–346).

Pachomius's background and the factors that led him to become a monk may provide insights about the nature of the cenobitic monasticism he initiated. The son of pagan parents, Pachomius served in the imperial army. During his period of service he became impressed with the kindness of Christians who brought the soldiers food and drink. The experience led him to seek baptism and then to join himself to an ascetic. Can we thus attribute Christian hospitality as well as the fellowship and discipline of military life that Pachomius experienced as formative factors in the creation of cenobitic monasticism? Or perhaps the Christian fellowship and disciplined life of monastic communities are rooted in the military lifestyle of Pachomius.

At any rate, let us return again to the Egyptian desert of the fourth century to observe monks in their cenobitic practice. As travelers came upon the monastic community, it was striking that they were encircled by a wall with a single entrance. Within the wall one might find several buildings, including a church, storehouse, refectory, and meeting hall. Modest living quarters were on the site.

The daily life of these monks included both work and devotion. No one, not even community leaders like Pachomius, was free from the most humble tasks. But in each of the daily tasks undertaken by members of the community, there was a mood of worship, as Psalms were sung and Scripture verses recited from memory. Twice a day the entire community gathered for corporate worship.

Although the lifestyle of these communities was far from lush, the exaggerated poverty typically practiced by some anchorites was not demanded. The basic rule of these communities was mutual service and absolute obedience to superiors. Superiors served those under them. But abbots (those above the superiors of each community) were given absolute authority. These communities of the desert made an inspiring witness. It is reported that many of the candidates who came to them and were eventually admitted had to be baptized and catechized. The cenobitic communities seem to have been effective evangelistic tools.

There is some debate among scholars about whether these monks and Pachomius's community in particular might have been influenced by Gnosticism. A few scholars believe that ancient Gnostic texts discovered in Nag Hammadi, Egypt, may have been remains of Pachomius's community. There is much dispute about this suggestion; it is by no means a proven fact. Certainly the life-denying ethos of the early African monks is consistent with the Gnostic devaluation of the material world.

As we reflect on the attractive features of the early monastic movement and of monasticism throughout history, it should be noted that women have been involved in the movement, even in leadership capacities. They formed their own communities, notably led by Pachomius's sister, Marie. Other prominent women of the desert include Theodora, Athanasia, Mary the Egyptian, and Syncletica. Although we do not know much about the biographies of these women, save the upper-class backgrounds of Theodora and Athanasia, the sayings of these African mothers (*ammas*) have been preserved in the oral traditions of the Church, just as with the *abbas*.

The fact that the Church so long preserved the memory of these women (what they said and did) certainly suggests that the feminist/womanist propensities we observed in the first centuries of the Church's history were not entirely extinguished by the Constantinian establishment. The compilations of their sayings indicate that their collective

theological profile is remarkably similar to that of the *abbas*, save perhaps a stronger emphasis than the *abbas* had on the nature of the
Christian life as a struggle. Of course, too rosy a picture of the situation in the African desert should not be painted. Women still faced all
the insults and bondage of patriarchalism. Perhaps the most compelling
testimony to this is the fact that several of the *ammas* found it necessary to impersonate men in order to function without harassment in the
desert.[11]

THE SPREADING OF MONASTICISM

At a very early date, monasticism was not confined merely to Africa but
also had practitioners in Syria and Asia Minor. It was soon to become
a truly catholic movement, spreading to other regions of the Roman
Empire. The spread of the monastic ideal occurred primarily through
bishops and scholars who saw great value in its witness for the daily life
of the Church, a development that in time had the effect of taming the
monastic movement's anticlericalism. Among these people were Athanasius (the great spokesman for the Council of Nicea), Jerome (himself
a monk who translated the Bible into Latin — the Vulgate), Augustine
(who was inspired by the *Life of St. Anthony* and who later established a semimonastic community for his followers, which eventually led
to the formation of the Augustinian Canons), and Martin of Tours (a
fourth-century Hungarian, who, among other monks, was drafted into
the episcopacy and whose reign greatly contributed to the popularity of
the monastic ideal).

The sort of monasticism most readers from Western societies have
experienced is a form of the movement that was largely influenced by developments in the Western Roman Catholic Church of the Middle Ages.
The ancient forms of monasticism have been more precisely preserved
by Eastern Orthodox monasticism, and it differs from the Western version in several significant ways: (1) the ancient forms were more likely
to punish the body for the sole purpose of renunciation, not just for a
practical purpose (although by way of qualification, it must be noted
that communal monasticism in the East did not demand exaggerated
poverty); (2) early African monasticism placed a premium on solitude;
and (3) it was born of a tension with the ecclesiastical hierarchy, not like
in Catholic monasticism, which has at times functioned as the right arm
of popes and bishops.

---

11. Bessarion, in ibid., 4; Sarah, in ibid., 4,9.

CONCLUDING QUESTION: DID MONASTICISM DISTORT THE FAITH OR ENRICH THE GOSPEL?

The roots of monasticism in Africa are established. The lives of the early monks and their female counterparts are indeed inspiring, perhaps no less to us today than to their contemporaries. Monasticism was also a movement with egalitarian impulses. Such egalitarianism is evident not just with regard to its implicit critique of the ecclesiastical hierarchy, but also insofar as it was the one institution of the Church in this period and for centuries that provided opportunities for women to exercise leadership.

The bottom-line question needs to be considered: Did monasticism distort the faith or enrich the gospel? If monasticism truly enriches the Church's testimony to the gospel, why are there no monks in Protestant churches? Or are there legalistic propensities in the monastic movement that ultimately rob God of glory by focusing too much attention on human spiritual accomplishments? This was clearly not what the early African monks intended, for they were merely yearning to live lives devoted to the gospel in times when the Church seemed to be changing radically.

CHAPTER 7

THE NICENE SOLUTION

The Trinity doctrine developed because the Church was stuck with the biblical formula for baptism: "in the name of the Father and of the Son and of the Holy Spirit" (Matt. 28:19; *Didache* 7). How do Father, Son, and Holy Spirit relate to each other given the Judeo-Christian commitment to one God? Gradually the early Church began to perceive the need to articulate with more precision the relations between the Father, Son, and Holy Spirit. However, such a task had not been an immediate problem for the Church in the first centuries of its existence. In fact, the first reference to the Trinity (*trias*) does not appear until A.D. 180 by Theophilus of Antioch (d. ca. 185/191) (*To Autolycus* 2.15). The New Testament church never employed the term "Trinity." Actually the issue of how Father, Son, and Holy Spirit relate to each other and to the Godhead only became a burning issue in controversies about Christology, specifically those posed by the rise of Arianism and to a lesser extent by Sabellianism (modalism).

It might seem strange that the early Church did not address the problem of the nature of the Godhead in and of itself, but did so only as a by-product of clarifying a christological question. However, it is really not so surprising after all. God is only known in Christ (John 14:9). Consequently it is not surprising that the Trinity doctrine was only spelled out in the context of describing Christ, that is, in explicating how a genuine incarnation happened in him.

ARIANISM

The roots of the Arian controversy and of Arianism itself are to be found in the apologetic efforts of relating the Christian view of God to classical Greek philosophy's conceptions of spiritual realities. Such realities were construed by these philosophers as immutable and impassable. The insights of the Apologists, especially of the so-called Alexandrian school (like Justin Martyr, Clement of Alexandria, and Origen), had been called on to relate this Greek worldview to the biblical picture of God. (Arius, the first proponent of this heresy, was himself a prominent Alexandrian priest.) As we have observed, the Apologists accomplished this by means of (1) an allegorical interpretation of Scripture (to rule out texts that seemed to contradict the idea of God, the ultimate spiritual reality, as impassable or immutable) and (2) the familiar appeal to the concept of the Logos, which served by permitting the argument that when the Bible reports that God spoke to the faithful, it was really the Logos (universal Reason) who spoke.

The next logical development was to regard the Logos as mediator between the immutable One and the mutable world. It was this line of argument, very much in the ecclesiastical air in the latter third and early fourth centuries, that eventually gave rise to Arian thought. Here was the problem: the Logos, as that mediating reality between the immutable, impassable God and the world, increasingly came to be viewed as belonging to creation. When Christ was identified as the Logos, as the Alexandrians and their sympathizers did, the logical conclusion was that Christ must be a creature inasmuch as he had not been immutable and impassable. We have here the essence of the Arian view. Arius (ca. 250–ca. 336) argued, contrary to the prevailing view that spoke of the Word as coeternal with the Father or identified Christ with God, that before anything else was made, the Word had been created (*Letter of Arius to Eusebius*).[1]

Insofar as the Arian view originated in the suppositions of the Alexandrian school, and Arius was from Alexandria, where the first real disputes over his views broke out, there is a sense in which the Nicene Creed, which was placed in its final form in order to refute Arianism, deals with a basically Eastern Christian issue. Since many bishops who eventually drew up this creed were from the West, they tended not to be deeply involved with or troubled by the Arian controversy. For them, when they referred to God as Father, Son, and Holy Spirit, it had been sufficient to affirm Tertullian's formula that God is "Three Persons and One Substance" (three *hypostases*, one *ousia*); (*Against Praxeas* XII,II–III,XIX).

In view of the clearly regional character of the original Arian controversy, it is appropriate from our modern viewpoint to raise the question of precisely what is wrong with the Arian view. Another way to put the question is to consider whether anything is really lost to the Church by a rejection of Arianism.

---

1. Cf. Ignatius *Letter to the Magnesians* 6.1; Tertullian *Apology* 21; Lactantius *Divine Institutes* IV.XXIX; Tatian *Address to the Greeks* V).

THE COUNCIL OF NICEA

Arianism is above all a christological problem. Its emergence had significant sociopolitical implications for the Constantinian empire, for it seemed to shred the unity of the very institution that Constantine had counted on for cementing unity in his empire. Public demonstrations in Alexandria by Arius's supporters were common. The authority of the Alexandrian bishop Alexander (d. 328) was in jeopardy. The schism had to be healed. At least in Constantine's view, the Roman Empire's unity was as much at stake as that of the Church. After all, the empire's unity and the Church's unity were closely related in Constantine's mind. With these aims in mind, in A.D. 325 he convened a council of about 250 bishops in Nicea, not far from Constantinople, to deal with the problem.

Essentially the council rejected the Arian formulation. Finally it was determined to agree on a creed that would express the faith of the Church in such a way that Arianism was clearly excluded. Historians have long contended that Eusebius of Caesarea presented to the council for this purpose a baptismal creed used in his own church (one that closely paralleled the ancient Roman creed with origins in the second century). (More recently some interpreters have maintained that the creed's origin was in a church of Syro-Palestinian location.) Except for Arian sympathizers, whose principal advocate was Eusebius of Nicomedia (d. ca. 342), the council basically accepted Eusebius of Caesarea's formula. Eusebius of Nicomedia and other Arian sympathizers continued to interpret this formulation in their own way throughout the remainder of the controversy.

At the suggestion of Constantine, the council amended the ancient creedal formula originally proposed, as it had nothing of significance for ruling out Arian teaching. Constantine proposed adding the word *homoousios* (of the same substance; that is, Christ, of one substance with the Father," as the creed in its final form reads). In view of the significance of this input from the emperor, it is readily apparent that the Nicene Creed is a political document in a number of ways. Given the roots of the Trinity doctrine in this creed and the impact that this doctrine has had on the Church through the centuries, we must reflect on whether Christianity's truth is somehow compromised by the political origins of its central affirmations. Of course, Jesus' death and the association of the messiahship with David's line are also rooted in the political dynamics of the era in which these events originally transpired.

The bishops proceeded to offer other amendments in addition to what Constantine proposed. The idea of the Son "begotten" of the Father was a compromise offered to the Arians, a way of affirming their subordination of the Son to the Father. In fact, it is little wonder that the Arians later tried to argue that the council had vindicated their view. Arius himself insisted the Son was "begotten," which, contrary to the council's intention, was roughly equivalent to claiming that the Son had been created (*Letter of Arius to Eusebius, Bishop of Nicomedia*).

The original creed probably proposed by Eusebius had only a passing reference to the Holy Spirit, and even the formula finally agreed to by the council does not provide the kind of details found in the final version of the Nicene Creed regarding the Spirit's office as Lord and giver of life, proceeding from the Father. Later the Western church added "and from the Son," that is to say, proceeds from the Son. This addition, called the "Filioque" clause, set up a controversy between Eastern Orthodox and Western churches that has still not been totally resolved. (We shall consider this point in much detail in chap. 11.) Thus it is evident that the creed finally formulated by the council is not identical with the Nicene Creed as we have it today. It only achieved its present form in 381 at the Council of Constantinople.

At any rate, we can say about the Council of Nicea that its purpose of stating a firm position about Christ's nature and a corresponding express condemnation of Arian teaching was fulfilled. In so doing, the council also more or less officially established the Trinity doctrine — at least insofar as it affirmed the equality of Father and Son with a reference to the Spirit. In a sense, then, the Church's ratification of the Trinity doctrine was only by accident. Perhaps this is why the Trinity, at least its implications for church life, has been largely ignored by the Church. Its formulation was accidental, it seems, in the sense that the term *homoousios* inserted to affirm Christ's divinity entailed an affirmation of the unity of God. By implication, then, God must be a unity, though at the same time Father, Son, and Holy Spirit. The Trinity doctrine as literally articulated by the council is merely a warning sign that reads as follows: Never talk about God in such a way that the unity of God is compromised, but never stress unity to such an extent that the distinctness of the three persons is compromised.

Implied in these formulations was a concern that the unity of the persons not be stressed in such a way as to construe that the Father suffered in the Passion (Patripassianism). This concern is implied insofar as proponents of the view at the council did not gain the council's sanction for it. On the other hand, some who study the results of the council fear that Patripassianism may be implied in claiming that the Son is *homoousios* with the Father.

Other important, less ambiguous implications were related to the affirmation of the Trinity by the Nicene Fathers. Effectively they mandated for the catholic faith that one must affirm a continuity between creation and redemption, that there is a continuity between the God who redeemed the world and the One who also created it. The God who created us must be the One who saved us. Consequently, Christ, our Savior, must be divine. In addition, the unity of the divine persons entails that the Spirit's ongoing work must always be in accord with God's revelation in Christ (as reported in Scripture). Proclamation that fails to give testimony to these points is not trinitarian, not truly Christian.

As already suggested, the statement of the Council of Nicea did not settle the matter in the early Church. Even with the backing of the emperor, the lack of effective means of communication and the unwillingness of the Arians, especially their most able spokespersons Arius and Eusebius of Nicomedia, to surrender meant that a "selling job" of the Nicene formulation was still necessary. The selling job would be made even more difficult by the fact that the Nicene party (defenders of the Nicene formulation) would soon not have full support of the emperor.

The prime mover in the push to gain consensus in the Church for the Nicene formula was the fourth-century bishop of Alexandria, Athanasius (ca. 296–373). (There is increasing consensus that Athanasius, mocked as the "black dwarf" by his enemies, was a black man.) Helpful clarifications of the doctrine came in the next generation from the Cappadocian Fathers: Basil the Great (ca. 330–79), Gregory of Nazianzus (329–89), and Gregory of Nyssa (ca. 330–ca. 395). In the succeeding generation, Augustine (354–430) also provided important elaborations and images. In a sense, these elaborations of the Nicene formula were reactions to the renewed push by the Arians after the Council of Nicea adjourned. In a strict chronological sense their consideration belongs in the next chapter, when the story of the post-Nicene Arian reaction and the final formulation of the Nicene Creed as we have it today will be told in full. However, in this context it is well to provide a full picture of the early Church's development of its trinitarian reflections. The Trinity is not just a negative doctrinal formulation, ruling out certain affirmations. It provides a framework for articulating some constructive images for depicting and glorifying God. If *nothing* constructive could ever be said about the Triune God, as is all too often the reality in most churches (where preachers piously proclaim that we cannot penetrate such a mystery), it should perhaps be asked if Arianism is so bad.

IS ARIANISM REALLY SO BAD?

The Arians present a logical treatment of Jesus' relation to the Father. If Christ is not fully equal to the Father, then Christians are not caught in the embarrassing situation of appearing to contradict monotheism by referring to the divinity of a Father and a Son (as well as the Spirit). One plus one plus one does not readily add up to one, as the Trinity doctrine seems to claim.

Also to be considered is the biblical witness, which frequently subordinates the Son to the Father (Matt. 26:42; John 5:30; 6:38; 17:1–26). The Nicene formulation itself takes this seriously insofar as it claims that the Son and the Spirit "proceed from the Father" and endorses biblical language regarding the Son's being "begotten of the Father" (Heb. 1:5; Ps. 2:7). These affirmations were the basis on which the Arians subsequently argued that the Nicene Council had in fact supported their position. In view of the more rational, commonsense character of its view of God and Christ, did the Church make a mistake in condemning Arianism at the Council of Nicea?

Of course there are reasons for rejecting Arianism. One thinks of biblical references that suggest the divinity of the Son (John 1:1; times when Jesus exercised divine prerogatives, such as Mark 2:5–7; Matt. 9:2–3; Luke 5:20–22). In addition, if Christ were a creature like us, and inasmuch as Christ is our Savior, then we would be giving ourselves, human creatures, credit for saving ourselves. Arianism effectively denies that salvation is God's work, that we are justified by grace. Has this been reason enough to justify the Church's condemnation of Arianism, despite the difficulties involved in claiming that God is three in one? Readers need to come to terms with how they truly feel about these questions, as the existential answers they give to them say much about their own working theology.

CONCLUSION: CAN WE MAKE SENSE OF THE TRINITY?

How do one plus one plus one equal one? Answering this question has been a baffling one for the Church. Its insolubility has led many Christians to throw up their arms in despair over the doctrine, to affirm it, but to say nothing more than that it is an inexplicable mystery. Of course when that happens, the Trinity effectively fails to function in any meaningful existentially significant way. Little wonder that so many Western Christians are effectively Unitarian in their piety.

It was not so among the leaders of the early Church. Very soon after the Nicene formulations a number of prominent theologians began to articulate concrete images for describing the Trinity. The power of their work seems to have had lasting impact in the Church as a whole (among the laity). Most of the theologians whom we shall consider have been particularly influential on the churches of Eastern Orthodoxy, and they have maintained a kind of trinitarian piety among the masses in a way that churches of the West have not. Could the fact that efforts were made by these theologians to portray the Trinity concretely and that their voices are still heard in the East be a factor in the sustaining of a trinitarian piety in these churches?

How can we make sense of the Trinity? We consider input from a number of previously noted theologians, some of whom are definitely post-Nicene and whose thought will be analyzed in later chapters. Of course, Athanasius, as the primary PR man for the Nicene formula, is the place to begin.

With Athanasius, the key to the Trinity was a firm insistence on the *homoousios* of the Son with the Father (*Letter concerning the Decrees of the Nicene Definition* 20). There is much historical-critical debate about whether the Athanasian Creed, an exposition of the Nicene formulation, is actually Athanasius's work. Like many pseudepigraphous writings, it may be a work of disciples of Athanasius who, believing themselves to be representing the authentic teachings of their master, attributed his name to the confession. There are even some suggestions that Augustine could have inspired it, long after Athanasius's lifetime.

In many ways, the creed is a kind of litany, most reminiscent of the repetitive form of verse characteristic of the African culture of its origins. A similar repetitive pattern for describing God is identifiable in Augustine:

> The Father eternal: the Son eternal: and the Holy Spirit eternal. And yet there are not three eternals: but one eternal.... So the Father is God: the Son is God: and the Holy Spirit is God. And yet there are not three Gods: but one God. (*On the Trinity* 5.8–9; 8.Pref.1; 8.1–2)

One can discern, then, in the Athanasian Creed, not so much an explanation of the Trinity, as a vehicle for stirring a trinitarian piety.

Athanasius did provide other arguments for, and ways of depicting, the Trinity. He argued for the Trinity on grounds of soteriology. In a manner similar to the Nicene Council's rationalization for condemning Arianism, he claimed that Jesus must be divine for only God can save (*Four Discourses against the Arians* II.21). He also taught deification (*On the Incarnation* 54.3).

Athanasius was also a skilled compromiser. At the Synod of Alexandria in 362, which he and his followers largely organized, it was proclaimed that meaning, not verbiage, was sufficient in dealing with God. This compromise position helped build the necessary coalition for facilitating endorsement of the Nicene formulation by the Church as a whole. The synod agreed that it was appropriate to refer to God both as three substances (*hypostases*) or as one substance (*hypostasis*), as long as this did not connote either an obliteration of the distinctions among the three or imply that there are three gods.

The decisions of this Athanasian synod account for why the Church never achieved a precise, universally accepted explanation of the Trinity. The coalition it achieved put Arianism to rest. The eventual demise of this heresy was also helped by the fact that in the West, Sabellianism was not a big problem. Consequently, the unity of God (the divinity of the Son) was more readily acceptable without as much fear as Christians in the eastern part of the empire had of compromising the distinctness of Father, Son, and Spirit.

It is relevant to assess the present ecclesiastical situation. Is the Church more inclined to be plagued by Arianism or Sabellianism? My instinct is that Arianism or a kind of tritheism (God as a "three-headed monster") is still our predominant problem in Western Christianity (in Protestantism and Roman Catholicism).

One reason why Western Christianity has been more prone to be victimized by a tritheism, why modalism and the obliteration of the distinctions of Father, Son, and Holy Spirit have not been a problem, could be a function of the dominance in the West since Tertullian of the formula of three persons, one substance. Contemporaneous with the Council of Nicea, Basil the Great and others had explicitly articulated this formula and others to explain the Nicene Creed. Basil introduced the idea of three *hypostases* and one *ousia,* which had been earlier affirmed by Tertullian.

Hypostasis refers to the individual subsistence of a thing (what makes it what it is). *Ousia* refers to the essence common to members of a species. *Hypostases* relates to *ousia,* as entities relate to a species, as, for example, Mark Ellingsen relates to humanity. Consequently in the West (the western half of the Roman Empire), where Latin, not Greek, prevailed, the Greek term *hypostases* was translated "persona." This is how Western Christians have come to speak of three persons of the Trinity. From this point, it is not too circuitous a route to the idea of God as a three-headed monster, which so plagues popular Western Christian piety.

Are we stuck with this problem of tritheism? There are several promising leads in the literature of the early Church.

ATHANASIUS

Athanasius had more to say constructively on the subject of the Trinity than the "official" positions of the Athanasian Creed and the Synod of Alexandria. He offers a concrete image for elaborating how Christ can be *homoousios* with the Father and still be begotten. Drawing on an image that had been employed earlier by Tertullian, he claimed that the brightness of the Father exists eternally and that this brightness is his Word. The relation between the sun and its brightness (rays) is analogous to the relation of the Father and the Son. As the sun begets its brightness as long as the sun has existed, and we commonly refer to its rays as the sun, so the Father eternally begets (radiates) the Son and is one with the Son, as the sun is in the brightness it radiates.[2]

Another image expressly addresses the distinctions among Father, Son, and Holy Spirit. They are one, yet distinct, Athanasius argues, rather as a river is generated from its source, yet is not separated from its source. The source is not the river, and the river is not the source; yet each is water. Likewise the Godhead flows from Father to Son (*Expositio Fidei* 1).

THE CAPPADOCIANS

Basil the Great also offered additional reflections besides his formula of three *hypostases*, one *ousia*. Addressing the impossibility of separating the persons of the Trinity, he claims that it is no more possible to separate them than it is to grasp one end of the chain without drawing the other end of the chain along with it.[3] Father, Son, and Holy Spirit are one, as the links of a chain are one and inseparable.

A colleague of Basil's, Gregory of Nazianzus offers other promising clues to formulating an understanding of the Trinity. He drew on a distinction between God as he is and as he is in his operations. Consequently God is three persons, or *hypostases*, in the sense that he undertakes three distinct operations. Actions constitute nature. Thus, God's actions make God who he is in his being. (There is an implicit break on Nazianzus's part with Greek philosophy and the static view of God that it entails. His suppositions are more like the Hebraic view of God as a being who is what he does.) Yet there are not distinct essences identified with Father, Son, and Spirit by their different actions, any more than one dog is more of a dog than another on the basis of its distinct behavior.[4]

Another image employed by Nazianzus is an effort to understand the Trinity is light. How can light be one yet emanate from distinct sources? God is one as the light of three suns combined would be mingled together as one.[5]

---

2. Athanasius *Four Discourses against the Arians* I.24–25; II.33; III.3–4; *Epistle to Seraplanem* I.20; cf. Tertullian *Incarnation of the Logos* Apol.xxi.
   3. Basil the Great *Letter to His Brother Gregory [of Nyssa]* XXXVIII.4.
   4. Gregory of Nazianzus *Theological Orations* 3.9–13.
   5. Gregory of Nazianzus *Fifth Theological Oration* 31.14.

Gregory's activist, almost Hebraic, view of God was developed further by Gregory of Nyssa, the brother of his colleague Basil. While still insisting that God is unchanging, Nyssa claimed that God is distinct in terms of operation or cause; that is, the Father begets the Spirit and the Son (*Letters* XVI). However the unity of the divine nature is affirmed insofar as no act of one of the divine persons is undertaken without the other persons of the Trinity. What one does the other does.[6] In *Against the Macedonians* (2.5), Nyssa elaborated on this point by claiming that Father, Son, and Holy Spirit are like three torches that pass their light one to another.

Half a century later these insights were developed more fully by Cyril of Alexandria (d. 444). In all divine actions, Cyril argued, the persons of the Trinity act together in harmony (*Against the Blasphemies of Nestorius* 5.6). When radiance can fall from light, then and only then will the Son and the Father do their work apart from each other.[7] If they all act together, they must be one. Elsewhere Cyril made this point concerning how divine action constitutes God's being in the sense of an appeal to the hypostatic union, so that God himself is said actually to suffer in Christ (*Third Letter to Nestorius* 6). (This manner of describing the Incarnation and its impact on God is typical of the so-called Alexandrian school of Christology. As we shall observe in chapter 11, it played a major role in the Church's formulation of the doctrine of Christ's two natures.)

At this point there is a total break with Greek philosophy and the logic of its suppositions that God is unchanging. The practical implications for Christian piety of this vision of the Trinity and Christology warrant consideration. If God has suffered when incarnate in the man Jesus, does he not seem more empathetic? Such a God has truly walked in our shoes. This is also a God conditioned in part by history. Time exists in Him. Such formulations anticipate Augustine's and later Martin Luther's contention that in God past, present, and future are one moment.[8] Is this (Alexandrian/Cappadocian) vision of the Trinity a fruitful vision?

The Cappadocian conceptualization of the Trinity distinguishes Father, Son, and Holy Spirit in what they do or in who causes whom, while insisting that they are one insofar as no person acts alone. Even for those attracted by this Hebraic trinitarian understanding of God as the one who is what he does, problems still may remain with how con-

---

6. Gregory of Nyssa *An Answer to Ablabius.*
7. Cyril *Answers to Tiberius and His Companions* 3.
8. Augustine *Confessions* XI.XIII–XIV; *Luther's Works* 30:114,196.

cretely to describe the idea of how the Father could beget the Son, how the Spirit could proceed from the Father, and yet God could still be one.

AUGUSTINE

Although he has not had an impact on the vibrant trinitarian piety of the Eastern churches, as have Church Fathers already considered, Augustine provides some fruitful images for dealing with the range of questions concerning the understanding of the Trinity. These images are best understood in the context of the full picture of his trinitarian reflections. Augustine employed the image of Athanasius and Tertullian to depict the Son's being begotten of the Father, claiming it is like the brightness being begotten of, yet simultaneous with, light (*On the Trinity* IV. 20.27). Also not unlike Athanasius, Augustine claimed that the Triune God is three in one, as a fountain, a river, and the drink we take from each are distinct, and yet all are water. Likewise, according to Augustine, a tree is composed of root, trunk, and branches, yet all three are distinct (*Faith and the Creed* 17).

Later in his life, in his classic work on the Trinity, Augustine tried to make the Trinity plain by arguing that our natural makeup is triadic in such a way as to give clues to the Trinity. Among his arguments and analogies, he notes that the nature of love is triadic, involving subject, object, and relation — and yet together they constitute one reality, love (*On the Trinity* VIII.10.14). The human mind likewise reflects a trinity, he asserts. Individuals who love themselves have self-knowledge, which is "begotten" of the mind, and the self-love "proceeds" from the givens of mind and self-knowledge (IX).

In a sense both of these images are combined in Augustine's idea of the Father's loving the Son and construing the Spirit as the love (between them) who makes them one. Recall that from a Christian perspective two become one in married love (Eph. 5:31). In imperfect human love, the two still retain some independence, but God loves perfectly. His love, in the Spirit, truly makes the many into one. Augustine's words are most reminiscent of the second-century Apologist Athenagoras:[9]

[With the Father and the Son] the Holy Spirit, too exists in this same unity of substance and equality. For whether He be the unity of the Father and the Son, or their holiness, or their love, or their unity because He is their love, or their love because He is their holiness, it is clear that He is not one of the two, since it is by Him that the two are joined, by Him that the Begotten is loved by the

---

9. Athenagoras *Plea for the Christians* 10.

Begetter, and in turn loves Him who begot Him. (Augustine *On the Trinity* VI.5.7)

For Augustine, God is truly a social being so full of love that he cannot be himself without loving someone. In eternity God has had himself to love, and so he begot the Son, an object for his love. The Father loves the Son, their love is mutual, and the Spirit is the love that makes them one.

Readers are encouraged to reflect on whether any of the concrete images for describing the Trinity are more helpful or compelling than others and, if so, why? At least they should be used as starting points in the construction of one's own trinitarian theology. If none of them is helpful or appropriate, what is it about the nature of God that precludes their viability? Recall, the Church is not bound to these descriptions. The Synod of Alexandria mandates that we agree in our intention to be faithful to the meaning of the Council of Nicea's decisions, not to the exact words and concepts it employed. We are faithful to this tradition as long as we reject the heresies that they reject — reject all efforts to deny the full divinity of any of the persons and reject efforts to minimize that they are distinct in essence.

SOCIAL IMPLICATIONS OF THE TRINITY

For those who do want to move beyond the idea of the Trinity doctrine as a mere boundary line for Christians, to mark Christian teaching off from false ideas, and proceed to describe the Trinity positively, there is much to gain in terms of the enrichment of Christianity's social implications. Again prominent figures in the early Church give clues.

Gregory of Nyssa believed that the idea that God truly assumed human nature has social consequences. That is, because what happens to humanity in Christ happens to God, then God's power permeates the whole of humanity. The entire human race is one in Christ's body.[10] This entails, he claims, that the distinction between male and female is not ultimate (*On the Making of Man* XVI–XVII). In Nyssa's view of the Trinity, in other words, the fact that what happens to one person happens to all means that God is totally incarnate in humanity. Just as God is one, the human species in which he is incarnate becomes one (for God himself tolerates no plurality, only harmony). God has a predilection for making many into one. As soon as he lays his hands on Jesus, he cannot but touch all of humanity in seeking to make them one. This is a necessary consequence of his being a Trinity, or three in one. The unifying force of the Triune God (that he makes one out of many) has that effect

10. Note that his argument at this point presupposes his endorsement of the concept of deification (Gregory of Nyssa *Address on Religious Instruction* 37).

on the human species once the human species is infected with divinity in Christ.

Augustine's picture of the Trinity clearly implies that because God is inherently social, always in relation to someone, he is always in relation to himself. Consequently his creatures made in his image cannot be isolated from each other and, like him, are inherently social. As each person of the Trinity shares all that he has with other persons, so likewise we creatures made in his image can do no other than to share all we have with others. Augustine himself did not explicitly make this point, but Clement of Alexandria did over a century before the Council of Nicea. Because the Father shares himself as the Word of God and makes all things common, so God wishes his creatures to share:

> God brought our race into communion by first imparting what was His own, when He gave His own Word, common to all, and made all things for all. All things therefore are common, and not for the rich to appropriate an undue share. (Clement of Alexandria *Instructor* II.XIII)

Do any of these theological options adequately assist Christians in understanding how one plus one plus one, when it comes to God, really does add up to one (divine nature)? Are any of them more helpful, better vehicles for communication, than others? Grappling with these questions can assist readers in developing their own ways of talking and thinking about the Trinity. The analysis has shown that the Trinity can help the Church to affirm more unambiguously that salvation is the work of God (since Christ and the Spirit are divine) and also aid the communication of the Trinity's implications for life in society. Perhaps more attention to the trinitarian images employed by theologians of the early Church could serve us well.

CHAPTER 8

MORE INTERNAL STRUGGLES IN A LESS FRIENDLY ENVIRONMENT

Immediately after the establishment of Christianity under Constantine, the Church experienced trying times. Indeed, all did not go smoothly for the Church under Constantine or under his successors, just as acceptance of the Trinity doctrine did not come easily.

Concerning the ongoing debate regarding Constantine and the virtues or vices of his establishment of Christianity, it should be noted that during his reign an impressive pro-Constantinian account of the history of early Christianity (the first post–New Testament church history text) was prepared by Eusebius of Caesarea (ca. 260–ca. 340), who was known as perhaps the most learned Christian of his time. Probably a native of Palestine, he became the bishop of Caesarea in A.D. 315. A great admirer of Origen's work, Eusebius collaborated very closely early in his intellectual development with Pamphilus of Caesarea (ca. 240–309), the student of a student of Origen's.

In the Arian controversy, Eusebius was initially attracted to Arius's teachings, and most of his career was spent fluctuating back and forth between it and the Nicene position (*Ecclesiastical Theology* 2.14). Some of this may have been motivated by political opportunism, some of it may have been a function of his concern to avoid modalism at all costs, and another factor was probably his concern, which he shared with Constantine, to maintain the unity of the Church.

Though Eusebius was neither a close friend nor a courtier of Constantine's, there was great mutual respect between them. Constantine, like many Christians in the Roman Empire, had genuine respect for the bishop and his reputation for learnedness. Eusebius, in turn, felt that God had raised up Constantine to save the Church from its earlier trials. It was in this historical and personal context that Eusebius wrote his great historical work, *Church History*. Its purpose was not merely to retell various events in the life of the Church; it was really an apology to show that Christianity was the culmination of human history, the completion of Roman tradition and the aims of the empire.

In making these points, Eusebius was standing in the tradition of Origen and of the entire Alexandrian tradition with its correlationist methodology. Justin Martyr and Clement of Alexandria had argued that both philosophy and the Hebrew Scriptures were preparation for the gospel.[1] Another idea in circulation at the time viewed God as having ordained the Roman Empire itself and the relative peace it had brought as a means of facilitating the proclamation of the gospel. Eusebius made the same point, only is a less explicit way.

Eusebius's position raises an intriguing question for readers about their own worldviews. Is it really the case that Christianity is the culmination of human history? The position one takes on this matter says much about one's view of divine providence (whether all things happen in accord with the divine will) and theological method (how one relates the Word of God to secular knowledge — that is, to philosophy, science, and the like).

One possible weakness of sharing Eusebius's and the Alexandrians' assessment of the relationship between the gospel and the world is the difficulty of taking a critical stance towards the events of one's own time. Given these assumptions, contemporary events presumably are vehicles for accomplishing God's will. The lack of critical perspective can blind one to developments that are happening to the institutions and values one loves. For example, Eusebius failed to note the negative implications of the ecclesiastical dynamics that the Constantinian establishment occasioned. Among those dynamics to which Eusebius offered no response was the Church's transformation from being a Church of the poor to an institution of the powerful, controlled by the establishment.

More and more, the Church was modeling the ways and values of the empire. Yet Eusebius joyfully described the ornate churches that Constantine erected and avoided any mention of an imminent eschaton. Beyond the present political order, Christians can only hope, according to Eusebius, for their own individual salvation. Such declarations represent a striking departure from the New Testament witness, though Eusebius and the Constantinian establishment never noticed it (Mark 1:14–15; 10:17–31). To some extent, Eusebius and those who shared his basic optimism about the direction of history flirted with something like the modern version of *civil religion* (the transformation of Christianity into a syncretistic set of beliefs shared by all members of a society that may serve to provide religious justification/undergirding for the society). Those who share Eusebius's optimism about God's working in contemporary movements need to keep in mind all these potential weaknesses of such a view.

---

1. Justin Martyr *First Apology* 44,46; Clement of Alexandria *Stromata* I.IV-V.

THE DEVELOPMENT OF PAPAL AUTHORITY: AN ANCIENT AND LEGITIMATELY CHRISTIAN PRACTICE?

As we consider how and by whom power was exercised in the Church during the years of Constantine's reign, it is well to be reminded of the previously noted sociological-ecclesiological reasons for the continuing concentration of power and influence in the church of Rome and its leadership. Since Rome was the capital of the empire, its economic, political, and intellectual center, it is easy to see why Christians throughout the empire naturally looked to the church in Rome for leadership. In addition, Rome was the largest city in the Roman Empire; there are indications that at least by A.D. 250 the church in Rome was the largest of all the churches. Big churches, it seems, have always had more clout than small ones.

Likewise, Constantine's relocation of the capital to Constantinople had the effect of enhancing the political power of Rome's bishop, as he stepped into the vacuum of power brought about by the emperor's departure. When subsequently the Huns and Vandals invaded Rome in the fifth century, later followed in the sixth century by the Lombards, the Roman bishop's political authority was even further enhanced since it was he who typically rallied the troops or carried on negotiations with the enemy.

Of course, claims to the primacy of the Roman church were based, not on these political dynamics, but on the tradition that Peter had founded it. Since Peter was respected as the prince of all the disciples — the rock on whom the Church was to be built (Matt. 16:8) — claims to Roman primacy were widely, but not unanimously (especially in the eastern part of the Roman Empire), thought to be rooted in Scripture and tradition.

Sometime during this period the bishop of Rome came to be called "pope," but he was by no means the only bishop of the Church to receive that title. The word "pope" derives from a Greek term that literally means "father." In early times it was used to refer to any respected and important bishop. The bishops of Carthage and Alexandria (including Athanasius), not just the bishops of Rome, were referred to as "popes." This practice has not completely terminated in the East, as to this day the presiding bishop of the Coptic Church carries the title. Eventually in the West, at some unspecified date, it became common to employ the title to refer exclusively to the bishop of Rome.

In addition to these largely sociopolitical and polity dynamics, there are clearly early theological precedents for appeal to the church in Rome and its leaders in settling disputes in the Church as a whole. In his second-century affirmation of the primacy of the Roman church, Irenaeus insisted that all churches must agree with it because of its position and authority. In the next century, Cyprian of Carthage argued for the primacy of Peter for the sake of the unity of the Church. In the fourth century and later in the fifth, the number of references to and the authoritative ("official") claims for Roman and even papal authority intensify. In 341 Julius, bishop of Rome (d. 352), wrote to the Council of Antioch (an Arian group of bishops) insisting on the restoration of Athanasius, claiming that consultation with the bishop of Rome in such cases was a tradition handed down from Peter. Two years later the Council of Sardica (Cans. 3,5) affirmed that Peter's memory is honored when the bishop of Rome is asked to adjudicate ecclesiastical cases involving a bishop is appealed. Four decades later, in 382, a Roman synod issued a parallel statement, requesting that the emperor give jurisdiction to the Roman church in trials of bishops and that the right of appeal to the bishop of Rome be permitted in cases where unfairness was suspected. This was certainly in the spirit of a decree made two years earlier by Emperor Theodosius I, who had ruled that his subjects should continue in the profession of the true religion delivered to the Romans by Peter.

  It is relevant to be reminded again of how appeals to and by the bishop of Rome were evident in the controversies surrounding the eventual reception of the Nicene formulation. In addition to the Roman bishop's efforts to exert his authority to ensure the restoration of Athanasius to his Alexandrian diocese, Jerome (ca. 342–420), the early Church's most renowned scholar and translator of the Bible into Latin, appealed to the papacy in 376 for an authoritative pronouncement on the validity of the Cappadocian use of the expression "of the same substance" (*Letters* 15). African bishops made a similar appeal concerning Pelagianism in A.D. 417, and Pope Innocent I in response claimed that there is nothing settled in the Church that does not come before the see (*Letters* 29). There was even political certification of these claims to papal primacy. In A.D. 445 Emperor Valentinian III claimed that the merit of Peter assured the preeminence of the apostolic see and that, therefore, one should hold as law whatever the apostolic see enacts.

  Generally speaking, appeals to papal authority have emerged in situations of controversy, much as the concept of episcopal authority did. To be sure, there was resistance to such claims for Roman authority even in the early Church. For example, the Council of Antioch in 341, with its Arian agenda, defied the Roman bishop Julius's urging of Athanasius's restoration, formulating instead its own Creed of Dedication. On at least two occasions African bishops defied papal authority. One instance occurred early in the fifth century, when the pope supported the teachings of (the heretic) Pelagius.[2] Again in 424 at the Synod of

---

2. Prosper of Aquitaine *Against Cassian the Lecturer* 5.3.

Carthage the bishops appealed to the Council of Nicea to authorize their insistence on local jurisdiction over clergy affairs. In fact, the tradition of challenging papal teachings continued into the seventh century. The Third Council of Constantinople in 680–681 condemned Pope Honorius I (d. 638) for apparently supporting the Monothelite heresy (to be considered in chap. 11).

Resistance to claims for papal authority by bishops from regions in the eastern half of the Roman Empire and elsewhere outside the sphere of influence dominated by Rome is not surprising. The Council of Sardica's formal proclamation of papal authority in the appeal of ecclesiastical controversies included no African or Eastern bishops in the process. It is evident that the papacy's power base from the earliest times was primarily in the West. Already we can sense Eastern and Western Christianity each going its own way.

As noted, with the transfer of the empire's capital to Constantinople, its presiding bishop came to be accorded higher honor. The First Council of Constantinople (Can. 3) in 381 and the Council of Chalcedon (Can. 28) in 451 made this official, as Constantinople was proclaimed the "New Rome" and its bishop was to be given comparable, if not identical, privileges as those conferred on the bishop of Rome.

•

It is evident that papal authority, papal supremacy, is an ancient practice and commitment of the Church (though not unambiguously accepted). To the extent that this is the case, why should the papacy not continue to be maintained? After all, the links between papal authority and apostolic succession are intimate, and both played important and constructive roles in the early Church's struggles with heresy. Is papal authority still a significant resource for overcoming the cultural and ecclesiastical permissive relativisms of our day?

THE POST-NICENE TRINITARIAN CONTROVERSY: IS THE TRINITY DOCTRINE A TRUE OR MERELY A POLITICAL COMPROMISE?

In view of Constantine's significant role in the formulation of the Trinity doctrine (a contribution not without political motivations), it is not surprising that he and his successors also played important roles in the Church's reception process of the Council of Nicea's decision. On the whole, Constantine and his successors made life pretty miserable for Church leaders committed to the Nicene decision and its trinitarian formula.

During Constantine's last years, he was approached by Eusebius of Nicomedia (d. ca. 342), a spokesman for the Arians. Eusebius was an able politician, and Constantine began to become more and more open to his Arian views. Eventually Eusebius demanded that Arius be restored to fellowship in Constantinople. Meanwhile Eusebius also got Constantine's ear concerning a dangerous enemy, Athanasius, the bishop of Alexandria, who emerged as the prime spokesman of the Nicene party. Athanasius's home was more than likely the Nile's shore in Egypt. We know that his mother tongue was Coptic. As noted, he seems to have had a dark complexion and was even labeled mockingly a "black dwarf" by adversaries. With Athanasius, we have a "black theology" incontestably manifest in the early Church (though one can make a good case for the prospect that many, though not all, of the Alexandrian theologians and African Christian martyrs we have already discussed may also have been black men and women). In this connection, given the great role Athanasius played in facilitating the Church's reception of the Nicene formula, it does not seem outlandish to refer to the African roots (or heritage) of the Trinity doctrine.

ATHANASIUS'S THEOLOGY

The impact of things African on Athanasius is apparent in other ways. African Christian monasticism profoundly influenced him. We have noted that he wrote the standard biography of Anthony, is said to have been one of Anthony's disciples, and counted Pachomius, the founder of cenobitic monasticism, among his friends. Much of Athanasius's theology endorses the themes characteristic of the theological suppositions of the early desert monks. He affirmed with them human free will (*Against the Heathen* 4), construed salvation as deification (*On the Incarnation* 54), at least in some contexts regarded Christ's atoning work in terms of a struggle with demons (6ff.), and seems to have affirmed belief in a sovereign God who orders all things in the universe (1).

One can readily detect how strong a defender of the core commitments of the Council of Nicea Athanasius was. We have already dealt with his own understanding of the Trinity in the previous chapter. Suffice it to note that he unambiguously affirmed the Son to be *homoousios* with the Father (*Four Discourses against the Arians* I.15–16) and with Nicea insisted on the continuity of creation and redemption (that God's work in saving us is intimately connected with his work in creating us; *On the Incarnation* 1,4,13).

Closely related to Athanasius's conviction about the continuity of creation and redemption was his view of sin as the contradiction of creation, as nonbeing (*On the Incarnation* 4). Whether he continued to affirm with the earlier Church Fathers that even in sin we continue to have free will is a matter of some uncertainty. When he spoke of the insatiable character of sin, he claimed that repentance alone would not be sufficient to save (6–7). Like the earlier Eastern Fathers and Mothers, he spoke of salvation in terms of deification (54), as the renewal of the image of God in humanity (13–14).

Some of the other convictions of the Alexandrian bishop reflect characteristic affirmations of the Alexandrian school of theology. Like his Alexandrian predecessors, Athanasius tended to identify the Son of God with the Logos. Consequently he claimed that all rational creatures know something of Christ (*On the Incarnation* 3,11). He was not an unequivocal advocate of allegorical interpretation, as typified most proponents of the Alexandrian School; however, he did opt for interpreting Scripture in light of one presupposition — that it must always be interpreted as giving testimony to Christ (37) — and claimed it is only properly understood by those with a pure mind and leading an honorable life (57).

Consistent with later fully developed Alexandrian christological commitments (see chap. 11), Athanasius claimed that what could be predicated of Christ's body may be predicated of him as the Word, a claim that came to be known as the *communicatio idiomatum* (*On the Incarnation* 18). Along the same lines, he referred to Mary as the Mother of God. Since she was Jesus' earthly mother, this may be predicated of his divine nature as well (*Four Discourses against the Arians* III.33). On the other hand, though, in a manner more characteristic of the soon-to-be-developed Antiochene School of Christology, he rejected this sort of attribution of what is appropriate to one of Christ's natures to the other (III.43). An intriguing question is whether there is in Athanasius at this point a frustrating inconsistency or whether his thought points us to a catholic consensus about Christology that would soon develop and has perdured for the last sixteen centuries.

These latter theological convictions, especially the ones not directly pertaining to the nature of Christ, did not get Athanasius in trouble. As much as his insistence on the Son's being construed as *homoousios* with the Father, it was his stubborn (or was it a loyal, heroic, and effective) style of advocating this affirmation of the Council of Nicea that landed him in trouble.

THE CONTROVERSY CONTINUES

As prime spokesperson for the Nicene formulation, Athanasius soon became the target of Eusebius of Nicomedia, who had successfully portrayed Athanasius as a fanatic to the emperor. Ultimately Constantine responded by exiling Athanasius from his episcopal responsibilities. Arianism increasingly gained favor in royal circles. Constantine's baptism on his deathbed was probably administered by an Arian.

Constantine was succeeded by his three sons, each ruling a portion of the Roman Empire. At first, the situation favored the Nicene party (those advocating the Nicene Creed against the Arians) because one of the late emperor's sons supported it. Athanasius was recalled from exile. His return to Alexandria touched off a period of tensions with Arians in town. To keep peace, he left and traveled to Rome, which turned out to be a fruitful development because he won most of the clergy in Rome over to the Nicene view.

Then another of Constantine's sons, Constantius II, the one in charge of the East, started obtaining the upper hand in military skirmishes with his brothers. Athanasius, who had returned with the people's acclaim, was under pressure from this brother. Part of the reason that Athanasius had been well received in Alexandria was because Arianism only appealed to the upper-class Hellenized citizens, whereas Athanasius had the support of the masses. This period of stability and growing support throughout the Church as a whole came to an end when the pro-Arian son, Constantius II, became the sole emperor. The whole empire was now Arian, with the support of even the bishop of Rome. It was A.D. 353. A synod was ordered to condemn Athanasius.

Several Arian-inspired creeds were produced during the controversy. One of these, the Dedication Creed of 341, refers to Christ as the first-born of all creatures.[3] It emerged from the Council of Antioch, which ignored a papal directive about Athanasius. The second, produced at a council held at Sirmium in 357, was especially concerned to affirm the superiority of Father to Son.[4]

Church leaders sympathetic with the Nicene position protested Constantius's efforts to inject the state and his Arian sympathies into church discipline. In this period, the Church recognized for the first time that there are risks and possible abuses associated with Constantinianism. This raises again the questions posed in chapter 6: Do these risks invalidate the establishment of Christianity by Constantine? Is it good for the Church that we are beginning to enter a post-Constantinian era in which the Church is so estranged from society that the state and social pressures will finally leave it alone and stop meddling in its affairs?

When Constantius died in 361, he was succeeded by his cousin Julian, called Julian the Apostate. Julian came to the throne with bad blood towards Constantine's immediate family, as it was widely believed that

3. Athanasius *On the Synods of Ariminum and Seleucia* 23.
4. Socrates Scholasticus *Ecclesiastical History* 2.30.

they had deliberately put to death all of Julian's family in order to elim-
inate competition for the throne. Julian matured into a great student
of philosophy who rejected Christianity. Ascending the throne, he instituted a program to restore paganism but borrowed much from Christian
Church polity in the way he organized a pagan priesthood. Julian came
to recognize that he could not strong-arm these reforms on the Roman
Empire. They were not popular, as the restoration of the old Roman religious ceremonies were frequently belittled. Consequently, he came to
realize that he could not persecute Christianity as earlier emperors had.
The best he could do was to use propaganda to undermine it.

Julian's tenure actually helped defenders of Nicene Orthodoxy, including their primary spokesperson, Athanasius. Julian, of course, had
no interest in supporting either side in the Arian versus Nicene debate,
so he simply canceled all orders of exile. Athanasius was now effectively free to operate as the PR man for the Nicene formulation. Thanks
largely to his efforts, the Nicene Creed in its present form came to be
and was accepted by the whole Church.

THE CREED TAKES FINAL FORM

Athanasius's previously noted insistence on the affirmation that the Son
is *homoousios* with the Father, introduced by Constantine to the Council of Nicea, is hardly surprising. He gradually came to the conclusion
that some were opposing the Nicene formula only because they feared
that the term *homoousios* neglected a distinction between Father and
Son. As we have observed, one of the reasons for the persistence of Arianism on the Eastern churches' agenda was because Sabellianism was
a bigger problem in the East than in the West. Consequently, in the
West it was not as problematic as in the East to stress the unity of God
(the divinity of the Son), as the Council of Nicea did, without fear of
compromising the distinctness of Father, Son, and Spirit. Readers are
again encouraged to reflect on which is a bigger problem in their church
today — Arianism or Sabellianism? Perhaps Arianism (tritheism) is a
bigger problem for Christians in the West.

In any case, Athanasius began to compromise in seeing as legitimate
the concerns of those who, though not Arian, preferred to speak of
Christ as *homoiousios* (of similar substance) with the Father. As we
noted in the previous chapter, in the Synod of Alexandria in A.D. 362, in
which Athanasius played a major role, it was declared acceptable to refer to Father, Son, and Holy Spirit as "one substance" as long as this
was not understood as obliterating the distinctions among the three.
Also, one could speak of three substances as long as this was not understood as referring to three gods. Was this compromise justifiable, or is

the concept of *homoiousios* more problematic than the synod and the Church have seemed to recognize?

At the Synod of Alexandria, the Church officially affirmed (at least by implication) the deity of the Holy Spirit for the first time. On the basis of the synod's preparatory work, the Council of Constantinople in 381 endorsed the Nicene formula, ratifying a creedal formulation that is like our present version of the Nicene Creed (without reference to the Filioque — the Spirit's proceeding "from the Son"). Constantinople was the council that definitively proclaimed the doctrine of the Trinity. Rooted in the work of the Synod of Alexandria and the controversy stirred by Montanism, the council was crucial in forcing the post–New Testament Church to take the Holy Spirit more seriously. (The council also condemned a budding heresy called "Apollinarianism" — i.e., the belief that Christ had no human soul, as it had been replaced by the Word of God — which will be considered in more depth in chap. 11.) The Council of Chalcedon in 451 ratified the same creed.

There is some speculation that the Constantinople Council did not formulate the Nicene Creed but that it had been circulating at least seven years before the council as the baptismal creed of Jerusalem. At any rate, we have in this narrative the origin of the Nicene Creed as we know it, as formulated by a circuitous route through the Council of Nicea, but dating from an ancient creed perhaps of the church in Rome. It should be reiterated that this more ancient creed is likely identical with the Apostles' Creed, which presumably originated in Rome (in the West), and so, not surprisingly, has been used only in Western (Roman Catholic and Protestant) churches.

Julian the Apostate turned on Athanasius, after recognizing Athanasius's heroic stature and the gaining influence of the faith he represented. Athanasius fled. The rest of Athanasius's life was a sequence of ups and downs from one emperor who favored him to another who was an Arian sympathizer. During Athanasius's old age, a new generation of Nicene sympathizers, the Cappadocian Fathers, emerged. We have already analyzed their important trinitarian reflections and subsequently will consider their theology in more detail.

The political maneuverings and compromises in the adoption of the final form of the Nicene Creed and the Trinity doctrine raise more sharply the question of whether the Trinity doctrine is a true affirmation or the result of a mere political compromise. Where is the Spirit's work in these seemingly accidental developments, or does the Spirit work through the accidents of history?

CHAPTER 9

AUGUSTINE AND THE AUGUSTINIAN SYNTHESIS

The acclaim that has been historically bestowed on Augustine (354–430), the bishop of Hippo in North Africa, is well deserved. In fact, the remainder of this book and its companion volume are in some sense the story of how the Western church since the Middle Ages, through the Reformation, and to this very day came to hold his thought in such high esteem.

Augustine was far from isolated in his greatness during his own lifetime. He was more or less a (younger) contemporary of Athanasius, as well as a full contemporary of the famed preacher Ambrose (ca. 339–97), the bishop of Milan; the equally renowned preacher and bishop of Constantinople John Chrysostom (ca. 347–407); and the eminent biblical scholar and translator of the Bible Jerome. Another group of famed contemporaries was the Cappadocians: Basil the Great, his sister Macrina (ca. 327–379), their brother Gregory of Nyssa, and their friend Gregory of Nazianzus. These four friends/relatives served the Church in the region of eastern Asia Minor (present-day Turkey) that bears the name of Cappadocia. Augustine's contact with at least one of these distinguished colleagues was one of the turning points of his life and spiritual development.

The analysis of Augustine, though, cannot focus merely on his theological views, profound and influential though they be. His greatness is intimately linked with his biography, with his spiritual pilgrimage. Much of that is recorded in his spiritually profound autobiography, the *Confessions*, which is a classic of Western literature.

LIFE OF AUGUSTINE: HOW A RESTLESS HEART FOUND REST

At the outset of his great spiritual autobiography (it is not truly an autobiography but an extended prayer), Augustine wrote the following words, which summarize both his life and his theology:

And man desires to praise Thee.... Thou does so excite him that
to praise Thee is his joy. For Thou hast made us for Thyself and
our hearts are restless till they rest in Thee. (*Confessions* I.I.1,
emphasis added.

Born in the small town of Thagaste in North Africa (specifically in
the ancient principality of Numidia, located in present-day Algeria),
Augustine lived in momentous times. He knew a post-Constantinian
era in which, save for the brief reign of Julian the Apostate, being a
Christian no longer placed one under serious threat. Yet it was still
not an era in which being a Christian was synonymous with being a
good citizen of the empire. There were still various viable meaning-
systems (philosophies) from which educated citizens could and typically
did draw. In fact, there are striking analogies between Western society at the end of the twentieth century and Augustine's times with
regard to the plethora of viable lifestyle choices, of which Christianity
is just one. Augustine also lived to see the fall of Rome to the Goths in
A.D. 410.

Augustine was born in a place and time that was enjoying the greatest period of economic prosperity that to date this region of Africa
had ever known, which is not to say, however, that the petty gentry
families of Thagaste like the one into which Augustine was born were
particularly comfortable. Yet it was an ethos in which upward social
mobility was a real possibility, and the sons of these families seem to
have been nurtured in a strong work ethic. The society was also multi-
cultural, populated by Italian immigrants; by Phoenicians (Punics), who
had been in the region for centuries; and by Berbers, a group of people
who in Algeria are characterized by black skin and curly black hair.
(Since we can likely discount Augustine's having Phoenician ancestry
given his criticism of the Punics, the possibility of his having been a
black man cannot be discounted.) Nevertheless, this was a culture that
was thoroughly Romanized/Hellenized. Africans in this region thought
of themselves first and foremost as Romans (as was also largely true
of the citizens of Carthage). Preexisting native traditions were largely
deemed as "Punic," as uncivilized. Given such cultural suppositions, it
is hardly surprising that great emphasis was placed on education, for
(Roman) education and a knowledge of the Roman legal system were
the ticket to status. Augustine certainly followed in this track of upward
social mobility.

Augustine was born into a peasant gentry family in Thagaste, a
family that was typical in some regards and extraordinary in others.
His mother, Monica, was a fervent Christian, a strong, unforgettable,
character and apparently rather possessive mother. Patricius, his fa-

ther and a minor Roman official, was a pagan, at least for most of his life. Both parents appreciated their son's gifts and provided him with the best possible education. In undertaking the quest for this education, young Augustine also undertook a quest for meaning in life. Along the way, he also had some fun — imbibing in all the pleasures of a cosmopolitan metropolitan area and the lively sex life that has been known to accompany such experiences (*Confessions* II.a–II.III.8; III.I.1ff.).

CLASSICAL STUDIES AND MANICHEE PHASE

There were various phases to Augustine's pilgrimage to faith. In childhood, he came to know of the Christian faith from his mother, Monica. Another factor in Augustine's development of a worldview was his undertaking of classical studies in Carthage, a first step on the way to a career in law or government service. Included in this education was the study of the famous Roman lawyer-orator Cicero (106–43 B.C.). These assignments helped convince the young student that the study of oratory, which was so fascinating to him, could not be divorced from the quest for truth. The encounter with Cicero was not only a key element in Augustine's career choice to become a rhetorician (speech-maker); it also launched him on a lifelong pilgrimage to search for truth, a pilgrimage that next led him to Manicheism. Along the way, of course, it was not all study and zeal. After launching a successful career as a teacher of rhetoric in his native region, Augustine took a concubine to ease his considerable sexual appetite. With her, he conceived a son.

Manicheism was a third-century syncretistic Persian religion founded by the prophet Mani (ca. 216–76), who had drawn on both the Christian view of salvation (likely in its Gnostic manifestations) and Zoroastrianism, an earlier dualistic Persian religion. According to Manicheism, the human condition is in the midst of a struggle between darkness and light, and salvation is the separation of two mixed elements so that our spirit can return to the true light. There is essentially no free will, as release is a matter of the good remaining passive in the face of darkness. Such passivity extends to procreation, for any mingling of the spirit and the darkness of the flesh was deemed evil. In Augustine's Hellenistic environment, these teachings seemed eminently rational.

Augustine's attraction to Manicheism made sense. It provided him with a helpful set of concepts for dealing with evil (a lifelong preoccupation for this African Father). The Manichees' critical perspective on unsophisticated, nonphilosophical writings like the Bible was music to Augustine's ears.

NEOPLATONISM

After a period of about nine years, Manicheism began to lose its attraction for Augustine. It seemed unable to deal with some of his further questions, both intellectual ones and those pertaining to the apparent conflict between his own lust for the things of the world and Manichee teaching regarding the rejection of these things. About the same time, the young scholar of rhetoric decided to relocate to Rome and then to Milan, where he hoped to find better teaching conditions.

In Milan, Augustine came to study and endorse the teachings of Neoplatonism. He found its preoccupation with seeking to reach the ineffable One, the source of all Being, as a most compelling lifestyle model. Its rejection of dualism and its insistence that evil is the result of moving away from the One also represented a break with his earlier Manicheism. In addition, Augustine found this philosophy superior to his former commitments insofar as evil and the soul were not described in a materialistic way. The stage was set, it seems, for the prodigal to come home to the faith he had learned on his mother's lap.

AMBROSE, MONASTIC IMPULSES, CONVERSION

In Milan, the great bishop and rhetorician Ambrose came into Augustine's life. At first Augustine only went to hear him preach in order to observe his acclaimed rhetorical style. He was frequently accompanied by his mother, Monica, who had goaded him his whole life about becoming Christian. She was very much a domineering influence on Augustine throughout his life.

The most helpful thing about Ambrose for Augustine was his propensity to interpret the Old Testament "spiritually" and "figuratively" (*Confessions* V.XIV.24; VI.IV.6–VI.V.7), an assessment that has led many interpreters to conclude that Ambrose was employing an allegorical approach to Scripture and that it was this sort of approach that strongly attracted Augustine. There are some indications that this was in fact the way in which Augustine appropriated his preaching. However, this conclusion overlooks the fact that Ambrose was not systematic in his employment of allegory. In fact, many of his sermons on the Old Testament aimed at audiences of catechumens took seriously the literal sense of Scripture, unlike an allegorical method of interpretation, and then represented a text's literal claims as a narrative portraying men who have been truly dependent on God.[1] This manner of biblical interpretation, usually designated as a *figural* approach, takes seriously a text's

---

1. Ambrose *De Abraham libri duo* 1.

literal sense but reads it in light of the overall message of the biblical/
canonical witness as a whole. (The New Testament authors' use of the
Old Testament seems to embody this approach. The existence of the Hebrew patriarchs and the truth of the stories about them were not denied.
They were interpreted, though, in light of God's work in Christ.)

Regardless of the precise nature of Ambrose's contribution to Augustine, Ambrose blazed a trail that allowed the African rhetorician to now
appreciate Scripture's value. He no longer regarded it as merely crude
literature but saw it as a viable tool for expressing eternal truths. In
addition, Ambrose's employment of Greek philosophical suppositions
about the nature of God and the spiritual character of the soul also
helped make Christianity more credible to Augustine, as he was still
much indebted to the insights of Neoplatonism.[2]

With Augustine's intellectual difficulties with Christianity overcome,
only conversion awaited. Yet Augustine struggled with all sorts of hesi-
tations, presumably related to the pleasures of the world that he felt he
would have to deny himself were he to become a Christian. One can debate endlessly whether his sense of needing to deny many of these goods
was more a function of his understanding and appreciation of the biblical witness, monastic ideals, or Neoplatonic spirituality. In any case,
he reflected on the profound human truth, not characteristic of Greek
philosophical views, that to know that something is good for someone
does not necessarily entail that the person will want (or will) that good
(*Confessions* VII.V.7–VII.VIII.12).

By Augustine's own account, crucial to his conversion experience
when it finally came at age thirty-one was the reading of Scripture and
a recollection of how it had moved Anthony to take up monasticism.
Augustine had earlier been moved by a story of two high civil servants
who had been inspired to convert to the faith upon reading Athanasius's
Life of St. Anthony (*Confessions* VIII.XII.29–30). Again we observe
African monasticism's impact on the giants of the faith. Overcome with
joy, Augustine, already a catechumen, sought baptism (on Easter 387)
and resolved to dedicate his life to spiritual pursuits. (Note that even as
late as the turn of the fifth century baptism was still being postponed in
Christian families, presumably because the baptism of an infant would
foreclose the possibility of repentance for young Christians who might
fall from faith during a period of sowing their wild oats. As previously
noted, there was no clear consensus that sins committed after baptism
were forgivable.)

Probably inspired by what he knew of Anthony (but also consistent
with the ideals of Neoplatonism), Augustine resolved to leave Milan and

---

2. Ambrose *Hexameron* 6.7.40,42; cf. Augustine *Confessions* VII.XX.26.

his teaching position, return to North Africa, and with some friends take up a kind of quasi-monastic lifestyle of contemplative retirement. The ideal he had in mind was certainly not identical with that of early African monasticism, as he planned a life devoted to reading and scholarship. In preparation for it, Augustine abandoned his pending marriage to a young heiress and dismissed his latest concubine. Under pressure during his engagement to the heiress, he had earlier dismissed his long-time concubine. Nevertheless, life as he was now planning it was not to be. Called to Hippo, a prosperous port city on the Mediterranean (about 250 miles east of modern Algiers), Augustine was reluctantly ordained as a priest in 391. Four years later he was consecrated as a bishop. Augustine devoted the rest of his life to ministry and writing on pastoral situations. These writings have made him the most influential theologian in the West since Paul.

As Augustine lived a life of faith over the years, Neoplatonism became less and less an influence on him. (This is not to say that he ever deemed the gospel and Platonic philosophy as he knew it to be in contradiction. In fact, some analysts refer to an Augustinian synthesis of philosophy and theology and have argued that in Augustine the two disciplines found a synthesis, superior even to that of the Middle Ages, in which both could thrive without distortion.) At the very least, one finds in Augustine's later theological reflections a diminished need to employ the sort of allegorical modes of interpretation that characterized the Platonic tradition. He was increasingly content to take guidance from the biblical story. In fact, he even came to speak of the Bible as infallible (*City of God* XI.6) and to claim that understanding is given in faith, that rational inquiry (and so philosophy) does not lead to faith (*Lectures on the Gospel of St. John* XXIX.6). Augustine did not believe that private interpretation of Scripture could provide this understanding. "For my part," he declared, "I should not not believe the Gospel except as moved by the authority of the catholic Church" (*Against the Epistle of Manicheus Called Fundamental* 5).

AUGUSTINIAN THEOLOGY: ITS DISTINCT PHASES

Summarizing Augustine's theology is hazardous, for its richness and the sheer volume of the Augustinian corpus do not lend themselves to brief summaries. Another factor rendering any summary of his theology difficult relates to its profound impact on Western theology for so many centuries. Most Roman Catholic and Protestant theology has endeavored to invoke the Augustinian heritage as an ally. Consequently any interpretation of Augustine's theology quite typically says as much about the commentator's theology as it does about Augustine's.

Part of the reason that Augustine's theology lends itself to so many distinct appropriations and uses is because it is so rich, which is a result both of Augustine's profundity and of the fact that his theology was developed over time in dialogue with distinct challenges. In a sense, he said different things in different pastoral contexts in response to different challenges, accounting for why interpreters with different theological agendas have been able to find Augustine saying things compatible with their own agendas. In one of his writings, Augustine conceded as much when he noted that he did not affirm predestination but rather spoke of free will in one of his treatises (directed against the Manichees) precisely because in that case the issue to be addressed was, not God's grace, but the origin of evil (*Retractations* I.9).

At least four phases are evident in Augustine's writings, each generally occasioned by the problems, challenges, and heresies he encountered. Within his corpus are writings (1) against the Manichees, (2) against Donatism, (3) against Pelagianism, and (4) against the charge that Christianity had undermined the Roman Empire. It is not necessary in the analysis in this chapter to reiterate Augustine's profound trinitarian reflections (see chap. 7), most of which belong to a later period. In addition to the four phases or categories of his writings, there is a distinct category of treatises that are of a general, summary character of his thought, works like the *Confessions* and his *Enchiridion*. Points made in these writings consistently reappear again in each of the four phases considered, as even in these general works there were times when Augustine needed to clarify his position against some of the false teachings or problems that in other works occupied him exclusively.

Another way of describing the diversity of Augustine's work might be to refer to his "Catholic side" and his "Protestant side." He has been the premier theological inspiration for Roman Catholic theology from the Middle Ages until this day. Thus, one would expect to find in Augustine many theological affirmations that are typical of the Roman Catholic theological tradition. To some extent, Augustine was the seminal influence in the development and appropriation of these themes by the Western (Catholic) Church. On the other hand, Augustine's role as the seminal influence on the Protestant Reformers means that much of his theology is characteristic of Protestant theology (esp. of the Lutheran and Reformed-Presbyterian traditions). This so-called Protestant side of Augustinian theology, though by no means absent in his general works, is especially prevalent in his writing directed against Pelagius and to some extent is reflected in his responses to the charges that the establishment of Christianity had undermined the Roman Empire.

AGAINST THE MANICHEES

Augustine wrote a number of responses to Manicheism. In examining these writings, we will observe some of the themes that have been most typical of later Roman Catholicism. Manicheism, recall, held that in a sense everything is predetermined. Evil is a function of the creation of the devil, a condition about which humans can do nothing. Indeed, humans can only be saved by remaining passive in face of the darkness of the flesh. In response, Augustine held that we do have a free will. Evil, he claimed, is produced by the human will, for it is a negation of the good (*On Free Will* II.20). Salvation is thus a work of free will assisted by grace. Augustine's view of soteriology later became essential to the theology of the Middle Ages (III.19; *On Grace and Free Will* 32–33; *On Rebuke and Grace* I.a; cf. *On the Spirit and the Letter* 52,60).

In many ways, Augustine's affirmation represented a continuation of the prevailing strands for describing the salvation process observed among virtually all of the prominent theologians of the pre-Augustinian early Church. In these writings, then, the African Father offers nothing essentially new. In one later work, directed against the Pelagians (*On the Spirit and the Letter* 56–57), while seeking to exonerate God from responsibility for the damnation of some, Augustine refers to the love of God (grace) as a reality, not identical with God's own love, but a reality that makes the faithful lovable, a reality that has become a kind of infused reality (infused grace) in the believer. In this regard, Augustinian literature again functions as a harbinger of the characteristic theology of the Middle Ages.

Augustine did not repudiate all of the characteristic Manichean emphases. We will note this in connection with his affirmation of the doctrine of original sin in his dialogue with the Pelagian heresy. Even at this earlier stage of his career, Augustine remained willing to construe evil as a force that overwhelms human beings and to speak of the devil. Consequently he characteristically understood the work of Christ in a way compatible with or characteristic of the African monastic tradition, as a conquest (entrapment) of the devil (*On Free Will* X.31). To be sure, Augustine did complement this characteristic understanding of the atoning work of Christ (the doctrine of the atonement) with the language of "sacrifice" as a metaphor for describing Christ's atoning work (*On the Trinity* IV.13.17). In fact at times, invoking a theme embedded in the early liturgies of the Church, Augustine referred to the work of Christ as a sacrifice to allay the wrath of God.[3]

---

3. *Enchiridion* 33; cf. *Didache* 14; Cyprian of Carthage *Epistles* LXII/LXIII.16.

CHRISTIAN FAITH AND THE EMPIRE

Late in Augustine's life, Rome came under siege by the less "civilized" people of northern Europe. As previously noted, it was finally conquered and sacked by the Goths in A.D. 410. The Eternal City was obviously not "eternal." Critics asked with glee whether it was not all Christianity's fault, that is, whether its adoption by Roman emperors had not ultimately and irreparably weakened the empire.

In response to these dynamics and charges, Augustine wrote one of his greatest works, the *City of God*. In order to understand the history of the world, he argued, one must view it as a history of the intermingling and the interaction between communities of spiritual beings (humans and angels), two cities — the City of God, whose denizens have been gathered together by their common love of God, and the earthly city built on the principles of self-love and the passion for domination (XIV.28; III.14; I.Pref.). Only the City of God will endure forever, Augustine taught. The Roman Empire, like all governments, must be construed as a manifestation of the earthly city that cannot endure forever. That is why the fall of Rome cannot be Christianity's fault, he argued. It was all part of God's plan that nothing of the earthly city can last forever (I.Pref.,8; II.2; V.21; XV.4).

Augustine's description of the two cities has implications for church-state relations. The earthly city is characterized by self-love; indeed, that is the way secular governments function — on the principles of self-interest or self-love. According to James Madison, such is the basis of the American constitutional system of government. If self-interest is the name of the game in government, then the state is not the place for the love of God. One cannot legislate divine love. All that can be done is to make sure that the rules of the game in society are fair enough so that all citizens have an equal chance to pursue their own interests.[4] Government's role is necessary in this connection, Augustine insisted, in order to restrain the evil and self-seeking that have characterized the human condition since the Fall (*Letters* CLIII.6.16).

Augustine's recognition that the state cannot be expected to reflect the teachings and values of the gospel but at its best may be governed by rational (philosophical) principles like justice, which may entail that Christian rulers employ force in its interest (*City of God* XIX.6,1), is evident in several of the government public policy proposals supported by him. As is well known, Augustine supported (and may even have been the first to devise) the concept of a *just war*, that is, the idea that the Christian may participate in a war when it is not for mere purposes of territorial

---

4. Augustine *City of God* XIV.28; XVIII.2; XIX.5ff.; cf. *Federalist Papers* Nos. 10,51.

expansion but is fought by duly constituted authorities to fend off evil powers (XIX.7; IV.15).[5] Although Augustine did criticize the institution of slavery and deemed it a consequence of sin, he also was apparently willing to allow it to remain in place (*City of God* XIX.15–16).

In the sixteenth century, Martin Luther picked up these Augustinian conceptions of a distinction between the ways of the state (its mandate to pursue justice) and the ways of the gospel (Christian love). Readers need to reflect on whether this is a legitimate political realism for Christians to affirm, a forerunner of the American separation of church and state, which is ultimately in the best interests of both the pursuit of justice and the Church. Proponents of this Augustinian view challenge alternative models of church-state relations with the question of whether it is realistic to believe that a civil government can reflect or legislate Christian values. But does this doctrine of the two cities ultimately relegate the gospel to such political irrelevance that it silences the Church in the public realm, paving the way to the modern Western division of reality into sacred and secular realms? These are crucial questions for students of Christian theology to answer for themselves in the development of their own Christian social ethic.

It should be noted that a number of interpreters have understood Augustine's views of social ethics in a manner more compatible with the sixteenth-century Reformer John Calvin than with Luther. If diagrams were used to describe the differences, this model would view Augustine as positing a church-state relation with one circle representing the state inside a larger circle representing Christian values, as the principles of the gospel are ultimately to govern the state. The more Lutheran perspective on Augustine's views on the subject might represent itself with two circles that overlap but are not concentric, one representing the state

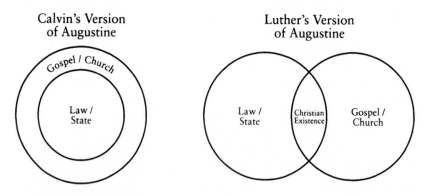

5. A similar affirmation was earlier espoused by Eusebius of Caesarea (*Life of Constantine* 4.56.3) and the Synod of Arles (Can. 3) in 314.

and the other the Church. The Christian lives in the territory where the two overlap, dwelling in both realms. The state is governed by principles of reason and justice (the natural law or the law of God), and the Church is the realm of the gospel. Since the spheres are distinct, the principles of the gospel are not to be imposed on the state.

Interpreters advocating the more Calvinist/Reformed model maintain that Augustine seemed to think that in an ideal state the precepts of the Christian religion (at least felicity and kingly glory) would be observed (*City of God* II.19). On some occasions, though not consistently, Augustine did claim that Christian princes should use their influence for the good of the Church (*Lectures on the Gospel of St. John* XI.14; cf. *Against the Letters of Petilianus* 2.97.224) when they use the state for the spread of Christianity (*City of God* V.24). These themes, most suggestive of Eastern Christianity, are more fully developed in the West in the Middle Ages.

There is clearly room in the thought of Augustine for affirming the goods of creation (like reason and natural science) and the hope that these goods may become beneficiaries of the conversion of man's love (*City of God* XV.4). In the same spirit of contending that Augustine may have subordinated the dynamics of the state to those of the gospel, one could note his remarks that the earthly city may be said to have been preserved for Christ's sake, that is, for the sake of the City of God (I.3,7).

All such affirmations are used by Calvinist/Reformed interpreters to contend that for Augustine church and state are not locked in paradox but that the gospel may indeed transform the state. Of course, most of these affirmations can be accounted for by the more Lutheran interpretation. To claim that the state is governed by principles of justice and reason is not to deny that its institutions and the virtues it espouses are good and subject to the Will of God. It is also uncertain how this more Calvinist/ Reformed, medieval interpretation of Augustine can account for those remarks by the African Father that distinguish a republic's legitimate public policy stands from principles of the gospel. What readers finally conclude, after their own study of the *City of God*, regarding Augustine's social ethics (views of the relationship between church and state) largely says as much about their own views on Christian social ethics as anything else.

DONATISM AND PELAGIANISM: DID AUGUSTINE AND THE CHURCH MAKE A MISTAKE?

Dealing with Augustine's polemic against Donatism and Pelagianism spawns two interesting questions. Were these heresies really so detrimental to the gospel? And would the Church have been much better off had it not followed Augustine's lead and instead endorsed Donatism and Pelagianism?

DONATISM

Donatism bears witness to one more instance when the Church was divided by the question of the lapsed and how to restore them, a problem that had emerged earlier in connection with the Novatian heresy. Donatism was a fourth-century North African movement occasioned by a violent persecution in the region instigated by Diocletian. In A.D. 313, some years after the persecution had ended, the election of two rival bishops in Carthage brought the controversy to a head. The rigorist party (those rejecting any accommodation of Christians who had lapsed during the persecution, even if they had only collaborated with the persecutors by turning over Bibles to the authorities) could not tolerate the regularly elected bishop, Caecilian. Allegedly he had turned over his Bibles to the authorities during the persecution or had been consecrated by a bishop who had done so.[6] Eventually the rigorists placed Donatus in the episcopacy, and that is the origin of the name of the movement.

The Donatists refused to recognize the ministry of any whom Caecilian ordained, and if any of the latter's party wished to join them, the rigorists insisted that they be baptized again. After all, these converts' original baptism, administered by one whose ministry was not valid, was itself invalid. The theological issue at stake in the controversy was whether sacraments or other pastoral acts performed by clergy who had lapsed are valid. What should the Church's policy be on this matter? If baptized or ordained by an unworthy pastor, is the ceremony valid in the eyes of the Lord and the Church? In a Constantinian era in which membership standards for the Church have declined, these are important questions.

There are other apparently attractive features to the Donatist cause. This African movement was originally a movement of the people, of the culturally disinherited. It clearly had some sociological roots. Most of the rigorists — the Donatists — belonged to the less Romanized classes of the earliest Christians in North Africa. As was typical of other regions in the Roman Empire, it was only when Constantine established Christianity that significant numbers of the Romanized upper classes in the regions surrounding Carthage joined the Church.

These dynamics were the cause of resentment among many of the longtime, rigorist members towards these "Johnny-come-lately" Chris-

---

6. Such Christians who had given up their Bibles under orders in the persecution came to be known in this region of Africa as *traditors*.

tians. Besides, many among these newcomers were perceived as less than wholeheartedly committed types. Also, the practice of the African churches had long included rebaptism if it was determined that the officiant of the rite was not a Catholic. Donatists could then claim their position had precedent over the new "Roman" rites. Soon after the election of Caecilian, the church of Rome came out against the Donatists, and this stance was ratified a year later when Emperor Constantine convened his First Synod of Arles. Undaunted, the Donatists continued to be a potent movement in the North African church, notably in the less Romanized regions of Numidia.

Just before Augustine's birth, some Donatists resorted to violence in hopes of gaining clout in the Roman Empire. Roman authorities responded with persecution, but the Donatist movement, which by now had certain nationalist connotations, was not snuffed out. It endured after the Vandals invaded the region putting an end to Roman rule; it survived the subsequent conquest of the region in the sixth century by the eastern part of the empire. The Donatist movement thrived until the seventh century, when the Moslem conquest of the region led to its total dissolution. It was very much a force with which to contend in Augustine's day.

AUGUSTINE'S RESPONSE TO DONATISM

Augustine's main response to Donatism was to insist on the validity of the rites of the Church even when the moral or spiritual virtue of the one administering them is suspect. If it were not so, Christians would ever live in doubt concerning the validity of baptism and of their salvation. The sacrament is holy because of what is given, because of whose sacrament it is. This is why, according to Augustine, baptism (or other ecclesiastical rites) need not be readministered because of the perverseness of the minister (*On Baptism* IV.16,18).[7] In essence, Augustine prioritized the Church and the sacraments, deeming them more important than the Church's leaders. In fact, the Church's perfection and holiness seem for him to have been a function of the grace it dispersed in its sacraments. In that sense, he conceived of the Church's holiness as objective, as not being a function of the holiness of its members, for sinners, he conceded, were to be found in the Church (*Against the Epistle of Parmenianus* III.iv.25; *City of God* XVIII.49). The Church is

---

7. Essentially this was a reaffirmation of the First Synod of Arles, which had been convened by Constantine in 314 to deal with Donatism. Political preoccupation with unity in the Roman Empire motivated Constantine's concern at this time no less than when such preoccupations motivated his convening of the later Council of Nicea.

more than its members; in fact, it bears its members, functioning as the Mother of all Christians (*Sermons* 191.2–3).

At the heart of Augustine's efforts to refute the Donatists is his commitment to the priority of God's work over human works in saving us. This is most consistent with his overall theological profile, especially as it came to be emphasized in his confrontation with Pelagianism. At stake in these commitments is not only a testimony to the glory of God and to our total dependence on God, which is such that we can only find rest in him. In that sense, these commitments unambiguously affirm the heritage of the Nicene Creed, that God alone, not we ourselves, is the Savior. However, Augustine's response is also a word of assurance that we can be sure of our salvation, for it is not contingent on our own piety or the piety of our pastors. The Word of God, an objective word manifest in the Church and the sacraments, provides this assurance. Given this emphasis on objectivity, it is not surprising to find it reflected in Augustine's complete view of the sacraments. He taught that we are regenerated in baptism (*On Original Sin* XLIV) and insisted that Christ is present in the elements, much as certain miracles were performed by angels (*On the Trinity* III.10.21). Christ is present even to unbelievers, as Judas Iscariot truly received him (*On Baptism* V.8–9). At other points, Augustine did modify his affirmations of Christ's presence in the sacrament, referring to the elements as "signs" (*figura*; see *Expositions on the Book of Psalms* III:1; *Lectures on the Gospel of St. John* XXVII.1).

Augustine's response to Donatism raises a number of important questions for contemporary readers facing modern forms of this heresy. One needs seriously to consider whether the Church and Augustine made a mistake in condemning Donatism. It is arguable that the Church's concern with purity and the faith commitments of its leaders is precisely what the Church needs in our own permissive society. Could it not also be argued that the main reason Donatism was condemned was because the upper-class Romanized elements of the Church could not bear this African "people's movement"?

On the other side, Augustine's theology offers a word of comfort for those who might be uncertain about whether they or their pastors are pure enough. It also offers a stirring testimony to God's grace. However, in order to have that, in order truly to refute Donatism, must one not endorse Augustine's emphasis on the primacy and objectivity of grace, on the real presence of Christ in the sacraments? If not, what alternative theological constructions would succeed in refuting Donatism? In a society in which authority is increasingly being called into question, in which some Christians have been known to leave churches over pastors they did not deem sufficiently "pious," Donatism is still a very contemporary heresy.

PELAGIANISM

Pelagianism is rooted in the thought of Pelagius (ca. 360–ca. 420), a monk from Britain (perhaps Ireland). Note the area from which he hailed. The spread of Christianity to the northern — considered to be backwater — regions of the Roman Empire was a comparatively late development. It had transpired through empire policies after Constantine and also through trading contacts, as in the case of England, which never formally became part of the empire. Here is yet another reminder that the origins of Christianity are to be found, not in northern Europe, but farther to the south, to other continents, meaning that Christianity is not an essentially "Western" religion. In any case, Pelagius was famous for his piety and austerity. Moral effort was, it seems, just what was needed in the Church in his view. The years he spent in Rome convinced him of that as he observed churches that bore little evidence of Christian conduct.

Pelagius's response to this pastoral context was to teach and preach a rigid moralism. Christian life was to be viewed as an effort to overcome our sins and attain salvation. We have complete freedom to sin or not to sin, he insisted. If not Pelagius himself, followers of his such as Coelestius rejected the doctrine of original sin, that is, the idea that Adam's sin damaged and corrupted the human race.[8] Yet Pelagius insisted that God's glory is not compromised by such beliefs. After all, God has given the possibility of free will and of doing good, and he ever assists us with his grace. At least two other related affirmations of Coelestius, and possibly Pelagius, should be noted: Pelagianism taught that children do not sin until they decide to sin; in addition, the law as much as the gospel leads to eternal life.

The Pelagian debate with Augustine was touched off by the African Father's prayer in his *Confessions* (X.XXIX.40): "Give what Thou commandest and command what thou wilt." Pelagius rejected the idea that God commands the impossible (*Letter to Demetriaden* 16), as Augustine seemed to imply. The two contemporaries would be locked in a heated debate for many years to come.

Initially Pelagius and his followers had support in the Church. This view was endorsed in 415 by synods in Palestine. But by 417/18, the Council of Carthage had condemned Pelagian views and mandated the practice of infant baptism, which by the fifth century was already universal practice, not even challenged by Pelagius. Various popes, notably Innocent I (d. 417), opposed Pelagius, but he did have the support of one, Zosimus (d. 418), who eventually retracted this advocacy of Pelagius and came to support the African bishop's position. Another official

---

8. Augustine *On Free Will*.

Church action against Pelagianism came in 431 at the Council of Ephesus, where it was condemned along with the Nestorian heresy (as a kind of payment of church-political debts by Cyril of Alexandria's anti-Nestorian supporters as a way of thanking the anti-Pelagian pope for support). These condemnations did not put an end to the struggle. The debate continued with no obvious or clear-cut resolution.

Among those having problems with Augustine's views was the Gallican (perhaps Italian) monk Vincent of Lérins (d. ca. 450; *Notebooks*). Vincent was clearly a man with a great sense of the value of Church history. The involvement of a thinker of his caliber on behalf of the Pelagian cause provides another indication, besides the communication problems in the period of disseminating information about official Church condemnation of false teachings, of why the Pelagian controversy was not readily put to rest. In this context, one can better understand the rationale behind the convening of the Synod of Arles in 473 for the purpose of trying to avoid extremes on both sides. The synod took a kind of Semi-Pelagian position, holding that we still have freedom but that our efforts must be united with God's grace. The Synod of Orange in 529 finally settled the matter with a condemnation of the core commitments of Pelagianism and Semi-Pelagianism. It endorsed Augustine's position on free will, affirming that one cannot think or do good apart from the Holy Spirit. The synod only broke with Augustine by not endorsing *double predestination* (the belief that God elects some to salvation and has eternally chosen to damn others). The decision of Orange has proven to be a most historic one. The most radical dimensions of Augustine's thought concerning grace were compromised and effectively lost to the Church for the next centuries. It was this tamed-down version of Augustine that Western Christians brought with them into the Middle Ages. Certainly, the claim that after grace has been received the believer may cooperate with grace and then have the power to perform all things necessary for salvation set the stage for medieval theology.

In taking a definitive stand on the relation of grace and free will, the Western church distinguishes itself further from Eastern churches. As such, the Pelagian controversy and its treatment may be said to represent a further cause of East-West differences. The aftermath of the Pelagian controversy explains why so much of the free-will rhetoric as well as the demands and strictures observed in the early Church (esp. by Jewish Christian theologians) sounds so legalistic and seems to connote works righteousness to our post-Augustinian ears. Or is such a reaction merely the consequence of Western Christian "hang-ups"?

Precisely what is wrong with Pelagianism? When consistently taught and practiced, it could make Christians begin to take their faith more seriously. Besides, we have observed rhetoric resembling the Pelagian emphasis on the responsibility of believers for their own salvation in the writings of earlier Church Fathers. Most of them seem not to have robbed God of the glory for saving them with such rhetoric because they presupposed the idea of salvation as deification, for, as previously noted, deification entails belief that in Christ the divine energies have permeated human reality, thus blotting out any distinction between God's act and human act. Consequently on these grounds, to claim that our obedience to the law leads to salvation is itself to describe a work of God, and Pelagius himself seems to affirm this (*For Free Will*). Could the real problem of Western Christianity with Pelagianism be a function of its (and Augustine's) failure to endorse the Eastern Christian concept of salvation as deification (or failure to appreciate how it was implied in Pelagius's actual writings)?

AUGUSTINE'S RESPONSE TO PELAGIANISM

The core of Augustine's response to Pelagius was his affirmation of the prevenience of grace. Grace precedes human action, making us will the good (*Epistles* ccxvii.30). Grace is irresistible. Once given, the faithful cannot but persevere, Augustine argued (*On Rebuke and Grace* XII.34,38).

These tenets were clearly related in Augustine's own mind to the hopelessness of the human condition in sin that he had experienced (*Confessions* I.V.5ff.). Free will leads only to sin (*On the Spirit and the Letter* 5). Consequently Augustine was one of the first formulators of the doctrine of original sin (*To Simplician* 9ff.; *Retractations* I.xiii.5), though earlier theologians had introduced the idea of an inclination to do evil from Adam's Fall.[9] This controversial doctrine became crucial in the debate with Pelagianism, becoming official teaching for the Western church, as per the Synod of Orange. Augustine's exposition as well as his spiritual autobiography represent a powerful testimony to (apology for) the truth of this doctrine (Rom. 7:14–23). Or is the doctrine just a product of an unfortunate, unnecessary (Pelagian) controversy, indeed a vestige of Augustine's Manicheism and its pessimistic determinism? In Augustine's view, one cannot become righteous simply by knowing the law and doing it (*Letter to Hilarius* clvii.5). The bishop makes this point by appealing to the Pauline distinction between the spirit and the letter, which does not merely refer to a distinction between the Bible's literal sense and its allegorical/spiritual sense. It also refers, he argued, to the idea that the law kills by revealing sin, while only with the Spirit

---

9. Tertullian *A Treatise on the Soul* XLI.

(with grace) can good be done and life be given (*On the Spirit and the Letter* 6). All the law (God's commandments) does is reveal sin (*On Rebuke and Grace* I.2). Rather than providing guidance for doing good, its only effect on this side of the Fall is to increase sin. The law makes us sin more because it is more attractive to do what is forbidden (*Confessions* II.IV.9; *To Simplician* 11). This is the sense for Augustine in which sin is concupiscence — a blind lust to satisfy oneself, which even for baptized Christians pollutes the deeds we do that are externally good (*On Marriage and Concupiscence* I.24–25). Sin, according to the bishop, affects even our good deeds. Is it not true that we find satisfaction in the good deeds that we do? Ultimately do we not do them in order to satisfy our own desires for gratification? As such, they are soiled by sin.

In order to explain how original sin is necessarily communicated to each generation, Augustine endorsed a notion, earlier affirmed by Cyprian of Carthage (*Epistles* LXIII/LXIV.5), that sin is transmitted through procreation (*On Rebuke and Grace* XIII.42). This belief had fateful consequences for the Middle Ages and the premodern Western Christian devaluation of the beauty of sexuality. This problem aside, it is tempting to challenge Augustine's contention that we can never be freed from the lusts that make us so miserable in sin. On the other hand, if we could be freed from such a curse on this side of the end times, would we need grace as much, would we so easily be able to steer clear of the Pelagian robbery of God's glory?

In Augustine's view, given how thoroughly saturated human nature is with sin, we cannot reach God on our own; sin gets in the way. The only way to receive God is through faith, which is itself a gift (*Confessions* I.I.1; *Enchiridion* 31). At this point the baptism of infants is such a powerful witness of Augustine's view. Nowhere else is it clearer that grace is prior to our willing than in the case of the baptized infant who brings no merit of his or her own yet is accepted by God (*On Grace and Free Will* XXII.44). Is Augustine correct in claiming that salvation by grace and infant baptism necessarily go together? From these commitments an affirmation of predestination is a necessary consequence — an election to grace which, for Augustine, quite logically entailed a rejection of others (*On the Gift of Perseverance* 35; *Enchiridion* 98).

Such an affirmation of double predestination inevitably led Augustine to address the concern of the faithful regarding whether they are among the elect. His response is that the elect of God persevere (*On Rebuke and Grace* VII.13). Is this sufficient comfort for those who struggle with questions of whether they are elect or not? For those who concur with the African Father's affirmations that we are in sin and that salvation is the result of God's prevenient grace, does not one logically have to go Augustine's route on predestination? Of course, the Church never officially affirmed this. (Recall the rejection of double predestination by the Synod of Orange.)

Some readers may experience a certain discomfort with these Augustinian commitments to the priority of grace. Augustine may have felt this as well. Consequently he never totally rejected the concepts of freedom and free will (*Letter to Hilarius* CLVII.5,8,10). How he integrated the affirmation of free will with grace is the subject of much debate. Both Catholics (as well as some Baptists and Methodists) on one side and Lutherans and Calvinists on the other continue to claim him, which is simply to observe that the presence of both the so-called Catholic and Protestant sides of Augustine's thought appear even in his anti-Pelagian writings. Themes most suggestive of the theological perspective of the sixteenth-century Reformers have been previously noted. The Catholic side of his thought (themes picked up in the Middle Ages by its most eminent theologian, Thomas Aquinas) demands immediate further attention.

Besides his express affirmation of free will, Augustine insisted on its capability of doing good works "if it receive divine assistance." Free will "is not therefore removed because it is assisted" (*Letter to Hilarius* CLVII.5,8,10). With comments most suggestive of Thomas Aquinas and other medieval Scholastic theologians, Augustine claimed that God helps us avoid evil and that the desire for the help of grace is the beginning of grace (*On Rebuke and Grace* I.2). Choices are our own; things would not happen if we had not chosen it (*City of God* V.10). The human will is divinely aided towards doing righteousness (*On the Spirit and the Letter* 5). These beliefs even affected Augustine's view of predestination, for in his great work the *City of God* (V.10), he referred to God's omnipotence as based on his foreknowledge.

Despite his strong doctrine of sin, Augustine insisted that human beings will virtues, yet God both prepares and aids the will (*Enchiridion* 9). Thomas Aquinas described how we are justified and saved in precisely this way (*Summa Theologica* I/2ae, Q.117, Arts.2–8). Augustine even anticipated medieval notions of accumulated merits as a cause of justification (*Letter to Sixtus* cxciv). It is important to note that at this point Augustine (and later Aquinas) did not opt for Semi-Pelagianism. Unlike proponents of this heresy, they never construed the act of the will as independent of grace. Grace, they insisted, must be given before the will is exercised. Characteristically Roman Catholic themes surfaced in Augustine's thought in other ways. They are evident in his treatment of the sacrament of the Lord's Supper, as he identified it as a sacrifice (*City of God* X.20).

On the other hand, more expressly Protestant-like themes can be identified in Augustine's treatment of freedom and grace. In some of his works, he claimed that we are free in the sense that sin no longer attracts the faithful (*City of God* X.30). Elsewhere he asserted that we are not really free until God gives grace (*Letter to Hilarius* CLVII.8). Typical of his overall anti-Pelagianism, he insisted that we only have freedom through grace (*On Rebuke and Grace* VIII.17). God's mercy goes before the unwilling human being to make him willing, so that "the whole work belongs to God" (*Enchiridion* 32).

It is possible to interpret the whole of the Augustinian corpus in accord with the Protestant model by interpreting his references to the work of grace on the will and free will as descriptions of the believer's conformity to Christ, a concept that maintains in justification the believer is brought into a relationship with Christ, not unlike what happens in a good marriage (1 Cor. 6:16b–17). Marriage partners truly become one, sharing all that they have in common. The sharing becomes so intense that sometimes the good qualities of one of the partners begin to reflect in the lifestyle of the other. This does not transpire by imitation.[10] In this model for describing the Christian life, good works are construed as happening spontaneously as the righteousness of Christ rubs off on the believer.

Augustine seems to come very close to explicitly endorsing this concept of the conformity to Christ in the *Confessions* (VIII.29) in his claim that when he put on Christ, the relationship infused his heart with light. Similarities between such an image and the Eastern notion of salvation as deification are apparent. In each case, something of God dwells in the faithful. Are the concepts of the conformity to Christ and deification ultimately compatible? Or is this particular Augustinian image more like the idea of grace as an element/substance cooperating with the will, as developed in medieval Scholasticism? These reflections in turn raise the question of whether there are any real distinctions between this medieval conception and the idea of justification as conformity to Christ.

Another point Augustine made in his polemic against Pelagianism that would have great impact on the Church during the Reformation was his treatment of the Pauline phrase "righteousness of God" (esp. Rom. 3:21). The African Father claimed that it refers to an external righteousness given to the believer. The righteousness of the believer is not our own but God's (*On the Spirit and the Letter* 15). Realize, however, that these commitments of Augustine, his *sola gratia* perspective, emerged from his existential sense of dependence on God, not merely from his polemics with Pelagius (*Confessions* XI.II.2.4; *Enchiridion* 2).

---

10. "Conformity to Christ" is radically different from the concept of the "imitation of Christ," which presents Christ as an example that the believer is self-consciously to emulate, not as a beloved mate whose attractiveness lures the faithful to new behavioral patterns.

AVOIDING HERESY:
IS THE AUGUSTINIAN SYNTHESIS
THE CHURCH'S ONLY HOPE?

The Pelagian heresy has taken many subtle forms that the Church has needed to address. In order to avoid this heresy, Christians do well to keep informed by insights of the 417 Council of Carthage, which first condemned Pelagianism (*Canons on Sin and Grace* 4): Grace is said to avail not only for remission of sins but is also involved in assisting the prevention of sins, that is, in living the Christian life. Much Pelagianism emanates from pulpits precisely because preachers forget this warning. They are willing to give credit to God for saving us but are not willing to give God credit for our practice of the Christian life.

To the degree that Pelagianism is a perennial problem in the Church, as human beings are always prone to want to take credit for what they have (allegedly) done to please God and to assert their freedom, the Augustinian response and the formative role that this theology played in the Church's rejection of Pelagianism pose a crucial question for all students of theology and church history. In the final analysis, is endorsing unequivocally the whole of Augustine's theology (notably its radical affirmation of the primacy of God's grace) the only way for the Church to purge all Pelagian (and Donatist) propensities? (Of course, perhaps the Church was mistaken in condemning them.) Are these heresies still around because the Church catholic has not unequivocally endorsed these particular dimensions of Augustine's theology? (Recall that the Synod of Orange did not endorse his affirmation of predestination.) In a sense, the remainder of this text and its companion volume can be read as providing data for framing a response to these questions. The next chapter, which examines other catholic/orthodox theological alternatives that were in the air in Augustine's lifetime, offers a first occasion to reflect on these questions. Augustine's contemporaries were apparently not as radical as he was in affirming the primacy of God's grace.

CHAPTER 10

THE GREAT CONTEMPORARIES OF AUGUSTINE

Augustine and his great contemporaries represent an important turning point in the history of the Church. For all the rich theological variety they embody (many of the recurring classical theological alternatives are rooted in their collective thought), they exhibit a remarkable similarity. We have already observed the impact monasticism, notably Athanasius's *Life of St. Anthony*, had at least indirectly on Augustine. Monasticism likewise had a significant impact on his contemporaries Ambrose, John Chrysostom, Jerome, and the Cappadocians.

The theological diversity among these contemporaries is significant for the present structural configurations of the universal Church. This diversity suggests the next stages in the gradual formation of distinct Eastern and Western theological profiles in the early Church, a diversity that would sow the seeds for the eventual schism of Eastern and Western Christianity. It is well to begin this analysis with one of the most profound influences on Eastern Christendom, the Cappadocians.

THE CAPPADOCIANS

The Cappadocians were four eminent fourth-century theologians (who were also friends and/or relatives) from Cappadocia, a region in present-day Turkey. Born within a few years of the Council of Nicea and the formal articulation of the Trinity doctrine, they became, along with Athanasius, the principal intellectual spokespersons for the concept. Intellectual heirs to the theology of the Alexandrian school and its use of Greek philosophy for articulating the faith, they were all heavily influenced by monasticism. In fact, some scholars have suggested that one could interpret the whole of their theologies as a rationalization for monasticism.

Precisely who were these three great men and one woman?[1] Three of

---

1. That a woman is numbered among these eminent teachers of the Church is in one sense surprising, given the increasing patriarchalism we have observed in the post-

the four were siblings: Basil the Great (ca. 330–79), who eventually became bishop of Caesarea; Gregory of Nyssa (ca. 330–ca. 395), who was the more scholarly, reflective, and mystical of the brothers; and Macrina (ca. 327–79), the older sister of these eminent bishops who was acknowledged at least by Gregory as his teacher (*On the Soul and the Resurrection*). The fourth Cappadocian was a friend of Basil's from their student days, Gregory of Nazianzus (329–89), a great orator and poet whose hymns have become classics in Greek-speaking segments of Christianity.

The family of the siblings had been Christian for at least two generations. The paternal grandparents and their father had "walked the walk," having spent seven years in hiding during the persecution of Decius. This father of Macrina, Basil, and Gregory became a famous lawyer and teacher of rhetoric; he married the daughter of a Christian martyr. The Christian roots of Gregory of Nazianzus are no less impressive. He was the son of the bishop of Nazianzus, also named Gregory.[2]

A number of common theological themes appear in the thought of the Cappadocians. All of them, save Macrina, wrote on the Trinity and were instrumental in the Church's eventual endorsement of the Nicene formula. Several of their other theological commitments are compatible with the themes of self-denial and Christian responsibility that were characteristic of the early monastic traditions. As is typical of Eastern theology, they conceptualized the process of salvation in terms of deification. Consequently, they did not embody the radical *sola gratia* (predestination) emphases of Augustine. All agreed that we must in some form make a contribution to our salvation.

Because the Trinity doctrine is at the heart of Cappadocian theology, and the struggle with Arianism heavily occupied much of their literary endeavor, it needs to be noted that the brief summaries below of the theological tenets of the Cappadocians are incomplete. They need to be understood as mere elaborations of the trinitarian reflections of these theologians previously outlined in chapter 7.

BASIL THE GREAT

Basil, who became bishop of Caesarea, was a monk who was later recruited in the struggle against the Arians. Throughout his career, he sought a middle ground between Sabellianism and Arianism, realizing that neither Aristotelian metaphysics (tending to make the oneness of

---

Constantinian church. On the other hand, it is not so surprising in view of the impact of monasticism on them. Monasticism's egalitarian propensities with regard to women, a dynamic that can be observed throughout much of Christian history, is again evident.

2. Note that in the fourth century bishops were still allowed to be married (1 Tim. 3:2).

God an abstraction) nor Stoic thought (tending to divide the Godhead) could be of much help to the Nicene cause.

As noted, Basil was raised in a Christian family in Cappadocia. In Caesarea he received the best education someone from the region could obtain, in preparation for a career in oratory like his father. He also studied in Athens, where he became friendly with a fellow student, Gregory, who would eventually become bishop of Nazianzus. In addition, Basil befriended a young man named Julian, who would eventually become emperor (Julian the Apostate).

Returning to Caesarea after completing his education, Basil took a position teaching rhetoric. His older sister perceived him as having become unduly vain and too preoccupied with secular knowledge. Basil first ignored Macrina's observations as the meanderings of an unlearned woman, but several subsequent family tragedies led Basil and the rest of the family to look to her for spiritual leadership. She advocated complete withdrawal from their lives of luxury to retreat to a more rural site where the family might live lives of renunciation and contemplation in service of God. In essence, she proposed a monastic lifestyle much like that of the African *ammas* and *abbas*.

Macrina not only succeeded in establishing a monastic community in nearby Annesi; she also persuaded her brother Basil, his friend Gregory of Nazianzus, and eventually her younger brother Gregory of Nyssa to take up such a lifestyle. Since Basil eventually became the leading theological apologist for such a lifestyle on the Asian continent, and most legislation in the Greek Orthodox Church regarding monastic life is based on his writings, one may trace the roots of monasticism in the Eastern (Greek-speaking) Church to a woman — his sister Macrina. (In this regard, we see another testimony to the way in which monasticism has functioned as an institution of the Church providing important leadership opportunities for women.) Basil's visit to Egypt soon after deciding to assume the monastic vocation points again to early African Christianity's impact on the universal Church.

It was Basil's intention, not unlike Augustine's, to devote the remainder of his life to a kind of monastic discipline, but after only six years of practicing this lifestyle, he was ordained a presbyter against his will. Not long after, he was thrust into the Arian controversy, eventually being recruited by the bishop of Caesarea as an ally against the Arianism of the emperor Valens. In Caesarea, Basil's heroic preaching of self-denial against the hoarding of goods that was transpiring during a famine (he himself sold most of his property for the sake of the poor) earned him so much stature that he was a virtual shoo-in for election as the next bishop upon the death of the present officeholder who was defending the Nicene position (*Homily Delivered in Times of Famine and Drought*

VIII,7). The election proved to be a test of strength between the Nicene and Arian factions. Basil was popular and politically shrewd, which meant that he was able to maintain his leadership and keep his diocese faithful to the Nicene cause in a period when few pro-Nicene bishops were able to fend off the emperor's pro-Arian advocacy. Without doubt, Basil's staying power in his diocese and his extensive writing on behalf of the Nicene cause played a most significant role in the final victory of the trinitarian formulation.

Besides his provocative and seminal treatment of the Trinity, including his affirmation of Tertullian's formula of God as three *hypostases* and one *ousia* and of the divinity of the Holy Spirit, his liturgical contributions (to this day one of the Eastern Orthodox liturgies bears his name), and his heavily influential articulation of monastic rules, there is not much that is atypical of early Eastern theology in Basil's thought. With regard to how we are saved, Basil claimed that works help discharge original sin (*Homily Delivered in Times of Famine and Drought* VIII.7). In his view, the Spirit does not abide in those whose wills are unstable and might easily reject the gift received (*On the Spirit* XXVI.61).

On the other hand, Basil also insisted that the creature is a slave, that it is the Spirit who sets free (*Letter to the Eupaterius and His Daughter* CLIX). In fact, the Spirit is said to pour out on the whole of humankind, rendering them spiritual in communion as a sunbeam renders transparent bodies bright (*On the Holy Spirit* IX.22). Although Basil does not explicitly affirm the concept of deification at this point, this image certainly suggests it. As such, we can interpret Basil's affirmations of the role of human works in the salvation process as we have considered other Eastern theologians, as remarks that convey the cooperation of God in every human work of the redeemed.

Other noteworthy theological tenets of Basil include his claim that the nature of the created order gives indications of God's existence (*Homilies on Psalms* 32, 3), an affirmation most suggestive of the cosmological argument for the existence of God. His views on the sacraments are revealing, especially when he explicitly invokes African Christian precedents for his advocacy of the practice of self-Communion in one's own home (*Letter to the Patrician Lady Caesaria* XCIII). Basil also advocated the practice of private confession to a priest (*Rules Briefly Treated* 288). An additional sacramentological commitment by Basil included his rejection of the idea of an indelible priesthood. It is not the case, according to him, that once one is ordained, he is always ordained, particularly when a priest joins a heretical group or engages in fornication (*Letter to Amphilochius* CLXXXVIII.1,3). Not surprisingly, the bishop of Caesarea was critical of divorce, except in the case of fornication. He lamented that in actual practice more strictness was expected of women in this matter (CLXXXVIII.9). He is also one of the first postbiblical writers to reject abortion (CLXXXVIII.2,8).

MACRINA

We have already reviewed Macrina's life and her influence on her brother Basil in awakening a sense of Christian vocation and monasticism in him and their brother Gregory of Nyssa. She had not originally intended to practice the monastic life, for she was betrothed to a young relative who planned to become a lawyer. When he died prior to their marriage, she used the family estate to establish a kind of monastic community. Her renowned learnedness and the influence she had on both Basil and Gregory of Nyssa have also already been observed.

What we know of Macrina's theology largely comes from a conversation she had with her brother Gregory of Nyssa, which he recorded in the treatise *On the Soul and the Resurrection*. She attempted to comfort him on the death of their brother Basil. Among her most noteworthy theological observations was one especially consistent with Basil's views: an insistence that the cosmos/universe declares God. (Again we observe the seeds of a cosmological argument for the existence of God.) She also taught the eternity of the soul. Her monastic commitments surfaced in the next move she made, following up on this affirmation. When divested of emotion and desire, she argued, the soul gets its divine form, becoming perfectly godlike. Obviously the concept of deification seems implied in these remarks.

Macrina's vision of the end is suggestive of her way of describing what salvation is like (soteriology). In this regard, she parallels her younger brother Nyssa, whose eschatology implied his soteriology. (This is hardly surprising in view of his role as author of the report of her views. Did he put such words in her mouth, or was she truly his teacher?) The concept of deification as developed later by Nyssa seems to entail that the whole of humanity is redeemed by virtue of God's incarnation in human nature (*Address on Religious Instruction* 26). Likewise, Macrina is cited as asserting that those departing evil are united with God, so that God will be *all in all*.

GREGORY OF NAZIANZUS

The son of a bishop (another reminder that clerical celibacy was not yet a universal catholic phenomenon), Gregory was a good friend of Basil's from the time of their student days. Soon after his schooling ended, Gregory became a monk, largely under the influence of Basil and his sister. Becoming a priest against his will, he fled for a time to Basil's monastic community, only to return to his pastoral duties with a sense of having been compelled by God. Subsequently Basil pressured him to assume the episcopacy of a small hamlet near Caesarea (a position in which he never actually served). Though the appointment did place a strain on their friendship, Gregory took up his friend's crusade against Arianism, shortly after the Caesarean's death, and did so with great impact in Constantinople, which at the time was firmly in the hands of Arian Christianity. When Emperor Theodosius I, a defender of Nicene orthodoxy, assumed the throne in A.D. 379 and the next year cast out Arians from Constantinople, it was not long before Gregory was proclaimed bishop of the city. Consequently Gregory was responsible for chairing the First Council of Constantinople, which met the following year and finally ratified for the Church the decisions of Nicea, placing the creed in final form as we have it today. Though to a great extent African in origin, the Nicene Creed is in large measure the result of the work of the Cappadocian Fathers.

With regard to Gregory's theology, the Trinity doctrine played a central role in his thought and piety (readers are thus referred to his views on the subject articulated in chap. 7). His basic methodological convictions are clearly manifest in his trinitarian reflections. His Stoic philosophical propensities are reflected in his contention that humans are only able to obtain knowledge by sense experience (*Second Theological Oration* 12). Given these suppositions, he operated with a distinction between God as he is and as he appears in his operations. Consequently, Gregory dealt with the Trinity more as an attempt to try to determine our experience of how God relates to himself, rather than as an unequivocal description of God as he is in himself (*Third Theological Oration* 16,9–13).

With regard to his view of salvation, much that Nazianzus said of creation and Christ relates to his affirmation of the concept of deification. He claimed that humans have a godlike and divine portion, our mind and reason (the image of God), which will ascend to God, its archetype, who will mingle with it (*Second Theological Oration* 28,17). Echoes of the concept of deification and its claim that the believer will become like God are clearly audible in these comments. Also suggestive of deification and its model of salvation as the collaborative work of God and the believer (albeit all God's work insofar as the divine energies have permeated human being) is Nazianzus's claim that God gives all good, even our choice of good things (*On the Words of the Gospel in Matthew 19:1*, XXXVII.XIII).

The concept of deification is only intelligible if Christ totally bore our human nature and yet was divine. Only in this way could the divine energies be at work in human nature to render it godlike. The concept of

Christ's having two natures, then, has been presupposed in most of the
theologians of the East thus far considered, but Gregory was one of the
first to state it explicitly (*On the Words of the Gospel in Matthew 19:1*
XXXVII.II). Part of the reason for making this explicit affirmation was
Gregory's finding himself in contention with a new heresy advocated by
Apollinarius (ca. 310–ca. 390), who advocated the deity of Christ to
such an extreme that he claimed that Christ had a human body but not
a human soul (see chap. 11 for details).

The situation, as Gregory saw it, demanded the unequivocal affirmation of Christ's full humanity. With this concern in view, as Athanasius
had done and as later advocates of the Alexandrian school of Christology would do, he referred to Mary as the Mother of God (*Letter to
Gregory of Cledonius the Priest, against Apollinaris* 101). Regarding the
work of Christ (the doctrine of the *atonement*), Gregory drew upon an
image characteristic of the monastic tradition and other early Fathers,
claiming that the blood of Christ was paid to the devil, which is the
so-called classic view of the atonement (38).

Nazianzus seems to have been the first Christian theologian to explicitly use the term "deification" (*theōsis*) to describe what happens in the
process of salvation (*Theological Orations* 30.21; 28.17). He was very
concerned about care for the poor, in keeping with the monastic ideal
(14.5). Such social concern fits well with his overall scheme of salvation, for he deemed *theōsis* as a prize for virtue (2.17). Of course, in a
manner typical of Eastern affirmations of salvation as deification, Gregory insisted that salvation involved both grace and free will (37.13,20;
40.34). To be sure, though, for Nazianzus, as for the Eastern tradition
as a whole, even the choice of the good is given by God:

> ...even to choose what is right is divine and a gift of the mercy of
> God.... However well you may run, however well you may wres-
> tle, you still need Him Who gives the crown. (*On the Words of the
> Gospel in Matthew 19:1* XXXVII.XIII)

Among his other theological commitments was Gregory's advocacy of
infant baptism (*Oration on Holy Baptism* 40.17,28). We have already
observed his concern for the poor and sick. Also noteworthy is his criticism, like that of his friend Basil, of laws that condemned only female
adultery, since God demands equality (*On the Words of the Gospel in
Matthew 19:1* XXXVII.VI).

GREGORY OF NYSSA

Gregory was the younger brother of Basil and Macrina. Primarily educated by his brother, he seems only to have become a monk after

an apparently happy marriage ended with the death of his beloved spouse. Theologically, he was more contemplative and mystical than his brother, and he was not the dynamic preacher that their friend Nazianzus was. Forced by Basil to assume the episcopacy of Nyssa, he, like the other Cappadocians, was thrust into the Arian controversy on behalf of Nicene orthodoxy. In his first confrontation with the Arians, he fled into hiding. Even prior to this action, he does not appear to have been a very good administrator. However, after the death of Basil, Gregory became one of the Nicene party's premier spokespersons and a theological advisor to Emperor Theodosius, all of which no doubt helps account for his renown. In addition to his obvious influence on the catholic tradition in general through his impact on the Church's appropriation of the Trinity doctrine and on Eastern Orthodoxy, Gregory seems to have had a direct impact on a significant segment of Western Christianity. A number of scholars suggest that he exhibited profound, albeit indirect, influence on John Wesley and the Methodist heritage as mediated through Macarius the Egyptian.

The full picture of Nyssa's theology, as with the other Cappadocian Fathers, emerges only if what follows is augmented by his reflections on the Trinity noted in chapter 7. Two interesting ontological commitments presupposed in his reflections should be noted. He claimed that there is an identity of motion and stability (*Life of Moses II* 243–44), an observation he used to account for how growth in grace is possible when we are firmly rooted in the divine goodness. Like Nazianzus, he was also concerned with God's actions/operations, not with what God is in himself (*Answer to Ablabius*).

Nyssa was probably the most influenced of all the Cappadocians by Greek philosophy, somewhat in the tradition of Origen, who also influenced Basil and Gregory of Nazianzus. The Alexandrian Apologist's impact is evident in Nyssa's use of an allegorical method of biblical interpretation (*Address on Religious Instruction* 2).

Although Gregory could refer to the divine inspiration of Scripture (in the sense that if its words that function as a kind of "bodily veil" were removed, Christ and the Spirit would be present), as is typical of the theology of the early Church, he found the tradition of the apostles to be authoritative in refuting heretics (*Against Eunomius* VII.1). Interestingly enough, he construes this tradition of the Fathers as proceeding by "succession" from the apostles (IV.6).

In his view of creation and human nature, Nyssa took a creative position (compatible with modern philosophical and scientific observations) combining the Stoic idea that the human mind belongs to the body with the Platonic notion that the soul images God (*On the Making of Man* Vff.). The influence of Origen with regard to speculative propensities seems to surface in his contention that God created all in innocence, but not in perfect righteousness. He construed the Fall as a mere event on the way to salvation, one that has predisposed us to sin (XXII–XXIII; *Sermons on the Beatitudes* 6). Infants die because God knew by virtue of his foreknowledge the evil they would do (*On the Untimely Deaths of Infants*).

Given Nyssa's vision of the rationale for creation — that is, to initiate a process culminating in salvation — it is hardly surprising to find Nyssa assert that the world is improving as a result of the Incarnation (*Address on Religious Instruction* 18). This belief is most suggestive of the concept of deification, which maintains that by virtue of God's becoming man in Christ, we are becoming more like God. In fact, the youngest Cappadocian did affirm the idea that God united himself with our nature in order that it might become divine (25,32,37).

Gregory appears to have affirmed the salvation of all, teaching that God wills all would be saved and that, therefore, damnation is one's own fault (*Against Apollinaris* 29). Elsewhere he refers to the restoration of the whole of creation, including the devil (*Address on Religious Instruction* 26). These views are related to the Greek philosophical supposition of an analogy between human nature and a single organism. Consequently the resurrection of one part of human nature, as happened in Christ, is communicated to the whole (32). Given the universalist thrust of his thought, it is not surprising that Nyssa expressly rejected slavery and expressed a concern for the poor (*Homilies on Ecclesiastes* 4; *Love for the Poor*).

The nature and work of Christ are crucial to the Cappadocian's vision of universal salvation through the deification of human nature. Regarding the nature of Christ, Nyssa followed the predispositions of Nazianzus, referring to Christ's divine nature and his perishable nature, and then proceeded to claim that in the Incarnation the qualities applicable to each nature "no longer seem to be in either Nature by way of division" (*Against Eunomius* V.5). This is in a nutshell the *communicatio idiomatum*, the idea that whatever is properly attributed to one of Christ's natures can be rightly attributed to the other. With regard to the work of Christ, Nyssa follows his Cappadocian and monastic colleagues by viewing the atoning work of Christ as a trick played on the devil (*Address on Religious Instruction* 21–24).

Nyssa's belief in the salvation of all did not lead him to abandon the concern with Christian responsibility (the role of the believer's works), which characterizes the concept of salvation as deification. Faith without works does not save, he claimed (*Homilies on Ecclesiastes* 8). In this connection, he also taught the possibility of Christian perfection (a concept that had great impact on John Wesley), as perfection is said to be the ultimate outcome of deification (becoming like God) and the process of growth in grace (*On Perfection*).

In several of Nyssa's comments, he affirms something like the later Roman Catholic doctrine of transubstantiation; he speaks of the bread being made over into the body of Christ (*Address on Religious Instruction* 37; *Sermon on the Day of Lights*). Comments that suggest similar affirmations of Christ's real presence in the sacrament are evident in the writings of Basil (*Letter to the Patrician Lady Caesaria* 93). In the writings of the Cappadocians, one can readily identify the core sacramental conceptions of the Eastern Orthodox Church.

AMBROSE

Likely born in A.D. 339, to non-Christian parents, Ambrose rose to significant political office in his native Italy. In 370 he became governor of an Italian region that included the city of Milan. Three years later the bishop of Milan, who was an Arian (Arians did not vanish in the generation following the Council of Nicea), died. Much controversy emerged between the orthodox and the Arians regarding who should become the new bishop. Ambrose attended the election to try to keep peace. Though already popular, his interventions made him even more impressive, and in the heat of the deadlock he was elected bishop. This was a rather strange occurrence given his vocational background and the fact that he was not yet even baptized. He was merely a catechumen at the time. He wished to decline but accepted the new position after it became clear the emperor welcomed his election.

Ambrose became one of the great theologians of the Western church of his day and was also the author of a number of hymns as well as the developer of the use of chanting in liturgical worship. Trained in the best rhetorical style of the day, he attracted many auditors. One whom he swept off his feet was a young faith-questing, philosophically oriented African named Augustine, who was subsequently baptized by the bishop. Ambrose became known as a defender of Nicene orthodoxy against the Arians, who always distrusted him. This courageous defender also clashed with the Empress Justina, standing up to her acts of repression against proponents of Nicene Orthodoxy (*Sermon against Auxentius 35*).

Regarding his trinitarian views, Ambrose wrote an influential work, *On the Holy Spirit*, which was a strong voice in the Nicene era advocating the divinity of the Holy Spirit (3.112; 1.8; 3.90–91). At some points in the work, he advocated the Spirit's procession from *both* the Father and the Son (2.134; 1.120). Given Ambrose's Western, Latin background, this affirmation would become crucial in the development of the Western church's insistence that the Spirit proceeds from the Son as well as from the Father. To some extent, the forging of a distinct Western theological identity was at stake in the development of this affirmation, as it became a crucial point in the West's eventual parting of the ways with Eastern Christianity.

Methodologically Ambrose prioritized faith over reason (*De libri duo Abraham* 1.3.2). Other significant aspects of his theology pertain to his soteriology. Much like Augustine, whom he influenced, Ambrose contended that all are born in sin, having been conceived in iniquity (*Explanation of David the Prophet* 1.11.56). Typical of other pre-Augustinian Church Fathers, he placed a strong emphasis on the contribution that the works of believers might make to their salvation. In the spirit of other Western theologians, such as Tertullian, Ambrose resorted to legal metaphors and spoke of the possibility of accumulating *merits* that could be to one's credit on the day of judgment (*Letter to Constantius* 2.16). This concept of merits and their accumulation would become central in the subsequent development of Scholastic theology in the Western church in the Middle Ages. To be sure, as did the best in medieval Scholastic theology, he insisted that grace is not bestowed as a reward for merit (*Exhortation to Virginity* 43) and that salvation involves the cooperation of human effort and grace, with the human work prepared for first by God (*Exposition of the Gospel of Luke* 2.84; 1.10). On the other hand, though, Ambrose seems to make the gift of grace (predestination) contingent on God's foreknowledge of who would merit it (*On the Faith* 5.6.83).

Additional aspects of Ambrose's thought most suggestive of the theology of the Middle Ages were his contention that the Eucharist is a sacrifice (*On the Sacraments* 5.25), that in the sacrament the elements are transformed into the flesh and blood of Christ (*On the Faith* 4.10.124), and his advice that the sinner not just confess sins but enumerate them (*Commentaries on Twelve of David's Psalms* 37.57). Of course, one also finds in his thought precedents for themes characteristic of the Reformation. He affirmed the concept of the priesthood of all believers; that is, all Christians have been made priests in their baptisms (4.1). Already in this period of the early Church, side by side strong affirmations of clerical authority, is this "lower" universal-priesthood view of ministry. It seems necessary to affirm the two views of ministry in order to embrace the catholic/orthodox heritage in all its fullness. In that connection, we have observed similar diversity on virtually all the other doctrinal themes (e.g., in soteriology we have identified the Protestant side of Augustine's thought and the emphasis on works by the Apostolic Fathers, and in theological method we have identified the legitimacy of both the correlationist and orthodox approaches).

There are strong indications that Ambrose had a fairly evenhanded attitude toward the equality of men and women, at least their equality in the eyes of God (*Epistles* 63). Another significant contribution to Christian social ethics was his endorsement (like Augustine's) of the idea of just wars, for example, when the empire is fighting in self-defense or on behalf of the weak (*On the Duties of the Clergy* I.27,129,176). Also like Augustine he apparently appealed to natural law (accessible to all through reason), not to distinct Christian teachings, as his criterion for making social ethical judgments about the common good (III.4.25). Also in a manner consistent with Augustine, Ambrose claimed that the Church has a certain independence from the state (*Epistles* 20.8,19).

For all his accomplishments, Ambrose made another contribution to the Christian tradition that is not so sterling. In a sense, he was responsible for making Christian anti-Semitism official public policy. Christians in a small town in the empire had burned a Jewish synagogue. The emperor at the time, Theodosius I, decided that perpetrators of the crime should be punished and that the state should rebuild the synagogue. Ambrose insisted that the Christian emperor should not force fellow Christians to undertake such a Jewish religious work (*Epistles* 40.14). After several stormy sessions, Ambrose got his way. This episode set the stage for the idea that Christian empires might not need to protect by law the rights of their non-Christian citizens.[3] There certainly is a long history of anti-Semitism and disregard for the rights of non-Christians in the life of Church, but is it a good tradition?

Ambrose had still other confrontations with Theodosius. The emperor ordered the massacre of several thousand subjects who dwelt in a city where a Roman commandant had been murdered. The fact that the emperor heeded Ambrose's rebuke illustrates the prophetic character of the Church that was developing in the West.

JOHN CHRYSOSTOM

John, known as "Chrysostom" (the golden-mouthed), was the late-fourth-century bishop of Constantinople. Recognized as the greatest interpreter of the Bible of his time, he did not typically employ allegorical methods of interpreting the Bible, preferring instead literal interpretation. In this regard, he broke with the Alexandrian school of theology, which characteristically employed allegory. In fact, Chrysos-

---

3. Anti-Semitism is clearly reflected in the actions of a younger contemporary of Ambrose, Cyril of Alexandria (d. 444), who by expelling Jews from Alexandria allegedly in retaliation for a Jewish assault became the first Christian leader to practice systematic persecution of the Jews.

tom, along with his friend Theodore of Mopsuestia (d. 428), was one of the first proponents of what would become known as the Antiochene school of theology, which on this and other theological issues became the prime alternative to the Alexandrian school in the early Church (see chap. 11 for the differences between these schools and their proponents in detail). Chrysostom was a native of Antioch and had much of his early education in that city.

Readers are encouraged to sort out for themselves which approach to biblical interpretation (the literal or the allegorical approach) they find most amenable, for example, whether they interpret the Bible's "historical" accounts like Jesus' miracles or the Hebrew exodus literally or prefer to seek some "deeper," spiritual meaning in these texts. In a sense, this question is identical to the issue raised in chapter 3 regarding whether one is more in the tradition of the orthodox approach of Tertullian or the correlationist approach of Justin Martyr and most other Apologists.[4] In developing one's own theological approach, students of theology need to come to terms with these questions.

Chrysostom was a gifted public speaker, a remarkable preacher regularly applauded by congregations when he spoke. This is why he was called "golden-mouthed." Like most of the figures considered in this chapter, he was heavily influenced by monasticism; after beginning a career in law, he practiced the monastic vocation. After several years in monastic withdrawal, John was ordained in Antioch, and his fame as a preacher began to spread. This renown led the Eastern emperor to notice him, and when the episcopacy in Constantinople became vacant in 397, he ordered John's appointment.

Chrysostom was quite a reformer and sought to clean up the financial scandals and moral irregularities of the church in Constantinople. In so doing, he stepped on many toes. He was indeed a prophet of social justice (*Homilies* 2.4). The powerful could not abide such critique. One was Emperor Eutropius, who felt he deserved special favors since he had been influential in John's appointment. Exile seemed in the offing, but John had the support of the masses. Yet on two occasions he surrendered, fearing that a riot would lead to suffering for the people.

An interesting contrast can be drawn at this point between Chrysostom's interactions with the Eastern Empire's authorities and those of Ambrose in his confrontations with the emperor in the West. Recall how Ambrose stood up to the emperor. From then on a pattern was set: What happened to Ambrose began to typify the practice of the Western church. It became progressively more influential in relation to society. In

---

4. The correlationists relied on allegorical methods of interpretation, whereas the orthodox approach characteristically relied more on literal methods of interpretation.

the East, where Chrysostom worked and where emperors would reign another thousand years, the Eastern church was often relegated to the status of a vassal of the state. To this day, this heritage of Eastern Christianity is manifest in a typically passive obedience of church to state not always characteristic of the Church in the West.

The emerging differences between Eastern and Western Christianity were becoming more and more self-evident. It was apparent in the development of different liturgies in these regions: in the East's tendency to talk about salvation as deification, which was not the case in the West; and in the West's more influential, even prophetic, stance in relation to the state, which is not typical of the East. The parting of the ways between Eastern and Western Christianity five centuries later was already beginning.

Regarding Chrysostom's theology, his literalist tendencies led him to a certain skepticism about the ability of philosophy to ascertain truth (*Homilies on I Corinthians* X.3). Another interesting methodological commitment of his, especially in light of the diversity we have observed in the tradition of the church, is his claim that the Church must trod the "middle path" among heresies (*On the Priesthood* IV.4). Though not insensitive to the insidious character of human nature (III.16), he seems to have rejected any idea of original sin (*Homilies on Romans* X) and, as did most of the great Eastern theologians, affirmed free will (*Instructions to Catechumens* II.3). This ambiguity in turn appears in his view of the relationship between grace and works in determining our salvation. He insists that faith and works are necessary conditions of salvation, that faith without right living will not save (*Homilies on the Gospel of John* XXXI.1). In fact, in one context he insisted that God only calls willing minds (*Homilies on I Corinthians* II.9). We must first do the good, and then God does his part (*Homilies on the Epistle to the Hebrews* XII.5). In these remarks, Chrysostom takes positions clearly compatible with Pelagianism and with late medieval nominalism (see chap. 14).

Chrysostom's links to nominalism can be made more validly than in the case of other Eastern theologians we have considered who also insisted on a necessary role for works in the process of salvation. Most of these Eastern theologians, recall, construed the salvation process in light of the concept of deification, which entails that all human works are permeated with the divine energies and so are also works of God. Chrysostom, however, in a fashion more typical of the theologians of the West, does not seem to have embraced the concept of deification. As such, he may share with post-Augustinian Western Christendom a bifurcation of human work and divine work *(Homilies on I Corinthians* II.3). In that case, his remarks about the human contribution in influencing

God in the giving of grace are intended as descriptions of *autonomous* human activity.

Other remarks by Chrysostom pertaining to divine-human cooperation in the salvation process are more compatible with Augustine's so-called Catholic side and with the mainstream of medieval Scholastic theology. He claims that divine grace (or providence) is at the beginning of every good act (*Concerning the Statues* VIII.5). Only those amply supplied with assistance can come to Christ (*Homilies on the Gospel of John* XLVI.1). The specter of Pelagianism is swept away by these remarks, as it is clear that even the human work contributing to the believer's salvation is inspired by grace. In fact, Chrysostom went so far as to argue that the good works that Christians do spontaneously follow from grace, rather like the sun not being able to cease shining (*Homilies on Acts* XX.4).

These and other commitments even suggest later Protestant appropriations of Augustine. Chrysostom went so far as to claim that we are saved by grace and faith, not by works. Like Augustine and the sixteenth-century Reformers he even claimed that God declares his righteousness by making us righteous (*Homilies on the Epistle to the Romans* VII.24, 27–28).

Chrysostom had a very high view of the office of ministry. The distinction between priest and laity is said to be as great as the one between rational man and irrational creatures (*On the Priesthood* II.2). He was, however, a realist about the fickleness of laypeople with regard to their veneration of their pastors. Laypeople, he noted, will try to bring down their religious leaders over trifles and tend to flit from one leader to another (V.1–8). Chrysostom's response was to call priests to realism and hold them to high accountability (III.10ff.).

Regarding his view of baptism, Chrysostom apparently construed it as the rite in which regeneration (being born again) actually happens (*Instructions to Catechumens* I.3). He did claim that as a result, when one who has been baptized falls away, it is impossible for such a one to be restored (I.2). In so doing, he expressed the sort of commonplace views of this period, which explains why so many Christian families did not baptize their infant children.

Chrysostom's view of the Lord's Supper presupposes the medieval notion of the sacrament as a sacrifice (*On the Priesthood* III.4). He refers to the believers' being translated to Christ's presence in heaven. This affirmation anticipates the understanding of Christ's presence in the sacrament that, as mediated through John Calvin, has come to be highly influential in much of Protestantism.

Despite his avoidance of confrontation with Eutropius, Chrysostom insisted that the rule of the Church demands more fidelity than the emperor (*Concerning the Statues* III.4; *Homilies on II Corinthians* XV.3). Though claiming that riches are not a sin, he insisted that, insofar as the common sharing of goods is more suited to our nature (*Homilies on I Timothy* 4), failing to distribute such wealth among the poor was a sin (*Homilies on I Corinthians* XIII.8). In fact, Chrysostom advocated a redistribution of wealth (*Homilies on the Gospel of Matthew* XLVI.3).

On some other social issues Chrysostom was not so egalitarian. The great preacher defended Paul's views on slavery, claiming that the Christian slave is already free (*Homilies on I Corinthians* XIX.5–6). His views of women tended to reinforce the patriarchalism of Roman society, and he expressly rejected the ordination of women (*Of the Priesthood* II.2; III.9; *Homilies on I Corinthians* XXVI.2,4–6).

JEROME

Jerome (Eusebius Hieronymus) may have been the greatest biblical scholar of early Christianity. A native of the region of Dalmatia (near present-day Bosnia, though perhaps in northern Italy), he is most famous for preparing a translation of the Bible into Latin, the Vulgate, which became the standard version of the Bible for scholarly use in European Christianity during the Middle Ages. Jerome himself was also influenced by monasticism and practiced its discipline throughout most of his career.

Jerome was an ardent admirer of classical learning. He gained knowledge of Hebrew, largely to sublimate the rampant sexual desire with which he grappled much of his life. As his fame as a scholar of many languages spread, Jerome journeyed to Constantinople and became friendly with the Cappadocians. Through his studies he also became an admirer of Origen. In the next phase of his life, he went to Rome and became a diocesan scholar. He attracted a number of wealthy admirers, especially women. Two of them, Paula (347–404) and her daughter Eustochium (370–ca. 419), formed an ascetic circle with Jerome and followed him the rest of his life, ostensibly practicing with him the monastic vocation.

A proud and often cantankerous man (no plaster saint), often preoccupying himself with criticisms of the local clergy (*Letter to Marcella* XXVII.1), Jerome began to lose favor in Rome. As a consequence, he and his women followers left for the Holy Land, where Jerome devoted himself to scholarly work, especially translations. He founded monasteries in the region: one for women under Paula, one for men under his leadership.

Earlier translations of the Bible in Latin had appeared, having been based on the Septuagint. What was special about the Vulgate, no doubt

accounting in part for its astounding impact, was that Jerome worked
with the original languages. In this connection it is interesting to note
his skepticism about the canonical authority of a number of the books of
the Apocrypha (*Preface to the Three Solomonic Books*). Protestantism's
eventual rejection of the canonical status of these books has ancient
precedent. Jerome's translation work was not just limited to the Bible.
He also translated into Latin the works of Origen and Eusebius of
Caesarea.

Controversy followed the great scholar's work insofar as his appeal to
original texts seemed to bypass the authority of the Septuagint, which
made it appear to many that Jerome lacked respect for the inspired
Word of God (as the Septuagint was widely believed in this period to
have been itself the work of divine inspiration). Young Augustine raised
such concerns (*Letters to Jerome* XXVIII.2). In the end, though, Jerome
became critical of Pelagius and relied on Augustine's insights to support
his critique.

Jerome's theological treatment of soteriology was by no means as unambiguously anti-Pelagian as was Augustine's. His main concern with
Pelagius, the concern of all anti-Pelagians, was that the heretic's emphasis on human autonomy failed to give God sufficient glory (*Letter
to Ageruchia* 133.7). Generally speaking, though, Jerome did not have
a strong doctrine of providence, believing that much happened in the
world in which God did not intervene (*Commentaries on Habakkuk*
1.1.14). Not surprising, therefore, is his teaching that whoever would
be faithful must first live a life of purity (*Commentaries on the Epistle to the Galatians* 2.3.11). Jerome believed that we have the power to
avoid sin and that no one is saved without having willed it (*Against the
Pelagians* III.12; *Commentaries on the Epistle to the Ephesians* 1.1.11).
We make the beginning, and God brings it to completion (*Against the
Pelagians* III.1). These commitments that, contrary to Jerome's intentions, sound so Pelagian were balanced by his claim elsewhere that
although we have a free will, it is God who brings our works to perfection (*Against Jovinianus* II.3). In fact, in a comment most reminiscent of
the so-called Catholic side of Augustine and Chrysostom's anti-Pelagian
remarks, Jerome claimed that we cannot repent unless God first gives us
his mercy or grace (*Letter to Demetrias* CXXX.12).

Standing in a tradition that would become more fully developed in
the Middle Ages, Jerome distinguished between mortal sins, which are
worthy of damnation, and venial sins, which do not deprive the soul
of grace (*Against Jovinianus* II.30). He also presupposed, as Augustine did (*Sermons* 87.6), the existence of different levels of blessedness
in heaven (*Against Jovinianus* II.32). Also in harmony with the later
medieval tradition, though commonly affirmed by many of his predeces-

sors, he believed that all human beings had at least an intuitive natural knowledge of God (*Treatise on Psalm 95*).

Jerome was a proponent of apostolic succession, a universally accepted supposition by this time in the Church (*Letter to Heliodorus* XIV.8). He advocated a kind of collegiality among the bishops, arguing that the strength of the Church depends equally on all the apostles (*Against Jovinianus* I.26). He went so far as to maintain that the office of presbyter and of bishop are identical (*Letter to Evangelus* CXLVI.1). He was also an advocate of the intercession of the deceased saints (*Against Vigilantius* 6.15).

Despite his commitment to the monastic life (*Homilies on the Psalms* 41.9), Jerome did not believe that the possession of private property was to be rejected by all Christians (*Letter to Demetrias* CXXX). Also in keeping with the monastic ideal, as well as perhaps the special bond he had with women, Jerome insisted that men had no more special privileges before God than women did (*Letter to Oceanus* LXXVII.3).

WHAT ARE THE BEST THEOLOGICAL OPTIONS OF THE AUGUSTINIAN ERA? DOES CHURCH HISTORY HAVE A NORMATIVE ROLE?

A good way to begin evaluating the theologians considered in this chapter (Basil, Gregory of Nazianzus, Gregory of Nyssa, Macrina, Ambrose, John Chrysostom, and Jerome) is to ask whether they have been faithful to the monastic heritage that influenced them. They do seem more in line with the theologies of their predecessors, more so than Augustine was (particularly the anti-Pelagian Protestant side of his thought). In that sense are these contemporaries of Augustine not more in touch with the catholic/orthodox heritage? In the differences between Augustine and his contemporaries, another indication of the Eastern church and the Western church going their separate ways is apparent. In view of this observation, do any of the theological perspectives analyzed in this chapter represent an option preferable to Augustine's? It could at least be argued that the majesty of the cosmic vision of salvation sketched by Gregory of Nyssa and the other Cappadocians is ultimately giving an even more powerful witness to the primacy of grace than Augustine.

A final point regarding the contemporaries of Augustine is relevant for any study of church history. In the previous chapter, Vincent of Lérins was introduced. Although a Semi-Pelagian, he offered insightful reflections on the value of the study of church history. According to

Vincent, the depth of Scripture is such that its statements are readily interpreted differently. Given these hermeneutical realities, and in order to have a way of avoiding false teachings, it is necessary to lay down a rule of interpretation in accord with the Catholic Church. He proposed that the Church hold "that which has been believed everywhere, always, and by all" (*Commonitorium* II). The study of church history is necessary in order for the Church to have access to this interpretive guide.

Vincent next addressed the question of what theologians are to do when ancient teachings are heretical. In this case, he contended, decrees of councils have the most authority in determining what is truly catholic. Where no conciliar decree on the subject has been made, then catholicity can be determined by comparing opinions of the Church Fathers (*Commonitorium* III[4]). Vincent's observations serve as a warning for Church leaders. If the Bible is as rich as he claims, can church history be denied a normative role in the doing of contemporary Christian theology and ministry?

CHAPTER 11

CHRISTOLOGICAL CONTROVERSIES, A DIVIDED CHRISTENDOM, AND A NEW ORDER

As we come to the end of the period of the early Church and begin entering the Middle Ages (from the fifth through the eleventh centuries), two very important controversies emerged: one pertaining to Christology and the events leading to the Council of Chalcedon and the other concerning the final separation of Eastern and Western Christianity. (The centuries now considered were also a period of profound and successful evangelism work.) We have observed that the East and West had been going their separate theological ways for some time concerning the development of distinct liturgies, the authority of the pope, church-state relationships, and how salvation should be construed — whether or not to portray it as deification. Augustine and his insistence on the primacy of grace against Pelagius contributed to the East-West Schism because in the East the issue was never posed so sharply. That is, what Western Christianity regarded as works righteousness or Pelagianism was never seen as problematic by Eastern Christians. God's work and the work of believers was never so sharply dichotomized in that region.

THE NEW ORDER

First, one must recognize that a new day in human history dawned late in Augustine's lifetime. The fall of Rome to the Goths in A.D. 410 created a dynamic that made possible further expansion of Germanic (barbarian) kingdoms into regions of the old empire. (The eastern half of the Roman Empire had formally separated from the western half, never to be reunited, in 395.) The pressure exerted by the Goths opened opportunities for another Germanic group, the Vandals, to take Carthage in 439. They became virtual masters of North Africa and then occupied Sicily. The next step was obvious. In 455 they sacked Rome. Twenty-one years later the Western Empire was destroyed forever.

The end of this epoch also marked the beginning of a new era in western Europe and in the East and in Africa. For centuries the empire had provided some cohesion among diverse peoples, holding back Germanic invaders. Now these barbarians were free to move about and plunder at will. An imperial church inaugurated by Constantine (one supported by an international empire) would survive another thousand years as long as the eastern part of the old empire, the Byzantine Empire, survived. However, the days of political unity and relative peace in the West were gone. As the new period dawned, only the Church was left to provide order and justice, functioning as guardian of what was left of ancient civilization.

The conquest of Rome served the Church in several ways. Many of the invading barbarians were potential converts. Eventually significant numbers of these people came to accept the Christian faith. It was the beginning of the saturation of the whole of Europe with Christianity. Others like the Vandals and Goths had been converted to the Arian version of Christianity during Constantine's reign. Their invasions functioned to bring Arianism back into the foreground in the West, but eventually the Nicene orthodoxy of those conquered prevailed through quiet persuasion.

IMPLICATIONS FOR THE LIFE OF THE CHURCH

With the empire no longer existing to provide stability, the Church in western Europe suffered in some ways. Under powerful kings, notably in the kingdom of the Franks (present-day France), church leaders deferred to rulers, who made appointments to episcopacies, and bishops increasingly became nothing more than politicians. Eastern Christianity, notably in North Africa, was particularly hard hit by the new circumstances, especially by the Vandal invaders who had conquered Rome. Their rule in the region was disastrous for the Church. Vandals were Arians, who effectively divided the Church in the region. Divided between Arian and pro-Nicene Catholic camps, as well as the remaining presence of some Donatists and by a Greek Orthodox faction that resulted from a sixth-century invasion of the region by the Eastern (Byzantine) Empire, the African church was an easier prey for Moslems when they invaded in the seventh century. North African Christianity in territories that had been part of the Roman Empire was severely decimated as a result.

After the invasion, North African Christians experienced social and political pressure to accept Islam. Were there, however, theological reasons why Christians in this region, many of whom were Arian, could so readily accept Islam? Perhaps the militant monotheism of Islam and its relegation of Jesus to the status of prophet may not have been really so foreign to the Arian Christian insistence that the oneness of God could not be compromised by Christ. The legalistic spiritual rigor demanded of faithful Moslems may also have resonated with the remaining Donatist Christians in the region, for whom such rigor was characteristic of their own spiritual life. Another factor in the decline of the Church in Africa was the emigration of pro-Nicene Catholics of the region to areas in southern Europe, where Catholics dominated. Perhaps because the Church in Egypt and Ethiopia was already accustomed to going its own way without dependence on the Roman Empire, these church bodies survived the conquest, though as a result they would henceforth be isolated from the rest of the Christian world, and the Egyptian Copts would endure centuries of sociopolitical restrictions and even at times outright persecution at the hands of their Arab conquerors.

The Moslem invasion included the conquest of other centers of early Christianity, including the Holy Land. From this time on until the fifteenth century, even Constantinople and the Eastern Empire would be under pressure from Moslem Arabs and Turks. Never again would Christianity in these regions exercise the influence it did in the first five centuries of the Christian Era. No longer would the growth zone for Christianity be along the Mediterranean. It was truly becoming a religion of the West. The sons and daughters of many of the first Christians in these regions are now and have been Islamic for centuries.

Back in the West, Christianity, which already had a foothold in the region of present-day Spain as a result of the Goths' domination of the region, gained influence in the territory of present-day France when the ruler of the Frankish tribes in that region, Clovis (466–511), converted to Christianity in A.D. 496, following his marriage to the princess of another Christianized tribe in the region, the Burgundians.[1] Although other Frankish tribes dominated the territories of the present-day Netherlands and Belgium, Christianity was not established in these regions until the eighth century.

One other opportunity for growth in western Europe was the Church's outreach to the British Isles. Great Britain had never been entirely under Roman control, but a segment of its Celtic citizens had been Christianized and remained so after the fall of the Roman Empire (recall that Pelagius had come from the British Isles). It was largely under siege by pagan tribes such as the Angles and the Saxons. Likewise

---

1. It is interesting to note a common pattern in the growth of the Church in Europe as well as in Africa, one that also conforms to the pattern of evangelizing the Roman Empire as a whole. The key to effective promulgation of the gospel on a regional basis has been the conversion of the ruler of the region in question. This is a pattern that, as we shall observe, has continued well into the twentieth century in many parts of the globe.

Ireland, which was never part of the empire, had been exposed to some evangelization efforts. Although the fifth-century missionary work in Ireland of Patrick (ca. 390–ca. 460) is usually credited as the primary means of the Christianization of the Emerald Isle, it was probably only one of several channels of evangelization.[2]

The son of a British clergyman, Patrick was kidnapped by Irish raiders, who took him to their home and enslaved him (*Confession* 1,16). After escaping captivity and returning home, Patrick had several visions (such visions were still construed as authoritative by many Christians in all regions during this period) calling him to return to Ireland to take up the missionary task (23–25).

With regard to Patrick's theology, it is common to take him at his word as being unlearned and to conclude that there is little insightful or original about the theological reflections of his authentic writings (*Confession* 1; *Letter to Coroticus* 1). This is true insofar as he was a man of the Church seeking simply to proclaim the Word. Patrick's starting point for all theology was the rule of faith, placing him in the tradition of Tertullian. This rule, which is enunciated in part in Patrick's authentic writings, is trinitarian in character. The similarities between Patrick's version of the rule and much of the Nicene creedal formulation are striking (*Confession* 4,14), which suggests that though the precise wording of the creed may not yet have been disseminated in Patrick's lifetime, there was a remarkable consensus about the Trinity and the incorrectness of Arianism throughout the Roman Empire.

Much debate concerns whether Patrick was influenced by monasticism. He clearly seems to have been an admirer and supporter of such a vocation (*Confession* 41–42). As did the monastic tradition, Patrick portrayed the Christian life as a struggle with Satan (20). He also expressed a strong sense of sin and unworthiness, combining this with a vigorous proclamation of the unmerited grace of God (*Confession* 1,15). He claimed that all that he ever accomplished was really God's work (62) and referred to a loving, forgiving God (46).[3] In the same vein, Patrick claimed to be bound in the Spirit (*Letter to Coroticus* 10). When we cut through all of the myths about Patrick's life, we find that his theology is quite profound, more deserving of attention than it has customarily received.

---

2. There are some ancient references to a Palladius serving as a bishop in Ireland in the fifth century in Ireland. See Prosper of Aquitaine *Chronicle*.

3. These affirmations are most suggestive of Augustinian themes. It is interesting to speculate whether Patrick's theological convictions could have self-consciously been shaped by a concern to distance himself and his church from the views of Pelagius, a fellow British Celt.

A STRENGTHENED PAPACY: GREGORY THE GREAT

Another most significant development in the Western church in this period was the further strengthening of the papacy. Previous developments had increased the authority of the bishop of Rome. In the period we now study, the Roman bishop came to be called "pope," as the barbarian invasions effectively strengthened the authority of this office. With the Eastern Empire too far removed to be of much help to the Catholic population, the papacy and the Church effectively became their guardian, the focal point for unity in beating back the invasions, as well as the guardian of what was left of the riches of the past. A prime example of this is Pope Leo I (d. 461), who is sometimes called the first "pope," in the modern sense of the office.

Leo was serving when the Vandals sacked Rome in A.D. 455 and was able to negotiate with their leader to prevent the burning of the city. Needless to say, his leadership in this and other ways greatly increased the prestige of his office among Catholics in Rome. More important for the history of Christian thought, Leo took the next step and began to articulate arguments for papal authority based on the office's derivation from Jesus' claim that the Church was to be built on Peter and, thus, on Peter's episcopal successors in Rome (Matt. 16:18). Of course, these arguments have continued to undergird claims to papal authority ever since.

With the increased cultural and political influence the papacy gained in the West as a result of these successful efforts, it is not surprising to see that tensions developed between the Eastern emperor and the pope. Some of the tensions were theological over Christology. Others were over political matters. We observe these dynamics in an East-West Schism in the early sixth century when the papacy came under Byzantine power. With the formal end of the Western Empire, the East believed that it had claim to the Italian territories. The situation was exacerbated by a controversy over the authority of a decision of the Council of Chalcedon concerning Christology in which the pope, in defending the council's decisions, engaged in an open breach with the patriarch of Constantinople and by the invasion of Italy by the Ostrogoths, who were Arian Christians. These barbarians appointed a pope in sympathy with their Arian commitments while the Eastern Empire recognized another pope. Eventually the tensions were relieved by the election of a single pope in A.D. 514 and his efforts five years later to restore the breach with the Eastern emperor.

All of these dynamics further foreshadowed the final schism between the Eastern and Western churches. Some of these East-West tensions are evident in the various councils called to resolve christological controversies (considered later in this chapter). The Council of Chalcedon, which formally resolved these controversies, took a position very much in line with later Roman Catholic conceptions of papal authority. It officially received a letter from Pope Leo I and proclaimed that "Peter has spoken through Leo....Anathema to him that believes otherwise." Likewise that council (Cans. 9,28) and the Council of Constantinople in 381, both largely Eastern church councils, seemed to elevate the patriarch of Constantinople to the level of Rome's bishop.

Another important turning point in the development of the papacy and for the Church as a whole was the reign of Gregory the Great (ca. 540–604), which followed the resolution of the controversies we have been discussing. In a power vacuum left by the eventual retreat of the forces of the Eastern Empire (it had dominated Italy and rendered popes as their vassals during much of the sixth century), Gregory functioned as the de facto political leader of the region. He was probably the inspiration for the forged eighth-century *Donation of Constantine*, which granted political power to the papacy over Rome and the rest of Italy as well as its ecclesiastical supremacy over other important episcopacies. Represented as Constantine's treaty, the document essentially authorized the French king's gift of Italian lands, which rightfully belonged to the Eastern emperor. The empire had not fully helped Italy (defended the pope) from Lombard invasions of the eighth century. With East-West tensions growing, popes after Gregory increasingly looked to the French king for military protection. This was another crucial factor in the eventual schism of the Eastern and Western churches.

The greatness of Gregory was not limited to the political sphere. Above all, he tried to be a religious leader. He took measures to promote clerical celibacy (a practice that was still not universally endorsed in the West). He also made it his business to intervene in various theological disputes, even if not always successfully. For example, African bishops largely ignored his interventions concerning Donatism. Gregory's most important contribution in evangelism was sending missionaries to the pagan Anglo-Saxons who dominated England after Patrick's lifetime. His strategy, albeit questionable, was to purchase Anglican slave boys for monasteries and then train them to do missionary work (*Epistles* vii.30). Another evangelism success was his role in converting the Visigoth king in Spain to Nicene orthodoxy.

Gregory's most significant theological contribution was his promulgation of his own version of Augustine as the Church's infallible teacher. This interpretation came to be *the* approved version of Augustine in the Middle Ages. The eminent pope made several significant amendments to Augustine's thought. He effectively set aside the African Father's view of predestination and implied affirmation of irresistible grace in favor of a new agenda — how we can merit the reward of eternal life (*Homilies on Ezekiel* I.IX.9.2; *Moral Discourses on Job* XXX.I.5). This is begun by us, he asserted, through obedient free will cooperating with the gift of grace (*Moral Discourses on Job* XXXIII.XXXI.40). Such obedience is exercised through penance (VIII.21.37; IX.55.83f.). In addition, Gregory proceeded to assert that the living can help the dead out of purgatory by offering Masses for them (*Dialogues* IV.LV). Gregory's affirmation of the doctrine of purgatory (IV.XXXIX), the state of existence where those who had died in Christ without sufficient merits could attain the merits still required to ensure entry into heaven (Matt. 12:32; 2 Macc. 12:39–45), may have been suggested to him by a few of Augustine's passing comments about the validity of praying that some of the dead might be granted salvation (*City of God* XXI.24). Gregory's assertion that the Eucharist is a sacrifice (*Dialogues* IV.58) has roots in a number of earlier theologians, including Augustine. In view of the resonance of all of these themes to medieval theology, it is readily apparent how important a transitional figure to the Middle Ages Gregory is.

After Gregory's death, the papacy reverted back to being controlled by the emperor in the East, and later popes in turn sought protection from the Franks. That Gregory himself seemed able during his reign to avoid this vacillation and to be no one's puppet is another mark of his greatness.

WESTERN MONASTIC ORIGINS

Another development in this period was the emergence of a unique Western version of monasticism, the Benedictine Order. The growth of this institution in the Western church in these centuries was especially significant insofar as Pope Gregory had been a monk, and we may understand some of his teachings and actions in that light. Although there had been many followers of the monastic life in the West before his time, Benedict of Nursia (ca. 480–ca. 550) was the main figure of Western monasticism in its formative years.

Born into a family of the old Roman aristocracy, Benedict was well aware of the persecutions that orthodox believers had suffered in their confrontations with Arians and of the meaningless flux that characterized daily life in the turbulent era in which he lived. Could it be that his sense of the Christian life as involving sacrifice and his desire for a stability that might image eternity in the midst of meaningless flux influenced him to resolve to take up the life of a Christian hermit? Word of the extreme asceticism he practiced began to spread (as Italy in this period was still an oral culture), manifesting itself in admirers who flocked about him. This was the beginning of a monastic community, which Benedict and his followers established in a section of Italy so remote (Monte Cassino) that the local inhabitants were still practicing pagan rites. Shortly thereafter Benedict's sister Scholastica (ca. 480–ca. 543) established a similar community for women.

Benedict's most perduring impact on the Church was his formulation of a rule for his community, the *Rule of Saint Benedict*. Its main commitments were, not asceticism, but rather the permanence of the monastic vow and the need for obedience to the *abbot* (the father or leader) of the community. Prayer was to be at the core of monastic life in Benedict's vision. Monks were to gather eight times a day for such corporate prayer. Physical labor was to be shared by all. Although Benedict himself had little to say about study, it became one of the main occupations of the monks. They became adept at copying the Bible and other books for future generations. Eventually this evolved into theological studies, which the monks carried out in the West and the East throughout the Middle Ages.

Given the chaotic political and religious situation that Benedict encountered, as Italy faced reality without a Western Empire to defend it and as the tensions between Arianism and Nicene orthodoxy continued to plague the Church, such discipline in the Christian life was an important word to proclaim. The permanence of the vows and the unchanging rhythm of monastic community were emblems of the hope for eternity in face of the meaningless flux of daily life. Such a Western manifestation of monasticism differed somewhat from the more ancient Eastern forms of the movement (see chap. 12 for a comparison of the two).

CHRISTOLOGICAL CONTROVERSIES ON THE PATH TO CHALCEDON: DO THE MONOPHYSITES HAVE IT RIGHT?

After the Council of Nicea, christological questions began to emerge: If Christ is *homoousios* with the Father, how could the Son be human? How are divinity and humanity joined in Jesus? These were burning questions in the East. Prior to this period, some theologians, such as the Cappadocians, were speaking of Christ as having two natures. Two distinct Orthodox approaches began to develop in dealing with these questions; in a sense, these two distinct theological perspectives had been emerging gradually in the preceding centuries.

ORTHODOX CHRISTOLOGICAL ALTERNATIVES

Antiochene Christology (so named because many of its proponents were influenced by theology in Antioch) insisted on the distinction of Christ's natures and were not so inclined to be specific about the nature of their union. For instance, these theologians would refer to Mary as the "Mother of God" only in a most qualified sense. Theodore of Mopsuestia (ca. 350–428), a friend of John Chrysostom's, was perhaps the primary spokesperson for these commitments and illustrates them well (*Incarnation* 5,8,1).

Alexandrian Christology (so named for its indebtedness to the theological style of Alexandria) stressed the union of the divine and human in Jesus. The two natures (*hypostases*) are distinct but cannot be separated. In that sense, its proponents affirmed that in Christ there was a hypostatic union. This in turn led to the affirmation of *communicatio idiomatum* (communion of idioms, meaning that whatever is said of one of Christ's natures can be attributed to the other in a derivative sense). On this basis, it was appropriate to say that Mary as the mother of Jesus' humanity was herself the mother of his divinity, the Mother of God (*theotokos*). Cyril of Alexandria (d. 444), the bishop of Alexandria during the last eighteen years of Augustine's episcopacy in Hippo, was the great spokesman for this view (*Letter to John, Bishop of Antioch* 39; *Five Books of Contradiction against the Blasphemies of Nestorius* 3.3; *Second Letter to Nestorius*). In a derivative albeit highly qualified sense, Cyril seemed to concede that the Word in Christ suffered (*Second Letter to Nestorius*). His hesitancy was a function of his endorsement of Greek philosophical assumptions about God, which mandated belief in God's unchangeable character. These assumptions have governed most Christian theology since their adoption by the Apologists. Nevertheless, a belief that the Word suffered in Christ had been affirmed at least by implication much earlier by Origen (*On First Principles* II.VI.3; IV.IV.4). Except for belief in the unchangeable nature of God, adherents of the Antiochene school were not sympathetic to any of these commitments.

Of course, all students of theology like to think that they find the "golden mean" when it comes to formulating their own positions. With regard to Christology, all of us want to believe that we have found the way to affirm the distinction of Christ's natures and the unity of his person. But in fact, history indicates that we will likely emphasize the unity a bit more than the distinctiveness (like the Alexandrians) or the distinctiveness of the natures a little more than their unity (like the Antiochenes). Virtually every theologian comes down on one side or the other. If they could not avoid emphasizing the unity of Christ's person more than the distinctiveness of his natures or vice versa, what makes us think that we can avoid emphasizing one more than the other?

Readers are asked to examine their own pieties and teaching styles with regard to this christological question and then determine for themselves with which ancient christological alternative they are in most agreement and why. Perhaps they will find themselves more in agreement with the alternatives to be sketched next. Could the Church have erred in condemning these views? In that case, precisely what is at stake in preferring one of these views over the others?

DISTORTIONS OF THE ORTHODOX ALTERNATIVES

Both the Antiochene and Alexandrian Christologies were subject to distortion. In the West, there was not so much of a stir over these options or the issues they addressed. After the barbarian invasions, the theologians in this region tended simply to revive Tertullian's old formula — in Christ, two substances (natures) in one person — without much elaboration (*Against Praxeas* 27).

This neutralizing of theological controversy in the West may at least in part have been related to the fact that barbarian invasions helped overcome a division that had not been totally resolved in the Western church. Christian members of most of the invading tribes from the north and west had sympathies with the Arian heresy. But this commitment began to wither among them as a result of encounters with the Nicene beliefs of those whom they conquered in the Western Empire. In this period of glowing theological harmony in the church in this region, it is little wonder that Western church leaders avoided attention to the sort of theological distinctions between the Alexandrian and Antiochene Christologies that might undermine the new harmony.

In the Eastern church, not affected by the barbarian invasions, nothing impeded giving further attention to the issues at stake in dividing the two Christologies. The dialogue resulted in further distortions of each.

Apollinarianism. The first distortion of the Alexandrian emphasis on the unity of Christ's person was by Apollinarius (ca. 310–ca. 390), the bishop of Laodicea. He was so opposed to Arianism that he emphasized Christ's divinity at the expense of his humanity, holding that the Logos took the place of the human soul in Jesus.[4] Apollinarius emphasized the unity of Christ's person, which certainly seems rational. Insofar as the soul is spiritual, according to the bishop, that which is divine/spiritual in Christ resided in the place of what is spiritual in all human beings. Nevertheless this view was condemned by the Church in 362 at

---

4. Gregory of Nazianzus *Epistles* 101.

a synod in Alexandria and again in 381 at the Council of Constantinople, where the Nicene Creed received its final formulation. At least by implication, the concern raised is that the Apollinarian view subtly compromises the humanity of Christ, in which case the specter of Docetism is raised anew.

Nestorianism. The next problematic teaching to appear was Nestorianism. Nestorius was a monk from Antioch, later bishop of Constantinople, who as a student of Theodore of Mopsuestia took an extreme Antiochene position.[5] He conceived of the union of the divinity and humanity in Christ to be like that of husband and wife, one yet each retaining separate natures. Nestorius was accused, perhaps unjustly, of maintaining the formula: two natures, two persons. In accord with the suppositions of Antiochene Christology, he rejected the idea of Mary as the Mother of God.[6] Later Nestorians rejected the prevailing eucharistic belief of the day that Christ's body is really in the consecrated elements, claiming instead that only by faith does the consecrated bread make possible an encounter with Christ's heavenly body (Babai of Kasker *On the Union* 4.16; 7).

No less than with Apollinarius, the key Nestorian images for depicting Christ help make sense of the Incarnation in a concrete way. Nevertheless, the Church, largely under the influence of Cyril and the Alexandrian school, condemned such teachings at a synod in Rome in 430 and at the Council of Ephesus in 431 (the council making the letters of Cyril [cited in n. 6] its own). Ephesus also condemned Pelagianism. In the christological controversy, Cyril had the support of the papacy. Some of this support for the Alexandrian cause may have been conditioned by Cyril's judicious disposition of Alexandrian wealth to influence certain authorities.

The rejection of Nestorianism had a biblical basis, for it seemed to the bishops at these meetings that to deny the unity of Christ was to undermine the Word's becoming flesh (John 1:14). From an Alexandrian perspective, believing in the concept of deification, a failure to unify the divine and human in the Incarnation would raise the disconcerting possibility that perhaps the divine energies that make us godlike may not have truly penetrated our human nature.

Nestorianism did not vanish following its condemnation. Several decades prior to its denunciation, the Church had been organized in Persia. After the condemnation of their leader, a number of Nestorius's followers fled from Antioch to Persia and established a school of their

---

5. He was also a supporter of Pelagius insofar as during his episcopal reign he offered asylum to a group of Pelagians who had been condemned in the West.

6. Cyril of Alexandria *Epistles* iv; xvii.

own, which became the main theological academy of the young Persian church. One of the attractions of Persia was the country's status as a traditional enemy of the Roman Empire, and so as enemies of the empire themselves, these Nestorian dissidents would seem to have been on safe territory.

In Persia, they encountered a young church whose members were composed of East Syrians, who had tended to distance themselves from the Church in Constantinople in order to gain the Persians, who were enemies of the Eastern Empire. Such a church, which had already declared its independence from Constantinople's patriarchate at a synod of Dadyeshu in 424, was more likely to accept the views of Nestorians, which contradicted the Eastern Empire's approved Christology. Consequently this Persian church, the forerunner of the Assyrian Church, has been and continues to be Nestorian in its orientation.

Though quite small today, largely due to the conversion of the Persian royal house to Islam late in the thirteenth century and subsequent exile in the twentieth century to lands of the Near East like Syria and Iraq, the Assyrian Church in its prime flourished and had a very successful evangelistic outreach. It planted churches in China in the seventh century (a mission largely comprised of Syrian immigrants that survived until the tenth century, which was revived again by Mongolians in the twelfth century and lasted until the fourteenth century) and in India in the sixth century (the Malabar Christians, who could have existed prior to this Nestorian missionary outreach, as they claim to have been established by missionary ventures of the apostle Thomas).[7] In any case, the perdurance of Nestorianism raises an interesting question: Within Christianity's catholic/orthodox heritage, is the predominance of the idea that Christ is truly one merely a function of sociopolitical accident? Had Nestorianism found more fertile political soil in Persia than the orthodox version did in Rome, would our theological convictions be quite different?

Eutychianism. An extreme Alexandrian position, Eutychianism was rooted in the teachings of Eutyches (ca. 378–454), a monk in Constantinople. He taught that Christ was of two natures before the union, prior to the Incarnation, but now (since the union) possesses only one nature. Generally speaking, Eutyches was so concerned to assert the deity of Christ that he preferred not to speak of Christ's being "consubstantial with human nature."

We can best understand Eutyches in light of the events that followed

---

7. In more modern times, Malabar Christians have renounced Nestorius either through uniting with the Roman Catholic Church in 1599 and again in 1662 or by joining a Syrian Monophysite body, the Jacobites.

the condemnation of Nestorius. After his condemnation at the Council of Ephesus along with that of his main supporter, John the bishop of Antioch (d. 441) — when neither was present due to travel delays — Nestorius, John, and their supporters convened a rival council, which declared Cyril of Alexandria (the main mover in the Ephesian Council) a heretic. At this point, the Eastern emperor Theodosius II, who had previously been on Cyril's side, arrested both John and Cyril and declared the actions of both councils null and void. Once again the characteristic model of church-state relationships in the East emerges: the state, as God's agent, rightly intervenes in the affairs of the Church. Cyril and John negotiated a formula of union, which essentially reconciled the Antiochene and Alexandrian views by admitting the appropriateness of referring to Mary as the "Mother of God" and by designating the Incarnation as a "union," not a "conjunction," of the natures.

The compromise character of the formula pleased no one. Consequently when Cyril died, radical Alexandrians like Eutyches were ready to enunciate their views more unambiguously. Flavian, the patriarch of Constantinople (d. 449), himself an Antiochene, condemned such views and Eutyches at a synod of Constantinople. In response, the Alexandrian bishop engineered a confrontation that led the Eastern emperor Theodosius II to convene a council at Ephesus in 449. The patriarch of Alexandria Dioscorus (d. 454) made sure that the council went his way, endorsing a radical Alexandrian line and fundamentally exonerating Eutyches. A letter from Pope Leo I was totally ignored, Flavian was physically abused, and the council concluded that the doctrine of Christ's two natures was heretical. There are indications that Alexandrian wealth helped influence initial political support for this decision, as it had at the earlier council in Ephesus in 431.

Pope Leo sought to negate the result of the council (referred to as a "robbers' synod"), but the emperor was not inclined to be dissuaded. Things changed dramatically when Theodosius broke his neck in a fall and his sister Pulcheria and her husband Marcian succeeded him. Pulcheria was sympathetic to the earlier Western position regarding Christ's two natures and the condemnation of Nestorius. She felt the meeting at Ephesus had gone too far. For this reason, and at the behest of the pope, she convened the Council of Chalcedon in 451 in order to condemn Eutychianism.

Eutyches' views appear to imply a kind of Docetism, which raises the question whether Christ, if not fully human, has really borne our sins. The strength of Eutyches' views is that the unity of Christ that he posited seems more intelligible than the idea that Christ is two and yet one at the same time. His views, which generated Monophysitism, have certainly had a lot of staying power in the Church.

THE COUNCIL OF CHALCEDON AND ITS AFTERMATH

The Council of Chalcedon was essentially Pope Leo's show. A letter by him was endorsed by all the bishops as the voice of Peter (*To Flavian* XXVIII). The council also articulated a definition that essentially affirmed the points in the letter, with some phrases drawn from the writings of Cyril of Alexandria. The definition affirmed that in Christ there is a union of natures (a hypostatic union). It did not, however, seek to define union but merely to set limits for appropriate ways of describing it. Its basic point was that the natures are to be distinguished but never divided or separated so as to compromise their union. In effect, the council authorized the legitimacy of both the Alexandrian and Antiochene alternatives: Never speak of Jesus in such a way that one fails to affirm that he is fully God and fully human, but do not make those points at the expense of the unity of Jesus' person.

The Chalcedonian formula effectively settled the controversies in the West, but not in the East. Nestorianism remained viable among the Assyrians who had settled in Persia. Likewise the Monophysite position continues to be represented to this very day, notably in the Coptic and Ethiopian Orthodox churches in Africa as well as in the Syrian Orthodox Church and the Armenian Apostolic Church. Just as political dynamics encouraged the spread and early preservation of Nestorianism, these dynamics were no less in evidence in the subsequent success of the Monophysite cause.

The kingdom of Armenia had a long history as a buffer state between Persia and the Roman Empire. The founder of Christianity in the region was Gregory the Illuminator (ca. 240–332), who had been raised as a Christian while in exile in Cappadocia. Upon returning home, he converted his relative King Tiridates III in A.D. 303. So Armenia was a Christian empire before Rome. By 450, when Persians tried to impose their religion on Armenia, the besieged leaders looked to the Eastern Empire for help, which never came. Overrun by the Persians at about the same time that the empire-inspired Council of Chalcedon was meeting, the Armenian church would have nothing to do with its christological definition, declaring the council to be heretical. Despite the conquests by the Persians, later by the Arabs, and by the Turks in the eleventh century, the Armenian church has flourished, perhaps partly because of the role it has played as the cultural glue of the people. This has been especially necessary in preserving any sense of an Armenian people since the eleventh century, as they have endured harsh persecution and a worldwide diaspora.

The Syrian Orthodox Church traces its origins to those residents of ancient Antioch who, led by their duly appointed patriarch Severus (ca.

465–538), refused to accept Chalcedon's condemnation of the Mono-physites. It has come to be known as the Jacobite Church, named for Jacob Baradaeus (ca. 500–578), who was appointed bishop of Edessa and proceeded to organize his own and assisted in the organization of other national Monophysite churches. His leadership eventually brought the Syrian Orthodox Church to become Syria's national religious insti-tution until the Mongol invasions of the fourteenth century. Heavily persecuted, the church, as noted, has had an impact on the conver-sion of a number of Malabar Christians in India to the Monophysite position.

The Jacobite Church is also notable among Monophysite churches for its theological contributions to the early and medieval church. Es-pecially significant in this connection is an early-sixth-century work appearing under the pseudonym of Dionysius the Areopagite; it is an early example of Christian *mysticism* (the belief that through spiritual discipline one may have direct, intuitive union with God). Reflect-ing many of Origen's positions, Pseudo-Dionysius sought to synthesize Monophysite thought and Neoplatonism, interpreting the Orthodox emphasis on deification in a kind of pantheistic conceptuality that sees that ultimately everything is God (*Epistles* 2; *Ecclesiastical Hierarchy* 1, 2.3, 7.2). The influence of this literature among medieval mystics in both the Eastern and Western churches has been profound.

With regard to the Egyptian Church, Coptic Christians felt exploited by the Eastern Empire (see chap. 1 for a description of its origin and that of the Ethiopian Orthodox Church). Greek speakers in Egypt at the time generally endorsed Chalcedon's definition and have come to be known as Melchites. With the Arab invasion, their ranks were largely deci-mated, and the Coptic Church became the predominant church in Egypt. Immediately following the decision of Chalcedon, though, the tensions between this group and the Monophysites were so high that Proterius, the patriarch of Alexandria, was lynched in 457 for his position on Christology.

Although deep-seated loyalty to Alexandrian suppositions about the unity of Christ's person is an undeniable cause of the Copts' rejection of the Chalcedonian formulation, one cannot totally discount as another cause the negative feelings that many Egyptian Christians had towards the Eastern Empire, especially when many perceived the Council of Chalcedon to be backed by the empire. Ethiopian Orthodoxy seems to have taken up the Monophysite position as a function of the church's ancient ties to the Egyptian mother church.

Eastern emperors tried to find a middle ground between supporters of the Chalcedonian statement and those opposed to it. One attempt was in 553 at the Second Council of Constantinople, which was called by Emperor Justinian. He hoped to placate critics of Chalcedon by condemning the most noted spokespersons of the Antiochene distinction of the two natures. Theodore of Mopsuestia was condemned, and the *communicatio idiomatum* was affirmed. Another endeavor to find a middle ground came from Patriarch Sergius of Constantinople (d. 638), who proposed that while Christ has two natures, there is only one will in him (that is, the divine will seems to have taken the place of Christ's human will).

Sergius's position came to be known as "Monothelitism." The objections raised to it were like those raised against Apollinarianism, for the proposal seems to say that Christ is not fully human. Monothelitism was also criticized for its suggestion that the whole of human nature, the will, cannot then have been deified by Christ. Concerned about remedying schism in the empire in light of Persian and Arab threats, the Eastern emperor used persuasion to have Pope Honorius take a position that would at least allow the permissibility of the Monothelite view, and for a while this view gained the support of the pope. His argument that two wills acting in unison are indistinguishable from one will is certainly an appealing defense of the view, which seems to provide a rational account of how God could be in the man Jesus.

Political (and so ecclesiastical) circumstances changed in the seventh century, that is, the Arab conquest of Syria and Egypt left no compelling reason to seek to mollify isolated Christians in those regions at the expense of the good will of the Western church. The largest of these groups of Christians who affirmed the Monothelite view is generally thought to be the Maronite Church, which claims its origin in a Christian hermit friend of John Chrysostom, Maro (d. 410). Members of this originally Syrian church, now concentrated in Lebanon, reject the Monothelite heritage, and it was probably renounced by the church in the twelfth century during the Crusades, when it became united with the Roman Catholic Church (as an Eastern-rite Catholic Church that maintains its indigenous language, ancient liturgies, and church law). In any case, with no perceived need by the Eastern Empire to mollify such Christians in the seventh century, a new council was convened, the Third Council of Constantinople (held 680–81). It condemned Monothelitism and also declared the deceased pope Honorius, who had supported Monothelitism, to have been a heretic.

That a pope could be deemed a heretic would be of crucial import for later discussions about papal infallibility. But could the pope have been correct in this case? What precisely is at stake in condemning Monothelitism and the other heresies, particularly in view of the coherence of many of these views?

THE MONOPHYSITE ALTERNATIVE

There is clearly an attractiveness to all the heresies of Alexandrian origin that stress the unity of the person of Christ. Since the Monophysite position is the most influential of these in the twentieth century, it seems valid to examine it in more detail, particularly how ancient churches still advocating it make their case for its viability. Readers affiliated with churches associated with the Chalcedonian tradition (Eastern Orthodox churches, the Roman Catholic Church, and Protestant churches) should ask why it is important to insist that Christ has two natures.

As the largest of the Monophysite churches (and in view of its other unique characteristics outlined in chap. 1), it is well to examine the Ethiopian Orthodox Church's treatment of this theological commitment. Besides, as will be apparent, its endorsement of Monophysitism is so qualified as to guard itself from many of the charges of heresy that proponents of the Chalcedonian formulation have historically lodged against the Monophysite position.

Both the Ethiopian Church and the Coptic Church agree with the ecumenical consensus in condemning Eutyches as a heretic. However, they reject the Chalcedonian doctrine of two natures in Christ. To preserve the unity of Christ, they just speak of him as having one nature. Two schools of thought have developed in the Ethiopian Church in explaining these commitments: the Sons of Grace and the Sons of Unction. The Sons of Grace (Walda-saga) teach that the unification of the divine and human natures takes place in such a way that the nature of Christ becomes a special nature, and this work is attributed to the Father. The unification takes place through the adoptive birth of Christ, his elevation to divinity, which happens when the Father anoints the Son with the Holy Spirit (Mark 1:8–11). This school rejects both absorption and distinction of the two natures. The Sons of Unction (Walda-qeb) insist on the radical unification of the two natures of Christ. Christ is the Son of God by nature. In eternity the divine nature has absorbed the human to such an extent that Christ's manhood is sometimes portrayed as a mere phantasm.

Though both schools of thought continue to have their adherents, the view of the Sons of Unction has tended to receive more sanction by the Ethiopian Church. Both hold that the unification of Christ's person takes place with no blending, no change, no confusion. Neither intends to deny that Jesus was "of one Substance with the Father" or that he "was made Man" (Nicene Creed). How can both be affirmed given the Monophysite position's commitments to unify Christ's person? Ethiopian theologians simply tell us that these are mysteries.

The previously noted contemporary Ethiopian Orthodox image for depicting the mystery of the Incarnation by comparing it to what happens when wine (Christ's divinity) is poured into a cup of water (Christ's humanity) is probably more in line with the Sons of Unction school. As the result of such a mixing of water with wine is still a cup of wine, so it is with Christ. An argument also still employed on behalf of the Monophysite view, which was articulated by some of its early post-Chalcedonian proponents, is to insist that there is no nature apart from a person/hypostasis. Thus if Christ is one hypostasis, as Chalcedon affirmed, the Logos after the Incarnation can only have one nature.

Do the Coptic and Ethiopian Monophysites have it right on Christology, such that Chalcedon is one of the Church's great mistakes? As with some of the other heresies considered, the Monophysite vision certainly seems more intellectually satisfying than the Chalcedonian idea that one nature plus one nature equals one. Defenders of the Chalcedonian formulation might respond by arguing that the Monophysite vision falls prey to the Arian or Docetic heresies, insofar as these churches do not make it unambiguously certain that the Savior is divine (as the Arians did not) or that he is human (as the Docetists did not). However, precisely why should avoiding these heresies matter? What is ultimately at stake in insisting that Christ has a divine and a human nature? Members of churches in the Chalcedonian tradition need to give special attention to these questions.

What would be the consequences for faith if Christ were not fully God? In that case, we would return to Arianism, in the sense of claiming that a creature — that we ourselves and not God — had saved us. Asserting that Christ has a divine nature is necessary if we are to give credit to God for saving us. Suppose Christ were not fully human. In that case, he could not have borne our sin. If Jesus were not fully human, he could not have identified with our human condition to assume our sin. It is necessary to insist that Christ has both a divine and a human nature, or the assurance that we have of our salvation would be in doubt. If he were not divine, we could not be sure that it was truly God's work that Jesus did on the Cross, and if he were not fully human, we could not be sure that he had really borne our sins.

In recent years, the Ethiopian Church and other Monophysite churches (often termed "Oriental Orthodox" churches) have been engaged in a dialogue with various Eastern Orthodox churches trying to resolve their differences, primarily pertaining to Christology. The conclusions thus far suggest that the differences are not so serious as for either side to consider that the other is heretical. Both sides have concluded that the differences between the Monophysite and the Chalcedonian positions can be reconciled and are, in fact, two sides of the same coin. Are the differences between these two distinct visions of

Christology enough to justify the continuing separation of churches espousing the different views?

THE EAST-WEST SCHISM: WERE THERE GOOD THEOLOGICAL REASONS FOR THE SPLIT?

As the first millennium of the Christian Era neared an end, the tensions between the Eastern and the Western churches had been building for some time. Different worship practices, polities, and theological profiles were emerging in each region. An outright schism between the Eastern and Western churches occurred in the late fifth century as a consequence of efforts to placate opposition to the Council of Chalcedon in Eastern territories. In hopes of effectively unifying his empire, Emperor Basiliscus annulled the decisions of Chalcedon in 476 and called for a new council, which never met. After Zeno (ca. 450?-91) regained the Eastern throne, he issued in 482, with support of the patriarch of Constantinople, the Edict of Union directing that all should return to what was commonly held before the controversy. Observe once again how Eastern church leaders typically agreed with heads of state, a model not typical of Western conceptions of church-state relations.

Of course, the pope in the West, Simplicius (d. 483), was critical of the edict and was determined to defend the decisions of Chalcedon since an imperial edict undermining this duly called council would enfeeble the authority of other conciliar decisions, such as Nicea and Constantinople. The teaching authority of the Church was at stake for Simplicius. A breach between Rome and Constantinople ensued. The pope proceeded to excommunicate the most prominent Eastern church leaders and the emperor himself. The schism continued until 519 when Pope Hormisdas (d. 523) and John the patriarch of Constantinople agreed to return to the decisions of Chalcedon. The tragic episode was a harbinger of the realities with which Christians would have to live for almost a millennium. The Eastern churches' general acceptance of Chalcedon led them to adopt the title "Orthodox" Church, in distinction from non-Chalcedonians. This is why we speak today of the Eastern Orthodox churches — Russian Orthodox, Greek Orthodox, etc.

The Arab conquest of Asia and North Africa in the late seventh century was a further spur to the deterioration of relations between Rome and Constantinople, not least of all because it began a process of isolating them from each other. It also changed evangelism strategies. Islam blocked the Church's access to the south and the east. In part, this accounts for the Orthodox expansion into eastern Europe and Russia. These regions were largely populated by Slavs, at least from the sixth century on. Some of their rulers were particularly concerned by the ninth century that Western missionaries in their regions might be serving as a spearhead for conquest by the Western Empire, which Charlemagne (ca. 742–814) had restored (see chap. 12 for details). Consequently contacts were made with the patriarch of Constantinople to ask for missionaries.

The patriarch was pleased to commission Cyril (826–69) and Methodius (ca. 815–85), two highly educated and accomplished brothers, to work among the Slavs. Their work was eventually undertaken in league with the pope's commission, and their prominence resulted in a most favorable reception by the Slavs. In 906 when the Magyars (Hungarians) invaded the area, the pioneer work of these missionaries had borne some fruit: when the Eastern and Western churches eventually split, some people from this region joined the Catholic Church and others joined Orthodox churches. It is for this reason that nations like Hungary, the former Yugoslavia (Serbia and Croatia), Czechoslovakia, and Poland tend to have both church bodies significantly represented among their populations. The more oriented a region was to the West, as was Croatia, which had been part of the Western Empire after the Roman Empire's division, the more thoroughly Roman Catholic it became.

Bulgaria adopted Christianity after being visited by both Western and Eastern missionaries. Following his baptism late in the ninth century, King Boris requested an (Eastern-oriented) archbishop from the patriarch in Constantinople. After some tense dynamics, the Bulgarian Orthodox Church was organized, but only after insisting on its autocephalous (independent) status, which was not actually achieved until A.D. 918.

The greatest missionary success of the Orthodox Church was the conversion of Russia. Around A.D. 950, Queen Olga was converted by German missionaries (for the discussion of the evangelization of Germany, see chap. 12). Under her grandson Vladimir, Christianity truly became planted. He sent for missionaries from the Byzantine Empire. An Orthodox church was established, probably to some extent through forced conversions. Monasticism functioned as the cutting edge of evangelism efforts. In the thirteenth century when the Mongols invaded Russia and throughout the next two centuries of their rule, Christianity functioned as the national bond that allowed the Russian people to survive.

Nonetheless the Russian Orthodox Church had its own internal problems during these years, especially in the fourteenth and fifteenth centuries. The practice of priests charging fees for sacraments developed. The Strigolniks (called "barbers" because their leader was a barber of the clergy) actively stood against these practices and established their own lay-led communities with no sacraments, save penance. The movement was rigorously persecuted. In the late fifteenth century, a movement of Judaizers began after two Orthodox priests had converted to Judaism and began active mission work. The movement succeeded in turning a number of leaders of the church in Russia to a crypto-Jewish perspective in the sense of advocating iconoclasm and embracing the Jewish philosophy of the day. This movement was also crushed, indicating how firmly rooted Christianity had become in Russia. After the conquest of Constantinople in the sixteenth century by the Ottomans, Russia declared Moscow the "Third Rome." This accounts for the prestige enjoyed by the patriarch of Moscow to this day.

ICONOCLAST CONTROVERSY

Deteriorating Eastern Christian-Western Christian relations were not helped by an eighth-century controversy. The Eastern emperor Leo III endeavored to purify a debased Christianity in his region. Christianity, it seems, was no longer at the cutting edge of society in education or culture. Islam had assumed that stature. In the high society of the empire, Christianity was increasingly seeming to be like an opiate for the masses. The solution, Leo thought, must lie with discarding as much of the popular superstitions as possible. An excellent target was the use of icons, which were easily misused by the masses as objects of worship. Leo's edict gave rise to rioting; Pope Gregory II (669–731), with the support of various Italian cities, denounced it. Leo responded by deposing the patriarch of Constantinople and seizing part of the papal lands.

Constantine V, a successor of Leo, convened a council in 754, which condemned the use of icons. The decision was likely related to Islamic influence and its rejection of all physical representation of spiritual realities. The empire was divided between *iconoclasts* (destroyers of images) and *iconodules* (worshipers of images). The West largely refused to accept the imperial edicts, for the use of images on catacombs and other places of worship was customary. The controversy continued for the next decades. In 787 Empress Irene persuaded the bishops to convene the Second Council of Nicea, which tried to mediate the dispute by distinguishing between worship in the strict sense (*latria*) and veneration (*dulia*). Images, it was asserted, are only entitled to veneration. Though the decree met with some resistance, by 842 images had been restored in the Eastern churches. In the West, the decision of the council was not well received, partly occasioned by the problems of making a distinction in Latin between *latria* and *dulia*. This problem became one more indication of East-West tensions.

Readers should come to terms with their own position on icons. The Second Nicene Council held that the use of icons was a way of recollecting what the icons represent. As such, they facilitate worship. There is also a christological overtone to the whole debate. Perhaps the greatest systematic theologian of the Eastern church, John of Damascus (ca. 675–ca. 749), a lifelong Greek Christian from Damascus, was a staunch defender of icons. He argued that Christ himself is an image, for his human nature is an image of the divine. All humans are images of God in a sense. We adore images for the same reason we adore each other — because they are made in God's image and give testimony to him.[8]

An argument such as John's challenges the anti-Catholic sentiments of Protestants, who strip all statues and images from the Church. Is it a valid argument, and should the Church as a whole reassess its position on icons? In any case, the controversy about icons still has significant ecumenical impact. Perhaps its most damaging effect with regard to Eastern-Western church relations was that it helped the West lose even more confidence in the Eastern church as it observed how readily the Eastern church had accepted the emperor's original iconoclastic decree that images be totally forbidden.

THE FILIOQUE CONTROVERSY

Relations between East and West further deteriorated over the Western church's insertion of the Filioque phrase in the Nicene Creed. *Filioque* is literally "and the Son." The Spirit proceeds "from the Father," the Nicene formulation stated. The Western churches affirm "from the Father and the Son." Although this phrase had some ancient precedents, the East never accepted it, properly claiming that the phrase was not part of the Council of Nicea's decision.[9] The alteration of the creed probably originated in Spain and was brought during the reign of Charlemagne to France, where the Filioque was regularly employed in the royal chapel. When some Frankish monks visited the East and recited the amended version of the creed, it touched off a huge controversy.

Political dynamics contributed to the Eastern church leadership's vitriolic reaction to the creedal addition. With the restoration of the Western Empire under Charlemagne, the popes no longer needed the

---

8. John of Damascus *Fount of Knowledge* IV.16.
9. The phrase was affirmed by Tertullian (*Against Praxeas* IV, VIII), the Athanasian Creed (22), and by Ambrose.

support of the Eastern Empire for military protection from barbarian tribes. The iconoclast controversy had increased the impression of Western church leaders that the Eastern church was little more than a tool of the Byzantine Empire. These impressions led Pope Nicholas I (d. 867) in the year of his death to support the deposed patriarch of Constantinople Ignatius, rather than his successor Photius (ca. 810–ca. 895), who had been installed through the emperor's intervention. In anger, Photius then declared the entire Western church heretical, noting especially its tampering with the creed by inserting the Filioque. When political circumstances changed, Ignatius was restored as patriarch, and eventually agreements were made by the Church to recognize Photius, but the bitterness engendered by the schism was a reality that would emerge again and again in the next centuries.

The widespread use of the Apostles' Creed in the Western church (it is not used at all in the Eastern church) owes its origins to this period. In order to avoid alienating either the Franks or the Byzantines by choosing one version of the creed over the other, the pope began to encourage use of the old Roman baptismal creed (now called "the Apostles' Creed"), which may have originally inspired the Nicene formulation. It had no reference at all to the Spirit's proceeding from any divine person, so none of the parties in the dispute over the Filioque would need to lose. It is well to keep this background in mind the next time readers confess this creed.

What is at stake in the Filioque? In the West, the insertion of this phrase in the creed may have helped the Church in combating a late-eighth-century controversy with those holding that Jesus was the "adopted" Son of God. If the Spirit proceeded from the Son, the Son must not have been adopted but rather had been God in eternity.[10]

The impact of Augustine's theology in the West also no doubt contributed to its endorsement of the Filioque. Recall Augustine's portrayal of the Trinity as the communion of the Father and Son united by the Spirit, who is their mutual love. This meant that the Spirit, who is also the Son's love for the Father, must proceed from the Son as well as from the Father. The East responded with an equally practical image that ruled out need of the Filioque. Photius of Constantinople compared the Trinity to a balance scale, in which there is a center (the Father) on which the two arms (Son and Holy Spirit) depend (*Amphilochia*). Given this image, the Spirit proceeds only from the Father.

There are other relevant issues at stake in the controversy. For the West, if the Spirit does not also proceed from the Son, then the Spirit might give new revelations not in harmony with the Son. The Filioque

---

10. Paulinus of Aquileia *Against Felix of Urgel* I.24.

guarantees a Christocentric revelation, safeguarding us from the Montanist heresy. From an Eastern perspective, besides safeguarding the integrity of ancient tradition (not arbitrarily adding to it), denial of the Filioque ensures that the work of the Spirit as a new initiative is not neglected, for if the Spirit proceeds from the Son, the Spirit seems chained to Christ's work in the past. When the Church fails to give testimony to the work of the Spirit as something present and new, it is faced with an untenable choice. It must either adhere to dead tradition (which as the Spirit's work could not by definition be a present reality and so could not be radically new) or to an individualistic spirituality that fails to celebrate its roots in tradition.

Which argument is most persuasive? Is it good to teach the Filioque, or should the Western churches abandon it? Granted the difference between these views may be significant, but is it significant enough to warrant the continuing schism between the Eastern and the Western churches?

THE SCHISM

The final break between the churches climaxed in 1054. The patriarch of Constantinople Michael Cerularius (d. 1058) precipitated the break. He feared that an alliance that could impede his diocese's independence was forming between the pope and the Eastern emperor. Opting to take action that might provoke schism, Cerularius ordered the closing of all churches of the Latin rite in Constantinople. Meanwhile another Eastern bishop, Leo of Orchid, accused the West of an error as it was moving to make clerical celibacy a universal rule (see chap. 12) and celebrate Communion with unleavened bread.

Pope Leo IX (1002–54) resolved to send an ambassador to deal with the problems; however, it seems he did not send his best ambassador. Cardinal Humbert of Silva Candida (d. 1061) was a committed reformer, but he knew no Greek, was committed to clerical celibacy, and was suspicious that the Eastern church had forfeited autonomy from the state. He and Cerularius exchanged insults. On June 16, 1054, Humbert delivered a letter of excommunication in the name of the pope to the patriarch. The excommunication was never retracted, and the schism remains to this day (though negotiations and dialogue aimed at resolving the schism have been undertaken).

Eastern and Western churches differ to this day on several issues:

1. The description of salvation (as *theōsis* in the East)

2. Distinct liturgies and liturgical calendars (the dates for Christmas and Easter)

3. The authority of the papacy

4. Married priesthood (in the East, though not the episcopacy)

5. Church-state relations

6. The Filioque

Are these issues enough to justify continuing separation, or is separation a mere historically conditioned tragedy?

CHAPTER 12

THE MIDDLE AGES
TESTS OF STRENGTH FOR CHURCH AND STATE

In the Middle Ages, the sphere of action regarding the Church's history began to switch geographically, coinciding primarily with the Moslem conquest of Orthodox regions. Thus, breaking significantly with the focus of analysis in previous chapters, attention here will be directed more on European rather than on African and the rest of the Eastern churches. The Moslem conquest effectively isolated these churches to the point at which less and less of what went on in their lives had much international significance. Under siege as they were, there was less opportunity for the luxury of theological controversy. In large part, these reasons and the fact that the modern Enlightenment and the Industrial Revolution and the problems they posed for the Church transpired in the West account for why so much of the focus for the remainder of this book and its companion volume will be on the Western church. The first concern we must address is the political and ecclesiastical structures that characterized the medieval church.

HERITAGE OF THE CAROLINGIAN EMPIRE:
THE CHURCH'S INCREASING POLITICAL INFLUENCE

We resume the narrative in the ninth century when the Frankish chieftain Charlemagne (ca. 742–814) was crowned by the pope as emperor of a revivified Roman Empire, after conquering much of the territory of western Europe that had been part of the western half of the empire in ancient times. This symbolic act, partly motivated by the new political realities of Charlemagne's power and as culmination of the political-military alliance between the papacy and the Franks in reaction to a period of Eastern domination of the papacy, was in effect a kind of testimony to a high level of papal authority.[1] The pope, it seemed, could give the crown.

---

1. Recall that the popes had had a special relationship with the Franks since the mid-eighth century, when the latter had functioned as protectors of Italy from invading Lombards.

In fact, papal authority in the Middle Ages was increasingly ambiguous, not unlike in the centuries immediately before and after the reign of Gregory the Great. In the ninth century, the papacy had significant international influence, especially in terms of a role in curbing hostile actions by sovereigns. The pope though had very little real power to effect things, even in Rome. Before pursuing the realities of papal power, though, we will examine the religious significance of Charlemagne's reign.

Charlemagne was more than a great military conqueror. Though not formally educated, he had a deep appreciation of culture and was an administrator par excellence. His almost legendary military exploits extended the borders of his empire beyond those of the ancient Roman Empire into the Saxon kingdoms. Having difficulties with counterinsurgency, he vowed to quash rebellions with a military-evangelistic policy. All heathens would either be baptized or slaughtered. This policy of forced baptisms had a good effect on the Saxons (who occupied much of present-day Germany). They apparently believed that in accepting this rite of entrance to another religion, they had forsaken their gods forever, and so with no other god to which to turn, many soon became true believers. In the late Middle Ages, Germans, and the Saxons in particular, were highly regarded throughout the Church for their piety. Consequently, filled with zeal (and ruthlessness), the Saxons began practicing this means of mass conversion among their neighbors. Indeed, this strategy was quite typical of the way in which Christianity was propagated in much of western Europe. In this way, thanks to Charlemagne, the region of Germany became largely Christianized.

Charlemagne ruled in the ecclesiastical as well as the civil realm. He exercised authority in appointing bishops. He ordered preaching in the language of the people (a practice that continued throughout the centuries when the use of Latin persisted in the Catholic liturgy). He also decreed that Sunday be a day of rest and that tithes be collected as if a tax. Another concern of Charlemagne's was that monasticism be reformed.

THE AFTERMATH OF CAROLINGIAN DECLINE

Charlemagne's empire did not long endure. His son Louis "the Pious" (778–840) was a great patron of the arts and a committed Christian who ordered that two-thirds of money received as tithes be given to the poor. He also tried to give the Church more autonomy by allowing the people and the clergy to elect bishops. Church leaders and local authorities hungry for power took advantage of his benevolence and forbearance. Various civil wars ensued. Even Louis's sons, who eventually held power in a divided empire, engaged in intrigue against each other.

By the ninth century all that was left of the Carolingian Empire was a nominal emperor. The empire had absolutely no control over the German territories, its power having been frittered away by a combination of ambitious local rulers and threats of foreign invasions by the Asian Magyars (present-day Hungarians) and the Vikings.

When the last nominal Carolingian ruler died, the German territories became *duchies* (sovereign territories each ruled by its own prince). They developed the practice of electing one of their number as sovereign. Otto I (reign 936–73), duke of Saxon, came to dominate most of the German territories and Italy and in 962 had himself crowned emperor of a "Holy Roman Empire" by the pope (just as Charlemagne had been so crowned). The very fact that he took this title to describe the territory over which he reigned is an indication of the deep impact that the ancient Roman Empire, though dead in the West for centuries, had made on the medieval Western social psyche (and so perhaps helps account for the ongoing preoccupation with Roman and Greek culture in much of the Western intellectual tradition throughout a good deal of its history).

Otto's rationale for going to Rome was another indication of the powerful symbolic significance that city and its heritage continued to hold for those seeking power. Rome had certainly fallen on hard times for almost a century, as it had come under the domination of several rival Roman noble families. They also controlled papal appointments, which inevitably led to a decline in the quality of papal leadership. The pope who crowned Otto was especially notorious for his degenerate indulgence of his own passions. Otto subsequently deposed this pope (John XII) and forced the Roman aristocracy to promise that imperial consent from then on would be necessary in all papal elections. For the next century, the papacy was a puppet of Otto's successors in the Holy Roman Empire or else the tool of powerful, often competing, families of the Roman aristocracy.[2]

The Holy Roman Empire continued with Otto's various successors holding power into the eleventh century until a number of controversies with the papacy (see the relevant section below) forced the emperor to cede most of his authority to local German princes. By late in the fourteenth century, and even earlier at some points, the emperor was customarily elected by the local princes. As a result, the empire was a

---

2. Recall the early period of the papacy's domination by the Eastern Empire, which was followed by a period of autonomy and power. This pattern of external domination followed by autonomy and back to external domination would continue again and again into the future. It has been a recurring trend in the history of the papacy.

weak confederation with little power. It had lost control of France and Switzerland (where, as in Germany, the real power was located in local judicatories/cantons) and had only sporadic control of Italy.

Meanwhile during the declining period of the Carolingian era in the western Frankish lands (present-day France), local hegemony developed, and this region was totally independent of the German rulers. After almost a century of contention between two prominent families for power in the region, a single king was elected just fourteen years after Otto I's death. Western Europe was beginning to witness the construction of the modern national states as we know them in the twentieth century.

The fracturing of a once-united Europe and, more importantly, the Arab conquests had enormous consequences for economic and political life in western Europe. Before these conquests, there had been a great deal of free trade, and so a quasi-capitalistic economy. But with these trade routes blocked, money ceased to circulate. When money no longer circulates, wealth comes to be measured by land. Kings and lords paid for services by granting use of their lands, which is how feudalism began.

THE NATURE OF FEUDALISM AND THE MEDIEVAL WAY OF LIFE

Feudalism is an economic system in which land-ownership is what constitutes wealth. Landowners (called "vassals" in this system) and their laborers (called "serfs") placed themselves under a lord for protection. In fact, serfs had been arranging this sort of agreement with larger landowners even before the demise of the Carolingian Empire.

Given the precarious character of life in the Middle Ages in western Europe, such a perceived need for protection is readily understandable. A contract was involved in gaining this protection. The vassal agreed to pay homage to the lord in return for use of the land. The lord in turn would be entitled to a certain portion of products produced on the land. Because the grant of land was for a lifetime, and in some instances the land in a given region was held by various lords, feudalism had the effect of institutionalizing hierarchical relationships and creating a permanent underclass. It also effectively institutionalized political and economic fragmentation of western Europe at the expense of any real centralized authority.

It comes as no surprise that post-Carolingian medieval Europeans were so concerned about protection that they would enter into feudal contracts. Life in this period had few affinities with late-twentieth-century Western lifestyles. Human existence in the Middle Ages was oppressively constricted. Variety in one's social life was nonexistent, at least not for the masses. Everything, even the lifestyle of the landed lords, was highly regimented. Why such regimentation arose and why it could be experienced by the masses as the divine order are easy to understand. Survival was the name of the game, and survival was a most precarious mode of existence in the medieval West. Western Europeans greeted the Middle Ages with a distinct sense of their powerlessness, which was no doubt rooted in the cultural inferiority many of the regions had experienced in the Roman Empire. With Rome's conquest, though, even the southern regions of the West, which had been the ancient empire's power base, had become second-class cultures in comparison to the Greek religio-political system and increasingly to the emerging Islamic civilization.

The sense of powerlessness experienced by western Europeans in this period was related to the more common experience of feeling politically and religiously powerless, the powerlessness that premodern peoples have always felt when confronting the horrors of plagues, famines, robbers, and local wars. Later in the Middle Ages, there would be plagues aplenty. In the absence of any central authority after the fall of the Roman Empire, local robbers and national invasions by Slavs, Hungarians, and Vikings were always present dangers. In addition, the loss of real profit-bearing economic trade after the Arab conquests in the ninth century effectively put an end to such trade and further contributed to declining standards of living. With this decline came a general decline in learning, for a culture that merely allows for subsistence living does not afford sufficient opportunity for study.

Nothing was certain in daily life for ordinary people in the Middle Ages. Any moment it could all come to an end. It was precisely the vulnerability of the ordinary farmer to the raids of robbers and barbarians that increasingly led such people to seek protection of a lord, who had an army that could defend the otherwise vulnerable family. The medieval town typically had its origins in this arrangement, that is, as peasant families made their homes around the lord's castle and from there went to work the fields. To be sure, even this arrangement brought uncertainty, for the lords were always at war with one another, and it was the peasants who were to be the victims of war. No matter, meaningless flux was all around. Even the lords' governments did not always endure for long.

Except for the culture developed by the Moors in Spain, daily life in these medieval towns was no bed of roses. The streets were narrow, crooked, dark, and filthy. They were not even paved. And we complain today of pollution! People threw all their garbage and rubbish into the streets. This was the origin of many of the catastrophic plagues of the era. There was no such thing as police protection. If you were crazy enough to go out at night, you better have your own servant bodyguards with you. Nights were dangerous for other reasons. The lamps typically used at night made the whole town a fire hazard. The city of Rouen, France, for example, burned to the ground six times between 1200 and 1225.

MEDIEVAL SPIRITUALITY

In the fleeting, transitory world in which the medieval commoners lived, the Church and monastic life had an important impact. In a world of meaningless change, people yearned for permanence, for certainty, for something immutable and eternal. The great cathedrals and the monasteries built during these centuries were living symbols of immutability and hope in the midst of frightful flux. In all the chaos, at least there was some order, something sure, stable, and magnificent in the midst of all the poverty, degradation, and uncertainty.

This was no fundamentally secular society like modern readers know, where religion is put on the shelf until Sunday (maybe dusting it off for Wednesday night). On the contrary, the practical meaning of religion, a sense of the divine intervention in daily life, a sense of the miraculous, was indelibly imprinted in people's minds. Such miracles were everywhere in evidence. They were revealed in the religious ceremonies (bread was miraculously transformed into Christ's body daily in Communion) and evident in saintly lives, in healings, and in holy relics allegedly having belonged to the great saints. Through these, powerless human beings had something to which to cling; with much regularity, the supernatural intervened to protect them from all the flux.

The medieval sense of total dependence on God and the loss of a central, uniting governing power in Europe in this period (even the Carolingian Empire lasted only from the conquest of Charlemagne through the ninth century) had important sociopolitical consequences. They combined to create a social milieu in which the Church (and its head, the papacy) came to play the powerful role of sanctifier of governments and coordinator of international military operations (such as the Crusades). In view of these social and economic factors that gave the Church such a dominant role in daily life, it is little wonder that scholars have begun to refer to the Middle Ages as the "age of faith." It was so in the sense that any conception of the world from which the supernatural was excluded was an impossibility to the mind of the medieval person. Even our rational capacities were subordinated to faith. For the most eminent theologian of the Middle Ages, Thomas Aquinas (ca. 1225–74), reason clearly has its limits, for some truths are beyond the reach of reason. But theology has no limits; its sphere is also the sphere of reason.[3] In the High Middle Ages, faith had the final say in every sphere of life.

The Church owned much property in this period. Consequently it effectively functioned as a feudal lord, the property held by bishops and monastic abbots. Their appointment, then, became a matter of enormous social, political, and economic import, and, as we shall observe, became a source of a number of problems and controversies.

THEOLOGICAL CONTROVERSIES: DID THE CHURCH RESOLVE THESE HELPFULLY?

There was a revival of learning in the Carolingian era and some theological activity. Wherever there is theology, there is bound to be some controversy. Whether the Church helpfully resolved the various controversies is something readers should decide and articulate for themselves.

John Scotus Erigena (ca. 810–ca. 877) was perhaps the one great scholar produced from Charlemagne's concern with education. This Irishman gained widespread influence for his contention that Paul was a Neoplatonic mystic. God, Scotus Erigena claimed, is totally unknowable, and yet he is also everything and all things are in him (*On Natures* 1.66,72). Given these suppositions, the great Irish theologian drew the obvious conclusion that there will be no punishment for the wicked: "All wickedness, will be abolished from the nature of things, what remains except that the whole of creation will remain" (5.27,8). God would be all in all.

Though Scotus Erigena had the full support of the Carolingian emperor of his day, his erudite works inspired a number of later heresies. His work was an ensign to those who followed him in this new era.[4] No matter how highly regarded Augustine's theology had become in the West (since its virtual canonization by Pope Gregory the Great), theologians of this new era deemed it necessary to go beyond Augustine at some points and generate their own distinct theologies. A number of medieval theologians who followed Scotus Erigena also saw the necessity of going beyond prior theologies. Are the directions he sketched, prodding a move beyond Augustine's thought, useful resources for our own era?

A controversy developed within the Spanish Catholic Church in the eighth century, in a church already plagued by tensions following Charlemagne's conquest of those regions formerly held by Arabs as a result of the Moslem invasion. During the period of Islamic rule, a number of Christians had remained and maintained a church, which came

---

3. Thomas Aquinas *Summa contra Gentiles* I.3.
4. Medieval intellectuals perceived themselves, not as forerunners of a modern era, but as thoroughly "modern" people.

to be know as "Mozarabic." Its liturgy and theology were of a period prior to the invasion, and after being liberated by the Carolingians, the Mozarabics resisted efforts to replace their traditions by the usages of France and Rome.

Claiming to be loyal interpreters of their historic liturgy and its traditions, Spanish bishops Felix of Urgel (d. 818) and Elipandus of Toledo (ca. 718–802) began advocating that Jesus was Son of the Father, but that according to his humanity, he was Son only by adoption.[5] Others like Beatus of Liébana responded by claiming that in Jesus the divine and human were so closely bound that God actually died on the Cross (*Epistle to Elipandus* I.4). Felix and Elipandus were not teaching an *adoptionist* Christology in the strictest sense, for they did not claim that Christ only became divine by God's adopting him but affirmed that in his divine nature he had been the Son of God eternally. Nevertheless, the papacy condemned both bishops.

The debate between these bishops and Beatus is suggestive of the ancient controversy between Alexandrian and Antiochene Christologies (with Felix and Elipandus coming down on the side of a radical Antiochene position). Both bishops insisted that a denial of Christ's adoption according to his humanity would effectively deny that he was a true man.[6] Were they rightly condemned?

Gottschalk of Orbais (ca. 804–ca. 869) was a German theologian condemned by two synods (in Mainz in 848 and in Quiercy in 849) and by various theologians, including Scotus Erigena, for calling the Church to return to Augustine's teachings on predestination.[7] For Gottschalk, the very character of God as omnipotent and unchanging demands this conclusion (*Responses* 6–7; *Brief Confession*).[8] But Gottschalk was going against the way in which Augustine had been received by the Church since the Synod of Orange. Must we endorse Gottschalk's conclusions in order truly to affirm God's sovereignty and omnipotence (Rom. 11:18)? Or is Scotus Erigena's universalism a more viable option (1 Tim. 2:4)? We should also assess the viability of the counterproposal of another participant in the dispute, Hincmar of Reims (ca. 806–82), who held that election is based on God's foreknowledge of the person's free will decision about faith (*To the Recluses and the Simple;* cf. Rom. 8:29).

A debate also emerged in the Carolingian era over the sense in which the Communion elements become Jesus' body and blood. The Benedic-

---

5. Elipandus *Epistle to the Bishops of Francia* 2.
6. Elipandus *Epistle to the Bishops of Francia* 15.
7. Scotus Erigena *On Predestination* II; XIV.1.
8. It is interesting to speculate about a possible relationship between Gottschalk's faith that everything is in God's hands and his own personal background as an *oblate* (one who had been dedicated to monastic service since childhood and raised in a monastery).

tine monk Paschasius Radbertus (ca. 790–865) held that transformation of the elements (transubstantiation) transpires in the sacrament so that the elements are no longer bread and wine (*On the Body and Blood of the Lord* 1,11). Some critics, especially the monk Ratramnus (d. 868), were inclined to insist that though the elements remained as they were, according to their "divine force" Christ's power was present. Ratramnus added, however, that the body of Christ present in the Eucharist is not identical with his historical body sitting at the right hand of the Father (48,57,69,72). The issue was settled in Paschasius's favor in 1215 when transubstantiation was affirmed by the Fourth Lateran Council. This was not the first time that prominent leaders of the Church had insisted that Christ is really present in the sacrament. Was the Catholic Church not correct in ultimately backing Paschasius?

Another theological development in this period grew out of reflections on *Mariology* (the doctrine of Mary). As more and more liturgical homage was given to Mary, some theologians, including Paschasius, began to refer to her *immaculate conception* (Mary's being born without sin) and her assumption into heaven.[9] The Roman Catholic Church's endorsement of these doctrines in the last two centuries has ancient roots. Given the ancient roots of these doctrines should Protestants not reconsider their validity?

PAPAL AUTHORITY AND REFORM
AFTER CHARLEMAGNE

The decay of the Carolingian Empire was also an evangelism opportunity for the Church. The various tribes of Poles united early in the eleventh century and became Christianized. Meanwhile a new round of foreign invasions on the territory of Charlemagne's empire was begun by Norsemen (Vikings) and the Magyars (who, because they reminded western Europeans of the Huns, have come to be known as Hungarians). Both had great success in the conquest of continental Europe, at least in pillaging much of its riches. But many converted and brought Christianity back to their motherlands. The story of how Christianity finally was established in Norway is especially revealing of this ethos.

Christianity took root in the land of the Vikings through the work of the king Olaf Haraldssön (St. Olaf; 995–1030) in 1016 after his conversion in England, presumably on one of his raids. An earlier king, Olaf Tryggvason (b. ca. 963) first brought Christianity to Norway, though

---

9. Paschasius *On the Parturition of Mary* 1.16; 2.64; *You Compel Me* 7–9.

without his namesake cousin's success.[10] After his conversion, Olaf Haraldssön gave Norwegians a choice they could not refuse: baptism or death. There are indications that Olaf's method, despite its apparent success, did not completely win the hearts of the Norwegian people. Aspects of their indigenous religion, especially belief in trolls (supernatural giants or dwarfs living in caves), persisted well into the modern period.

With regard to papal authority, specifically how did it develop from the time of Charlemagne to the High Middle Ages? After the demise of Charlemagne's empire, powerful Italian families dominated the papacy. Many times rival popes reigned simultaneously. One of the first emperors of the new Holy Roman Empire explicitly sought a reformer for the papacy. That pope, Sylvester II (ca. 940–1003), was not entirely successful in his efforts. Nevertheless, there was general yearning for reform throughout the Western church, even for reform of monastic life.

THE CLUNIAC REFORM AND ITS BROADER IMPACT

At least by the tenth century, monasticism was in dire straits. Invading Norsemen and Magyars had destroyed many monasteries. Worse yet, the rigor of monastic life was being neglected. It had become a comfortable way of life for the rich, who could become abbots of monasteries and wallow in their wealth.

In the midst of these anxieties, the Cluniac movement, a monastic reform movement, was a significant development. It was initiated by Duke William of Aquitaine, who early in the tenth century founded a monastery in Cluny. For a noble to establish a monastery was nothing particularly unique in this era, but William made some noteworthy and significant decisions in founding this community, not least of all was his calling on the devout monk Berno to establish it. Under Berno and his successors' devout and capable leadership, Cluniacs became the center of monastic reform through strict enforcement of the Rule of Benedict, though with more emphasis on divine office (on daily public prayer) than on physical labor. The monastery was also placed under direct jurisdiction of the papacy so that nearby bishops and feudal lords could not meddle in its affairs.

In time, the horizons of this monastery began to broaden, and its abbots set out to reform other monastic houses in accord with this

---

10. In a similar manner, Christianity was first brought to Denmark when the Danish chief Harold was baptized in England in the century before Olaf's conversion, though it was not until the eleventh century that the Christian faith became generally accepted. Although Christianity was first brought to Sweden in the ninth century by Anskar (801–65), who also worked in Denmark after Harold's conversion, it was not permanently planted until the eleventh and twelfth centuries by the British. From Sweden and Russian, the Church also made its way into Finland in the twelfth century.

model. Eventually, as the papacy sank into another period of decay and bondage to extraneous sociopolitical agendas, the Cluniacs and others began dreaming of being a paradigm for papal reform and for reform of the whole Church. By the eleventh century, this dream had the support of many who were not Cluniacs. Its components, all of them embodied in the motherhouse in Cluny, included (1) freedom of church leaders from civil authorities, (2) overturning *simony* (the buying and selling of ecclesiastical posts), and (3) clerical celibacy. It was believed that clerical marriage must be rejected lest clergy try to pass on their authority to their children, a dynamic that would forever have the Church reflect only interests of the rich and powerful. It is well to recall this intention when reflecting on the virtues and vices of the Catholic Church's insistence on clerical celibacy (1 Cor. 7:8). Does the Church not still face these problems (the "clergy dynasties" of Protestantism and the bourgeois character of many churches) that require some remedy?

Pope Leo IX (Bruno of Toul; 1002–54), who had been named pope by a Holy Roman emperor who supported the Cluniac reform, and his immediate successors tried often heroically to implement these reforms. For example, he went uninvited to France, where ecclesiastical corruption was especially intense, and convened an Easter Synod in 1049, which decreed that all clerics should be celibate. The synod also deposed several French clergy who had practiced simony. Unfortunately, Leo's reforms were not fully implemented, and he was the pope that presided over the East-West Schism. He showed his loyalty to the emperor who had made his appointment happen, both by excommunicating a leader of a revolution and reaffirming that the emperor could rule the life of the Church in his domain.

There was much controversy over how to elect a successor to Leo. Not wanting to overturn the Cluniac stricture against governmental interference in the Church, the Holy Roman emperor called on the Romans to elect the new pope, with the stipulation that they must elect a German (in order that the office not fall to one simply holding the position as a local political tool). The new pope who was elected, Victor II, exercised significant political influence on the empire, as he effectively functioned as the regent for the boy emperor Henry IV (1050–1106).

The next popes continued to be reformers. One reform came to pass with the calling of the Lateran Council in 1059, which created a formula for electing popes.[11] It was at the Third (Ecumenical) Lateran Council of 1179, which also held that no Christian should be held as a slave, that this method of papal elections was certified. The formula

---

11. This council was not to be deemed one of the ecumenical councils, which the whole Church recognizes as authoritatively binding.

agreed upon was that the pope was to be elected by *cardinals* (bishops who may function as the pope's representatives) with the consent of the Roman people. This move was shrewdly political. The cardinals in this period were predominantly reformers, so this would ensure election of reforming popes.

The system worked well for some time. In England, during the reign of William the Conqueror (ca. 1028–87), the reforms enjoyed their strongest royal support and greatest success. The reformers did encounter staunch opposition, especially in France, on clerical celibacy from a coalition of powerful prelates who were gaining economically from their posts and married parish clergy who would have otherwise supported reforms against simony. It should be highlighted at this point that as late as the final decades of the eleventh century it was still common practice for Catholic clergy to marry. By no means was clerical marriage totally eradicated in the next centuries, as it often went underground replaced by the practice of priests taking concubines.

THE LAY INVESTITURE CONTROVERSY

Among the problems reforming popes of the eleventh and twelfth centuries encountered was the practice of *lay investiture* (the practice of royalty appointing bishops and abbots and conferring the prelate's insignia of office in a formal worship setting). Pope Gregory VII (Hildebrand; ca. 1021–85) forbade the practice in 1075, touching off the controversy. The papal position was clearly in accord with the suppositions of the Cluniac reform, specifically its commitment to upholding the freedom of church leaders from political authorities. From the side of the Holy Roman emperor Henry IV, this decree was a disaster. To his mind, his power depended on having bishops in place who would support him. A long controversy followed with charges that Gregory did not in fact validly hold the papal office and with papal threats of excommunication issued to the emperor. Henry responded in various ways, including lending support to papal pretenders. This had the cumulative effect of stripping Gregory of all power before his death.

With the principal parties deceased by 1109, a compromise was established. The new emperor, Henry V, gave up the right to invest bishops (ceding this to the pope) as long as the Church gave up all feudal privileges. This was a key issue for the emperor because political rulers would be foolish to give up the right to name the bishop if bishops held political power. Conflicts developed over this agreement. Clergy raised objections. They saw themselves deprived of temporal power. Under pressure, the emperor tried to renege on the agreement. From then on, the popes looked to France more and more as an ally and not to the Holy Roman Empire.

The Concordat of Worms, a lasting compromise, was finally worked out in 1122. The compromise, which was aided no doubt by the fact that the new pope Callistus II (Guido of Burgundy; d. 1124), was a relative of the royal house, formalized somewhat the earlier agreement and clearly was achieved through the pressure exerted by local German princes who were progressively gaining more and more power in the empire. The Concordat was itself confirmed by the First Lateran Council held the next year. Its main points were that (1) bishops and abbots are to be elected, without simony or coercion, though in the presence of the emperor; and that (2) investiture was only by the clergy, but the emperor was entitled to an oath of loyalty from each new bishop before he was consecrated.[12]

The overall record of the reforming popes in this era is an impressive one. They succeeded in instituting clerical celibacy. Simony almost disappeared for several centuries. Papal power grew. But the wealth and sociopolitical power that the Church had accumulated continued to be a haunting issue that never ceased plaguing the Church.

THE CRUSADES

The Crusades were a turning point in medieval history, another apparent high point in the development of papal authority and influence. Their aim was to defeat the Moslems who threatened Constantinople, to reunite Eastern and Western Christianity, and to reconquer the Holy Land (and in so doing win heaven). As a result of these military endeavors, Constantinople was able to survive until the fifteenth century, there was a brief period of East-West reunion, and Christians succeeded in holding the Holy Land for a century before returning it to the Moslems.

The Crusades were motivated both by apocalyptic hopes and a poor economic situation in Europe, which made such an adventure attractive. This was particularly true of the First Crusade, the one that in many respects was the most successful. Among others are five particular consequences that the Crusades had on the life of the Church: the Crusades (1) built up enmity between Christians and Moslems, as well as suspicions between Rome and Constantinople; (2) exacerbated anti-Semitic Christian tendencies, as the Second Crusade showed sentiment towards exterminating Jews; (3) advanced the power of the papacy; (4) had an impact on Christian piety (as contacts with the Holy Land

---

12. The emperor, though, must recognize bishops installed elsewhere but could still bestow the appropriate regalia.

led to greater focus on the Bible's narratives and the humanity of Jesus); and (5) had an influence on monastic life in that the military preoccupations of the Crusades influenced the emergence of several military-style orders, notably the Templars (who were mandated to protect pilgrims on public roads in the Holy Land) and the Order of Santiago (a military order designed to expel the Moors, or Spanish Moslems, from Spain).

The First Crusade (1096–99) was occasioned by the hope that such an endeavor to rescue Christ's sepulchre from the Moslems would advance the kingdom of God (by helping to realize the heavenly Jerusalem) and also by a dire economic depression and series of plagues, which had ravaged Europe. Pope Urban II (ca. 1042–99) promoted this expedition. He was responding to a series of urgent requests from the Eastern emperor for help in defending the empire from Turkish armies. Of course, the idea of raising a Western army to save Constantinople and retake the Holy Land had been proposed by the early reforming popes, like Gregory VII who envisaged a world united under the one papal shepherd.

Largely led by French feudal barons, the Crusaders joined with forces of the Eastern Empire culminating in a successful conquest of Jerusalem. Numerous Jews and other innocent citizens were tortured or put to death during the conflict. Jerusalem was again in Christian hands! The Crusaders established a Latin kingdom of Jerusalem. Waves of new Crusaders came and went in the next half century, yet sufficient recruits were garnered to protect the new Western kingdom in the Holy Land from Moslem assaults. These developments were also sufficient to keep Europe in a fever pitch of religious-military fervor.

The Second Crusade (1147–49) was initiated as a result of the Moslem reconquest of portions of the kingdom of Jerusalem. In Europe, it was inspired by the sermons of various notable preachers, including the renowned and highly respected Cistercian monk Bernard of Clairvaux (1090–1153), who advocated the organization of an army of relief for the Jerusalem kingdom. The crusade was led by the Holy Roman emperor and the French king. Along the way to the Holy Land, these Crusaders engaged in the extermination of Jews, and they failed in their originally intended mission, for they never reached Jerusalem.

The Third Crusade (1189–92) was occasioned by the Moslem reconquest of Jerusalem in 1187, the news of which deeply shook western Europe. Pope Gregory VIII called for a renewal of the crusading spirit, and all the major sovereigns of the region, including England's Richard the Lion-hearted (1157–99), temporarily put aside their rivalries and participated. The crusade did succeed in recapturing one of the cities of the Jerusalem kingdom, but it failed to regain Jerusalem itself. The endeavor also degenerated when internal European rivalries led the Holy Roman emperor to take Richard captive, holding him for some time.

Inspired by Pope Innocent III (1160–1216), the Fourth Crusade (1202–4) was an even greater disaster. Though its aim was to attack the Moslem leader at his headquarters in Egypt, the Crusaders rerouted to Constantinople, which they captured, and installed one of their own as emperor of the East, establishing the Latin empire of Constantinople. A Latin patriarch for the Church was also named. The Church had been reunited! It did not last long. The Byzantines retook the city in 1261, ending the Latin empire and its ties to the Catholic Church. The net result was more bitter and intense enmity between the East and West.

Later crusades, which continued until 1291, had little success, save one notable accomplishment. The Holy Roman emperor Frederick II (1194–1250) and the Moslems entered into an agreement that in 1229 placed Jerusalem, Nazareth, and Bethlehem in Christian hands. He was crowned "king of Jerusalem." However, the city was recaptured by the Moslems in 1244.

AFTER THE CRUSADES: THE FATE OF THE EASTERN EMPIRE AND ITS CHURCH

The Fourth Crusade and the period of Latin rule had seriously weakened the Eastern Empire. When the empire was restored to governing Constantinople, most of the territories it had once held were not returned. The Byzantine Empire was little more than Constantinople and its surroundings. Immediately upon the restoration of Byzantine rule, the new emperor entered into negotiations with the papacy with an eye towards establishing political security. This culminated in a Roman Catholic decree of unity with the Eastern church in 1274 by the Second Council of Lyons. The overwhelming majority of the Byzantine Church, though, rejected the decree.

The Ottoman Turkish menace to the Eastern Empire grew, and in 1422 the Turks laid siege on Constantinople. The Byzantine emperors had no choice. They needed help from the West. The pope would only grant their request for aid subject to another ecclesiastical reconciliation, which occurred in 1439 at the Council of Ferrara-Florence.[13] Various Eastern church patriarchs rejected the agreement. Constantinople fell to the Turks in 1453; the Eastern Empire was no more. Many Byzantine Christians interpreted this event as an act of God, as a liberation from

---

13. Union was also subsequently declared with the Armenian church and with the Coptic Orthodox Church in 1442.

a tyrannical emperor who had forced them into union with a heretical Roman Catholic Church.

Initially the conquering Ottoman Empire granted Christians a measure of freedom, allowing the new patriarch (the old pro-Roman one had fled) to function as the de facto civil and ecclesiastical authority for Christians. When the Ottomans conquered Syria and Palestine in 1516, these churches were likewise placed under the patriarch.[14] A similar status among Egyptian Christians was granted to the Alexandrian patriarch, who functioned as their de facto governor. The drawback of these arrangements was the patriarchs' lack of freedom to govern. If the patriarchs did not follow the sultan's wishes, they would be rapidly disposed. Of course, this sort of intimate, uncritical church-state relationship had long characterized the Eastern church ethos.

AFTER THE CRUSADES: THE CHURCH'S CONFRONTATION WITH JUDAISM AND ISLAM

The Crusades served to increase enmity between Christianity and Islam; they also contributed to hampering further relations between Christians and Jews. In several respects, this was a tragedy because there are indications that relations among these three monotheistic faiths had not been bad prior to the High Middle Ages.

Jews had endured a special fiscal tax during the earlier period of the Roman Empire. Constantine initiated a conscious policy of segregation in the empire after his conversion in order that the faithful not be polluted by Jewish false teachings. Remember also the callousness of Ambrose in his unwillingness to have the Roman Empire aid Jews who had been victims of synagogue burning and Cyril's banning of all Jews from his diocese in Alexandria. In the same period, Christian heretics, notably Nestorians and Arians, came to be referred to as "Jews," presumably because their Christologies were thought to give insufficient witness to the messiahship of Jesus. This was certainly consistent with the earliest traditions of postbiblical Christian theology, since the Apologists directed much of their theological defense of Christianity's credibility against perceived Jewish "errors."

Nevertheless, relations between the Christian masses and their Jewish neighbors were apparently quite wholesome in the patristic period and the early Middle Ages. Some Orthodox Christians preferred to refer to themselves as "Israelites" or "Jews." There is evidence that a number of Gentile Christians continued to attend synagogues on Saturdays

14. We observe in this development another reason why the patriarch of Constantinople has continued his role as the preeminent bishop of the Eastern Orthodox Church.

and celebrate Easter on Passover. In North Africa, many Christians were buried in Jewish cemeteries. After all, despite the agenda of many Apologists to refute Judaism, the religion of Abraham's heirs contributed most profoundly to the postbiblical church (recall the development of Jewish-Christian theology in the period of the Apostolic Fathers).

Such good will seems reflected in the early Middle Ages. Jews in Spain prior to the Islamic invasion established an intellectual climate of great significance to the European Jewish community. Well into the thirteenth century Jews in France and Germany still had permission to bear arms. From the ninth through the eleventh centuries, they were permitted to trade and transact business without restriction. In Germany, the Jews were pressed into service as merchants, providing the link between the farmer and the nobility. Many succeeded building stately homes.

Jews ranked with knights and Christian vassals in the feudal economy of the era. Ecclesiastical law protected their lives and basic possessions. The Fourth Council of Toledo in 633 decreed that Jews must not be compelled to join the Church but should only be persuaded to do so of their own free will.[15] Not until the tenth century were Jews pressed into service as moneylenders. The Cluniac reform strongly prohibited the money trade, as the monastic ideal came to be regarded as a paradigm for the lifestyle of all Christians (Luke 6:34–35). Contrary to popular impressions, Jews do not seem ever to have dominated the field.

Things changed dramatically with the Crusades. Extermination of Jews on the way to the Holy Land (blotting out all unbelievers) was espoused and practiced particularly in the Second Crusade. The Fourth Lateran Council of 1215, as part of its program of regulating the use of the *inquisition* (a judicial persecution of heresy by ecclesiastical courts, which may lead to temporal punishment), opened the way for authorization of plunging the Jews into a life of shame. As a follow-up from the council, they were to wear yellow badges and cone-shaped hats. That made them easy prey for their tormentors. Growing popular animosity towards the Jews was a function of the rising interest rates that began to emerge as the capitalist economy made inroads in the late Middle Ages. Even in this vocation, though, they were not secure. Christians began to enter the banking field in large numbers, and Jews were pushed out, permitted to lend only on a small level.

By the thirteenth century, society defined Jews as "king's serfs," and so their welfare depended on the whims of the ruler. Their goods could be expropriated anytime. At the same time, vicious slanders were spread among the populace about the Jews, such as the accusation that they

---

15. As has been observed, children of the Vikings and other European Gentiles did not receive such protection.

drank the blood of Christian children at their Passover observances. Popes, to the credit of the office, did take steps to proclaim the falseness of these accusations, but to no avail. Victimization by mob action became a consistent threat for medieval European (Ashkenazi) Jews. One of the new mendicant orders of monks, the Dominicans, worked especially hard in converting Jews and Moslems. What success they had, though, was largely related to the threats of force used by Spanish Christians (without regard to the decisions of the earlier Council of Toledo) against the Jewish community during later crusades. In this same period, Jews were expelled from England and France.[16] Some German Jews, under pressure, migrated to eastern Europe. In this period, ghettos, as we have come to know them, came into existence. Many of the stereotypes about the Jews in the Middle Ages, concerning their suffering at the hands of Christians, particularly as a result of the Crusades, are accurate. But as we have seen, that is not the whole story, particularly in the earlier centuries.

The Crusades also took a toll on Christian attitudes towards Islam, though not to the point of militating against a certain degree of appreciation for it. The threat its adherents posed to the Holy Land and the Eastern church led medieval theologians to lump it together with Judaism as a heresy.[17] As such, it was conceded that Islam did teach some things accurately.[18]

The Church's encounter with Islam forced theologians to reconsider the relationship between this new religion and Christian faith. In fact, at least one Eastern Orthodox theologian of the Middle Ages, Nicetas of Byzantium, found Judaism preferable to Islam.[19] The Fourth Lateran Council authorized stigmatizing Moslems, thereby plunging them into a life of shame, just as the council had targeted the Jews. Moslems were also targets of Dominican evangelistic endeavors, which were usually accompanied by threats of force, especially in Tripoli, Spain, and Portugal (after the reconquest of the Iberian peninsula). The encounter with Islam also put Western Christians in touch with a highly developed Arab culture and sophisticated philosophy.

PAPAL AUTHORITY AFTER WORMS

During the Crusades, further developments in the evolution of papal authority transpired. The Concordat of Worms and papal leadership of the

---

16. Only in the papal province of Avignon were they permitted to remain.
17. Peter the Venerable *Against the Sect or Heresy of the Saracens* 12.
18. Peter the Venerable *Epistles* III.
19. Nicetas of Byzantium *Refutation of the Falsely Written Book of the Arab Mohammed* 5.52.

Crusades by no means ended the papacy's difficulties. Several papal pretenders emerged, Roman citizens and various regions of the papal states rejected papal rule, and several twelfth-century emperors of the Holy Roman Empire sought to control the papacy.

The reign in the early thirteenth century of the most politically powerful of all popes, Innocent III, whose power was clearly reflected in part by his initiation of the Fourth Crusade, put these trends that tended to weaken the papacy to rest. In a case that was contested by the German nobles among rival claimants for the office of emperor after the death of Henry VI, the pope himself settled the matter by choosing the new emperor. Innocent justified his intervention by claiming that the emperor received his power from the pope, as the moon receives its light from the sun (*Sicut universitatis conditor* Ep.i.401). Consequently the pope had the authority to determine the rightful emperor. Eventually Innocent reversed his choice, but the episode demonstrates the power that he and the papal office in this period could exercise.

Innocent successfully intervened in the lives of virtually all the European monarchies. For example, he reprimanded the king of France for his efforts to put away his present wife in favor of another. He also reprimanded the king of England when he refused to accept a new archbishop of Canterbury, who was duly elected by the cardinals. The Fourth Crusade's conquest of Constantinople, though apparently against the pope's wishes, also served to increase his temporal power.

During Innocent's reign two great mendicant orders, the Franciscans and the Dominicans, were founded. He also convened the Fourth Lateran Council in 1215. Among the decisions made at the council were (1) the endorsement of transubstantiation; (2) the rejection of the founding of new monastic orders with new rules; (3) the mandate that every cathedral provide educational opportunities, even for the poor; (4) the establishment of strict lifestyle standards for clergy regarding abstinence from theater, games, and hunting; and (5) the decree that all the faithful must confess sins at least annually. Regular use of the sacrament of confession was mandated by the last decision, an expression of piety that would be most crucial for the Reformation. The council also instituted episcopal inquisition (giving each bishop the responsibility of seeking out heresy in his diocese and destroying it) and authorized indulgences (the remission by the Church of punishment deserved by the sinner, in effect releasing the believer from time that should be served in purgatory) for penalties due unto those who participated in actions aimed at exterminating heretics (such as the Crusades).

In connection with the institution of a more generalized use of the inquisition, we have already noted how the council stigmatized the Jews and Moslems, requiring all adherents of these religions living in Christian lands to wear distinctive garments that would separate them from Christians. Several other heterodox movements or persons were condemned, notably Peter of Waldo and the Waldensians, Flagellants, and the Albigensians (also known as Cathari).

The Flagellants were a mass movement of men, women, and children who marched through the streets naked except for loin cloths, crying to God for mercy and beating themselves until they bled. They sought out enemies to reconcile with them. The movement began in the mid-thirteenth century and spread from Italy to Germany and Bohemia, but subsided not long after it initiation. The movement revivified again in the fourteenth century but suffered persecution when adherents began to speak of their ritual as a form of penance.

Albigensians were Manicheistic in their belief structure (see chap. 9 for details) and flourished in southern France in the twelfth and thirteenth centuries, which in this period was a region where the Catholic Church and its leadership were infamously corrupt. Members of this sect held that Christ was an angel with a phantom body, who did not suffer and die. His redemptive work consisted only in his teachings. They rejected the sacraments, believing that all matter is evil created by the forces of evil. They also disdained the practice that had developed since the time of Pope Gregory the Great of praying for the dead. In addition, the Albigensians held an extremely rigorous ethic but recognized two classes of humans — the perfect who, baptized in the Holy Spirit, keep the precepts in all their rigor and ordinary believers.

The Albigensians were so called because their strongest concentration was in a city of southern France, Albi. The sect's adherents in Italy were known as Cathari (which in Greek means "pure," for purity is what this sect aimed to achieve). Innocent III had called for a crusade against the Albigensians even before the Lateran Council met, and they were as persecuted as the Moslems. These undertakings were remarkably "successful," as there was scarcely a trace of the sect remaining by the end of the fourteenth century.

The Albigensian doctrines were much akin to an earlier Manichee sect from the East (specifically, the Balkans) known as the Bogomils. Many scholars believe that the Albigensians appropriated their views directly from this group. In the sixteenth century, the Ottoman Empire invaded the territories where this heresy was continuing to thrive. Many adopted Islam, and so practically no trace of the heresy remains.

Pope Innocent's stature led many to conclude that he was somehow superhuman, that the pope had authority extending to every human endeavor. These popular attitudes contributed to the eventual attribution of infallibility to certain papal teachings and to Protestant misunderstandings of the idea. Innocent's successors established the autonomy of the pope's rule over the papal states. This political hegemony rendered the papacy the political guardian of Western culture, a role that contributed to a decision in the mid-thirteenth century to send Catholic missionaries to Mongolia and China, both for purposes of evangelism and for spying. These missions continued into the fourteenth century, even as papal power went into some decline as early as the late thirteenth century. At the turn of the fourteenth century, some Nestorian Christians already in China converted to Catholicism, and the Catholic Church was planted. Along with much of the earlier Nestorian Church, it was largely wiped out as the fourteenth century waned, primarily because most Christians in China were Mongolian and came to be persecuted.

Meanwhile back in Europe, papal power did decline beginning in the late thirteenth century. Boniface VIII (ca. 1234–1303) did much to stabilize that power, especially in Italy. Also in 1300 he declared a Year of Jubilee, promising indulgences to all who visited the Tomb of Saint Peter in Rome.[20] He used moral pressure (and the pressure of ecclesiastical discipline) against the Holy Roman emperor and the kings of France and England, who were threatening war with each other (which eventually led to the Hundred Years' War). Tensions were especially high with the French king Philip IV after he took some actions that deliberately provoked the pope, including confiscating ecclesiastical land and forbidding the transport of gold and other valuables to Rome. In response, Boniface issued a bull in 1302, *Unam Sanctam*, claiming that temporal authority was to be judged by the spiritual authority (Jer. 1:10).

Precedent for such claims had been set at least as early as in 1081 in Pope Gregory VII's previously noted dispute with the Holy Roman emperor Henry IV (*Letter to the Bishop of Metz*). Another relevant precedent is the previously noted 1198 papal bull (official decree) of Innocent III, in which he claimed that royal power is derived from pontifical authority. In addition, we should note the efforts made by Pope Innocent IV (d. 1254) to depose the Holy Roman emperor Frederick II on account of his failure to submit to papal authority concerning the Crusades and papal political power over the papal states in Italy. The First Council of Lyons meeting in 1245 officially declared Frederick deposed, though it failed to implement its decree. Given the political realities of the time, could the papacy have done anything other than seek to exercise the political influence it did? Or should church and state always be kept distinct?

---

20. This was a most fateful development for the sixteenth-century Reformation.

PAPAL AUTHORITY IN DECLINE: IS IT GOOD FOR THE CHURCH TO HAVE POLITICAL POWER?

The political power amassed by the papacy did not endure. Philip IV of France resolved to remove Boniface, and he succeeded. He carefully ensured that an eventual successor to the papacy was indebted to him, and this happened in 1305 when a pro-French party of bishops succeeded in electing Bertrand de Got (1264–1314), who became Clement V, as pope. Succumbing to Philip's pressure, the new pope relocated to Avignon, France, where he could be kept under the French king's thumb. For the next seventy years, popes would reside in Avignon, as little more than puppets of the French king (a period known as the "Avignon papacy").[21]

In view of the perils that the papacy and the Church as a whole endured in the Avignon period and the general sociopolitical pressures and manipulations it experienced throughout the Middle Ages, did the Church in this era not do well to gain all the political influence it endeavored to obtain? When the Church is not influencing society, it seems more readily victimized by the latest social trends and whims of its gurus. To remedy the risks of such victimization and in order to best use the Church's sociopolitical influence, is it worthwhile to have a centralized locus for that authority, such as the papacy? Also, were the medieval popes truly serving the gospel by accumulating as much power as they sought to obtain?

WAS THE MEDIEVAL REFORM OF MONASTICISM AN AUTHENTIC DEVELOPMENT OF THE GOSPEL?

Recall that monasticism began largely as a reaction to the establishment of Christianity in the Roman Empire, a way to live a life of total commitment to Christ in a manner no longer possible where being a Christian was now "legit." In the Western church, it has differed from its characteristic Eastern forms in at least three ways:

1. Western monasticism was more practical; it punished the body, not for the sole purpose of renunciation, but only to train for mission in the world.

2. The West never placed a premium on solitude, as in the East.

---

21. The story of how the pope finally returned to Rome and regained some, but by no means all, of its former political power will be told in chapter 14.

3. Western forms of monasticism did not live in constant tension with the ecclesiastical hierarchy, as was the case in the East.

As we previously noted, the main figures of Western monasticism in its formative years were Benedict and his sister Scholastica. Though there may have been Western monks before Benedict's time, his *Rule* organized the institution. In fact, in this earlier period, women's monasteries had largely been for the upper class. Even as late as several centuries after Benedict's and Scholastica's time, such monasteries were still quite independent. They were places for women to exercise freedom, which was only lost later in the Middle Ages when a more structured society brought convents under male control. Nonetheless significant women leaders emerged in the convents in this era, such as the eminent Benedictine mystic Hildegard of Bingen (1098–1179), whose prophetic gifts and eschatological visions inspired popes during her lifetime.

The monastic ideals of Benedict (permanence, obedience, physical labor, and prayer) had fallen on hard times in the tenth century, and the institution of monasticism in general was in disrepute. Great abbeys had become means of personal aggrandizement because with all the property they had accumulated, the income they realized made for a most comfortable living. The *Rule of Saint Benedict* was largely ignored. The pain and despair felt over these developments by devout Catholics as the ninth century ended must have been excruciating, considering what monasticism had meant to western Europeans in the previous centuries. In the midst of the fleeting, transitory character of earthly existence as medieval Europeans experienced it, how good it had been for them to have in their midst a replica of eternity, which the hospitable (the weary traveler could always find a home), stable, and immutable lifestyle of the monastic communities provided. In addition, monastic communities had made an important contribution to the economic life of medieval Europe. Many such communities had been established on marginal lands. The hard work of the brothers and sisters, though, had brought these lands into production. Thousands of acres of once unproductive land were now contributing to the welfare of Europe. Alas, by the tenth century it was all being polluted.

Given all that monasticism had meant to early medieval people in Europe, it is little wonder that the monastic ideal and the hope for its reform never died. The tenth century would witness a number of significant efforts to bring about such reforms. It is in this context that one can better understand the significance and hope that the Cluniac movement brought to the Western church. In a sense, the movement was a victim of its own success, as it increasingly accumulated power, influence in the Church as a whole, and wealth from an admiring laity.

CISTERCIAN MONASTICISM

The wealth of the Cluniacs eventually led to their demise. And so the reform required more reform. The Cistercian movement began in the late eleventh century as a reaction. Its most famous member was Bernard of Clairvaux, a mystic devoted to the contemplation of Christ, champion of ecclesiastical reform, and chief recruiter for the Second Crusade.

Much of Bernard's theology focused on the erotic, mystical marriage of Christ and the believer. Like Augustine, he drew on the Pauline image of the Christian as the bride of Christ (Eph. 5:31–32). However in Bernard's case, this was combined with themes most suggestive of the Song of Solomon. He referred to believers receiving kisses from God. As recipients of the divine passion, believers will necessarily quest for more intense fellowship with God. In the spirit of Augustine, Bernard claimed that "He Who moved my will to penitence should further give me the power to persevere." Yet Bernard did posit a hierarchy of holiness and claimed that forgiveness of sins is no good if we do not yearn to avoid sin (*On the Song of Songs* 3.3.5).

Bernard related these commitments to staunch advocacy of the classical Nicene and Chalcedonian formulations. Concerning the Trinity, he reiterated Augustine's notion of the Holy Spirit as the love that unites Father and Son (*On the Song of Songs* 8.1.2). Regarding Christology, he embraced the Alexandrian idea of the communication of idioms (*On Consideration* V.IX.21). Bernard also maintained the anti-Pelagianism of Augustine, insisting that a proper distinction be made between what comes from God and what we did ourselves (*On the Songs of Songs* 32.3.7) and that the merits God demands of the faithful were those that he had already given by prevenient grace (*In Praise of the Virgin Mother* IV.11). Given its catholicity and its richness, is Bernard's a theology that could still communicate in our day?

MONASTIC ORDERS WITH NEW PARADIGMS

At least two other types of monastic orders had their origins in the Middle Ages as reactions to its social dynamics. We have already alluded to the development of military orders, such as the Templars and the Order of Santiago, which grew out of the military dynamics of the Crusades. The next phase in the development of monasticism was the emergence of *mendicant orders* (monastic orders forbidden to hold property in common and whose adherents work or beg for a living). Their emergence was in part a function of the growth of cities at the height of the Middle Ages and the emergence of a monetary economy in the thirteenth century. In this new context, it was difficult for the traditional parish to minister to all who were flocking to town. The mendicant orders challenged the new urban preoccupation with wealth.

Peter of Waldo (Peter Valdes; d. ca. 1205), a French merchant, was a forerunner of the development of this new style of orders. A relatively successful entrepreneur, he was moved by stories of a monk who practiced extreme poverty to sell all that he had to devote himself to a life of poverty and preaching. In this respect, there are close parallels between Waldo's vision and that of the mendicant orders that gained the Church's sanction.

Waldo and his followers came to be known as the Waldensians. They sought papal approval but only received it for their vow of poverty. Sanction to preach was withheld, possibly because they were perceived as ignorant. They were clearly committed to seeking to restore what they regarded as the simplicity of New Testament Christianity. Despite the papal judgment, the Waldensians carried on their mission. As a result, they as we have noted, were persecuted and condemned by the Fourth Lateran Council. Under persecution, Waldo's followers fled to the Alps, where the group eventually accepted Reformation teachings and evolved into the Waldensian Church, which still exists today largely in Italy.

The Franciscans (Order of Friars Minor) follow Francis of Assisi (1181/82–1226), the son of a rich Italian merchant and his commitment to a life of poverty. He claimed to have wed "Lady Poverty" and then proceeded to give away his inheritance to the poor. Having given away even his clothes, he went naked into the woods to enjoy the beauty of nature. In time, his original vision altered slightly as he came to the conviction that poverty should be joined with preaching, that his place should not be in solitude but among the poor — a vision reflected in the *Rule of Saint Francis*, which still governs the order to this day. Francis never abandoned his love for the beauty of God's creation. He seems to offer a model for an ecological theology, one that includes communing with animals (*Canticle of Brother Sun*).

According to the *Rule*, brothers are to live in obedience without personal possessions and in chastity (1). Besides rubrics on corporate prayer (3), as in the *Rule of Saint Benedict*, there are also strictures on how subsistence may be obtained (often by begging) and in what circumstance one might preach (5–7,9). The Franciscan is to give all to the poor (2). The order certainly articulates a most impressive concern to identify with the plight of the poor, though it is stated in the *Rule* that a "good will" regarding these matters is sufficient if one is not able to do all this (2).

Although Francis received papal sanction for the order and traveled widely, he was never at the forefront of its institutional development. In fact, he feared that success of the order would corrupt it, though success it certainly had, and he voluntarily gave up its leadership. The Franciscan model even had an impact on female monasticism. One of the hundreds who joined his cause was Clare of Assisi (1194–1253). An Italian of noble birth, who left behind her wealth at eighteen and dedicated herself to "Lady Poverty," she eventually established the Poor Clares, an austere, contemplative order.

Shortly after Francis's death, a conflict developed in the order over how rigorously the Franciscans were to practice poverty. In response to those who believed that the order should be able to own property where it furthered its mission, Pope Gregory IX (ca. 1148–1241) decreed in 1230 that the will of Francis was not binding on the order. A rigorist party dedicated to literal fidelity to Francis's vision balked. They began to invoke the prophetic teachings of the deceased Cistercian monk Joachim of Fiore (ca. 1132–1202). He had taught *dispensationalism* (a view of history as different stages within each of which God works differently), thus placing more emphasis on the end times than had been typical of the medieval church. (Joachim had been condemned for such views by the Fourth Lateran Council.) The rigorists proceeded to argue that different believers have different rankings, that in the new age of the Spirit monks were heralds of the new age while the pope and other church leaders were of a lower level.

Given the number of Franciscans holding such views, the order was approaching a heterodoxy not unlike what became of the Waldensians. When Bonaventure (ca. 1217–74) became minister general of the order, he was able to reconcile these rigorists with the papal order allowing Franciscans to hold property.[22] No less than the continuing credibility and contribution of the order was at stake in these developments.

The Dominicans (Order of Preachers) were founded by the Spaniard Augustinian monk Dominic (1170–1221) later in the thirteenth century after the formation of the Waldensians and Franciscans.[23] Motivated by a desire to have in his native Italy a Catholic alternative to the Waldensians that was as attractive in its asceticism as the Waldensians (presumably he did not believe that his present order, the Augustinians, practiced sufficient rigor), Dominic proceeded with his own work stressing rigorous study and discipline. He gained papal sanction with the proviso that he adopt one of the existing monastic rules, as the proliferation of new monastic orders in this period was troubling to

---

22. His impressive theological contributions are discussed in the next chapter.
23. Augustinian Canons were communities of clerics devoted to a common life of poverty, celibacy, and obedience. They did not withdraw from the world but remained committed to a ministry to the faithful. The order was first formed in the middle decades of the eleventh century.

the hierarchy. Dominic and his followers adopted the *Canons of Saint Augustine*, which still govern the order.

Dominicans have always had a strong emphasis on study and the refutation of heresy, more so than the Franciscans. Poverty was merely a means to that end, a way of gaining credibility for the arguments of the monks because of their impeccable lifestyle. Historically it has produced, as have the Franciscans, some of the Roman Church's greatest theologians. The period when these orders were forming was also the time when theological study was beginning to find a home in the developing universities of Europe. The great medieval theologians of these orders became university professors.

ASSESSMENT

The typical Protestant reaction to the dynamics that led to the formation of these various monastic orders is to challenge them as not being in the best interests of the gospel. The concern may be akin to that expressed by the sixteenth-century Reformer Martin Luther that monasticism directs the believer away from Christ to oneself and one's works (*Next Book of Duke George* WA 38:159). Would the Church have been better off without monasticism, especially this Western form?

When one considers the profound impact that the medieval monastic reforms had on the Roman Church (notably the Cluniac role in overcoming corruption and instituting clerical celibacy as a universal practice), the inspiring character of the lifestyle it engendered, and the thoughtful theology that it nurtured, must we not conclude that the monasticism that resulted from these reforms has been good for the gospel? Has Protestantism been impoverished by its neglect of this office?

CHAPTER 13

SCHOLASTIC THEOLOGY IN THE HIGH MIDDLE AGES

A most telling characteristic of the Middle Ages is its theology. Scholars increasingly characterize the Middle Ages as the "Age of Faith," an era in which any conception of the world that excluded the supernatural was supremely alien to the minds of the people. Nothing could characterize such an age more than its theology. The style of theological reflection that developed in this period has been termed "Scholastic theology." The burden of this chapter is to understand and to assess Scholastic theology, to seek to determine whether this style was all wrong, as militant Protestantism and some strands of modern Catholic theology have alleged. Could the theological insights of the premier representatives of this theological approach still have something to say to us and to our experience of the faith?

The thirteenth century probably marked the apex of papal power and also the birth of mendicant orders; it was likewise the high point of Scholastic theology. Early roots of this theological style were in the monasteries, as most of its practitioners were monks. However, in the twelfth century, cathedral schools (authorized by the Fourth Lateran Council) became the center of theological activity, only to be supplanted in the thirteenth century by universities. One of the reasons why the theology done in this era has been termed "Scholastic" is because of its connection with these schools. The term also relates with the distinct method most theologians employed in this period. As we examine the character of its unique method, and the thought of each of the major figures of Scholastic theology, it would be well for readers to evaluate each particular theologian and sort out with whom they are most in agreement and why.

ANSELM

Probably the most important forerunner of Scholasticism was Anselm (ca. 1033–1109). A native of Italy, he was a Benedictine monk who late in his life became archbishop of Canterbury. As bishop, he clashed with England's king Henry I (1068–1135) over the authority of the Church in relation to the state and over enforcement of the papal strictures against lay investiture. As a result, much of his episcopacy was spent in exile. He used these periods to produce many of his greatest works.

THEOLOGICAL METHOD

Anselm's key theological and methodological commitment was "faith seeking understanding." That is, human beings only really understand when and because they believe (*Proslogion* I). Such commitments were implicit in Augustine's later thought, especially as he moved more and more away from Neoplatonism.[1] Though perhaps not as critical of reason as Tertullian, Anselm's commitments at this point clearly have more in common with the African Father's theological method than that of Justin Martyr.

An evaluation of the validity of Anselm's approach gives rise to at least two related questions. Must one believe in order really to understand? Or is it more helpful to seek to understand by reason in order to render faith credible, to understand in order to believe (as many of the Apologists held)? Anselm would have us engage in the use of reason for the sheer joy of contemplating what we believe. A number of scholars contend that it is precisely this commitment of Anselm's that renders him a forerunner of Scholastic theology. Though subordinating reason to faith, he clearly affirmed that reason is legitimately applied to questions of faith. This systemic commitment to the legitimate use of reason in extrapolating the nature of faith is the core characteristic of Scholastic theology.

Anselm's prioritization of faith over reason underlies his ontological argument for the existence of God. The concept of God, he maintained, is that of which nothing greater can be conceived. Consequently God must exist because God's failure to exist would imply a violation of the definition of the concept of God. If God did not exist, something greater than God could be conceived. God has to exist, or he wouldn't be the greatest. And if he is not the greatest, the reality considered is not God. Given the absolute logical necessity of God's existence, only a fool would deny God's existence. Again it is evident that faith is necessary to understand; without faith, one is foolish.

It is important to note that Anselm's "proof" is really in the form of a prayer. In that sense, it is an argument made from the perspective

---

1. *On the Trinity* VII.6.12; *Exposition of the Gospel of John* XXVII.9; XXIX.6.

of faith. If you really understand God, you cannot help but believe he exists (*Proslogion*). Is this argument persuasive?

OTHER DOCTRINAL COMMITMENTS

With regard to Anselm's treatment of certain core doctrines, his view of the atonement, his answer to the question of why Christ had to die, merits attention. In dealing with this doctrine, Anselm operated with the suppositions of his feudal culture — with symbols of honor, dishonor, obedience, reward. He conceived of sin as an affront to God's honor and majesty. God's justice requires satisfaction. God could not arbitrarily cancel debt because that would contravene (cancel out) divine justice. Human beings must atone for sin. Of course, though, they cannot. They owe everything to God. Consequently they cannot pay him anything extra for their sin that they do not already owe (*Why God Became Man* 1.19–20,23). Human beings must do the work of satisfying the divine demands, but sin is only recompensed adequately by giving what is greater than all that exists, except God. Only God is above God, so only God can save (2.6). Consequently the divine-human Jesus died a death of perfect obedience, satisfying the requirements of divine justice. Since God needs nothing, Jesus transferred the reward to sinful humanity (2.19; 1.9).

To be sure, Anselm's conception of Christ's atoning work was not dominant in the early Church, where the predominant image was that of Christ's death conquering the devil and the forces of evil (the so-called classic view of the atonement). However Anselm was by no means the first theologian to construe the work of Christ as a satisfaction of the demands of divine justice, which is called the "satisfaction theory" of the atonement (Eph. 5:2; Heb. 10:12). Images suggestive of this theory (at least the need to make satisfaction to God for sins), sometimes combined with those of the classic view, appear to some degree in the writings of Tertullian, Athanasius, Augustine, and others.[2] The difference between these conceptions raises the question of how to integrate them or how to determine whether one of them is more in touch with the New Testament witness. At any rate, in the Middle Ages, largely after Anselm, the satisfaction theory became the prevailing version of describing the atonement; indeed, it was perceived to be the only legitimate one.

Anselm's treatment of the doctrine of the atonement placed an emphasis on election as the basis of the creation and redemption of human beings (*Why God Became Man* 1.18). This compelled him to address the question of predestination, a topic in Western Christianity whose

---

2. See Tertullian *An Answer to the Jews* XIII; Athanasius *On the Incarnation* 7–9.

agenda Augustine had set, given his eminence among medieval theologians. Concerning this question and the related issue of soteriology, Anselm was uncomfortable with the full implication of Augustine's anti-Pelagian thought. Anselm claimed that God can be said to have destined all things, including evil deeds, only in the sense that he caused them as deeds, not that he caused these deeds to be evil (*On the Harmony of the Foreknowledge, Predestination, and Grace of God with Free Will* II.II). Freedom and foreknowledge as well as predestination are not incompatible. God foreknows without necessity that we will sin (1.1; 2.2–3). Because there is neither past nor future in God, but only an eternal present, God must not have predestined anything since all things are present to him at once (2.2). Immediate successors of Anselm tended to treat predestination in light of foreknowledge. They avoided, as did Anselm, any emphasis on the divine volition.

Given Anselm's unwillingness to forfeit the affirmation of human freedom, it was certainly consistent for him to claim that natural free will assists grace in saving us. Of course, he insisted that grace receive the credit, for without it free will could not attain to salvation (*On the Harmony of the Foreknowledge, Predestination, and Grace of God with Free Will* III.III–IV). If such a view is not perfectly consistent with Augustine, it clearly reflects a loyalty to the African Father's theological commitments in the sense of expressing a concern to repudiate Pelagianism. In fact, Anselm's soteriological reflections at this point seem reconcilable with the so-called Catholic side of Augustine's theology. Was Anselm a true interpreter of the African Father? At any rate, his general orientation of viewing salvation as the outcome of the cooperation of human works and divine grace, with a priority on grace, is symptomatic of much medieval Scholastic theology.

PETER ABELARD

Another famed forerunner of Scholasticism was the brilliant French scholar Peter Abelard (1079–1142). A bombastic, brilliant student who delighted in taking issue with his famed teachers and making numerous enemies along the way, Abelard became a renowned teacher acclaimed for his debating skills on the philosophical and theological topics of the day. He opened his own school of theological instruction, one independent of the cathedral (breaking with the Fourth Lateran Council's concept of cathedral schools). This institution was a forerunner in the development of the medieval (and modern) university. His renown brought him many students who would become famous, including numerous future cardinals and bishops. One of his pupils was Peter Lombard.

Abelard almost lost his career when a canon of the cathedral in Paris entrusted him with the education of his gifted niece Heloise. Abelard and Heloise proceeded with a passionate and infamous affair. The uncle had him emasculated, and Abelard left his school in Paris to become a monk. His enemies followed him. After other controversies in this and other new venues (he also became abbot of a cathedral in his native Brittany), he was able to return to Paris to resume his teaching. Controversy followed him again, as he was accused of heresy by the saintly Bernard of Clairvaux (*Epistles* 191.1), and several of his propositions were condemned. In death he was reconciled with the Church and with his lover, Heloise.

A major problem with Abelard, in the minds of his intellectual critics, was his bold use of reason. This in itself is qualification enough for ranking him as a forerunner of Scholastic theology, which is characterized by the presupposition that reason is legitimately applied to questions of faith. However there is a sense in which Abelard went another step along the way in proceeding from Anselm to Scholasticism proper. His theological method seems to employ reason, if not in a more autonomous way, at least as much as Anselm's did. Also his method deeply influenced his former student Peter Lombard, the man who wrote the standard theological textbook for the Middle Ages.

THEOLOGICAL METHOD

The key to Abelard's influential method was the compilation of apparently contradictory opinions of early Church theologians on points of doctrine, such as the atonement, theological method (correlationist or orthodox), and justification and the role of the law in the Christian life. Abelard's purpose in highlighting these contradictions was to force critical evaluation of the issues by the contemporary Church. He was aiming ultimately to synthesize this diversity into a meaningful whole. It was precisely this "yes-no," dialectical approach to theology and its related project of seeking to synthesize apparent opposites into a single system that his student Peter Lombard picked up and developed into the question-and-answer method of Scholasticism.

OTHER DOCTRINAL COMMITMENTS

Abelard addressed one very controversial philosophical issue that came to a head at the end of the Middle Ages — the status of universal forms. In classical Greek philosophy, universal forms are real — more real than individual physical objects. In the Middle Ages, proponents of this position (virtually every scholar in the High Middle Ages) were called "Realists." Abelard took a position between Realism and the denial of the reality of universal forms, insisting that universals name things that actually exist. Therefore, they are not empty thoughts, yet there is a sense in which they only exist in the mind (*Logica Ingredientibus*). This distancing himself from Realism was an important precedent for future development in the late Middle Ages.

Questions were posed to Abelard by his contemporaries. One set of challenges pertained to his treatment of the Trinity. Abelard had been locked in a debate with Roscellinas (d. ca. 1125), who had taught a kind of tritheism in the sense of arguing that there are three substances in the Trinity (*Epistle to Abelard* 10,13). In response to this apparent overemphasis on the distinctions within the Godhead, Abelard stressed the unity of the persons. However, his claim that God was triune, not according to a diversity of substance, but according to distinct properties of the person led some to conclude (including the Synod of Sens, which condemned him in 1140) that he taught that power and other divine attributes only belonged to one of the persons (*Christian Theology* I).

Abelard took a different approach (a third option) as to why Christ had to die (the doctrine of the atonement). He was especially critical of the satisfaction theory and its idea that Christ's death was pleasing to God the Father. In his view, Christ's Passion makes us more righteous, inspiring greater love to God in us (*Exposition of the Epistle to the Romans* II). This model has come to be known as the "moral influence theory" of the atonement. Is this an improvement on or decline from the other two models? It clearly emphasizes human responsibility in the salvation process. Bernard of Clairvaux criticized Abelard on this point, claiming that such a view belittled the need of redemption and was effectively a return to the Pelagian heresy (*Epistles* 190.9.23). Was he correct in this assessment?

Consistent with his view of the atonement, Abelard considered the question of whether those who came before the Incarnation might still be saved. He argued that those who strove to please God according to what they knew of him through the natural law accessible to all rational human beings would not be damned for their efforts.[3] However since salvation must be through Christ, he believed that God would reveal the saving truth of what is to be believed about Christ either through a special messenger or by divine inspiration (*Problems of Heloise* XIII).

---

3. Such an emphasis on the role of works in contributing to salvation is most consistent with the idea of the moral influence theory of the atonement and its claim that Christians are saved by following Christ.

Abelard also tried to make clear that Christians are saved, not by their works, but freely by grace. Of course, in the spirit of Anselm and the moral influence theory of the atonement, Abelard also argued that the love of God inspires love in us (*Exposition of the Epistle to the Romans* I,III).

PETER LOMBARD

An Italian, Peter Lombard (ca. 1100–1160) spent most of his career in Paris as a teacher in its cathedral school and later as bishop of Paris. His greatest contribution to the life of the Church was his composition of a systematic treatment of the main themes of Christian doctrine in question-and-answer form called the *Sentences*. The work became the main textbook for teaching theology in European universities for centuries. Subsequent theologians developed their own ideas by writing commentaries on these volumes. That is how important Lombard's work has been.

European universities emerged as outgrowths of the cathedral schools mandated by the Fourth Lateran Council. Instruction usually proceeded with the presentation of commentaries on the Bible and Lombard's great work, followed by debates on a theme related to the commentaries, which forced the students and professors to interact and stake out their own distinct theological positions. One wonders if this instructional method still has validity and why it has largely fallen in disuse. In the Middle Ages was none of today's "don't pin me down" or "don't evaluate me" style of education.

One theological controversy in the Middle Ages developed especially among Spanish Mozarabic Christians, who had not succumbed to Islamic domination during the period of Islamic rule in Spain. Some of them had espoused a kind of adoptionist Christology (see chap. 12 for details). Lombard refuted such adoptionism, making his case by marshaling witnesses of early Church Fathers and by appealing to Scripture that Christ's humanity and divinity are his by nature (*Sentences* III/X/II). We need to assess whether the careful citation of such precedents for one's position is still a viable way of doing theology or if such a style is anachronistically bound to its medieval context.

Regarding his sacramentology, Lombard offered only a qualified affirmation of transubstantiation (*Sentences* IV/VIII–X), which did not become official Catholic teaching (as affirmed by the Fourth Lateran Council) until after his death. He recognized the philosophical difficulties entailed in any precise statement of transubstantiation, speaking only of a substantial presence under the accident of the Communion elements.

With regard to his conception of God, Lombard argued that the Trinity is manifest in all humans. Creatures manifest the triune character of unity, form or beauty, and order (*Sentences* I/III/I). In his treatment of predestination, he apparently followed Anselm's tendency to make it to some extent contingent on divine foreknowledge. Thus he claims that when the Bible attributes the hardening of the heart to God (Exod. 9:12; 14:8; Mark 6:52), this act of God was merited by the sin of the entire mass of humanity (*Collections on the Epistle of St. Paul* Rom. 9:18).

Not everyone who followed Lombard agreed with the whole of his theology. His impact on the Church, though, as a result of the medieval church's widespread use of the *Sentences*, was truly enormous.

THE REDISCOVERY OF ARISTOTLE
AND ITS CONSEQUENCES

Later in the thirteenth century Western society was shaken by the reintroduction of Aristotle's thought. From the time of Justin Martyr in the second century, Plato and Neoplatonism had been the primary conversation partners for theologians. However, the Crusades and renewed contacts with Moslems in Spain and Sicily, where Aristotle had been and was still studied in the Middle Ages, led to this reintroduction of his thought.

Recall the differences between Plato and Aristotle. Both agreed that what is really real are the universal forms in which all individual entities participate. The key difference between them on issues related to this matter is that for Aristotle the form is *in* each individual thing (*Metaphysics* I.9). Each individual human being bears within himself or herself the universal form of humanity. Not so for Plato. For him the form exists in another dimension serving as an ideal to which the changing material world only approximates (*Timaeus* 1.51–52). Aristotle, then, was a bit more open to empirical approaches as a way to find truth, since the form is in what we perceive. Plato was more the pure rationalist.

Another difference surfaces between Aristotle and the version of Platonism that had prevailed in the West during the Christian Era (Neoplatonism). While the Neoplatonic agenda focused on the individual's relationship with eternity and a strategy for overcoming the anxieties of sensual experience, Aristotle's philosophy (like Plato's) was primarily preoccupied with explaining or understanding the world. In that sense the "new" Aristotelianism appeared atheistic in character, only concerned with the temporal world, while the (Neo) Platonism of the early Scholastics was perceived as concerned with the higher (spiritual) things.[4] This was probably the main reason for the resistance to Aristotelianism in the medieval Catholic Church.

The first medieval Westerners to appropriate Aristotle received his philosophy from the work of the great Islamic philosopher of the era, Averroes (1126–98). That the Western appropriation of Aristotle was mediated through Islamic philosophy meant that when Aristotle's insights were appropriated, it was done so without regard for to their consequences for Christian faith. The early medieval advocates of Aristotelianism argued that reason must be independent from any constraint imposed by faith and theology. In the Age of Faith, which characterized medieval western Europe, it is little wonder that the rediscovery of Aristotle was a most controversial development. Some theologians responded with a determination to defend the "old" Platonic Christian traditions.

A CRITICAL REACTION: BONAVENTURE

Bonaventure (Giovanni di Fidanza; ca. 1217–74) was probably the most famous Franciscan theologian of the period. His role was most important in stabilizing the order during a period of crisis when he served as its minister general, and he launched a kind of theological protest against the impact of Aristotelianism. A native of Italy, he was educated in Paris and spent most of his monastic career in the French capital. Along the lines of Anselm and Tertullian, he argued that faith (or at least eternal reason functioning as the regulator of the mind) is necessary in order to achieve understanding. In a way, he was in dialogue with Platonism at this point in arguing that all knowledge comes from the Word Incarnate in Christ. To claim knowledge apart from the Logos is to deny the very core of all knowledge (*Quaestiones disputatae de scientia Christi* 4).

That Bonaventure worked with something like Anselmian suppositions is evident in his employment of an ontological argument for the existence of God, for which he expressly cited the Canterbury archbishop. Granted, he also made an argument for God's existence akin to Thomas Aquinas's cosmological argument (*Quaestiones disputatae de mysterio Trinitatis* I.1). Reason can prove that there is a God, but only with faith is what reason knows of God brought to a higher order. Only with faith does reason become what it ought to be (*III Sentences* 24.2.3). One must believe in order truly to understand. Is this a valid presupposition, or should one's theological style be more inclined to try to relate faith and reason than to subordinate reason to faith? If so,

---

4. Bonaventure *Collations on the Hexaemeron* XVII.

the most influential of all the medieval Scholastic theologians, Thomas Aquinas, may be a viable alternative.[5]

To the extent that Aquinas was engaged in an endeavor to relate the gospel to Aristotle's philosophy (albeit not in a thoroughly systematic way), similarities are apparent to Justin Martyr's efforts to correlate the gospel with Plato. Likewise parallels can be observed between Bonaventure, Anselm, and Tertullian in their prioritization of the Word to the claims of reason. We have returned once again to the issues at stake in the ancient debate between Tertullian and Justin Martyr.

When Aquinas relates faith to Aristotle's philosophy, his theological method closely resembles the correlationist approach of Justin Martyr and the Alexandrians. However on some issues Aquinas was not as systematic about it. (In his view, on some issues Aristotelian philosophy was not relevant for faith.) In addition, Justin Martyr and the Alexandrians correlate faith with Platonic philosophy, not with Aristotelianism as Aquinas did. Nevertheless, formally, the commitment to and method of relating faith and philosophy is the same. Aquinas differs from the earlier correlationists only in details. Bonaventure and Anselm, by contrast, seem to be more in the heritage of Tertullian, insofar as they prioritized the Word of God over the truths that reason apart from faith can obtain. To the degree that the two great theological alternatives are either this sort of "orthodoxy" or the correlationist approach of Aquinas and the Apologists, which one seems more viable?

Among his core theological commitments, Bonaventure claimed that God aims to restore us through the hierarchization of the soul. The soul must be reorganized, and this is to happen through its progression through various stages of spiritual illumination. God is seeking to restore the image of God, rendering the soul *deiform* (*De donnis Spirit. Sancti* III.5).[6] Bonaventure spoke of the soul's illumination, at its highest stages, as the "mystical" elevation to God. At this stage, an immediate knowledge is given of God through one's experience (*The Journey of the Mind to God* VII; IV.4; III.1). This idea that God may be known immediately through personal religious experience is a logical outcome of the notion of the soul as deiform. If my soul has taken on the character of God, of course my experience will put me in direct touch with the divine.

---

5. Yet some claim that, no less than Anselm, Aquinas was merely using reason to interpret faith. See the discussion below of Aquinas's cosmological argument for the existence of God.

6. Although the precise meaning of *deiform* is unclear, to the degree it connotes humanity taking on the character of God, the similarities between Bonaventure's reflections on the soul becoming deiform and the Eastern theological notion of deification are certainly suggested.

Such direct contact with the divine is the essence of mysticism. Bonaventure cited Francis of Assisi, the patron of his order, as one who likewise espoused this sort of mystical theology. Certainly the legends about Francis's immediate encounters with Christ, which are somewhat akin to Bernard of Clairvaux's descriptions of his experience as the bride of Christ and its sensual character, suggest that both Francis and Bernard were mystics who believed that they had immediate access to God through their own personal religious experience.

In explaining how we are saved, Bonaventure claimed that God infuses grace, which penetrates the whole substance of the human soul and functions as the foundation of the will when it does the good (*The Journey of the Mind to God* I.7–8). In positing this sort of divine-human cooperation, with the priority of grace, Bonaventure demonstrated his continuing loyalty to the Augustinian tradition. In fact, there are obvious affinities between this approach to soteriology and the Catholic side of Augustine's thought. It also links with the views of Aquinas.

Bonaventure's views on how we are saved have several implications for his treatment of the doctrine of predestination. God, Bonaventure insisted, did not impose constraint of human free will and so is not himself the author of the hardening of the heart (*Commentary on the Sentences* 1.40). Reprobation is not a positive act on God's part, but a negative act of divine permission. The great Franciscan did not elaborate this point but stressed the need for concealment of God's ways. He did, however, elaborate some other aspects of the doctrine, claiming that predestination was not only grounded in God's foreknowledge but also in the unchangeability of his plan and ordinance. This affirmation breaks with the Anselmian tradition and the authoritative reinterpretation of Augustine provided by Pope Gregory the Great in favor of something more like the so-called Protestant (anti-Pelagian) side of Augustine's thought. Was this a beneficial development for the Church?

The prioritization of faith over reason and the concept of the soul's becoming deiform manifested itself in Bonaventure's views of the relationship between Church and state. His conclusions may also reflect his social context and the medieval church's vision of a Christian society in which the Church wielded supreme authority. From these suppositions, it logically follows that the state is to be hierarchically subordinate to Christian principles. Bonaventure came to this conclusion in a somewhat indirect route (most suggestive of the views of his contemporary Thomas Aquinas). He appealed to the concept of the *natural law* (the idea that all rational human beings have at least a sense of the contents of God's demands in the Decalogue) and proceeded to argue that the natural law dictates a hierarchical order (*Quaestiones Dispu-*

tatae, De Perfectione Evangelica IV.I). Justice is only achieved when the proper ordering of society has been established. Bonaventure also asserted that the worship of God is the foundation of such justice (1.Conc.), for reason is dependent upon faith as its proper starting point. Consequently, the state has a legitimate role in guiding subjects to faith (*Op. VIII; The Six Wings of the Seraph* c.v.), and its rulers are properly regarded as the Church's secular arm (*Commentary on the Sentences* 4.24).

THOMAS AQUINAS

Thomas Aquinas (ca. 1225–74) was an Italian scholar who joined the Dominican Order against his aristocratic family's wishes, for they desired better things for him than life in a monastic order dedicated to poverty. He spent most of his life in Paris, first as the student of the West's greatest scholar of Aristotle in the period, Albert the Great (ca. 1200–1280), and then after a slight interruption as a lecturer. The Dominican, whose primary project was the endeavor to reconcile faith and the new Aristotelianism, is generally recognized as the greatest of all the Scholastic theologians. The sixteenth-century Council of Trent officially declared Thomas's to be the dominant theology in the Catholic Church, and it still officially plays that role.

THEOLOGICAL METHOD

Was it a good development for the Church that Aquinas took on the task of undercutting Platonic influence? Platonism does effectively undermine the present and the physical. This in turn could make it easier to push the Incarnation in the background, focusing faith only on the Logos. Aristotelianism has the virtue of taking the empirical more seriously. Is it good that Thomas made such Aristotelian suppositions more of a dialogue partner for faith?

Aquinas did not unequivocally correlate Christian faith with the tenets of Aristotelian philosophy. To his mind, there were some aspects of the gospel that are radically autonomous. Granted, some truths about God are accessible to reason, however, others are not. With regard to the second sort of truths, one can only appeal to Scripture. Nevertheless, the truths of faith can never be opposed to the principles of reason (*Summa contra Gentiles* I.IV). Grace presupposes nature and completes nature, but does not abolish it (*Summa Theologica* I.2.2; *Summa contra Gentiles* III.XXVI).

Aquinas's commitment to relating nature and grace, reason and faith, manifested in his regular employment of an allegorical method of biblical interpretation (*Summa Theologica* I.1.10). The whole point of opting for the possibility that the Bible might mean more than its literal sense, he argued, was because the Bible must be shown to surpass all the sciences (i.e., be intellectually credible). Given the fact that the overall Scholastic agenda was to present an intellectually credible version of the faith, it is hardly surprising that many other Scholastics relied on the method of allegorical interpretation, often citing Augustine's spirit-letter distinction and early employment of the method.[7]

That these theologians, committed to demonstrating the intellectual credibility of the faith, not unlike the ancient Apologists, should have shared the allegorical method of the Apologists is hardly surprising. The history of Christianity reveals that whenever one does Christian apologetics, tries to make the faith rationally credible as the primary agenda, an allegorical approach to Scripture, which liberates one from what the Bible literally says, is the inevitable consequence. In the debate on theological method between Justin Martyr and Tertullian, such theological commitments will always lead to the conclusion that Justin is one's principal ally.

Like the other Scholastics, Aquinas argued that belief in God was rational and that the divine existence could be demonstrated by rational argumentation. He argued for God's existence a posteriori from his effects, rather than a priori, as is characteristic of Anselm's ontological argument. Aquinas was not willing to embrace the idea that the existence of God is self-evident. Such an argument is not possible because we do not know the essence of God; we can only know God by means of things known to us, by his effects (*Summa Theologica* I.2.1). This is Aquinas's cosmological argument, which he developed in five ways, with arguments from (1) motion, (2) efficient cause, (3) possibility and necessity, (4) gradation found in things; and (5) governance (*Summa Theologica* I.2.2–3).

Basically Aquinas's argument is that for every reality known to us, there is a relationship between that reality and the whole. It must have been caused, or there must be some other reality that is greater or more powerful than the reality first considered. What is said of this initially observed reality must also be said of its cause or superior. Something must have caused the cause or be of higher quality than something else. There must be some ultimate cause, something greater than everything else. That First Cause or Greatest Good is what everyone calls "God." Thus our experience of the world entails that God must exist.

---

7. Isidore of Seville *Against the Jews* 2.20.1; Aldhelm *On Virginity* 4.

It is possible to interpret Aquinas's arguments as depending on faith. In each case, the argument proceeds with the presupposition that the conclusion reached is that there must be a First Cause, a Greatest Good, a Governor whom "we call God," and this conclusion "all men call God." Is it not faith that authorizes the conclusion that we can call these realities "God"? In that case, the cosmological argument presupposes faith. Regardless of how one responds to the preceding question, is the cosmological argument credible, at least more credible than the ontological argument for the existence of God?

Another Thomistic methodological commitment worth noting is the distinction he drew between knowledge and belief. In the case of knowledge, he argued, assent depends on reasoning. With belief, reasoning follows assent and so is a matter of the will (*De veritate* XIV.1).

OTHER DOCTRINAL COMMITMENTS

Too often when Aquinas's theology is considered by non-Catholics, the Augustinian intentions of his views are not sufficiently considered, and he is portrayed as a man more concerned with philosophical questions pertaining to God's existence than with redemption. A study of his major works quickly belies that assessment. For him, the Incarnation is predicated on the concern with salvation. He claims that it was necessitated by, is contingent upon, the Fall (*Summa Theologica* III.1.1–3).

Aquinas insisted that sin has not destroyed all good in humanity. We still have reason. What has been lost is the original justice that Adam and Eve possessed prior to the Fall (*Summa Theologica* I/II.85.2). It is important to adjudicate whether this in any way compromises the anti-Pelagian perspective of Augustine. If the two disagree at this point, whose view is preferable?

With regard to the work of Christ, Aquinas typically endorsed the satisfaction theory of the atonement, the idea that Christ rendered satisfaction to the justice of God (*Compendium of Theology* 200–201). Of course, he did intersperse some references with it to the classic view of the atonement and its idea of Christ's overcoming the forces of evil (*Summa Theologica* III.1.2; III.48.4).

Besides Aquinas's predictable affirmation of post-Fourth Lateran Council Roman Catholic sacramentology, notably transubstantiation (*Summa Theologica* III.75), he also supported inquisition (including the death penalty, even for those who lapse a second time). He was willing to readmit heretics who would renounce their views and receive penance (II.11.3–4). Such uncompromising strictness towards those who are not true believers also manifests itself in his position towards the

Jews. Aquinas claimed that they are subject to perpetual servitude and that their goods are to be at the disposition of the ruler. He only cautioned that so much not to be taken from the Jews that they be deprived of the means of life (*De Regimine Judaeorum ad Ducissam Brabantiae*). Though willing to defend their well-being to a certain extent, Aquinas clearly intended to relegate Jews to the status of second-class citizens.

Aquinas presupposed a hierarchical view of church-state relations, which was typical of Bonaventure and medieval Catholic intentions. Government seems to be natural in Thomas's view (*Summa Theologica* I.96.4). There is a natural law to which the human laws of the state should conform (I/II.91.3; I/II.95.2; Rom. 2:14–15). Insofar as the end of human life is the enjoyment of God, so likewise this should be the proper end of the state. Consequently, the subordination of the state to the Church is explicitly affirmed (*De Regimine Principum* I.14).

Making a final determination of whether Aquinas (and so the Roman Catholic tradition) continued to maintain the Augustinian heritage is best determined with reference to the Scholastic's treatment of how one is justified. He argued that the infusion of grace is required for justification (*Summa Theologica* I/II.113.2). In fact he noted four causes of justification: (1) infusion of grace, (2) movement of the free will towards God by faith, (3) movement of the will from sin, and (4) remission of sin. Although logically the idea that these causes concur in justification seems to indicate that the redemption of the faithful is a process, Aquinas insisted that it happens as an instantaneous event (I/II.113.2–7). What is to be made of this scheme of justification as the outcome of the believer's cooperation with grace? Thomas effectively argued that free will contributes to salvation but is itself moved by grace. Is this consistent with Augustine? It certainly seems compatible with the Catholic side of the African Father's thought. Is this a golden mean for affirming Augustine's emphasis on the priority of grace while still taking seriously the role of human responsibility in being saved? Or does this view of soteriology ultimately fall prey to a subtle Pelagianism?

The whole story on Aquinas's theology and the adequacy of his portrayal of how we are saved cannot be assessed until his views on predestination are considered. On this doctrine, he took a position much like Bonaventure's. The number predestined is determined, not by reason of God's knowledge, but by reason of his election and determination (*Summa Theologica* I.23.7). Like Augustine, he taught double predestination; that is, some are elected, and others are rejected (I.23.5). Though God loves all, this does not mean that God wishes the same good for all of them (I.23.3). Withholding eternal life from some is the Will of God (I/II.79.3). Is our salvation by grace through faith (Rom. 3:24) sufficiently affirmed by Aquinas?

ASSESSMENTS OF SCHOLASTIC THEOLOGY: CAN WE USE THESE THEOLOGIANS TODAY?

Medieval Scholastic theology made a rich contribution to the Church's life. It helped to preserve Christianity's intellectual credibility for centuries by persuasively "synthesizing" it with the new data drawn from the rediscovery of Aristotle and all other areas of medieval knowledge. Regarding Aquinas and his colleagues, we can truly speak of a synthesis of reason and faith, a synthesis that characterized the worldview of the Middle Ages in western Europe. No society can remain a Christian society as the Middle Ages were if theological convictions are not unquestionably accepted as that society's most profound wisdom. The impact of this theological approach, notably the theology of Thomas Aquinas, on the Roman Catholic Church is incalculable. In addition, one can only praise and marvel at the care and thoroughness of argumentation with which the Scholastics went about their tasks.

On the other hand, one could argue that this style of theology effectively divorced theology from the masses, while the older, more practical style of theology as embodied in Augustine, the great bishops of the patristic era, and the monastic tradition succeeded, it seems, in bridging this gap. Was Scholastic theology and its development bad for the Church? A related question concerns the relationship between the proponents of this approach and Augustine's theology, which they claimed to be interpreting. A further question of the Scholastics is whether some are more in touch with the issues for proclaiming the gospel in the contemporary context than others? If they are all equally credible or equally unhelpful, readers need to come to terms with and decide what to make of the very obvious disagreements among them on issues such as proofs for the existence of God, the proper realm for philosophy and other secular spheres of knowledge, and the atonement.

CHAPTER 14

DAWN OF THE REFORMATION

Historians have long debated whether the situation in Western (Roman Catholic) Christianity in the late Middle Ages (the mid-fourteenth through the early sixteenth centuries) represented a decline of the Catholic Church or whether the problems we can identify in that period were simply a consequence of what is wrong with the Roman Catholic heritage. A third option is to regard the late Middle Ages as a true development, a harvest of the medieval Roman Catholic tradition, which in turn legitimately sowed the seeds for the Reformation and the emergence of modernity as we know it.[1] We can neutrally characterize the period as a time of monumental social and economic change.

BREAKDOWN OF MEDIEVAL SOCIETY

The medieval way of life started to become unglued in the late thirteenth and early fourteenth centuries. At least three factors account for this: (1) socioeconomic changes, (2) corruption in medieval church life, and (3) significant intellectual developments.

SOCIOECONOMIC CHANGES

One of the major developments in the late Middle Ages in western Europe was the gradual evolution of a capitalist economy, including international trade. As previously noted, during the High Middle Ages, from the time after Charlemagne in the early ninth century, the West largely organized itself politically and economically by means of a system rooted in both Roman and early Germanic practices called "feudalism."

Recall that feudalism was an economic system that emerged as a consequence of the dearth of trade and the failure of money to circulate, which occurred in the Middle Ages in Europe due to the demise of the

---

1. On these grounds, the Reformation is understood as a fundamentally late medieval, very premodern development.

Roman Empire and the loss of the stability it once provided as well as the Islamic conquest, which cut off free trade. Consequently, in the feudal economy, wealth was defined by how much land a person owned. Local landowners and peasants placed themselves under the protection of a lord because of the unruly circumstances of early medieval society, which were caused both by the invasion of barbarian nations and by local marauders and land-grabbers. What effect did such contracts of protection have on those who ceded their land? Originally the contract ceding ownership of the land or entitling the lord to a percentage of it had only been for the lifetime of the parties. In time, however, the system evolved into something hereditary. For example, let us suppose that a landowner ceded his land to a lord. In that case, the landowner's son too would have rights to work the land after his father's death. It would still be owned, though, by the heirs of the lord, to give to others for use if the landowner's son, the lord's vassal, should die without an heir.

Towards the end of the Middle Ages, the feudal system began to break down. As living conditions worsened, the masses came to recognize how the system exploited them. The catastrophic plagues and declining living conditions of the era led to a population decline, which in turn contributed to a shrinking of both the supply of labor and the market for such labor. It was in this context that capitalism began to emerge in the West. To be sure, the High Middle Ages had already sown the seeds for its development. The emergence of towns in the eleventh century led to some revival of trading for goods and services in these locales. Indeed, in several Italian towns, notably in Venice and later in Genoa, where feudalism had never gained a strong hold, a kind of city-state atmosphere not unlike the days of ancient Greece had never abated.

The new tide of trade in the more northern sections of western Europe may in part have been a function of the scarcity of food and produce that began to develop in the fourteenth century. As early as the eleventh century, medieval farmers had learned the wisdom of bringing their surplus crops to areas of famine and to sell them to the hungry. Manorial lords began to specialize in crops on which they could realize a profit and then use the currency gained to purchase what they were no longer raising. With money's new importance came a desire for luxuries, which skilled artisans could produce. The artisans, who no longer needed to work the land in order to support themselves and their families, moved into the cities, which had become the centers of trade. The city dwellers, who became the new capitalists, were called "bourgeois" (inasmuch as the first towns were gathered around royal castles, termed *bourg* in French and *Burg* in German).

Trade particularly began to flourish to new heights for very logical reasons in western Europe in the midst of its fourteenth-century tribulations. As disease wiped out between one-fifth to one-third of the population in more densely settled regions, laborers became scarce and expensive. Peasants found that they could insist on financial remuneration from the lords, and not merely a share of the land's produce as compensation for their service. With this increase in trade, wealth and social relationships came again to be determined, not in terms of land, but in terms of cash to pay and accumulated goods. A natural rivalry began developing between the new bourgeoisie and the feudal lords, a rivalry that further undermined feudalism. Petty royal wars, after all, were bad for business; they stifled trade. Kings, whose power had been markedly reduced during the period of feudalism (for in some cases lords controlled more land, and so more loyal troops, than the kings), could now bypass the lords and hire their own troops.

In a sense, the Crusades had played a role in the resurgence of the power of kings. During the Crusades a number of vassals with significant landholdings but no male heirs had met death in battle. In these cases, their land had reverted automatically to their royal lords, which in the waning stages of the feudal economy translated into further wealth and power for the royals. Even more significantly, in the late Middle Ages these kings also gained the support of the rising class of merchants. The end of feudalism marked the beginnings of the creation of strong national states in Europe, such as England, France, and eventually Spain as we know them today.

Capitalists need to expand their markets. The system requires growth. Trade with other continents, with the Far East, seemed the answer. This quest for new markets in the East, the search for more direct travel lines to the Asian continent, was of course the dynamic that drove the Portuguese to Africa and the Spanish, with Columbus at the helm, to the New World. The lands in Africa and the Americas could be exploited in the interests of a profit. Portugal's discovery of gold in Africa in the fifteenth century and its establishment of a trade monopoly with the continent are good examples of the capitalist dynamic in action.

In time, the need for cheap labor in both Europe and America coupled with the natural capitalist inclination to make a profit wherever possible created the slave trade. A summary of economic developments in the late Middle Ages can be offered quite concisely: it was a period when the decline of feudalism and the emergence of modern capitalism created colonialism and the institution of slavery. In that sense, it is a tragic chapter in human history.

The pathos of these socioeconomic dynamics can be experienced more sharply if we try to put ourselves again in the shoes of these medieval folk. Given the deprivation that they were experiencing, given the exploitation many of their forebears had endured under feudalism, is it possible to understand how these basically good Christian, hardworking late medieval European capitalists could enslave and exploit other human beings, with no apparent awareness of how evil the system was? In that case, the reader understands what the doctrine of original sin is teaching — how sin is a corporate, institutional dynamic that traps people in evil.

SECULAR POWER CORRUPTS

A second characteristic of the late Middle Ages that contributed to its disintegration was the corrupting influence of secular power and the quest for such power in the Church. One would logically expect that the new materialism associated with the emergence of capitalism, a dynamic that in turn locates power in the secular realm, would have had an impact on all the institutions of late medieval society, including the Church. And it did.

Such corrupting power is evident to some extent in the Church's foreign missions work in this era. Power was at stake for the Catholic Church in the colonizing efforts because these efforts provided the Church with the chance to extend its sphere of influence and serve the sovereigns who requested its presence in the colonies. Granted, there were bright moments. The Church enjoyed its greatest period of expansion in these years. Some of the missions displayed sensitivity of the indigenous cultures in the era of colonization (see chap. 15). On the whole, though, the Roman Catholic Church failed miserably on the dynamics that created slavery, and some, if not all, of its missionary work in this period was driven by the dynamics of colonialism.

On the European continent, the Church was clearly corrupted by its leaders' quest for power. In the old feudal economy, a clerical career provided an opportunity for social advancement or a way of preserving the social status of one's kin. Nobles or the wealthy often guided their younger sons to the priesthood in order that those who could not inherit the estate might still lead the good life. In a feudal economy where wealth was determined by land owned, and the Church owned a significant amount of land, ecclesiastical leadership entailed wealth. Consequently, simony was widespread. Many held clerical posts, profiting monetarily, but were never on the scene to give pastoral care. Clerical celibacy was frequently violated publicly. Bishops and local priests often flaunted their illegitimate children. Educational requirements for the priesthood were virtually nil. Corruption was even evident in monasteries, which were now in the late Middle Ages often little more than houses of pleasure.

Of course, these dynamics might be expected when one considers that matters were little better at the top, with the papacy. Several cataclysmic events in the fourteenth and fifteenth centuries rocked the papacy and the whole Western church. These included the Hundred Years' War (a consistent series of military actions largely fought between England and France from 1337 to 1453) and the bubonic plague of 1347–48, which decimated western Europe's economy and approximately 30 percent of its population. This pneumonic disease resulted in gruesome death for its victims, who in later stages coughed blood and produced excreted body fluids with unbearable stench, which often led to the abandonment of dying victims. Widespread fear of the epidemic eroded cultural norms and hope. The fall of Constantinople in 1453 also had a significant impact on the Western church, for it effectively cut the Church in the West off from contact with its Eastern counterpart.

After a period of weakness in the early fourteenth century, the papacy came so much under French royal influence that from 1309 to 1377 seven successive popes were compelled to reside in Avignon, France — a period known as the "Avignon papacy." This, of course, was a travesty of all standards of polity and pastoral care. When the first of the Avignon popes, Clement V, came to papal power, he assumed residence in Avignon as a virtual vassal of the French monarchy. Subsequent Avignon popes were also little more than tools of French policy. Simony was widespread in the period, and long episcopal vacancies were encouraged in order that the diocesan funds of the vacant episcopal office would be diverted to Avignon to support its lifestyle and French military actions. Of course, the call for a return to Rome and an end to papal corruption was heard throughout the Church. And the Avignon papacy was corrupt. Virtually all of the Catholic Church's resources were placed in the service of the French during the Hundred Years' War. These dynamics created a sense of alienation towards the papacy among France's rivals — England and the Holy Roman Empire.

Several popes from 1352 on made overtures about returning to Rome and/or reforming corruption. The turning point came in 1370 when the great, internationally renowned Italian mystic Catherine of Siena (1347–80) began a mission to have the pope return to Rome. Widely admired for her almost legendary spiritual discipline and for her service to the poor, the imprisoned, and the victims of medieval plagues (the Mother Teresa of her day), she marshaled much popular support for her mission to bring the pope home to Rome. Seven years later, she succeeded in her mission, and Pope Gregory XI (1329–78) returned.

Gregory's return, however, did not settle the problems, for the same political dynamics that had created the Avignon papacy continued to exist. He was pressured to return to Avignon. With his death, a French successor seemed a shoo-in for election, since in the Avignon period the French had come to compose the majority of cardinals (electors of the pope). Under pressure from Roman mobs, the cardinals elected an Italian, the archbishop of Bari, who became Urban VI (1318–89). Urban was very reform minded, but he was too radical in his reforms for the Church hierarchy as a whole. He was particularly concerned to condemn ostentation and wealth among the hierarchy. Disgruntled cardinals (mostly Frenchmen) elected a pretender, Clement VII, who took up residence in Avignon.

After years of controversy in which separate parties continued to elect different popes (a period known as the Great Western Schism), the controversy was finally resolved by the development of the *conciliar movement* (the theory that a universal council has more authority than the pope; Council of Constance, *Sacrosancta*). Rival popes bowed to the call for a council to be held at Pisa in 1409 but sought to circumvent it by calling councils of their own. The Pisa Council's efforts to depose both rival claimants and elect a legitimate pope had the effect of creating three rivals for the office. Finally, in 1415 at a new Council of Constance, the schism was resolved by the resignation of two of the pretenders, the eventual total discrediting of the Avignon pretender, and the election of a new successor to the Pisa-appointed pope, who took the name Martin V (1368–1431).

The new pope and his successors successfully diffused subsequent councils, which seem to have been more committed to the project of reforming the Church than they were. Eventually the conciliar movement became discredited. In 1430 a group of bishops already meeting in a council in Basel refused to adjourn to a new venue in Ferrara and later in Florence, to which the pope had directed them and then angrily elected a papal pretender. The conciliar movement, which had been instituted to unify the Church, wound up fostering schism. The papal pretender it elected, and so the movement, gained virtually no support, and eventually its pope, Felix V, renounced claims to the office. From then on, the councils of the Roman Catholic Church would ever remain subordinate to the pope (Pius II *Exercrabilis*).

Following the disposition of these controversies, in fact even before conciliarism was fully put to rest, the papacy was politically strengthened. In fact, it was so strengthened that it began exercising political, if not military, dominance over certain regional states. These dynamics are especially evident in the reigns of Nicholas V (1447–55), Callistus III (1455–58), and Julius II (1503–13). Callistus and a successor, Sixtus IV (1471–84), were particularly notorious practitioners of nepotism, truly turning the church into a family business (whose every activity and clerical appointment was aimed at enriching brothers and nephews).

Other popes of this era are reported to have believed in "family" in a more intimate way (though, to be sure, they were no practitioners of family values). Innocent VIII (1484–92) publicly acknowledged several illegitimate children (while authorizing and advocating numerous witch hunts), and Alexander VI (1492–1503) took concubines from the spouses of colleagues in the papal court and publicly acknowledged several of the offspring they bore him.

All of the popes and their successors/predecessors following the papacy's restoration in Rome (during the late fifteenth and early sixteenth centuries) were very influenced by the *Renaissance* (a rebirth of interest in classical Greek and Roman civilization). As a result, it could be argued, the gospel played a less influential role during their reigns. In any case, the prime agenda of these popes tended to be the restoration of the glories of ancient Rome by whatever means it took — bribery, intrigue, war — you name it.

Good Renaissance men that they were, many of these popes were great patrons of the arts, sometimes devoting more attention to beautifying Rome than to the care of souls. The best cases in point are the popes who reigned just before and during Martin Luther's time, Julius II and Leo X (1513–21). They supervised the decoration of the Vatican and completion of the Vatican's Sistine Chapel and St. Peter's Cathedral. Of course, this cost money, and to afford the cost, Pope Leo authorized the sale of indulgences. This was a most significant decision, which had a great impact on the Reformation.

Many committed Christians were outraged. A sense that the shenanigans must stop increasingly marked the Western church. On the eve of the Reformation in the sixteenth century, in the waning stages of the Middles Ages, a call for ecclesiastical reform was clearly in the air.

INTELLECTUAL DEVELOPMENTS

The major intellectual developments of the Middle Ages were nominalism, Renaissance humanism, mysticism, and the pre-Reformation. We shall examine these movements in a kind of inverse chronological order, starting with the most recent movement, which was self-consciously concerned to work for reform of the abuses noted above.

The pre-Reformers. The yearnings for reform manifested themselves in the work of the pre-Reformers of the late fourteenth and early fifteenth centuries. Foremost among these figures were a British theologian and professor at Oxford University John Wycliffe (1330–84) and his admirer from the next generation John Huss (1372–1415), a Bohemian Catholic.[2]

---

2. An Italian Dominican friar, Girolamo Savonarola (1452–98) was another Catholic

Wycliffe was not only a much-admired professor of theology at England's most prestigious university; his political connections were most impressive, as he served as a diplomat for the British throne. Assembling an impressive group of largely elite English followers, called the "Lollards," he and they argued against the exercise of authority by the Church for its own benefit or the exercise of such authority for purely secular purposes. Wycliffe's stand on this matter is certainly understandable given the fact that during his lifetime the papacy resided in Avignon, France, totally under the French king's thumb. These commitments led him to reject all efforts by the Church to collect taxes for its own use (*On the Pastoral Office* I.6–7; *Lollard Conclusions* 1). In view of the political situation, it is hardly surprising that Wycliffe's views were initially well received in his British homeland. They supported the rising tide of British nationalism. Besides, Wycliffe was a man of no little prestige.

The next stage in Wycliffe's career occurred during the Great Western Schism, when rival popes made claims to be the true pope. Disillusioned, echoing anticlerical sentiment of many in the late Middle Ages, Wycliffe and his followers began to teach that the true Church is not the pope and the hierarchy, but the invisible body of the predestined. This Augustinian point was developed more fully by Protestant Reformers, especially Luther. Along the same lines, Wycliffe urged putting the Bible back in the hands of the laity, maintaining something like the priesthood of all believers at this point. Wycliffe's followers developed these commitments further, working to ensure that the Bible was translated into English (*On the Pastoral Office* II.2a).

Perhaps Wycliffe's most controversial position was his rejection of the characteristic Roman Catholic position of the Lord's Supper — transubstantiation (see chap. 12) — in favor of claiming that though the body of Christ is present in the sacrament, his presence does not destroy the bread (*On the Eucharist* 2[1]-[2]). Such a view is suggestive of the later views of Martin Luther and John Calvin.

Wycliffe's followers, the Lollards, went so far as to deny the value of pilgrimages, indulgences on behalf of the deceased, and even the value of the sacrament of confession. They also condemned the exercise of political authority by the episcopacy (*Lollard Conclusions* 6–9). These were attacks at the very heart of medieval Catholicism. No wonder he and his followers were eventually condemned, especially when they began applying the servant model of authority to recommend ways in which the

reformer of this era. His outreach to the poor, critique of the luxuries of society (he built a pyramid on which vanities like dresses, jewelry, and ostentatious furniture were burned), and political alliances he forged on behalf of the city of Florence with the king of France led him to become a thorn in the side of the hierarchy, which culminated in his execution.

state should exercise authority. Politically influential supporters of the Lollards began to distance themselves from Wycliffe and the movement, for it was now evident that the implementation of its reforms could cost them power.

Wycliffe died in communion with the Church. His treatment of soteriology as the cooperation of prevenient grace with works of merit was a Catholic position, in the sense of Thomas Aquinas (*Pastoral Office* II; *De dominio divino*). This affirmation of prevenient grace took an Augustinian character with Wycliffe's understanding of predestination as an election either to salvation or to reprobation, which is otherwise known as "double predestination" (*Sermons* 1.52; 2.24). His views were only formally condemned posthumously by the Council of Constance in 1415. In Wycliffe's native England, though his early support from the nobility gradually began to erode, the Lollard movement (a pejorative title derived from a word meaning "mumblers") became a popular movement exerting much influence on Parliament. Although most of the Lollards among the nobility recanted as the pressure against Wycliffe intensified and as it became evident that the movement jeopardized their own self-interest, the movement went underground. Early in the sixteenth century, it enjoyed a revival. Lollard loyalists were an important part of the eventual success of the Reformation in England later in the century.

John Huss, himself a noted preacher and eminent academician at the University of Prague (its rector), was a student of Wycliffe's work, though he was more moderate in his theological views. Huss's concern was to restore Christian life to its highest ideals, not to alter doctrines (*On Simony* 10). Though younger than Wycliffe, he too lived during the time of the Great Western Schism. A controversy developed at the university and later in Bohemia as a whole over the validity of teaching the works of Wycliffe. (Interest in the English situation in Bohemia was quite natural in this period, inasmuch as the British king Richard II was married to a Bohemian princess.) During the controversy, the Bohemian hierarchy backed a papal decree banning the works of Wycliffe and also ordered (no doubt with Huss in view) that preaching could only take place in cathedrals, parish churches, and monasteries. Huss's primary pulpit qualified under none of these categories.

Huss refused to be silenced. For his disobedience, he was excommunicated by the pope, who had been elected during the Great Western Schism by the Council of Pisa in 1411. Since Huss was still supported by his king and the Bohemian people, the excommunication was of no practical effect. This conflict, however, led Huss to assume more radical positions. He came to the conclusion that an unworthy pope ought not be obeyed. The Bible, he began to claim, must be the final authority by which popes are to be judged (*On Simony* 4).[3] Like the sixteenth-century Reformers, he also proceeded to reject indulgences.

Huss's followers (largely members of the nobility and the bourgeoisie) joined with a lower-class Bohemian Christian movement, which later came to be known as the Taborites. Apocalyptic in orientation, this latter group taught that the Church should reject anything not found in Scripture. Hussites, by contrast, only condemned what the Bible explicitly condemned. The two groups formed a coalition, which made these two demands: (1) that Communion be given in both kinds (since the Church's endorsement of transubstantiation, only bread had been distributed to the laity so that they not run the risk of desecrating Christ's blood by dribbling the wine as they drank) and (2) that clergy be deprived of all wealth.

Huss himself was condemned by the Council of Constance and executed in 1415. His followers achieved a compromise with the Bohemian Church with several of their concerns addressed. Those who remained dissatisfied, most of whom were Taborites living in nomadic, communist-style communities, left the established church. The least militant formed the Union of Brethren, a movement that spread to Moravia, which was located in present-day Germany. This group eventually evolved in the eighteenth century into the Moravian Church, under the leadership of Ludwig von Zinzendorf (1700–1760). It is quite clear that many of the concerns and commitments that were to be articulated in the next century by the Reformers did not come "out of the blue" but had already been raised by Wycliffe and Huss. In that sense, they truly deserve to be designated as pre-Reformers.

Mysticism. The quest for reform was also evidenced in the growing impact that mysticism began to exert on the Western church in the late Middle Ages, particularly in Germany and in the regions of present-day Netherlands and Belgium. Such commitments have the (sometimes unwitting) effect of undercutting the authority of the Church and its external rites. To the extent that one can have access to God through one's personal spiritual experience, as the mystics maintain, it follows at least by implication that such Christians do not require intermediaries.

To be sure, mysticism was no new development in the late Middle Ages. Bernard of Clairvaux, Hildegard of Bingen, and Francis of Assisi in the High Middle Ages had been prominent mystics. In the late Middle Ages, the big names of the movement were Meister Eckhart (1260–1327); John Tauler (ca. 1300–1361); Thomas à Kempis (1380–1471); an anonymous German work called *German Theology;* two women mystics, Julian of Norwich (ca. 1342– after 1413) and Catherine of

---

3. The Reformation commitment to *sola scriptura* is clearly prefigured at this point.

Siena (1347–80); as well as a mystical order founded by Gerhard Groote [Geerte de Groote] (1340–84), the Brethren of the Common Life. Generally speaking, save for Catherine, we do not know much about the personal lives of these renowned mystics. Most of these men were well educated, and they all entered monastic orders. We know more of their renowned spirituality and their often provocative theology.

Some of these prominent mystics, notably Eckhart, were heavily influenced by the philosophy of Neoplatonism, which identifies the human soul (as a universal form) with the divine insofar as God enters the soul and identifies with it with no mediation (*Sermons* 1).[4] Others, like à Kempis, unwittingly endorsed a kind of Semi-Pelagianism. For example, à Kempis claimed that Christ will come if we make ready for him (*Of the Imitation of Christ* 1.25; 2.1). Such views were very much in the air in the late Middle Ages. On the other hand, in the *German Theology* (2,9) we observe language reminiscent of Augustine's anti-Pelagian rhetoric concerning the worthlessness of good works and recognition that salvation depends only on God and his working.

In the work of the two women mystics, unambiguous affirmations of God's unconditional love in joining himself to the soul despite our sin (an Augustinian theological profile most suggestive of the thought of the first Reformers) are even more readily apparent (Catherine of Siena *Dialogue* 148; Julian of Norwich *Showings* 82,58). In fact, Julian took the next (Augustinian) step by claiming that all good in the world is done by God (*Showings* 11). Another intriguing aspect of Julian's thought is her fourteenth-century teaching that God is Mother, Brother, Savior. The second person of the Trinity is our Mother, she wrote, in the sense that as the second person, in becoming incarnate, God has taken on our sensual nature. Presumably Julian, in accord with cultural suppositions of the era, understood that womanhood is to be defined in terms of sensuality. God's motherhood is also manifest for Julian insofar as the second person of the Trinity is identified as Wisdom (*Sophia*), who creates us in our sensuality.[5] Finally Christ is Mother as the Mother of mercy by whom we are reformed and restored (58).

The timeliness of Julian's reflections for our present context, as the Church struggles to come to terms with the gender of God in light of feminist/womanist agendas, is readily apparent. Her reflections have never been censured by the Church catholic. Perhaps it is time for participants in the debate to stop thinking that they are creatively avant-garde.

---

4. Eckhart's theology was also characterized by a critical perspective on the inadequacy of language for describing the undifferentiated oneness of the Godhead. For Eckhart, even the Trinity is not quite an adequate depiction of the divine reality but is a mere manifestation of it.

5. Presumably the Father's role in creation is to protect our substance/essence.

Could the whole matter have been indirectly settled more than half a millennium ago, and we need only take seriously the historical sources? Regardless of the possible contributions of late medieval mysticism to the modern theological agenda, this late medieval movement made several significant positive contributions to the Reformation. Erasmus, the greatest of the Renaissance humanists, was trained in Brethren of Common Life schools. There is considerable debate among scholars concerning whether much of Luther's theology is fundamentally indebted to mysticism. Indeed, some of these mystics endorse themes suggestive of Luther's Pauline emphases on sin, unconditional forgiveness, and the character of the Christian life as a constant struggle. The relationship between mysticism and the founders of several of the Protestant denominations is an issue that continues to warrant consideration.

Renaissance humanism. A yet more sweeping intellectual development, the humanism of the Renaissance eventually undermined medieval life. The Renaissance is the era of late medieval Western society's rediscovery of the glories of ancient Greek and Roman cultures and their art. The movement was intimately related to the hope that these new sources and opportunities for learning (the printing press had just been invented) could help reform the Church.

One immediate consequence of the movement was an outburst of great artistic interest and creation. The work of the great painters Michelangelo (Buonarroti; 1475–1564) and Leonardo da Vinci (1452–1519) come to mind. Significant stylistic shifts became apparent in their work and careers. Both focused much more on human potential than on extolling the glories of heaven, as was more characteristic of the art of earlier medieval centuries. This stylistic shift, then, provides one more indication of the end of the medieval "Age of Faith." Artists and other educated persons were now free to begin to consider human existence and reality, even without reference to God. To be sure, such observations sound normal to our modern ears, but they were astounding to the medieval mind-set.

The Renaissance preoccupation with ancient texts eventually led to the emergence of the discipline of textual criticism. Soon questions began to emerge about the authority of the West's Latin translation of Bible, the Vulgate, which had been Western Christianity's only authoritative Bible since its preparation by Jerome in the fourth century. We see in this agenda the beginning of Western scholarly concern to consider the Bible in its original languages, a task that the Reformers and the pre-Reformers readily assumed. Already in the Renaissance, then, the stage was being set for our modern approach to exegesis. A development related to the emergence of textual criticism was the challenge to the authenticity of the *Donation of Constantine.* Soon it could no longer be invoked without ambiguity by church leaders in support of papal claims to political authority. In many ways, the Renaissance was a tool of liberation for humanity from old God-centered structures and visions of reality. The greatest Renaissance figure was a Dutch humanist, the illegitimate son of a priest and a physician's daughter, Desiderius Erasmus (ca. 1469–1536), a man who was truly an international scholarly star during his lifetime. Erasmus sought a reformation of the Church through classical learning. He urged educated Christians to seek a balanced life. In his view, the ethics of Jesus, purged of Scholastic speculation, was the key to such a balanced life. Such an ethic, sometimes said to be made possible by grace (*Concerning the Immense Mercy of God*), closely resembles the Stoic philosophy we covered in chapter 1. Like the Stoics, Erasmus insisted that Christians must practice discipline (*Enchiridion Militis Christiani* I.5; II).

In addition, Erasmus maintained that the Church does well to purge all pomp (*Enchiridion Militis Christiani* II.5). He was also critical of monasticism. We seem to hear echoes at this point of Martin Luther's doctrine of vocation (that is, the belief that all stations in life and legitimate jobs are equally valid opportunities to serve God). In the view of Erasmus, discipline was more important than doctrine. There almost seems to be a kind of mystical piety in operation here, like one Erasmus learned with the Brethren of Common Life. We are to find God through inwardness. Given these commitments, it is hardly surprising to learn that as the sixteenth-century Reformation transpired, Erasmus took the middle ground between Catholics and the Protestant Reformers in the dispute (*De Sacrienda Ecclesiae Concordia*).

A last word on the Renaissance should be one of mixed judgment: its optimism and anthropocentrism are unquestionably harbingers of the modern era. Without it, Western, if not global, society in the late twentieth century would be very different. Yet as a human-centered movement, it could not of itself reform the Church.

Nominalism. The oldest of the intellectual currents that transformed the Middle Ages, nominalism is rooted in the philosophy of two eminent later medieval philosophers from the British Isles — William of Ockham (1285–1347) and, to some extent, John Duns Scotus (1265–1308). Other prominent late Scholastic, nominalist theologians include Robert Holcot (d. 1349) and one of Martin Luther's main posthumous theological sparring partners, the fifteenth-century German Catholic philosopher Gabriel Biel (d. 1495).

Nominalism was committed to demystifying the use of reason and asserting its independence. Though Scotus was not himself a nominalist, the process began with him and his insistence that reason and faith do not intersect at all points, that some truths of faith are beyond the sphere of reason. Of course, Aquinas had made this point with regard to some truths of faith, but Scotus greatly increased the list of revealed truths that a Christian should believe but cannot prove (*On the First Principle*). These commitments were also related to Scotus's emphasis on God's sovereign freedom (*Oxford Commentary on the Sentences* I.41), a theological affirmation that would also greatly influence nominalism.

The aim of the nominalists was to explain what is the case in the simplest way. William of Ockham developed a principle, known later as "Ockham's razor," that went beyond Scotus's claims.[6] The razor's principle is to cut away whatever is not necessary to an argument (*Reportatio* II,Q.15); therefore, the Aristotelian-Platonic idea that an eternal form is more real than the perceived individual thing itself has to go (*Summa totius logicae* I, C. xiv). In other words, when a person sees a number of books on a shelf, he or she need not posit the idea of an eternal form of "bookness" in order to recognize each individual volume as a book. That is, what you see is what you get.

What are we to make of this rejection of universal forms? It has clearly won the day in the Western intellectual tradition. The nominalist emphasis on the reality of the individual physical things and the unique experience of them, not spiritual-rational entities like the forms, focused academic inquiry on the truth to be gained by our experience of the physical world in a way that made the rise of modern science possible. That may or may not be a good thing. Setting reason free to investigate the physical realm entails recognizing its limits. In contrast to most Scholastic theologians, notably Thomas Aquinas, nominalists claimed that reason could not prove virtually any of the core doctrines of the faith, not even the existence of God (*Quodlibeta* V, Q.i).

Given such a critical assessment of the competence of reason in spiritual matters, authority for Ockham and other nominalists was a crucial question. On this matter, he tended to share the general late medieval skepticism towards ecclesiastical institutions in a way most suggestive of the theology of subsequent Protestantism. Thus he claimed that the pope and a council could err (*Brief Statement on the Tyrannical Principate* 3.15). The Bible, he insisted, was by contrast more authoritative than they or "the entire company of mortals" (*Dialogue* 1.2.2; *Against Pope John XXII* 15). These commitments, like those of the pre-Reformers clearly set the stage for subsequent Protestant appeals to the authority of Scripture alone.[7] The nominalist skepticism about reason seems to en-

---

6. Duns Scotus still believed in the reality of universals (*Oxford Commentary on the Sentences* I.43).

7. This extolling of the unique character of the biblical witness also prefigures an affirmation of biblical infallibility. Something like the concept began to develop in Western Catholicism in this era (Johannes de Vrevi Coxa *Treatise on Faith, the Church, the Roman*

tail that faith must be deemed "trust," for reason can lead to doubt. This understanding of faith would appear in the theology of the Reformers, notably in Martin Luther.

There is a wholesome commitment at stake in the nominalist insistence on the discontinuity of reason and faith. Virtually all of the nominalists, indebted as they were to Scotus, were concerned to affirm God's sovereign will. There is nothing above God; not even reason may judge God. Consequently, one should not say that God always does good. No, what God does is good only because he does these things. If God acts, it is good even if the action is evil according to standards of human reason. By the same token, God did not need Jesus to redeem human beings: however God had decreed to save us would have worked. God's solemn (predestining) will is the final reality (Ockham *Quodlibeta* VI,Q.vi; Duns Scotus *Oxford Commentary on the Sentences* III.19).

Such emphases on the sovereignty of God's will seem quite Augustinian and suggestive of Luther and Calvin; however, important differences exist between nominalists in general and the Reformers, even between Scotus and the Reformers. These differences, which may be what the Reformation was all about, may have been occasioned in Ockham's case, as a Franciscan, by his militant defense of his order's commitment to poverty without compromising it, as had occurred since Francis's death (*Work of Ninety Days* 9.6; see chap. 12). Another factor in the shaping of Ockham's thought was probably the general preoccupation with reform and Christian commitment that characterized the thought of many Christian scholars in the late Middle Ages. In any case, and perhaps as a result of such preoccupation with issues of the Christian lifestyle, nominalists modified the characteristic mode of Scholasticism for describing the process of redemption.

All Scholastics employed the concept of preparation for grace and human will's responsibility, as in James 4:8 (NRSV) — "Draw near to God, and he will draw near to you." Human beings must do something, it was taught, in order to prepare themselves to receive God's saving grace when it is given. Thomas Aquinas, the great Scholastic theologian and recognized spokesman of the Catholic Church, seems to have endorsed these commitments without falling into works righteousness. To be sure, he insisted that there is a role for the human will in receiving grace, in preparing for grace; however, just as clearly, Aquinas insisted that even that act of preparation by our wills ("the movement of the free will toward God") is an act of God's grace that is infused in the

---

Pontiff, and the General Council 1.1) and eventually became the official teaching of the Catholic Church (Council of Trent *Decree concerning Canonical Scriptures*, which teaches that the Bible was divinely dictated by the Spirit).

believer (*Summa Theologica* I/II.113). In this sense, he has affirmed that salvation is *sola gratia;* God does everything. Even our turning to God in preparation is God's act. Could Luther, Calvin, and other Protestants object to such a theological formulation?

By contrast the nominalists, borrowing from Scotus and Ockham, used the scheme of preparation for grace, but many of them failed to give credit to God's grace as the driving force of the human will in preparing to receive the grace that saves. When humans do their very best, God accepts what they have done of themselves as adequate preparation (Biel *Commentary on the Sentences* II.27, 28; Holcot *Super Libros Saientiae* III.35). In other words, along with Aquinas, the nominalists taught that we are saved through the cooperation of grace and works. However, unlike Thomas, they held that the human work of preparation precedes the gift of grace.

To be sure, not all of the nominalists made these affirmations without qualification. John Duns Scotus had insisted on a strong, Augustinian doctrine of predestination, whereby God elects without regard for merit (*Quodlibeta* 16.17). Given these suppositions, it could be argued that he has successfully balanced his concern to assert human freedom and the responsibility of sinners for their own damnation with a strong affirmation that salvation is by grace. There is no need for God to accept anything from a creature. But why, then, did he not make it clearer that the act of the will in meriting grace is itself the work of unmerited grace?

William of Ockham and his followers, the majority of notable nominalists of the era, seem to have applied the "razor" to explaining the reality of justification. They basically adopted Scotus's scheme in toto but amended its concept of predestination. In their view, God elects on the basis of foreseen good works by the elect.[8] Given these commitments and their endorsement of Scotus's view of the role of the will in justification, it follows that for most nominalists human freedom is at both the beginning and the end of the salvation process, prior to God's election (which is de facto based upon human response) and God's acceptance of the sinner (which given this nominalist model is contingent upon human responses).

Granted, it is not an outright Pelagianism that operates in Scotus's thought, and perhaps not even in the mainstream of nominalist theology. Nevertheless, in both cases, their collective insistence on the cooperating role of the will, unaided by grace in the process of justification, seems to be an endorsement of a kind of Semi-Pelagianism. For all of these nominalists, God does not act alone in the process of salvation. The

---

8. Ockham *Ordinatio* D. XXXVIII, Q.unica; *Predestination and the Foreknowledge of God* 1.

believer is a kind of junior partner. It was precisely against this teaching — that humans can contribute to their own salvation — that Luther rebelled. These commitments are certainly characteristic of the nominalist theologians and of the late medieval Catholic Church. It is less clear, though, that they adequately represent the teaching of Aquinas and of the Catholic heritage. One could in a sense say, then, of nominalism that it not only undermined the security of the medieval worldview and its dependence on ontological categories of Greek philosophy; nominalism also unwittingly undermined the security of the faithful in making salvation to some extent dependent on themselves.

THE LATE MIDDLE AGES: HARVEST OR DECLINE OF MEDIEVAL CATHOLICISM?

Any attempt to pass some sort of historical judgment on medieval Catholicism is by necessity complex. Was there something about the Roman Catholic heritage that mandated the sort of (negative) developments we have noted in the late Middle Ages? If all of these developments were negative, then one must regard the Reformation as a necessary corrective to all that was wrong with Roman Catholicism.

In some aspects of medieval Catholic theology (at least with reference to the question of how we are saved or forgiven), the late Middle Ages represents a decline from High Scholasticism. Of course, it could be argued that the very logic of Scholasticism, as represented by Thomas Aquinas, with its insistence on the faithful's cooperation with grace, sowed the seeds for the Semi-Pelagian inclinations of nominalist theology.

With regard to ethics, the reforming instincts of the late Middle Ages, save its countenancing of slavery, might represent a harvest, of the best traditions of the medieval Roman Catholic tradition. On the other hand, some of the evidence could be viewed as so ambiguous as to call this conclusion into question. For example, an inherently sexist bias in Roman Catholicism seems reaffirmed by the fact that women were denied the priesthood in the late Middle Ages, as they have been throughout much of the history of the Catholic tradition. On the other hand, there are some indications of a significant role for women in the late medieval Church (see chap. 15). Not to be forgotten in considering the late Middle Ages is the significant impact of women mystics, Catherine of Siena and Julian of Norwich. The fact that as early as the fourteenth century the Catholic Church was countenancing such a "feminist theologian" as Julian, who referred to God as Mother, could perhaps be taken as an argument against an essential patriarchal bias in the Roman Catholic heritage.

Also to be noted is the abysmal record of the Roman Catholic tradition in Africa during the late Middle Ages. It is combined, though, with a number of intriguing successes in indigenizing the gospel in some regions during this period. What to make of these dynamics in the Church's missionary work is a question that students of this period and of the heritage of the Church universal must answer for themselves. The scholarly community has not reached a consensus on these matters, which are of great ecumenical import.

The theological issues of the late Middle Ages are crucial for understanding the Reformation and the validity of the continuing existence of Protestantism. Perhaps the greatest failure of the late medieval Church was in the area of theology, in its treatment of the doctrine of justification, with its insistence on a role for the believer, unaided by grace, in the salvation process. But this is not what the Roman Catholic Church authoritatively teaches. However, should the Scholastic theological traditions of the High Middle Ages, themselves rooted in certain developments of the early Church, not be held responsible for creating a climate in which the questionable nominalist commitments emerged? Furthermore, to the degree that Luther and the other Reformers were reacting primarily to a distinct theological strand within the Roman Catholic Church of their time, not to the official theology of the church, what are the implications for the Reformation and the continuing validity of Protestantism? How readers answer these questions will say much about their ecumenical and theological positions.

CHAPTER 15

THE BEGINNINGS OF COLONIAL CHRISTIANITY AND ITS IMPACT ON THE CHURCH IN EUROPE

The issues raised in this chapter bring us to the brink of the modern period, for with colonialism, capitalism truly indigenizes itself in the West, and of course capitalism, giving rise to the Industrial Revolution, is what modernity is all about. The European settlement of many regions in the so-called New World and the Southern Hemisphere in effect tells the story of the Church's (particularly the Roman Catholic Church's) globalization as well as the tragic story of the dislocation of many indigenous people of these regions, the beginnings of the suppression of Native Americans and the enslavement of Africans. It is not a story of one of the Church's better moments. In another sense, though, in a way not previously recognized by modern historians, perhaps some of the trends related to missions were not so bad. The Church's spiritual and theological wealth was enriched by many of its encounters with the previously unreached cultures. In considering how the late medieval Western church may or may not have abetted the persecution of many, one ought not overlook the status it conferred on another, too often persecuted minority — women.

The whole story of late medieval missionary work really extends into the sixteenth century, into the period known as the Catholic Reformation (covered in vol. 2). Consequently, some of the material noted in this chapter properly belongs in that book. Yet the violation of strict chronological order seems desirable in order to provide the full picture of the heritage of the late medieval missionary work of the Western church. After all, the first period of colonial Christianity in Africa, Asia, and the Americas extended from the late Middle Ages until the Industrial Revolution began to make its presence felt on the European continent.

THE CHURCH AND THE COLONIAL AGENDA

Recall the three factors responsible for the breakdown of the Middle Ages. One of these was the corrupting influence of secular power. Secular power and economic power are what colonialism and even to some extent what late medieval missionary work were all about. Consequently, another factor in the breakdown of the Middle Ages, the socioeconomic changes experienced in western Europe, particularly the breakdown of feudalism and the emergence of capitalism, were what really made colonialism and the slave trade happen.

The capitalists' need to expand their markets led to the western European outreach to other continents, especially to the Far East, in order to gain new markets. It was by accident in quest for new markets in the East, in searching for more direct travel lines to the Asian continent, that the Portuguese came to Africa and the Spanish, with Columbus at the helm, came to the New World. It was the same capitalistic concern to obtain cheap labor that created the slave trade. These socioeconomic dynamics raise a crucial question: To the degree that medieval Catholicism's missionary outreach was begun in earnest during the period of late medieval colonial ventures, was this outreach fundamentally a manifestation of European colonialism?

Remember that the quest for power that corrupted the Catholic Church in the late Middle Ages resulted to some extent in the Church's foreign missions work in this era. Power was at stake for the Church in the colonizing efforts because these efforts provided the Church with the chance to extend its sphere of influence and serve the sovereigns who requested its presence in the colonies. There were bright moments. The Church enjoyed its greatest period of expansion in these years, and some sensitivity to certain indigenous cultures was shown in the missionary work done. However, the Church failed miserably on the dynamics that created slavery and colonialism.

MISSIONS IN AFRICA

The Church's outreach to the African continent as well as to Asia and the Americas was inextricably linked to sociopolitical and economic developments in Portugal and Spain in the fifteenth century. Portugal's Christianization had largely coincided with that of Spain's, as no real distinction existed between the two regions during the period of the Roman Empire. In the fifth century, the Visigoths had invaded the region that today is Portugal and, as happened in Spain, thereby became Christianized. At the time of the invasion, the Goths were Arians, who had been restored to Nicene orthodoxy during the reign of Gregory the Great in the late sixth century.

The entire region of Spain and Portugal and the Church in particular had endured a period of Islamic domination beginning in the eighth century. This period of Moslem rule was prosperous, but by that time Christianity had become so embedded in the social psyche of the earlier inhabitants that the Church became the rallying point in the hope for liberation. That time finally came in the late eleventh century, as Spanish Christians began to reconquer the whole of the Iberian Peninsula (present-day Spain and Portugal). In 1094 the Spanish king Alfonso VI awarded Henry of Burgundy, a French knight who was aiding in the struggle against the Moslems, the counties that today make up Portugal. With the reconquest well on the way to culminating in the complete success it eventually achieved, he assumed the title "King of Portugal" in 1143. Portugal has henceforth been an independent kingdom.

By the thirteenth century, Portugal had completely rid itself of Moslems, doing so almost two hundred years before Spain accomplished this. In the course of the next century or more, it became increasingly evident that there was little local regional opportunity for expansion and increased prosperity for the new nation. As a result, its royal and business elite looked to the sea as their sole viable means of achieving these ends.[1] This is the background for Henry the Navigator's (1394–1460) exploration of the west coast of Africa early in the fifteenth century.

One aim of Henry's and the general Portuguese agenda was to reach the Orient in order to open more avenues of trade; the hope was that by sailing around Africa, the Portuguese could reach their economic target without interference from militant Moslems whom they might otherwise encounter on the journey. Another motivating factor was the hope inspired by the rumor widespread in the Western world that somewhere on the way to the Orient was a Christian kingdom (i.e., Ethiopia).[2] However, accurate information about it had been lost, probably due to its church's status as heretical in the eyes of the Catholic Church and also due to its isolation from Europe brought about by the Islamic invasion of North Africa. It was hoped that perhaps an alliance could be established with this kingdom, which together might make possible a new crusade against the Moslems. A related concern of Henry's grew out of his deep and apparently sincere faith commitments. Soon another,

---

1. As noted, the capitalist revolution had already been initiated in western Europe by this time, and the capitalist economy requires expanding markets.

2. Presumably the oral tradition of the ancient Roman Empire regarding Ethiopia had never been entirely extinguished over the centuries. The occasional contacts that medieval Catholics had had in the Holy Land with Ethiopian Orthodox pilgrims to Jerusalem may also have helped rekindle this awareness.

insidious rationale for the ventures in Africa developed: the slave traffic began to dictate further exploration and colonization of the continent.

Subsequent expeditions brought the Portuguese farther along Africa's western coast until 1488 when they reached the southern tip of the continent. Almost a decade later, in 1497, Vasco da Gama (ca. 1469–1524) discovered that by sailing north along Africa's east coast one could reach India. The next step was to land in India. The Portuguese had a monopoly on unimpeded trade with the Orient!

With each of these early explorations, the Portuguese established alliances and colonies on the African coast. It was through these settlements that the Catholic Church began to be planted anew on the African continent. Of course, the Catholic Church (at least its predecessor prior to the East-West Schism of 1054) was not new to the region. It had existed in the Roman Empire's territories of North Africa in the early centuries but had perished in the Arab invasion.

Having established contact with China and India and their rich opportunities for trade, the Portuguese took steps to create a monopoly on these markets by organizing a network of military bases along the routes. The quest for a passage to the Orient also led the Portuguese, again by accident, to the Americas. A 1500 expedition sailing for the Orient gave the coast of Africa too wide a berth and wound up sighting Brazil. In later expeditions, the Portuguese discovered they could exploit the region for the production of valuable dyes.

As Portugal sought to establish its trade monopolies, Spain began to authorize expeditions to find new trade routes to the Far East. This was the framework in which King Ferdinand V (1452–1516) and Queen Isabella (1451–1504) commissioned the famed 1492 voyage of Christopher Columbus (1451–1506). Columbus died thinking that he had reached Asia in his various voyages. During the next years, new explorations were initiated in hopes of discovering a way through the Americas to the Far East. Among the most famous were those of Vasco Núñez de Balboa (1475–1519) and the round-the-world expedition led by Ferdinand Magellan (ca. 1480–1521). The settlement of the Americas and the eventual planting of the Church in the New World were now possible.

Obviously Spain and Portugal had been locked in potentially explosive competition over the new territories. Both governments appealed to Pope Alexander VI (Rodrigo Borgia; 1431–1503), a Spaniard who had originally come to the office through bribery. Of course, this sort of papal exercise of significant political influence was quite typical in the late Middle Ages. In 1493 he conferred on Spain the right of possession over all the lands and islands discovered or to be discovered (save those that might already be occupied by a Christian power). He affirmed his earlier grant to Portugal of the coasts of Africa. Subsequently diplomats at the Treaty of Tordesillas rearranged the boundaries slightly to the west so that Brazil might be awarded to Portugal. This territorial arrangement proved to be binding in the subsequent history of the Americas (esp. for South and Central America). It also proved to be significant in inspiring the late medieval church's missionary outreach. Both the papal decree and the treaty made these land grants contingent on the condition that the European powers would propagate the Christian faith among the native inhabitants.

In Africa, the Portuguese began their missionary work primarily on the west coast of the continent and its islands after establishing settlements like Cape Verde in 1444, Sierra Leone in 1460, the Gold Coast (present-day Ghana) in 1482, Sofala (on the east coast) and Mozambique in 1505, as well as Angola in 1575. In addition, Portugal claimed lands in the interior of the continent, albeit without settling or even visiting them, and also established contacts with the African tribal kingdoms of the Kongo and Benin. A new rationale for these African settlements, as well as the desire for strong military bases and a headquarters for the emerging slave trade, developed with the discovery of gold.[3] In Africa as well as in other segments of their empire along the coasts of India and China, the Portuguese did not establish large settlements. Their interest was in trade. Consequently, few Portuguese came to Africa. Even significant numbers of soldiers were not necessary in order to keep the indigenous Africans under control. Instead the Portuguese left the tribal chiefs and ruling groups in control as they found them. Initially the only real impact on the natives, save those "Eur-Africans" who learned the language and received a European-style education, were the Western goods that might be obtained through trade.

In view of this pattern of Portuguese colonization, it is hardly surprising that the primary focus of the ministry of the early Catholic missionaries in Africa was, not on the indigenous peoples, but on Portuguese colonists and Eur-Africans. We see this pattern illustrated in Portugal's settlement of the Gold Coast, Angola, and Africa's Atlantic Islands like Cape Verde. In the case of the last of these, both black men and Eur-Africans were employed as priests and evangelists. In Sierra Leone, there is evidence that the faith nurtured among the mixed community of the Portuguese and the Eur-Africans endured. Nearly 150 years after Portugal founded the community, a Jesuit missionary (a member of a monastic order founded about the same time as the Protestant Reformation) observed in the community the pres-

---

3. A similar new rationale for establishing settlements in the New World by the Spanish developed in the Americas with the discovery of gold and silver.

ence of Christians who had been reared by the Portuguese. Capuchin missionaries in the mid-seventeenth century subsequently baptized thousands, but the Catholic Church did not maintain a consistent ministry throughout the premodern period. In Mozambique, the first clergy on the island were Portuguese priests, who functioned more as chaplains to the Portuguese military than as evangelists to the natives. A Dominican community was established soon after Portuguese occupation early in the sixteenth century.

With regard to Sofala and the area inland in East Africa surrounding the Zambezi River and the area of present-day Zimbabwe, Catholic missionary work was apparently inextricably intertwined with the Portuguese political and economic agenda. Baptisms of hundreds of natives were recorded, but there is little trace of instruction and virtually no sign of subsequent nurturing. Reports from the sixteenth century maintain that Dominicans ministering in the area were so concerned about trade that they rarely preached and taught. On the positive side are stories of heroic efforts by Dominican and Jesuit missionaries. After some successful missionary work, Gonzalo de Silveira died a martyr when the king of Zimbabwe turned on him and had him killed. In addition, it appears that at least two princes of the Mutapap tribe in Zimbabwe became friars in the late seventeenth century. In a pattern typical of the few indigenous African clergy in the late medieval–early modern period, they lived out most of their professional service elsewhere, in their case in one of Portugal's settlements in India. Those natives who were ordained as priests, usually members of the ruling class, tended to receive little respect from the Portuguese — a pattern one can note again and again in these early African missions.

In regions where Islam dominated, such as the northern east coast (the so-called Swahili Coast) and the former stronghold of ancient Christianity, Roman North Africa, Portuguese missionary work took the form of forced conversions, which had little or no lasting impact. In contrast, some of the finest moments of the Church's mission on the African continent in this period were in places where the Portuguese dealt with tribal kingdoms as partners whose autonomy and traditions were more or less to be respected. The Portuguese first made contact with the Kingdom of the Kongo in 1483. The turning point came in the early sixteenth century when King Mbemba Nzinga (Christian name Afonso) was baptized. One of the reasons for the royal court's ready acceptance of the European missionaries and their message may have been related to the Kongo's traditional cosmology, which linked the color white with the color of the spirit. Furthermore, there was not a significant difference between the worldviews of the missionaries and those of the Kongolese. As much as Africans, medieval Europeans regarded religion as permeating all dimensions of life and with the Africans believed in witchcraft, magic, and the veneration of ancestors.

Virtually all the African tribes held such a worldview, and at least a few tended to find special spiritual significance in "whiteness." Yet not all of them reacted as positively to the proclamation as the Kongolese. It is evident, therefore, that other factors were involved in the Kongoleses' conversion. Also aiding the sympathetic hearing that these white men received was the very favorable impressions of the wonders of European civilization that were made on four members of the Kongolese royal court who were invited to Lisbon for a visit. From these contacts, Portugal pledged military support as an ally of the Kongolese for any wars against their African neighbors and also shared craftsmen with the Kongo, with a view towards improving the economics and lifestyle of the tribe. Another reason for the successful planting of the Church in the Kongo was the missionaries' respect for cultural traditions, such as allowing polygamist converts to retain additional wives as "consorts" and employing traditional religious terminology to describe Christian concepts. For example, the missionaries allowed themselves to be identified as *nganga* (traditional religious leaders) rather than as priests.

There is much scholarly contention over the degree to which the conversion of the Kongo nation was sincere or merely a matter of political expediency. Nevertheless, unlike in other Portuguese colonies, Catholic Christianity in the Kongo continued to survive, if not thrive, through the nineteenth century, albeit sometimes in a *syncretistic* mode (unsystematically combined with other indigenous religious beliefs).[4] In the Kongo, then, is another reminder that missionary activity that is sensitive to and appropriates local cultural traditions is most likely to thrive. Or should it be argued that such efforts at indigenizing inevitably nurture a syncretistic, heretical version of the gospel?

With regard to the evangelization efforts in the kingdom of Benin (a medieval West African monarchy with territory in the area of present-day Nigeria and Benin), Portuguese missionaries reached the capital in 1515. The king's response was originally favorable, and his son learned Portuguese and was baptized. A handful of conversions were recorded in the sixteenth century (the first Nigerian Christians). They apparently acted as interpreters and brokers for the Portuguese with the Beni. This sort of "Westernization" of converts has been a more or less typical pattern in Africa, which explains why the principal target of evangelization was the Euro-African community. In Benin, the Westernization

---

4. This assessment of Catholicism in the region may say more about the cultural predispositions of its contemporary nineteenth-century European observers than anything else. Most definitely, when the political fortunes of the kingdom declined in the late seventeenth century, church life seemed to have suffered.

manifested itself in the missionaries' intolerance of Beni traditional religion and culture. Given these dynamics and the fact that the missionary enterprise was sporadic prior to the nineteenth century, it is hardly surprising that formal Christianity made no lasting impact in Benin. This is a significant contrast to the successful efforts in indigenizing the gospel in the Kongo.

Consideration of the desirability of indigenizing the gospel is closely related to the mandate to indigenize the Church's leadership. It has been noted that the churches of the West African Portuguese colonies produced a number of indigenous priests, mostly Eur-Africans. Many were brought to Portugal to be educated. In general, though, when they returned to Africa, they were treated with hostility by Europeans on the scene. For example, in the Kongo there is at least one report of the ordination of an African cleric in the early sixteenth century, Henrique, the brother (or the son) of the king. He was eventually consecrated by the pope as bishop of an Islamic province of North Africa. However, when Henrique assumed the position and returned to the Kongo, most European clerics on the scene tended to ignore his decrees. He died a broken man. In 1518 Pope Leo X (Giovanni de' Medici; 1475–1521) decreed a general approval of ordaining qualified Africans, Ethiopians, and Indians. However, like other papal decrees in the era pertaining to Africa and the colonies, its impact on the life of the Church was minimal. The colonial agenda and a sense of Western cultural hegemony were often more formative than the gospel for the life of the Church.

The Western church's dreams of cultural hegemony are manifest in the sixteenth-century efforts of the Catholic Church to plant missions in Ethiopia, the very land on which an ancient Orthodox church had existed since the first century. In the seventeenth century, such missionary efforts succeeded with the Ethiopian king, and during his brief reign, reunion between the Catholic and the Ethiopian churches was restored. With his death, the reunion was suspended, which accounts for the continuing separation of the two. These developments also laid the groundwork for the establishment in the nineteenth century of an Eastern rite (Uniat) church, a branch of the Roman Catholic Church that retains its indigenous liturgy and canon/church law, which in Ethiopia entails a continuing acceptance of married parish priests.

Perhaps the greatest misstep of the Church in this era was its complicity in the development of slavery. As early as 1434, in a papal decree, the Church even provided authorization or rationalization for slavery and colonization, claiming that the slave trade at least rescued the heathen from perdition. Of course, this rationalization meant nothing when it was bad for trade. In those instances, many Christians would not allow for the conversion of some slaves (as it was bad for discipline and besides, it was alleged, they had no souls) or the freeing of converts (even though the gospel sets the faithful free; 1 Cor. 7:22). Slavery did not perturb clergy; a number of priests serving in Africa owned slaves.

Many of the slaves were practitioners of traditional religion, and the rest were Islamic. A significant number of the former group who remained in Africa converted to Christianity. In the late seventeenth century, a Eur-African Catholic layman from present-day Angola, Lourenço da Silva, petitioned the Vatican regarding the abolition of perpetual slavery. The papacy accepted a series of propositions that essentially made the slave trade unworkable. At other times the institution was condemned by various popes. Unfortunately these condemnations were not enforced in practice.

Focusing only on the coastal regions with little penetration of the interior except as carried out by the Jesuits and Dominicans, the Church failed to do much lasting, truly evangelical work in Portugal's African colonies. The failure of most of the churches that were established in this period to endure was no doubt also related to Portugal's increasing preoccupation with the Far East.

MISSIONS IN THE FAR EAST

Despite the Catholic Church's failures in Africa, there were some bright spots in the late medieval–sixteenth-century missionary outreach. On several occasions the missionaries displayed sensitivity to indigenous cultures of the Far East. However, the Portuguese and Spanish mission to this region was plagued with some of the same imperialistic policies observed in the mission in Africa.

Spain, moving west from its colonies in the New World, reached the Philippines in the sixteenth century. Ferdinand Magellan discovered and conquered the islands in 1565. Many Moslems were encountered, but the results of evangelization particularly among those practicing an indigenous religion were phenomenal. Part of the reason for this phenomenal success is likely related to the colonial strategy of investing Catholic priests with most of the political power on the islands. In any case, the missionary strategy exhibited little sensitivity to the indigenous cultural traditions of the island. Nevertheless, by early in the next century, the Church's membership was in the millions, and in the twentieth century was the only Catholic nation in the Far East.

Missionary work in India, China, and Japan was a function of Portuguese travel to these lands for purposes of trade. Settlements were established only for this purpose. In many instances, the national authorities allowed this to happen, as trade was in their interest. The agenda for the Portuguese in this region, then, was never conquest. The key to the Portuguese Catholic outreach to the East was the ministry of the Spanish-Basque Jesuit Francis Xavier (1506–52), whom both the king of Portugal and the pope authorized to undertake his mission to the Orient. This Basque nobleman, one of the first Jesuits and highly regarded for his spirituality and intelligence, undertook this commission only because one of the Jesuit missionaries fell ill the day before the boat was to sail from Portugal. Xavier stepped in as a substitute with outstanding results.

Churches had already been established in some of the Portuguese settlements prior to the 1541 initiation of Xavier's mission. In the primary settlement in the Orient, Goa, Xavier developed a unique evangelistic style, one perhaps still worth consideration at least in modified form. He would walk along the streets, ringing a bell to attract children, and then invite them to follow him to church. There he would provide them with catechetical instruction. Then he would send them home to share with their parents what they had learned. "Get to the adults through the children" proved to be a most successful strategy for Xavier, and his ministry was characterized by its significant impact, evident in many instances of mass penance.

Xavier and his colleagues proceeded to the Indian coast. A number of Indians had previously converted to Catholic Christianity, probably as a result of the contacts they had had with Portuguese traders.[5] He himself had success with the lower castes, which was in part related to the outcastes' impressions that by becoming Christian they could at last have a caste. Presumably the sense of self-respect that the gospel message and Xavier's attention to them offered was a major factor in their conversion. For obvious reasons, many members of the higher castes reacted negatively to Xavier's mission and to the gospel.

Leaving others in charge of this ministry, Xavier proceeded in 1549 to Japan, where his ministry met even more profound success. The Church flourished until a persecution broke out shortly after his death. The persecution, which was the most severe any church has ever endured (producing at least four thousand recorded martyrs), seemed to decimate the Christian community, but in fact three centuries later Protestant missionaries found that a community of about one hundred thousand had survived. Indigenous Japanese priests served this church. The Church's success in Japan owed to certain economic factors. Though the Japanese regarded Europeans as barbarians, they were interested in the mechanical arts of Europe and the prospect of Portuguese trade. The Jesuit missionaries were pleased to facilitate such exchanges. This iden-

---

5. These earlier converts were not the first Indian Christians, for there are references to the planting of Malabar Christianity at least as early as the fourth century.

tification of the Church with Western interests primarily occasioned the subsequent persecution.

Xavier next proceeded to China in 1552. As previously noted, Christian missionaries (Nestorian Christians) had visited China in the seventh century and established a Nestorian church, which, after disappearing in the tenth century, was revived two centuries later by the Mongolian invasion of China. In the thirteenth century, the Franciscan John of Monte Corvino (1246/47–1330) undertook a successful missionary journey, which planted a Catholic church. A late-fourteenth-century persecution of Christians wiped out both of these movements. Xavier was never able to enter the country, for the government was averse to any foreign influence. It would be up to the next generation of Jesuit missionaries to bring the gospel to this land.

The success of Xavier's mission in the Far East was not related to his sensitivity to these ancient cultures. He and his colleagues did not make a clear distinction between European culture and the Christian faith. Mass baptisms were the norm for his conversions.[6] Spanish missionaries also employed this technique in the Americas. However, one can raise questions about the quality of Christian nurture that this method provides. In addition, we should note that in Xavier's case, he was not above employing secular means of coercion to "encourage" conversion.

To his credit, Xavier did try to leave behind him schools and priests to nurture the newly baptized. Unfortunately, his concern was to place European priests on these sites. In this regard, he did not show the sort of sensitivity that characterized the Portuguese missionary outreach in general, for the Portuguese tended not to be hesitant in the East about ordaining indigenous Christians. In fact, Portuguese Catholics were even more open to this possibility in Asia than they had been in Africa.

The cultural imperialism of some of Xavier's methods brought about a reaction from the next generation of Jesuit missionaries, notably from two Italian Jesuits — Matteo Ricci and Roberto de Nobili — who continued to minister under Portuguese auspices. In many respects, their work represents the high point in indigenizing efforts in Far East.

The Jesuits' strategy in China contended that the Chinese reverence for ancestors, so integral to their social system, was a social, not a religious, act. If it were deemed a religious act, it could be regarded as something like prayers for dead. They tried to present Christianity, not as a replacement, but as the highest fulfillment of China's cultural aspirations. Matteo Ricci (1552–1610) especially took the lead in trying

---

6. Of course, it could be argued that given the importance of the extended family in these cultures, this method of conversion was an instance of sensitivity to indigenous cultures.

to penetrate the Chinese intellectual elite in this way, intriguing them first with his erudition and then informally proselytizing. His work successfully planted the Catholic Church in this land. Ricci's approach to missions came to be known as "accommodation." After his death, a protracted debate about its legitimacy emerged in Catholicism.

In India, the Jesuits undertook a serious dialogue with the caste system. Notable in this connection was the ministry of Roberto de Nobili (1577–1656). Of course, Xavier's earlier success in evangelizing the lower castes was a kind of precedent for de Nobili. In seeking to reach out to the higher castes, de Nobili studied Indian culture with *Brahmans* (those of the priestly Hindu caste), took up with them a vegetarian diet, permitted converts to continue celebrating Hindu feasts, indigenized worship, took the Brahman title of "teacher" for himself, and in the tradition of Indian/Hindu culture did not allow lower castes to worship with upper-caste converts. All but the last of these missionary strategies seem unimpeachable by the standards of today's commitments to multiculturalism. But the de facto practice of segregation in the Church that de Nobili advocated is another matter. Should the Church always respect venerable cultural traditions? Is it ever necessary to critique such traditions in the name of the gospel?

Less controversial was the openness of the Church to ordaining native priests in India. A Brahman Christian, Matthew de Castro, was even consecrated as bishop in 1637. Unfortunately, he met the same fate as his Kongolese colleague Henrique with regard to a lack of acceptance by the Portuguese government and Portuguese clergy. The Catholic Church has not made a wide impact on Indian society, but it has persevered.

MISSIONS IN THE NEW WORLD

The Church's missionary outreach during the late medieval–early modern era in the Spanish colonies in Central and South America provides some of Christianity's finest moments. As with the Portuguese colonization efforts, though, the good was mixed with some bad. Except for Brazil, the Church's pre-Reformation outreach to the New World was under Spanish auspices. Its colonization strategy was different from that of Portugal's elsewhere in the world.

The strategy developed during the reigns of Ferdinand V and Isabella, who were determined not to allow the settlers too much power. Having successfully curbed the power of feudal lords in Spain and centralized power, they were determined to maintain control of the colonies. The strategy took the form of efforts by the crown to enact laws that would guarantee protection of the Native American communities whose conquest by Spanish troops had been the presupposition for the settlements.

This policy continued with their successors, as in 1542 and again in the seventeenth century laws were established which granted freedom to the Indian slaves. Since feudalism was still a force in Spanish economics in the late fifteenth century, the accumulation of property and wealth by military leaders would infuse them with such a spirit of independence as effectively to negate royal power. Ferdinand and Isabella believed that if the Spanish conquistadores were curbed in exploiting the Indians, they would not accumulate such unlimited property and hence would not threaten the power of the throne.

Not surprisingly, Ferdinand's and Isabella's laws were neglected in the New World. The Native American communities were the losers. Those not killed in the military raids were pressed into the lowest echelons of the labor force by the conquerors, often as slaves. Ferdinand and Isabella tried to address these dynamics by establishing strong central administration of the colonies. Before long, though, the colonial bureaucracy was managed by colonists. The rivalry between them and new immigrants sent by the Spanish royalty severely undercut the motherland's power in the colonies and would be an ongoing dynamic in the history of Latin America.

Another way in which the Spanish monarchy tried to enforce a centralized power over the colonies was through the exercise of centralized religious authority. Shortly before the discovery of the New World, Iberia (a predecessor of modern Spain) had conquered new lands, and the papacy had given the crown extraordinary powers over the Church in these lands. This precedent was now applied to the New World. Popes Alexander VI (1431–1503) and Julius II (1443–1513) gave the Spanish monarchy the right of "royal patronage" over the Church in the New World, which effectively gave the kings the right to appoint bishops in the region as well as to administer church funds. The Portuguese had earlier received similar authority over the Church in their African colonies from Nicholas V in 1452 and from Leo X in 1514.

Committed to establishing settlements, and not just centers of trade, the Spanish colonials required laborers, either for gold mining or for farming. Native Americans, who were often the losers in a military campaign of conquest, were pressed into service, usually as forced labor (slaves). In some regions where the Indian population was small or decimated (as in the Caribbean), African slaves were imported. This happened first in 1502.

Religious policies in the New World closely followed the agenda of the Middle Ages. Just as the Crusades and the subsequent European campaigns against Moslems and Jews had practiced principles of conquest against the "infidels," so in the Americas the strategy was to conquer the Indian infidels. This was certainly not a promising start for propagating the gospel among Native Americans. Necessarily committed to evangelizing their captives, as per Alexander VI's 1493 directive, the Spaniards undertook the task of both evangelizing and civilizing the inhabitants of the territories. For example, Columbus took seven missionaries with him on his second voyage to the Caribbean. The conqueror of the Aztecs in present-day Mexico, Hernando Cortés (1485–1547) was a devout Catholic, who expressly requested that the king of Spain send mendicant friars for mission work among the Indians. The natives needed to be civilized, it was thought, in order to be economically useful as a labor force. However, given their treatment by the conquistadors and the ethically questionable behavior of these "Christian" soldiers (a significant segment of the Spanish army and its clergy in the New World was the social scum of late medieval Spanish society), Native Americans became highly suspicious of Christian claims. On the other hand, at least in Mexico among the conquered Aztecs, their conquest by Cortés was perceived as proof of the superiority of the Christian God to their own gods. This became an opening for effective evangelism practiced by a number of devoted monks belonging to the mendicant orders.

Certainly a bright spot in the missionary activity of the Spanish colonies in Central and South America was the significant work among Indians carried on by monastic orders (notably by the Franciscans, Dominicans, and Jesuits). Many of these monks lived with the Indians and knew their plight. The mendicant lifestyle of these monks' orders brought them credibility with the Indians, and they became advocates of these Native Americans. To be sure, this did not sit well with the Latin American Catholic hierarchy, who generally owed their posts to colonizers. Tensions between an unresponsive Church hierarchy, concerned about the interests of the powerful and wealthy, and the parish priests and friars dedicated to the poor were a way of life in the American colonies. In our century, Latin American Catholicism continues to live with this tension.

Generally speaking, the Spaniards, unlike the Portuguese in Africa and the Orient, denied American Indians education as well as the possibility of eligibility for ordination. Even the idealists among the Spaniards who ministered to the Native Americans tended to regard the Indians as children, not worthy of the priesthood. It is true that in Mexico the Franciscans planned a native clergy and founded a school to train priests in the sixteenth century, but it never produced a single native priest. The first ordination of a Mexican was delayed until the seventeenth century, and elsewhere in the Americas it was another century until the ordinations of Native Americans.

Part of the reason for the unresponsiveness of the Catholic clergy was

likely a function of the ecclesiastical authority that the popes had conferred on the Spanish crown. Since the episcopacy and the parish clergy
owed their positions to the secular authorities, it is hardly surprising
that they were more concerned with the interests of these authorities
than with justice to the oppressed. In the region of the former Inca
Empire (present-day Peru), the colonial agenda clearly contaminated
the Church. The wealth of the colonies even corrupted many of the
friars. In addition, it was decided without protest to develop separate
churches for European colonists and Indians. Christianity soon came to
be perceived by Native Americans as a "white-man's religion," and the
Indians who joined the Church were ostracized or threatened with violence. To be sure, here and elsewhere in the Americas the first wave
of missionaries brought some of these perceptions on themselves. Most
of them displayed no sensitivity to the indigenous culture, to the point
of deliberately destroying all the temples and idols of the old religions.
Such iconoclasm was especially virulent in the territories of present-day
Mexico.

In territories that are now Argentina, Uruguay, and Paraguay, immigrants depended on Indians for their subsistence and so were very
moderate in their treatment of the indigenous folk. Franciscans gathered
the Native Americans into small towns (called *reductions*), where they
were taught European technology and agriculture besides receiving instruction in the Christian faith. This method for handling the "Indian
problem" was typical of other regions in the New World; it was not just
employed in many of the Spanish colonies. Portuguese Jesuits also uti-
lized something like such a missionary strategy in Brazil. These Indian
towns (forerunners of North American Indian reservations) were almost
theocracies. Native Americans elected their leaders, but they were under
the final authority of the missionaries. So successful were these missions (sometimes economically successful) that they became the target
of raids, not only from other Native Americans but also from white
settlers. The Spanish monarchy developed an anti-Jesuit policy in the
eighteenth century, which created vacancies in the leadership of these
communities. Civil authorities began exploiting the Indians who resided
in them.

The Catholic Church first came to the territory of what has become the United States, specifically into the Southwest, in the early
seventeenth century, as settlers proceeded north from Mexico. Some
missionary work among the Native Americans in these regions was
undertaken as thousands were baptized. The mission was always precarious, though, due to much general Indian hostility. In Florida, French
Protestants (the Huguenots, whose origin and history fall just outside
the span of years covered in this book) established a settlement in

the early 1560s. A few years later, the Spanish moved in, settled, and eventually wiped out the Huguenots. Spanish-supported Jesuits and Dominicans did make concerted efforts to evangelize the Native Americans. Under pressure from the expanding British Empire, this outreach to the Indians and Spanish life in Florida virtually collapsed by the middle of the eighteenth century (see vol. 2).

Spain was not the only colonial power present in the Americas in the late Middle Ages. Portugal had also gained access to Brazil, but the Church faced serious problems in that region. Brazil's potential prosperity and the pressures the Portuguese felt from other colonial powers in the region were the major causes of these problems. The colonizers' cruelty to Native Americans and the colonists' wild living characterized colonial life. In response, the king of Portugal sought to establish order in 1549 by declaring Brazil a royal colony and sending Jesuit missionaries. The leader of the delegation was Manoel da Nobrega. These Jesuits founded typical Indian settlements but placed them near the plantations so that the Indians could serve as virtual slaves. Furthermore, these missionaries presented the gospel as specifically teaching the submissiveness of slaves (Eph. 6:5; Col. 3:22). Needless to say, this sort of Christianity encouraged the creation of sects among the indentured servants who were converted. Both the Indian and the black slaves developed belief structures that combined elements of their indigenous religions and Christianity.

Despite these various examples of insensitivity to the oppressed and apparent compromises of the gospel, there were some sterling moments in the late medieval–early modern Catholic Church's missionary outreach. Noteworthy is the work in the Americas of a Spanish priest, Bernardino de Sahagún, who undertook a significant, empathetic, and realistic anthropological study of the tribes of Native Americans. Not surprising, given the paternalism of much of the priesthood in this era, his contemporaries were very critical of the study. Missionaries to the Americas were not ready to see the indigenous American religions as primitive approximations of Christian truth in the positive way that the accommodationists did in the Far East with the religions of that region.

Crucial in the evangelization of Indians in Central America was a Spanish monk, Juan de Estrada Ravago, about whose background little is known except that he was a renegade Franciscan. Central America was a region with a mixed record regarding Native American–Spanish settler relations. The leader of the first effort at colonization of the region, Vasco Núñez de Balboa distinguished himself not only by the illicit way in which he seized leadership of the expedition but also by his efforts to establish cordial relationships with the local Native Americans. When the Spanish royalty removed him from the leadership, the new governor enforced strict discipline on the Indians, "entrusting" most of them to settlers, ostensibly to civilize and evangelize them but in fact to provide the settlers with forced labor. This system, called *encomiendas*, was the way in which the Spanish colonies maintained slaves while getting around official condemnations of slavery as an institution.

Ravago was by no means a purely spiritual man. He had joined the conquering conquistadors. As a renegade Franciscan, he had been ordered to return to Europe when he learned of the needs of a proposed expedition to Costa Rica. He proceeded to provide funding for the expedition and joined it as its head. He worked at indigenizing the gospel, in the sense of learning the language of the people. He also bought food, clothes, and seed for the Native Americans and the European settlers. The Church developed rapidly. By the end of the sixteenth century, most of the original inhabitants of Central America called themselves Christian. When the preaching of the gospel is accompanied with a concern for the material needs of the poor, missions seem to be most effective.

The Church in the New World finally marshalled an open protest in 1511 against the system of *encomiendas*. The Dominican preacher Antonio Montesinos preached a sermon in Santo Domingo condemning the practice. One who heard the sermon was the Spanish missionary Bartolomé de Las Casas (1474–1566), the first priest to be ordained in the New World.[7] Some three years after hearing the sermon, he was moved to conclude that the Christian faith was incompatible with exploitation of the Indians. He proceeded to devote the rest of his career to this cause, crossing the Atlantic repeatedly to gain legislation that would condemn the practice. His urgings gained the favorable response of Pope Paul III (Alessandro Farnese; 1468–1549), who in 1537 issued a bull condemning the enslavement of Native Americans. In struggling for implementation of this bull, Las Casas was joined by other episcopal colleagues in the region, notably Antonio de Valdivieso of Nicaragua. There was much resistance to both Las Casas and the papal directive, which the New World colonial establishment generally ignored. Even the legislation of King Charles I (1500–1558) of Spain (also known as Charles V of the Holy Roman Empire) in 1542 condemning slavery failed to gain much attention.

Las Casas's own record with regard to African slaves was less admirable than his advocacy on behalf of Native Americans. In his zeal for protecting Native American rights, he suggested in 1516 that slaves be imported from Africa. He did recant this position later in life and became a defender of African slaves as well as Native Americans. Colombian settlers found slavery economically advantageous and en-

---

7. He eventually joined the Dominican Order.

slaved both Native Americans and Africans. An important name to remember in this region is Pedro Claver (1580–1654), a Catholic priest who is especially notable for his work with the African slaves. Claver came to America as a Jesuit missionary in 1610. His first project was to get his order to treat slaves as equals. Subsequently he began a ministry of evangelism and welcome to the slaves. He provided them with health care and even organized them to give mutual ministry to each other. Most of his life Claver lived without acclaim but with some criticism among Spanish settlers. In his later years, he began to receive the attention he deserved. He was declared a saint of the Catholic Church in the nineteenth century.

Archbishop Toribio Alfonso de Mogrovejo of Lima in the sixteenth century is another shining example of Roman Catholic missionary concern for the oppressed. In 1582 he convened a regional synod (the Third Lima Council), which passed laws to defend the liberties of Indians and the relatively few African slaves in his diocese. He advocated the education of the slaves and prepared textbooks in original Native American languages. Though never breaking outright with the Spanish colonial regime, he repeatedly clashed with it over the issue of more just treatment of Native Americans. Another prominent figure in Peru was Martin de Porres (1579–1639), who entered a Dominican monastery but was never allowed to join because he was the son of an African slave and a Spanish colonist. He devoted his life to caring for the sick, both human and animals, in hopes that they would someday help those who were hungry.

WAS THE MEDIEVAL CHURCH'S MISSIONARY OUTREACH FUNDAMENTALLY A MANIFESTATION OF EUROPEAN COLONIALISM?

To be sure, there were dismal failures and much that was bad in the life of the Roman Catholic Church in the early colonial period. Yet there is much to celebrate — some intriguing successes in indigenizing the gospel and advocating the cause of liberation. Was such successful indigenizing of the gospel and witness for social justice on behalf of the oppressed a continuation of the Catholic tradition's faithful witness to the biblical heritage (as expressed in the Church's mission to the Gentiles)? Could one consider the failure of the Catholic Church in Africa and with colonialism in general, not so much as a shortcoming of the Roman Catholic tradition, but rather as a tragic example of what can go wrong whenever the Church allows itself to be co-opted by political-economic interests?

Or could it be that the authoritarian, largely Western orientation of the Roman Catholic tradition is to blame for the dismal failures on the missions field that we have observed?

DEVELOPMENTS IN
THE INDIGENOUS AFRICAN CHURCHES

While emerging Western powers colonized regions of Africa and established Christianity there, developments took place in the indigenous churches of the region as well. The two most prominent of these indigenous churches are the Coptic and Ethiopian Orthodox churches. While Romanized North African Christianity totally succumbed to the Islamic invasion, the indigenous churches in these regions persevered.

In Egypt, the initial relations between the Christians and their Islamic invaders had been good. Some Egyptian Christians at the time of the seventh-century invasion had regarded Islam as a Christian sect. The Moslem invaders regarded the Christians as "Peoples of the Book" (Koran 3:64–66, 69–72, 98–100, 113–15, 187, 199) and granted them toleration in return for a poll tax. Apparently there were economic reasons for the initial Arab toleration of Egyptian Christianity.

Successive waves of Arab immigration to Egypt during the centuries of persecution from the mid-thirteenth to the early sixteenth centuries, however, led to the decline of the Christian population to its present minority status. The Crusades seem to have been a factor in their declining fortunes. The Coptic Church's declining fortunes in the Middle Ages may also have been related to the corrupt leadership that plagued it. Many bishops practiced simony, charging fees for ordination. Furthermore, a controversy over the administration of confession had introduced turmoil in the church earlier in the second half of the twelfth century. After the Coptic patriarch gave the faithful permission to confess in privacy, a movement developed that made confession to a priest necessary for salvation. The hierarchy's openness to making confession before a priest optional eventually prevailed.

CONFLICTS IN ETHIOPIAN ORTHODOXY

In Ethiopia, Christians have remained as the vast majority of the population, though not without enduring persecution. Initially amiable Christian-Moslem relations were probably related to an earlier decision of a Christian king to give sanctuary to some of the first Moslem refugees fleeing from Mecca in the early stages of the religion's development. Changing dynasties in Ethiopia, though, brought interruptions to these relationships, as in the tenth century the Ethiopian Christian community endured pressure from Moslems in the north and from proponents of traditional religion in the south. One tenth-century queen of the latter group is especially infamous to this day among Ethiopian Christians for her hostility to the faith. Her acts of desecration are the reason some churches still continue to bar women from entering. When her dynasty was replaced by a new dynastic line, which laid claim to Solomonic descent, Ethiopian Christianity began to appeal to the Solomonic tradition as the cornerstone of national identity.

Several interesting controversies developed within the Ethiopian Orthodox Church in this period. At least from the sixth century on, the patriarchate of Alexandria denied the Ethiopian Church, especially its native clergy, independent authority. One should note that there were ancient precedents for such policies, relating to the commission of Frumentius's ministry by the patriarch of Alexandria (see chap. 1). Prelates and clergy attached to the royal court in Ethiopia used their influence with the king to direct internal policies that were in competition with regular clergy in the monasteries. Tensions flared into public confrontation in the fourteenth century, manifesting themselves in theological disputes over questions like observance of Christmas and other feasts as well as questions of royal inheritance. In the second half of the fifteenth century, a settlement was reached, which continued until well into the twentieth century: the Coptic patriarch of Egypt retained authority over the whole Ethiopian Church. Monastic clergy were given autonomy.

In the same period, perhaps earlier, a great dispute among two powerful monastic orders in the church, nearly resulting in schism, flared regarding when to observe the Sabbath. The dispute was finally resolved in the mid-fifteenth century, by establishing the present practice of worshiping on Sundays while still observing the Hebrew Sabbath. This development should not be construed as a sign that relations between the church and the Ethiopian Jewish community were amiable. As in medieval Europe, Jews in Ethiopia feared Christians, and Christians despised Jews. From the fifteenth century on, Jews were not permitted to own land and were regularly shunned. It was also in the late fourteenth century that Ethiopian Orthodoxy was spread to other tribes (located in present-day Ethiopia) primarily through military consolidation under the Amharic people.

In the fourteenth and fifteenth centuries, the Ethiopian Church contended with two heresies. The Mikaelites taught a Gnostic dualism contending that God cannot be known and so only can be approached by degrees under the guidance of certain teachers who can interpret the secret meaning of Scripture. The Stephanites venerated neither the Cross nor the Virgin Mary. Although repressed by Ethiopian kings, especially

Zare'a Ya'qob (1436–68), these heresies persisted in some monasteries through the end of the sixteenth century. In that century, largely prompted by Portuguese Catholic missionary endeavors in the region, renewed attention to the unique Monophysite Christology of the Ethiopian Church led to the development of distinct schools of Christology in the church, which are manifest in the Sons of Unction–Sons of Grace debate described in chapter 11.

A KONGO HERESY

With regard to African heresies, one other intriguing indigenous heresy is worthy of note, although it emerged in a church planted by European settlers (in the Roman Catholic Church) in the Kingdom of the Kongo. Sometime during the period of declining fortunes of the kingdom, probably in the late seventeenth or eighteenth century, several women prophets emerged, notably Appolonia Mafuta and Vita Kimpa (d. 1706). The latter, a member of the nobility, claimed to be a medium of Anthony. Both claimed to be possessed by the Spirit, an idea linked to traditional Kongolese religion. Vita destroyed the symbols of both Christianity and traditional religion, proclaiming that they were powerless to save. She also taught that Jesus was black, a native of the Kongo. (The idea of a "black Jesus" is not really so new after all.) The prophets had widespread support but were eventually condemned as heretics and executed.

WERE WOMEN TOTALLY MARGINALIZED BY THE CHURCH IN THE MIDDLE AGES?

Back in the European homelands, the increased prosperity that capitalism and colonialism nurtured was both good and bad. Women were denied the priesthood in the late Middle Ages and throughout the history of the Roman Catholic tradition. However, monastic life since the inception of female orders provided women as much freedom as they could achieve anywhere in the first centuries. Monastic life in the pre-medieval and early medieval period was the equivalent of a career. It is difficult to indict monasticism as a sexist institution.

So popular were the opportunities the monastic life seemed to afford women that in the late Middle Ages convents were flooded with candidates. Soon male leaders in the Franciscan and Dominican Orders put limits on those admitted. The policy did not stop the flood. In response, some women formed their own small groups in order to live together in prayer, devotion, and poverty. This came to be known as the Beguine movement. By the late thirteenth century, the papacy said no to the movement, insisting that the monastic profession must be lived out in official monastic orders. The movement was further suppressed by a council convened in Viénne in 1311. Similar strictures were imposed on men. The papacy also placed convents under the guidance of friars and priests. This was through the work of Innocent III's (1160–1216) negotiations with female orders. It was all part of a general trend in the High Middle Ages to permit less and less self-government by the nuns of their convents, less and less freedom of movement, on grounds that they needed protection and proper spiritual guidance. Were these dynamics sexist?

Generally speaking, medieval female Christian leaders experienced visions, which were often the source of their influence. They also typically practiced asceticism. Of those who experienced visions, perhaps the most famous was Joan of Arc (1412–31). The daughter of a French peasant, she experienced several supernatural visitations, which she described as voices accompanied by a blaze of light. While still a teenager, she approached the French king (Charles VII) at a difficult time for him. English troops, whose king claimed to be the rightful heir to the French throne, had barricaded Charles in Orleans. Joan convinced him that it was her mission to save the kingdom. She succeeded and also persuaded Charles to accept his coronation. She was now a national heroine! The king persuaded Joan to continue to lead military campaigns on his behalf. She was captured in one in 1430, sold to the English, and charged with witchcraft and heresy. A 1456 revision of her trial found this great military leader and religious visionary posthumously innocent.

The great Italian Dominican nun and mystic Catherine of Siena (Caterina Benincasa; 1347–80) was internationally renowned for her holiness, spirituality, and service to others, as well as for being an influential advocate of the Second Crusade and a key agent in urging the Avignon pope Gregory XI to return to Rome. Catherine's theological insights, dictated to her secretaries, were often produced while she was in a state of "ecstasy." Her church has recognized their profundity, declaring her a doctor of the Church in 1970. Her mystical commitments surface in her visions of experiencing a kind of mystical marriage to Christ (*Miracles; Dialogue* 84). Tied with this is her Augustinian-like claim to be accepted by God despite sin. After all, she insisted, she was loved before she existed (*Dialogue* 148,134).

Not surprisingly, with her mystical commitments Catherine did not merely affirm God's unconditional love; she was also very concerned with the practice of the Christian life. Consequently she emphasized perseverance in light of faith (*Dialogue* 148; *Letter to Brother Raymond of Capria*) and aimed for perfection in the Christian life, that is, the eradication of self-will (*Letters to Blessed Daniella of Orvieto; Dialogue* 11). Of course, she added that we love others with God's own infinite love (*Dialogue* 148), which suggests the Augustinian theme that even the good we do is God's work. Catherine's involvements in the Church of her day ensured that she was well acquainted with ecclesiastical abuse. Typical of the mystical tradition, she strongly criticized these abuses (*Dialogue* 113).

Clare of Assisi (ca. 1194–1253) was an early-thirteenth-century Italian nun, a woman of noble birth, whom Francis profoundly influenced (*Testament of St. Clare* 2–4,7–14). Dedicating herself to total renunciation of her wealth, she organized a monastic order, the Poor Clares, which was formally established during the papacy of Innocent III. It was noted as the most severe and rigorous of all the women's orders. Many themes characteristic of the Franciscan Order appear in Clare's and her order's theological convictions. Mandated is a life of poverty (10,14,17; *Rule of Saint Clare* VI) and obedience (*Testament of St. Clare* 20; *Rule of Saint Clare* I), much like the Franciscan vow. Clare also frequently proclaimed God's great kindness (*Testament of St. Clare* 5), while insisting that the merits of Mary and the saints will aid the Christian's perseverance (23).

Umilta of Faenza (1226–1310) was another late-thirteenth-century Italian nun. She was an illiterate member of the nobility, who claimed to have acquired literacy through a miracle. With her husband, she joined a Benedictine-like Order, but yearned for more solitude. She attracted many followers during the course of her ministry. At the heart of much of Umilta's theology are her calls on Mary to forgive her sins (*Sermons* 5.1–3). Is Marian piety a help or hindrance to the Christian feminist cause? Such a piety seems closely and naturally connected to the theology of these medieval Christian women. It is manifest in the thought of Angela of Foligno (*Book of the Experience of the Truly Faithful* 9) and Catherine of Siena (*Letter to Brother Raymond of Capria*). In any case, Umilta urged Christ to come, for she claims to have had much yearning for divine love (*Sermons* 6.1).

Angela of Foligno (ca. 1248–1309) was a late-thirteenth-century to early-fourteenth-century Italian nun, related to the Franciscans as a layperson who, while not taking vows, along with others of a similar ecclesiastical status, formed chapters, which for the most part were governed by monastic rules under the direction of a priest (an order called "Tertiary").[8] Angela undertook a complete renunciation of property after the death of her husband, children, and mother, losses she viewed as the removal of hindrances in following the way of God. Her

---

8. Catherine of Siena was a Dominican Tertiary.

powerful spiritual life in the wake of these tragedies attracted the notice and admiration of many.

Angela identified eighteen steps in her penitential period (*Book of Divine Consolation* I). Not surprisingly given her Franciscan commitments, she included as one of these steps a commitment to the practice of poverty (*Book of the Experience of the Truly Faithful* 12,15,22). There are reports that Angela was so full of love that she screamed whenever God was mentioned. Such behavior no doubt contributed to the accusation that she was demon possessed (21). Even her confessor (the author of a treatise about her) was embarrassed (34).

Angela claimed that the Holy Spirit wooed her while on pilgrimage; according to her, the Spirit vowed never to cease communicating with her. The Spirit is said to have called Angela daughter and bride (*Book of the Experience of the Truly Faithful* 35). She referred to God as the Lover of the soul, for God dwells in it (*Book of Divine Consolation* II.I). Of course, because God is so much greater than the mind and all other things, we are not able to measure, speak, or think of him. God's goodness cannot be perfectly explained. The encounter with the Spirit, Angela claimed, leads first to a profound sense of sin (*Book of the Experience of the Truly Faithful* 35; *Book of Divine Consolation* I). In the presence of God, we truly know our sin. However, this is not the final word. We also experience total forgiveness and affirmation. Angela claimed to have heard that all aspects of her life were now pleasing. The Holy Spirit is said to have entered her, never to leave as long as she loves him (*Book of the Experience of the Truly Faithful* 35).

We do not know much about the personal life of the English mystic Julian of Norwich (ca. 1342–after 1423), except that she lived in contemplative seclusion attached to a parish church in Concord. (Her residence was likely attached to the church.) Her theological insights, like those of many other women mystics of the period, emerged from ecstatic visions she experienced. Among the unique characteristics of her thought is the sophisticated conceptuality that she employed in describing her visions. Julian was an accomplished and creative theologian, as we previously observed in her reflections on the gender of God (chap. 14).

These are impressive women. The patriarchalism of the Western church in the Middle Ages did not succeed in silencing them. Should one still say that women were totally marginalized in this era? We should consider a question not unlike the one raised concerning the Catholic Church's missionary work in the early colonial period: Is there anything about the nature of the Christian faith, at least as it was proclaimed in the Roman Catholic tradition of the Middle Ages, that accounts for the role women played in that era and continue to play?

WAS THIS A GOLDEN AGE?

One cannot deny the harshness of the Middle Ages. But at least the
Church in the West was still one and the Thomistic synthesis of reason and faith was not totally dislodged. That would all change in the
sixteenth century. Is the vision of the Church described in this volume,
including the unity of faith and reason, the ultimate subordination of
society to faith, as well as the Church's Asian and African roots, a vision that should still inform us in our ministries today? At least to some
extent, the emergence of Protestantism, which was on the horizon at
the end of the Middle Ages, represented a negative response to these
questions. But has Protestantism's apparent no to many of the trends
reported in this volume really served the Church well?

Appendix 1 *Significant Events for the Church in the Pre-Christian Era*

	POLITICAL EVENTS	RELIGIOUS/PHILOSOPHICAL DEVELOPMENTS	THEOLOGICAL SIGNIFICANCE
B.C. Late 13th century	Settlement of Hebrew tribes in Israel		
12th–11th centuries	Amphictiony (period of the Judges)		
ca. 1005	United Kingdom under Saul		
ca. 1000–961	Reign of David		
961–922	Reign of Solomon	Temple in Jerusalem built	
ca. 922	Division of the kingdom		
721	Fall of Samaria		
587–586	Fall of Jerusalem and Babylonian exile begins (586–539)		
Late 6th–4th centuries	Persian domination	Temple in Jerusalem rebuilt Plato (428–348)	Beginnings of Hebraic separatist impulses

	POLITICAL EVENTS	RELIGIOUS/PHILOSOPHICAL DEVELOPMENTS	THEOLOGICAL SIGNIFICANCE
Late 6th–4th centuries (cont'd)		Aristotle (384–322) Stoicism	
333–163	Greek domination -Alexander the Great -Ptolemaic (Egyptian) rule -Seleucid (Syrian) rule	Maccabean Revolt (175–163)	Hellenization of region and Jewish reaction against it
141–63	Hasmonean dynasty	Septuagint Pharisees Sadducees Essenes	Development of eschatological consciousness
63–	Roman rule -Hasmonean puppet rulers -Herodian puppet rulers	Birth of Jesus	

Appendix 2 Significant Events for the Church in the Christian Era

	POLITICAL EVENTS	RELIGIOUS/PHILOSOPHICAL DEVELOPMENTS	THEOLOGICAL SIGNIFICANCE
A.D. 1–395	Roman Empire as united entity		
14–37	-Reign of Tiberius	Philo and continued thriving of Jewish community in Alexandria Birth of Church Early missionary outreach of Paul	Development of method of correlation and use of allegory applied to Scripture
41–54	-Reign of Claudius; Herod Agrippa's reign as his surrogate in Israel	Local persecution of Christians initiated; James killed and Peter harassed (Acts 12) Jerusalem Council (Acts 15) Expulsion of Jews from Rome (Acts 18:2)	Admission of Gentiles to Church
54–68	-Reign of Nero	Persecution of Christians –Pomponia Graecina indicted as Christian Zealot revolution begins (66)	

	POLITICAL EVENTS	RELIGIOUS/PHILOSOPHICAL DEVELOPMENTS	THEOLOGICAL SIGNIFICANCE
69–79	-Reign of Vespasian	Conquest of Jerusalem and destruction of the Temple (70)	Beginnings of modern Judaism
81–96	-Reign of Domitian	Persecution of Christians	
98–117	-Reign of Trajan	Clement, bishop of Rome Persecution of Christians –Martyrdom of Ignatius	Work of Apostolic Fathers and re-Judaization of Christianity Church begins to refer to real presence of Christ in Lord's Supper and begins to develop idea of apostolic succession
117–38	-Reign of Hadrian	*The Didache* *The Letter of Barnabas* Surge of Gnosticism –Marcion	Christian worship continues to be ritualized
138–61	-Reign of Antoninus Pius	*The Shepherd of Hermas* Martyrdom of Polycarp	Church begins process of forming New Testament canon and affirming goodness of creation

	POLITICAL EVENTS	RELIGIOUS/PHILOSOPHICAL DEVELOPMENTS	THEOLOGICAL SIGNIFICANCE
138–61 (cont'd)		Development of baptismal creed in Rome Montanism	Church gives renewed attention to Holy Spirit
161–80	-Reign of Marcus Aurelius	Persecution of Christians –Martyrdom of Felicitas and her sons Justin Martyr (ca. 100–ca. 165) Athenagoras Tatian (b. ca. 120)	Apologetics and method of correlation introduced in Christianity
180–93	-Reign of Commodus and his successors	Persecutions ease Irenaeus (ca. 130–ca. 202) Catechetical school of Alexandria established Debate over date of Easter	Criticism of Gnosticism; development of doctrines of creation and *theosis*; Eucharist construed as sacrifice

POLITICAL EVENTS	RELIGIOUS/PHILOSOPHICAL DEVELOPMENTS	THEOLOGICAL SIGNIFICANCE
180–93 (cont'd)	Sabellius and Modalist heresy	Church's response ensures it would posit a distinction between Father, Son, and Spirit
	Christians begin to refer to Church as "catholic"	
193–211 -Reign of Septimius Severus	Policy of syncretism instituted in Roman Empire, and dissenting Christians persecuted –Martyrdom of Perpetua and Felicitas	
	Tertullian (ca. 160-ca. 225)	Theology in accord with Rule of Faith (Christocentric Orthodoxy)
	Clement of Alexandria (ca. 150-ca. 215)	
	Infant baptism practiced, but not yet generally endorsed for centuries	
	Sacrament of ordination practiced; marriage increasingly practiced as religious ceremony	

POLITICAL EVENTS	RELIGIOUS/PHILOSOPHICAL DEVELOPMENTS	THEOLOGICAL SIGNIFICANCE
217–22	-Reigns of Macrinus and Elagabalus	Hippolytus (ca. 170–ca. 263)	Church's rejection of Hippolytus's unwillingness to forgive fornicators opens way to development of sacrament of confession
238–44	-Reign of Gordian III	Mani (ca. 216–76) and development of Manicheism	
249–51	-Reign of Decius	Sought restoration of worship of ancient Roman gods Christians persecuted	
		Origen (ca. 185–254)	Framer of idea of universal salvation. His theological approach and dualistic tendencies had great impact on Eastern church through monasticism as well as on Church in West, and his Christology also influenced heresies like Arianism.
		Extreme unction (last rites) practiced	
		Cyprian of Carthage (d. 258)	

	POLITICAL EVENTS	RELIGIOUS/PHILOSOPHICAL DEVELOPMENTS	THEOLOGICAL SIGNIFICANCE
251–53	-Reign of Gallus	Ends persecutions Synods of Carthage (251) (252) Novatian reaction Gradual development of church buildings and Christian calendar	Formula for restoring to Church those who lapsed during earlier persecution; outside Church, no salvation. Further contribution to the development of the sacrament of penance
253–60	-Reign of Valerian	Renews policies of Decius; forbids Christians to assemble	
ca. 260–68	-Reign of Gallienus	Christian basilicas and freedom of worship restored	
284–305	-Reign of Diocletian (established system of shared rule with Galerius [292–311], Maximinus Daia [305–13], Maxentius [306–12], and Constantine [306–24]); Licinius (307–24) added to governing coalition	Repealed Edict of Gallienus, stripping Christians of government positions After further persecution of Christians, Constantine issues Edict of Milan (313)	Christians given freedom of religion

	POLITICAL EVENTS	RELIGIOUS/PHILOSOPHICAL DEVELOPMENTS	THEOLOGICAL SIGNIFICANCE
284–305 (cont'd)		Council of Elvira (ca. 300)	Numerous strictures on women and sexuality posited
		Gregory the Illuminator (ca. 240–332); Church established in Armenia	
		Donatism emerges (313)	
		First Synod of Arles (314)	Condemns Donatism; advocates just war theory
		Evidence that Church had been planted in England	
324–37	-Sole rule by Constantine and establishment of Roman Empire's capital in Constantinople (330)	Establishment of Christianity	
		Effectively enhances power of bishop of Rome; begins to be called pope	
		Helena (ca. 255–330) supervises founding of churches built on holy sites in Holy Land	
		Confirmation widely practiced	

POLITICAL EVENTS	RELIGIOUS/PHILOSOPHICAL DEVELOPMENTS	THEOLOGICAL SIGNIFICANCE
324–37 (cont'd)	Use of music in worship becomes typical	
	Frumentius (ca. 300–ca. 380) undertakes missionary work in Ethiopia	
	Many churches built on sites of martyrdom; alleged holy relics increasingly venerated	
	Emergence and dynamic growth of monasticism –Anthony (ca. 251-356) –Paul of Thebes (d. ca. 340) –Macarius the Egyptian (ca. 300-ca. 390) –Moses the Negro	
	Cenobitic monasticism –Pachomius (ca. 290–346); Marie; Theodora; Athanasia; Mary the Egyptian; Syncletica; Bessarion; Sarah	

	POLITICAL EVENTS	RELIGIOUS/PHILOSOPHICAL DEVELOPMENTS	THEOLOGICAL SIGNIFICANCE
324–37 (cont'd)		Council of Neocaesarea (ca. 314–25)	Advocates removal of married presbyters
		Eusebius of Caesarea (ca. 260–ca. 340)	
		Arius (ca. 250–ca. 336) and beginning of Arian controversy –Eusebius of Nicomedia (d. ca. 342)	
		Council of Nicea (325)	Condemns Arianism; adopts ancient baptismal creed with affirmation of *homoousios* of Father and Son
		Arian attempts to reassert credibility	
		Athanasius (ca. 296–373)	
337–61	-Reign of Constantine's sons	Arian Council of Antioch (341)	Rejects papal pleas (by Julius) to reinstate Athanasius; develops an Arian creed (*Creed of Dedication*)

	POLITICAL EVENTS	RELIGIOUS/PHILOSOPHICAL DEVELOPMENTS	THEOLOGICAL SIGNIFICANCE
337–61 (cont'd)		Council of Sardica (343)	Appeals involving bishops in ecclesiastical cases to be made to pope
		Council of Sirmium (357)	Develops another Arian creed
361–63	Reign of Julian the Apostate	Some refer to Christ as *homoiousios*	
		Apollinarius (ca. 310–ca. 390)	
		Synod of Alexandria (362)	Affirms deity of Holy Spirit, since appropriate to refer to God as three hypostases, yet one; condemns Apollinarius
364–78	Reign of Valens (in Eastern Empire); Valentinian I rules in Western Empire (364–75)	Athanasius prepares first list of biblical canon to include all books of the Bible (367)	
		Synods of Rome (374–80)	Condemn Apollinarius

	POLITICAL EVENTS	RELIGIOUS/PHILOSOPHICAL DEVELOPMENTS	THEOLOGICAL SIGNIFICANCE
379–95	-Reign of Theodosius; Valentinian II rules in Western Empire (375–92)	Macrina (ca. 327–79)	
		Gregory of Nazianzus (329–89)	
		Basil (330–79)	
		Gregory of Nyssa (ca. 330–ca. 395)	
		Ambrose (ca. 339–97)	Confronts Theodosius over the Eastern Empire's policies towards Jews; first stirrings of institutionalized anti-Jewish sentiment
		First Council of Constantinople (381)	Affirms Nicea; places Nicene Creed in final form; condemns Apollinarius; accords patriarch of Constantinople privileges comparable to that of pope
		Synod of Rome (382)	Asks emperor to give papacy jurisdiction in ecclesiastical cases involving bishops

	POLITICAL EVENTS	RELIGIOUS/PHILOSOPHICAL DEVELOPMENTS	THEOLOGICAL SIGNIFICANCE
379–95 (cont'd)		Council of Hippo (393)	Affirms Athanasius's version of biblical canon and apocryphal books
		Augustine (354–430)	Primary shaper of Western theology
		Donatist controversy	Priority of Church and sacraments over holiness of priesthood affirmed
		Pelagius (ca. 360–ca. 420)	
		Jerome (ca. 342–420) and translation of Vulgate	
		John Chrysostom (ca. 347–407)	
		Maro (d. 410)	
395	Roman Empire divides permanently into East and West	Council of Carthage (397)	Affirms Athanasius's version of biblical canon and apocryphal books
		Council of Alexandria (400)	Condemns views of Origen

	POLITICAL EVENTS	RELIGIOUS/PHILOSOPHICAL DEVELOPMENTS	THEOLOGICAL SIGNIFICANCE
408–50	Reign of Theodosius II in Eastern Empire		
410	Fall of Rome; Eastern Empire continues until 1453	Synods in Palestine (415)	Endorses Pelagianism (with support of Pope Zosimus [d. 418])
		Council of Carthage (417/18)	Condemns Pelagianism; mandates infant baptism
		Cyril of Alexandria (d. 444)	Leads systematic persecution of Jews
		Alexandrian Christology (largely through work of Cyril) and Antiochene Christology (largely through the work of Theodore of Mopsuestia [ca. 350–428]) come to mature expression	
		Nestorianism emerges	
414–18	Visigoth invasion of Spain	Spanish Church brought under Arian influence	

	POLITICAL EVENTS	RELIGIOUS/PHILOSOPHICAL DEVELOPMENTS	THEOLOGICAL SIGNIFICANCE
414–18 (cont'd)		Synod of Carthage (424)	Insists on local jurisdiction over clergy affairs
		Synod of Dadyeshu (426)	Persian Church (eventually becoming Nestorian) declares its independence from the patriarchate of Constantinople
		Synod in Rome (430)	Condemns Nestorianism
		Synod of Alexandria (430)	Condemns Nestorianism
		Council of Ephesus (431)	Condemns Nestorius and Pelagianism; views Mary as Mother of God (*theotokos*)
		Nestorianism spreads to Persia (Assyrian Church)	
		Formula of union (433)	Reconciles Alexandrian and Antiochene Christologies, putting an end to controversy between Cyril of Alexandria and John of Antioch (d. 441)
		Patrick (ca. 390–ca. 460) works in Ireland	
		Synod of Orange (441)	Refers to confirmation
		Eutyches (ca. 378–454) and Monophysite Christology	
		Synod in Constantinople (448)	Condemns Eutyches

	POLITICAL EVENTS	RELIGIOUS/PHILOSOPHICAL DEVELOPMENTS	THEOLOGICAL SIGNIFICANCE
414–18 (cont'd)		"Robber Synod" Council at Ephesus (449)	Acquits Eutyches
450–57	Reign of Marcian in Eastern Empire	Council of Chalcedon (451)	Condemns Eutyches; affirms hypostatic union of Christ's two natures, in a way compatible with both Alexandrian and Antiochene Christology; reaffirms christological affirmations of Councils of Constantinople and Nicea; accords patriarch of Constantinople privileges comparable to that of pope
		Some Egyptian bishops reject decisions of Chalcedon; Coptic and Ethiopian Orthodox churches become Monophysite. Armenian Apostolic and Syrian Orthodox follow; Melchites reject Monophysite views in Egypt.	
		Proeterius martyred in christological controversy in Egypt (457)	
		Papacy of Leo I (d. 440–61)	
455	Vandals sack Rome	Synod of Arles (473)	Affirms a Semi-Pelagian position

	POLITICAL EVENTS	RELIGIOUS/PHILOSOPHICAL DEVELOPMENTS	THEOLOGICAL SIGNIFICANCE
474–91	Reign of Zeno in Eastern Empire (interrupted briefly by Basiliscus)	Decisions of Council of Chalcedon annulled by Basiliscus (476)	
		Edict of Union (482)	Directs all engaged in christological controversies to return to positions held prior to controversy
		East-West Schism precipitated by Edict of Union; resolved in 519	East eventually embraces decisions of Chalcedon
		Christianity planted in France (496)	
		Papal Schism—one Arian, one Chalcedonian (498–514)	
		Nestorians undertake mission in India, perhaps planting Malabar Church	
		Dionysius the Areopagite (ca. 500)	

	POLITICAL EVENTS	RELIGIOUS/PHILOSOPHICAL DEVELOPMENTS	THEOLOGICAL SIGNIFICANCE
527–65	Reign of Justinian in Eastern Empire	Synod of Orange (529)	Condemns Semi-Pelagianism, adopting Augustine's theology, save predestination
		Benedict (ca. 480–ca. 550) and Rule of St. Benedict	Origins of Western monasticism
		Jacob Baradaeus (ca. 500–578) turns Syrian Orthodox Church in Monophysite direction	
		Second Council of Constantinople (553)	Condemns Origen and Antiochene Christology
570–632	Mohammed	Third Council of Toledo (589)	Renounces Arianism; refers to confession as sacrament
		Papacy of Gregory I (590–604) -*Donation of Constantine*	Institutes liturgical chanting; commissions missions; asserts supremacy of Church over state; establishes his own version of Augustine as infallible teacher of Church (emphasizing penance); affirms doctrine of purgatory; views Eucharist as sacrifice
		Missions to Anglo-Saxons in England; ministry of Augustine (d. 604/5)	
		Spain returns to Nicene Orthodoxy	

Significant Events for the Church in the Christian Era

	POLITICAL EVENTS	RELIGIOUS/PHILOSOPHICAL DEVELOPMENTS	THEOLOGICAL SIGNIFICANCE
630	Mohammed takes Mecca	Fourth Council of Toledo (633)	Decrees Jews not be compelled to join Church
634–732	Islamic invasions	North African Christianity eradicated	
		Sergius of Constantinople (d. 638); rise of Monothelite heresy	
		Nestorian mission planted in China (635ff.)	
		Third Council of Constantinople (680–81)	Condemns Monothelitism and Pope Honorius I for supporting it
		Church planted in Netherlands and Belgium	
717–41	Reign of Leo III in Eastern Empire	Iconoclast controversy (ca. 725–842)	
741–75	Reign of Constantine V in Eastern Empire	Adoptionist Christology controversy in West (8th century)	

	POLITICAL EVENTS	RELIGIOUS/PHILOSOPHICAL DEVELOPMENTS	THEOLOGICAL SIGNIFICANCE
741–75 (cont'd)		Second Council of Nicea (787)	Condemns Iconoclasts
800–40	Carolingian Empire (Charlemagne)	Church planted in Germany	
		John Scotus Erigena (ca. 810–ca. 877)	
845	Vikings take Paris	Cyril (826–69) and Methodius (ca. 815–85); Christian missions planted among Slavs	
		Orthodox Church planted in Bulgaria (ca. 864; autocephalous in 918)	
		Bogomil heresy emerges	
		Paschasius Radbertus (ca. 790–865) and controversy over transubstantiation (with Ratramnus [d. 868])	Also teaches immaculate conception of Mary and her assumption into heaven
		Synod of Mainz (848) Synod of Quiercy (849)	Condemn Gottschalk of Orbais for teaching Augustine's view of predestination

Significant Events for the Church in the Christian Era

	POLITICAL EVENTS	RELIGIOUS/PHILOSOPHICAL DEVELOPMENTS	THEOLOGICAL SIGNIFICANCE
845 (cont'd)		Second East-West Schism, as Western Church excommunicated by Photius of Constantinople (867); schism eventually healed in 879–80 by Fourth Council of Constantinople	
		Nestorian Church in China wiped out	
		Order of Cluny founded (909)	Monastic reform
		Christianity planted in Russia (950) and other eastern European regions	
962–1806	Holy Roman Empire	Church planted in Norway (by Olaf; 995–1030) and elsewhere in Scandinavia	
		Cluniac reform initiated with Easter Synod (1049)	Mandates clerical celibacy and rejects simony
		Permanent East-West Schism (1054)	

	POLITICAL EVENTS	RELIGIOUS/PHILOSOPHICAL DEVELOPMENTS	THEOLOGICAL SIGNIFICANCE
962–1806 (cont'd)		Lateran Council (1059)	Creates formula for electing popes; approves Order of Augustinian Canons
		Lay investiture controversy initiated (1075) when practice forbidden by Pope Gregory VII	
		Anselm (ca. 1033–1109)	Frames ontological argument
		Peter Abelard (1079–1142)	Origins of Scholastic theology
		Cistercian Order founded (1098)	Monastic reform reinitiated
1096–99	First Crusade	Concordat of Worms (1122)	Bishops to be elected; investiture only by clergy
1099	Crusaders capture Jerusalem	First (Ecumenical) Lateran Council (1123)	Confirms Concordat of Worms
		Knights Templar Order approved by Council of Troyes (1128)	
		Second (Ecumenical) Lateran Council (1139)	Mandates clerical celibacy

POLITICAL EVENTS	RELIGIOUS/PHILOSOPHICAL DEVELOPMENTS	THEOLOGICAL SIGNIFICANCE
1099 (cont'd)	Synod of Sens (1140)	Condemns Abelard's view of the Trinity
	Hildegard of Bingen (1098–1179)	
1147–49 Second Crusade –Practices extermination of Jews	Bernard of Clairvaux (1090–1153)	
	Peter Lombard (ca. 1100–1160)	Preparation of Scholasticism's primary textbook
	Waldensian and Albigensian heresies emerge	
	Averroes (1126–98)	Writings aid Western society's recovery of Aristotle
	Third (Ecumenical) Lateran Council (1179)	Determines extant formula for papal elections; declares no Christian could be enslaved
	Maronite Church affiliates with Roman Catholic Church (1182)	
1187 Fall of Jerusalem		
1189–92 Third Crusade	Papacy of Innocent III (1198–1216)	

	POLITICAL EVENTS	RELIGIOUS/PHILOSOPHICAL DEVELOPMENTS	THEOLOGICAL SIGNIFICANCE
1202–4	Fourth Crusade		
1204–61	Latin Empire of Constantinople	Fourth (Ecumenical) Lateran Council (1215)	Mandates annual observance of confession and Eucharist; endorses transubstantiation; regulates inquisition and establishment of new monastic orders; establishes strict lifestyle standards for clergy; mandates that each cathedral provide educational opportunities; grants indulgences; authorizes stigmatizing Moslems; condemns Waldensians and Albigensians
1215–1368	Mongol conquest of China	Nestorian Church restored and Catholic Church planted in China until end of Mongol Empire	
		Francis of Assisi (ca. 1181/82–1226); Franciscan Order founded	Establishment of mendicant orders in the West

	POLITICAL EVENTS	RELIGIOUS/PHILOSOPHICAL DEVELOPMENTS	THEOLOGICAL SIGNIFICANCE
1215–1368 (cont'd)		Clare (1194–1253); Poor Clares founded	
		Dominic (1170–1221); Dominican Order founded	
		Controversy in Franciscan Order, led by Joachim of Fiore (ca. 1132–1202), over decree of Pope Gregory IX (ca. 1148–1241) to diminish the rigor of its commitment to poverty	
		Recovery of Aristotle's philosophy in the West	
		Bonaventure (ca. 1217–74)	Heals controversy in Franciscan Order over poverty; launches protest against appropriation of Aristotelian philosophy
1244	Jerusalem permanently in Moslem hands		
		First Council of Lyons (1245)	Declared Emperor Frederick II deposed, thereby exercising authority over the state
		Controversy in Coptic Church over confession	Validity of private confession affirmed
		Flagellant movement flourishes	

	POLITICAL EVENTS	RELIGIOUS/PHILOSOPHICAL DEVELOPMENTS	THEOLOGICAL SIGNIFICANCE
1261	Byzantines recapture Constantinople; restore Eastern Empire	Thomas Aquinas (ca. 1225–74)	Applies Aristotelian philosophy to Scholastic theology
		Umilta of Faenza (1226–1310)	
		Second Council of Lyons (1274)	Nominal reunion of Eastern and Western churches
		Angela of Foligno (ca. 1248–1309)	
1291	End of Crusader presence in Holy Land	Meister Eckhart (1260–1327)	
		John Duns Scotus (1265–1308)	
ca. 1300	Rise of Ottoman Empire (continued until 1918)	Jubilee Year declared by Pope Boniface VIII (1300)	Indulgences given to those making pilgrimage to Rome
	Portuguese begin exploring Africa	*Unam Sanctam* (1302)	Pope Boniface VIII claims Church to judge state
		Council of Vienne (1311–12)	Suppressed the Templars and unauthorized monastic movements (the Beguines)
		William of Ockham (ca. 1285–1347)	Nominalism begins to make an impact on Western society and the Church
		Robert Holcot (d. 1349)	

	POLITICAL EVENTS	RELIGIOUS/PHILOSOPHICAL DEVELOPMENTS	THEOLOGICAL SIGNIFICANCE
ca. 1300 (cont'd)		Avignon papacy (1309–77)	
		John Tauler (ca. 1300–1361)	
		German Theology	
1337–1453	Hundred Years' War Joan of Arc (1412–31)	Controversies over Christmas and other festivals in Ethiopian Orthodoxy	
		Emergence of Mikaelite and Stephanite heresies in Ethiopian Orthodoxy	
		Emergence of Strigolnik heresy in Russian Orthodox Church	
		Papacy of Clement VI (1342–52); issues papal bull authorizing indulgences (1343)	
1347–48	Bubonic plague	Gerhard Groote (1340–84) and founding of Brethren of the Common Life	

	POLITICAL EVENTS	RELIGIOUS/PHILOSOPHICAL DEVELOPMENTS	THEOLOGICAL SIGNIFICANCE
1347–48 (cont'd)		Julian of Norwich (1342–after 1413)	Increasing impact of mysticism
		Catherine of Siena (1347–80)	
		Great Western Schism and rise of conciliar movement (1378–1415)	Period of rival claimants/ pretenders to papacy
	Spain and Portugal initiate settlements in Africa	Council of Pisa fails to resolve schism (1409)	
		John Wycliffe (1330–84) and the Lollards	Pre-reformers
		John Huss (1372–1415) and the Hussites and Taborites	
	Period of Henry the Navigator's explorations	Council of Constance (1414–18)	End of Great Western Schism with election of single pope; condemns Wycliffe and Huss

	POLITICAL EVENTS	RELIGIOUS/PHILOSOPHICAL DEVELOPMENTS	THEOLOGICAL SIGNIFICANCE
1347–48 (cont'd)		Council of Basle/Ferrara–Florence (1431–45)	Designates seven as the number of sacraments; proclaims nominal reunion with Eastern Orthodox, Armenian Orthodox, and Jacobites; in early stages, council meeting in Basle defies Pope Eugenius IV and illegitimately elects Martin V as pope
		Pope Eugenius IV decrees a rationale for slavery (1434)	
1453	Fall of Constantinople and Eastern Empire	Union of Brethren secede from Catholic Church in Bohemia	
	Renaissance begins to flower -Leonardo da Vinci (1452–1519)	Settlement reached with Coptic Church in Ethiopian Orthodoxy regarding Egyptian patriarch's role of leadership of Ethiopian Church; monastic clergy given autonomy	
	-Michelangelo (1475–1564)	Has theological controversy with Luther (1525)	
	-Desiderius Erasmus (ca. 1466–1536)	Sabbath controversy in Ethiopian Orthodox Church resolved	Both Christian and Jewish Sabbath observed
		Judaizers in Russian Orthodox Church	

	POLITICAL EVENTS	RELIGIOUS/PHILOSOPHICAL DEVELOPMENTS	THEOLOGICAL SIGNIFICANCE
1474–1504	Reign of Ferdinand and Isabella in Spain	Reform in Spanish Catholic Church	
		Francisco de Cisneros (1436–1517)	
		Girolamo Savonarola (1452–98)	
		Church planted in Kongo (1483)	
1492	Columbus lands in the Americas	Gabriel Biel (d. 1495)	
		Royal patronage over Church in Americas granted by papacy to Spain and Portugal (1493ff.)	
1497	Vasco da Gama discovers route to India	Martin Luther (1483–1546)	
	Vasco Núñez da Balboa explores the Americas		

	POLITICAL EVENTS	RELIGIOUS/PHILOSOPHICAL DEVELOPMENTS	THEOLOGICAL SIGNIFICANCE
1509–47	Reign of Henry VIII in England Pope Julius II grants Henry a dispensation to marry Catherine of Aragon (1509)		
1516	Ottoman Empire conquers Syria and Palestine	Fifth (Ecumenical) Lateran Council (1512–17)	Condemns conciliarism

INDEX

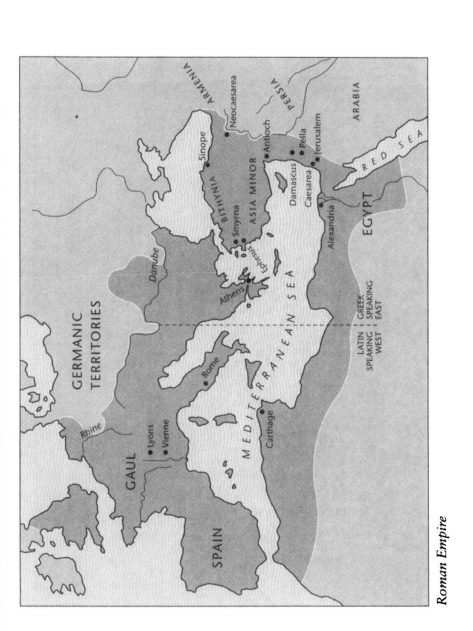

Roman Empire

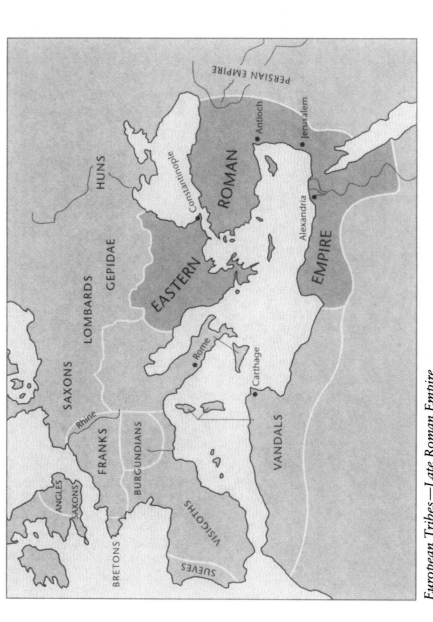

European Tribes—Late Roman Empire

Americas in Early Colonial Period

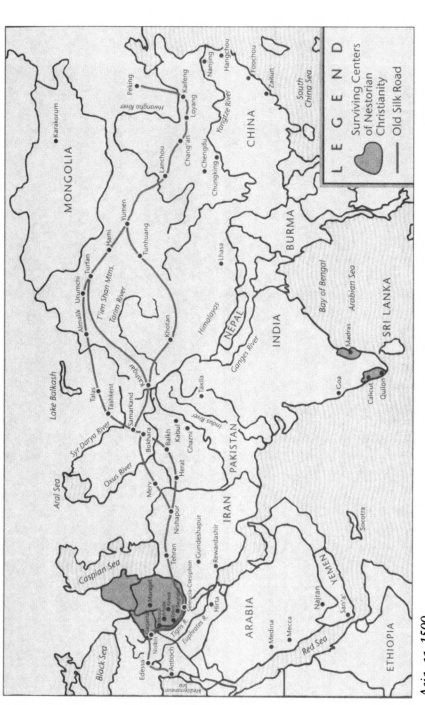

Asia, ca. 1500

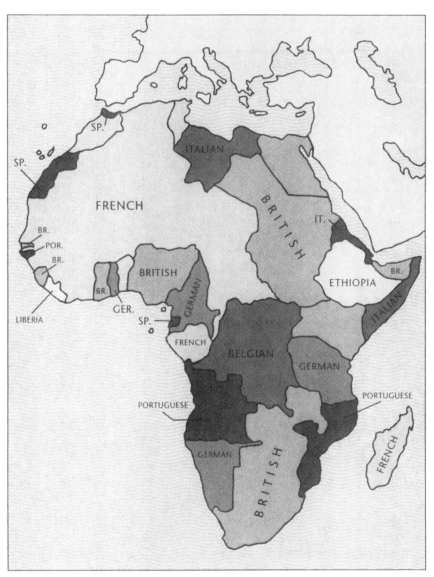

Africa at the height of Colonial Expansion

CPSIA information can be obtained at www.ICGtesting.com
Printed in the USA
LVOW06s0244210714

395258LV00002B/142/P

9 781563 382758